PARTNERSHIP POWER

American Alliance of Museums

The American Alliance of Museums has been bringing museums together since 1906, helping to develop standards and best practices, gathering and sharing knowledge, and providing advocacy on issues of concern to the entire museum community. Representing more than 35,000 individual museum professionals and volunteers, institutions, and corporate partners serving the museum field, the Alliance stands for the broad scope of the museum community.

The American Alliance of Museums' mission is to champion museums and nurture excellence in partnership with its members and allies.

Books published by AAM further the Alliance's mission to make standards and best practices for the broad museum community widely available.

PARTNERSHIP POWER

Essential Museum Strategies
for Today's Networked World

MARSHA L. SEMMEL

ROWMAN & LITTLEFIELD
Lanham • Boulder • New York • London

Published by Rowman & Littlefield
A wholly owned subsidiary of The Rowman & Littlefield Publishing Group, Inc.
4501 Forbes Boulevard, Suite 200, Lanham, Maryland 20706
www.rowman.com

6 Tinworth Street, London SE11 5AL, United Kingdom

British Library Cataloguing in Publication Information Available

Library of Congress Cataloging-in-Publication Data Available

ISBN 978-1-5381-0313-5 (cloth: alk. paper)
ISBN 978-1-5381-0314-2 (pbk.: alk. paper)
ISBN 978-1-5381-0315-9 (electronic)

♾™ The paper used in this publication meets the minimum requirements of
American National Standard for Information Sciences—Permanence of Paper for
Printed Library Materials, ANSI/NISO Z39.48-1992.

Printed in the United States of America

CONTENTS

List of Illustrations

Acknowledgments

MARSHA L. SEMMEL

I N MY LONG CAREER IN THE MUSEUM sector and in federal service, I have been tremendously fortunate in meeting, and learning from, generations of museum and public service leaders who have generously shared their wisdom and experiences with me, and who have shaped my own perspectives and knowledge. This list includes each of the many contributors to this volume, who have candidly shared their own partnership stories, philosophies, and practice. Thanks to each of them for their contributions. Other powerful thinkers and leaders are recognized in the chapters about my own partnership journey as well as in the resources section.

There are others, however, who were equally influential in shaping my experience in collaboration and understanding of its power (and challenges), who are not mentioned by name in this volume. This list is long, and I'm certain that I will unintentionally omit some key people. It includes Stephen E. Weil, Elaine Heumann Gurian, David Carr, Harold and Susan Skramstad, Gabriel P. Weisberg, Deborah Mack, Wendy Luke, Lynn Dierking, and Nina Simon. During my decade at the Institute of Museum and Library Services (IMLS), I owe a great debt to Director Robert Martin for recruiting me as the first director for strategic partnerships and to his predecessor Acting Director Beverly Sheppard, as well as to Martin's successor, Anne Imelda Radice, and IMLS colleagues, including Mamie Bittner, Nancy Weiss, Nancy Rogers, Abigail Swetz, and Allison Prabhu. Some of our hard-working partners on IMLS collaborations need to be called out, including Cheryl Williams, then at the Corporation for Public Broadcasting; Ken Kay and Valerie Greenhill, who worked with us on *Museums, Libraries and 21st Century Skills*; and Ralph Smith, Ron Fairchild,

Andrea Camp, and Ellen Galinsky, who were invaluable for our *Growing Young Minds: How Museums and Libraries Create Lifelong Learners* collaboration. There were many employees of other federal agencies, including the National Endowment for the Arts and the National Endowment for the Humanities, who navigated the development and implementation of various multiagency partnerships with which I was involved. Rachel Goslins, as director of the President's Committee on the Arts and the Humanities, enlisted our collaboration, with Scholastic, in the creation of the annual National Student Poet competition. Connie Yowell, the architect of the MacArthur Foundation's Digital Media and Learning initiative, along with her colleague An-Me Chung, were inspiring and supportive partners in the development of the IMLS-MacArthur Learning Labs collaboration. For each of the major IMLS partnerships with which I was involved, there were also task forces and advisory committees comprising busy museum and library professionals (and others) who took the time and made the effort to make our collaborative processes, resources, and ultimate products better and more resonant and relevant to the field.

When I left IMLS in 2013 to work on a more sustained basis with the Noyce Leadership Institute, Ann Bowers, Lynn Luckow, Geno Schnell, and David Coleman played powerful roles in my personal growth and in reinforcing the importance and power of an ecosystem perspective for science-focused informal learning organizations. Moving beyond the domain of out-of-school learning organizations, the invitation from founder Stan Gryskiewicz to join the international group Association for Managers of Innovation (AMI) expanded my network of peers and colleagues, my awareness of strategic innovations across a broad spectrum of organizations, and my knowledge of the power of collaboration well beyond the world of museums. The insights I've acquired in the years since I joined AMI have added enormously to my practice.

With regard to this book, special thanks to Charles Harmon, of Rowman and Littlefield, who has helped to shepherd this volume and never failed to coach me, gently but firmly, through some of the writing dry spells. As a person who cringes whenever she is confronted with massive style guides that dictate every dimension of a manuscript, I was elated to meet—and recruit—Helen Santoro as my research assistant. Helen embraced and contributed to the "big ideas" of this book with the same enthusiasm she had for the minutiae of style sheets. Thank you, Helen!

Finally, I want to thank my parents and my son for their love and support. I grew up in Detroit, Michigan, in a family clothing business that dated to 1918, and I continue to become more conscious that the experiences I had working from my tween years through high school (and occasionally beyond) at one or more Klein's stores were formative in powerful ways. Putting the customer first, rotating and updating merchandise displays ("exhibits") regularly to keep the store "fresh," creating a positive and supportive work culture among the sales staff (and being part of them and their lives), keeping a close eye on finances, tracking accounts payable and receivables, staying current on fashion trends, consumer behavior and changing community demographics—all of these skills and experiences made me a better museum professional and a better public servant. Similarly, observing my son David's growth and development as a kind, generous, knowledgeable, and committed Gen X exemplar of a "glocal" citizen, reflecting and balancing, in his work and life, both local environmental and community values with the power of digital resources and awareness of global issues, continues to inform my multigenerational sensibilities.

As I write this, there are those who might question the value of such institutional bulwarks of the knowledge society as museums, libraries, and public broadcasting stations. Similarly, there are those who take an almost perverse delight in demeaning and questioning the commitment, dedication, and expertise of those in the public sector—the government workers who, literally and figuratively, keep the wheels of government turning at the federal, state, and local levels, and who maintain a deep commitment to the public trust. This book is dedicated to you—the professionals and volunteers who strive to keep the foundations and structures of our democracy strong and vital.

Introduction

MARSHA L. SEMMEL

> *"Survival of the fittest" is out. "Survival of the connected" is in. Cloud storage, telecommuting, mobile access, data analysis, machine learning—we're living in a transformational era where societal change fueled by digitization and automation is altering how we work and live like never before. The social impact and nonprofit space . . . is not immune to these changes, and organizations of all sizes are now seeking out collaborations across geographies and in real time with the aim of finding more partners with complementary assets to execute a shared vision.*
>
> *–"ADVANCING THE ART OF COLLABORATION"*[1]

About This Book

THIS BOOK FOCUSES ON PARTNERSHIPS as a professional practice in the museum sector, not as "one-off" relationships but as a way of life, an essential strategy in this networked age. Accordingly, the partnership perspectives and the case studies have been selected for their focus on sustained relationship building with others in the community, the state, or nationally—relationships that are now part of the organization's DNA and are reflected in governance, leadership, organization charts, staff responsibilities, and strategic goals. Fortunately, there are many such examples within the museum sector, in all types of museums—size, focus, geographic location—and what is represented in this book reflects my own "partnership playlist" of the many partnerships about which I have been privileged to learn. I have tried to select the examples based on diversity of thematic focus, museum size, and geography. It was very difficult to limit the book to these examples. The reader should understand that partnerships, by their very nature, are dynamic. Their success and failure (like so many other complexities of life and work today) can rise or fall based on a number of factors: change in leadership, change in community context, economic changes. Even when a single partnership may not survive, there can often be, as the wonderful Ron Thorpe from WNET once noted, "important sticky residue" from a "completed" partnership that remains and can be invested in a new set of strategic alliances. This "important sticky residue" can include lessons learned, relationships, new contacts, or new strategies. While there have been several studies and accounts of museum-school partnerships, the focus of this volume goes beyond this important, yet well-documented, type of collaboration.

There are many useful and important books and articles about partnerships—in the corporate world, in the nonprofit sector, in the funding/philanthropic community—that examine, explore, and collect recent partnership practices, but literature within the museum community is sparse. That's why this compilation of recent museum examples now exists. Despite significant and increasing activity in this area, many museums have not built a partnership mindset into their ongoing work, and do not necessarily create resources or conditions for successful partnerships as part of the organizational chart, mission, vision, or overall infrastructure.

The book tries to capture the attitudes and mindsets that are conducive to successful partnerships as well as the conditions for fertile partnerships and the challenges that partnerships inevitably pose. Although a number of sections offer useful and practical advice, this is not a recipe book. Each partnership has its own special conditions, opportunities, and constraints. Many of the partnerships profiled in this book have been built on or have generated formal agreements, memorandums of understanding, contracts, or other binding documents. These formal partnership codifications are useful and typically necessary to ensure clarity of terms, expectations, and deliverables. They provide continuity should any of the principals or conditions change. Yet, in my experience, the most successful partnerships are largely a matter of conviction, commitment, shared vision, trust, and good faith. One of my favorite partnership quotes comes from Hilary Mantel's novel, *Wolf Hall*. It is voiced by Thomas Cromwell, who has been mentored by Thomas Wolsey, Archbishop of York, cardinal, papal legate, Lord Chancellor, and who rises to be a key advisor to King Henry VIII.

Wolsey always said that the making of a treaty is the treaty. It doesn't matter what the terms are, just that there are terms. It's the goodwill that matters. When that runs out, the treaty is broken, whatever the terms say. It is the processions that matter, the exchange of gifts, the royal games of bowls, the tilts, jousts, and masques: these are not preliminary to the process, they are the process itself.[2]

What this quote says to me is that the process of developing partnerships—the courtship, the trust building, the getting to know each other—is crucial.

Partnerships are work. As I learned in a conference during my time at Institute of Museum and Library Services (IMLS)—and through my own first-hand experience—the root of the word "collaborate" is "labor." Partnerships are about people. They are about relationships. And the most enduring partnerships address real needs. They address the needs of each institution as well as the intended audiences and pay attention to the partnership process as it develops and evolves.

Why Partnerships?

Museums may believe that they can quite effectively fulfill their missions by not engaging in partnerships, so why is partnership an essential strategy today? Across multiple sectors, it is widely acknowledged that contemporary challenges require collective action. Whether dealing with increasing economic and educational inequity, climate change, demographic changes, immigration and migration, or homelessness, stakeholders such as government entities, social service organizations, and other nonprofits are recognizing today's challenges as complex and multidimensional. These challenges require a system-oriented approach in order to "move a needle" on effective change.

Many corporations today have also moved into the domain of corporate social responsibility and worked with others to achieve, beyond increased returns to shareholders, a "double bottom line" of impact that shows social as well as financial benefits. Funders—both governmental and private—are increasingly demanding measures and evidence of impact from any nonprofit in the competition for funds. Collective impact—which relies on different organizations coming together to develop measurable systemic, positive change in dealing with wicked or complex societal problems—is increasingly a funder priority. Our contemporary challenges, as well as potential solutions, have been facilitated, of course, by the digital revolution, which has changed the environment for all social, economic, and cultural interactions.

While partnership practice is an essential strategy and can often be effective in small doses that involve two or more organizations—and indeed a museum often needs to start at that point—we have moved beyond the domain of partnerships into the world of networks and ecosystems, where multiple actors engage in fluid and dynamic relationships with like and unlike organizations that have entire systems as their focus. Partnerships are the building blocks for successful network engagement; hence, proficiency in partnerships, especially a partnership mindset, can lead to easier and more effective engagement in these larger system-wide efforts.

Beyond Partnerships:
The World of Networks and Systems

Increasingly, limited partnerships, as fruitful as they may be for specific projects and purposes, are being complemented (and in some cases, overshadowed) by a focus on broader ecosystems and systems-level outcomes and impacts. In a world where many interactions are connected, or hyperconnected due to the internet, the exponential growth of connected devices, mobile devices, and the growing influence of artificial intelligence, no museum can afford to be an island. For museums to remain relevant institutions that "make a difference" in a world facing such challenges as global warming, demographic shifts, increasing economic inequity, and rapidly changing workforce skills, they need to acknowledge their role as part of a dynamic, larger social, cultural, and educational whole.

In *Networked: The New Social Operating System*, Lee Rainie and Barry Wellman explore "how networks among people have profoundly transformed how we connect, in person and electronically."[3] Acknowledging the impossibility of predicting future technological directions with any certainty (although they offer some potential scenarios), they express confidence that "the internet and mobile phones have facilitated the reshaping of people's social networks, . . . and they have reconfigured the way people use their networks to learn, solve problems, make decisions, and provide support to each other."[4]

In the corporate sector, the conversation has already moved beyond partnerships and into the world of ecosystems. In an October 2017 podcast conversation among David Schwartz of McKinsey Publishing, and other McKinsey partners Miklos Dietz and Venkat Atluri, the *McKinsey Quarterly* explored the dissolution of sector borders. The group defined an ecosystem as "a complex network of interconnected businesses that depend on and feed on each other to deliver value to their customers, to the end users, and their key stakeholders." These ecosystems have been driven by the exponential growth of technology, driving the pace of change ever faster; an accelerating rate of innovation, due to technology and data availability; and changing customer expectations. This is forging new business models, requiring different mindsets, and changing the nature of partnership: "we urge CEOs to think less about just one partnership, and more about what's the ecosystem you are building with their partnership mind-set." In the developing, highly complex, and nuanced world of emerging ecosystems, Schwartz notes, "many of the biggest winners are companies which are in the middle and connecting the dots."[5]

In "Relational Networks, Strategic Advantage: New Challenges for Collaborative Control," John Hagel III, John Seely Brown, and Mariann Jelinek[6] note a similar shift in strategic focus based on "the contemporary rapid-paced world of constant learning and innovation" that requires "frequent network configuration—building new relationships, adding partners, and creating ad hoc assemblages of willing, capable collaborating partners for changing goals."[7] They posit a taxonomy of four types of networks: "innovation networks," "transactional networks," "relational networks," and "relationship process networks."[8]

In addition, "Influencing Complex Systems Change" by Natasha Winegear, Susan Misra, and Ashley Shelton, in *Nonprofit Quarterly*, suggests that "complex times require complex responses,"[9] describes six "evolving" practices that augur positive results in multiorganizational, systems-focused efforts, and provides nonprofit-centered examples of each:

- Rethinking boundaries to address intersecting constituencies, issues, and geographies
- Learning how to surf the waves of irrational and unpredictable developments
- Drawing on multiple ways of knowing to surface, include, and transcend differences
- Centering deep equity in all aspects of systems change
- Developing an ecosystem of leaders who are systems thinkers and doers
- Understanding that influencing complex systems is a marathon, not a sprint

In another take on the potential of networks, this time as the basis for more efficient business practices, "Star Trek and the Future of the Nonprofit Sector" by Vu Le draws on the *Star Trek* "Community Alliance" model to make analogies with the nonprofit sector.[10] As in *Star Trek*, there is a "prime directive" in nonprofits; for our sector it has to do with "making the community better overall." But, by operating with the understanding that each organization is "expected to do its own [human resources], finance, evaluation, communications, [information technology], fundraising, governance, etc.," as well as competing with each other and being woefully ignorant of what other nonprofits are doing, we have created an "incredibly inefficient" system that "perpetuates the Nonprofit Hunger Games, screws over grassroots organizations led by marginalized communities, and leaves us scrambling to respond to the horrifying social and political climate bearing down on our community." Vu Le hopes for a future where shared administrative, operating, and fundraising support will allow "each organization significant time and resources to focus on individualized programmatic work as well as collective efforts to address systemic issues."

Despite the many examples of networks and systems in the business, philanthropic, education, and nonprofit worlds, I suspect some museum professionals may still ask why museums, with their unique features, resources, and assets, need to move beyond the "usual" partnerships and more actively engage in the current environment of systems and networks?

First and foremost, most museums, as nonprofits, have a responsibility to contribute to the public good and to demonstrate their public value. The IMLS, long a supporter of museum-library partnerships and other collaborations, has a current Community Catalyst Initiative that "challenges museums and libraries to transform how they collaborate with their communities" in order to bring about "positive community change by drawing on the unique relationships, knowledge, and spaces of museums and libraries. It also encourages the exploration of partnerships with other organizations, including local non-profit and community development organizations."[11] IMLS is far from the only organization incentivizing these efforts.

Second, as places of lifelong learning, museums must recognize their role in existing learning ecosystems, with responsiveness to the challenges and opportunities of the digital age. The twenty-first-century skills highlighted in *Museums, Libraries, and 21st Century Skills*[12] remain more relevant than ever, and, in addition to several pieces in this volume, there is a burgeoning literature that supports the complementary roles of learning in a multitude of formal and out-of-school settings, including museums.

STEM Learning Is Everywhere, a Summary of a Convocation on Building Learning Systems includes a graphic representation of such a learning eco-system, with the individual learner at the center, surrounded by concentric rings representing, in the nearest circle, family, caregivers, friends, and mentors, and, in the next, a variety of organizational settings, including school, the internet, church, afterschool, and hobby clubs.

The Connected Learning Alliance, spawned largely from the Digital Media and Learning Initiative of the John D. and Catherine T. MacArthur Foundation, draws on research that demonstrates, in a networked world, "Young people learn best when actively engaged, creating, and solving problems they care about, and supported by peers who appreciate and recognize their accomplishments. . . . While connected learning is not new, and does not require technology, new digital and networked technologies expand opportunities to make connected learning accessible to all young people."[13]

Finally, as Vu Le notes in the *Star Trek* article cited previously, there are business-related as well as mission-related reasons to consider operating within a networked environment. As Ann Rowson Love and Yuha Jung have demonstrated in their recent edited volume, *Systems Thinking in Museums: Theory and Practice*,[14] a systems approach yields benefits within a museum as well as in ways that benefits museums' interactions with other likeminded or complementary organizations. Participation in networks can work to museums' advantages in terms of new business and strategic efficiencies, as well as more effective community and learning engagement.

How to Use This Book

T HE ESSAYS IN THIS BOOK, taken together, answer the following
questions:

1. Why are partnerships an essential strategy today for museums in
fulfilling their missions?
2. Why is it important to participate in broader, multi-institutional
collaborations in a world increasingly oriented toward systems,
networks, dynamic and fluid boundaries, and an ecosystem approach?
3. What is the spectrum of partnership/collaborative relationships?
4. What are common features of successful museum-related partnerships?
5. What kind of leadership and other skill sets do partnerships require?
What are implications for the organization charts, organizational
culture, and staff competencies?
6. How can a museum measure the impact of a partnership?
7. How can organizations sustain and manage dynamic partnership
relationships?

The Perspectives and Profiles

The book includes partnership case studies, focusing on specific museum-
related partnership initiatives, as well as partnership perspectives, observations, and advice from people in related fields who have extensive
experience working with museums. Some perspectives are from leaders
who have been deeply rooted in museums, whereas others are in different,
but related, sectors.

These leaders include **Chris Ernst**, formerly of the Center for Creative Leadership and currently Global Head, Leadership and Organizational Development at the Bill & Melinda Gates Foundation, whose work on boundary-spanning leadership has implications for creating successful partnerships with other organizations and also navigating and fostering an internal organizational culture for productive collaboration. A former museum professional, **Kate Goodall**, co-founder and chief executive officer of Halcyon, a social and arts incubator and innovator based in Washington, DC, sheds light on her journey as a leader in a start-up with a mission for public good, building and demonstrating value through public-private partnerships. **Richard C. Harwood**, founder and chief executive officer of the Harwood Institute for Public Innovation, has worked nationally and globally across a huge range of organizations, including United Way Worldwide, the Corporation for Public Broadcasting, and the American Library Association, on ways that these organizations can "turn outward" to connect more effectively with their communities in order to effect positive change. Harwood has developed and field-tested a number of tools for effective community listening and engagement, including *The Harwood Index: Five Stages of Community Life* and the community *Aspirations Facilitator's Guide*, that focus on ways in which organizations can successfully join forces with others to achieve lasting impact. The Harwood tools have been used to great effect at places like the Explora Museum in Albuquerque. Similarly, Explora has benefited from the strategic planning expertise of **David La Piana**, whose organization has worked for decades to help nonprofits navigate strategically along an entire spectrum of collaboration, as the perspective authored by him and his colleague **Melissa Mendez Campos** explains. Based in the Office of Strategic Partnerships at the Smithsonian's newest museum, The National Museum of African American History and Culture, four staff members—**Nicole Bryner**, **Marion McGee**, **Allison Prabhu**, and **Auntaneshia Staveloz**—share their experiences and insights in forging intra- and inter-museum relationships. **Felton Thomas, Jr.**, director of the Cleveland Public Library, describes his continued efforts at embedding the library ever more firmly in the urban fabric of that city, by evoking the library's original purpose as a "people's university" and reimagining ways in which this goal serves the needs of contemporary Cleveland residents.

Other contributors to this volume have been leaders in defining, creating, fostering, researching, and funding emerging learning ecosystems—those networks of diverse formal, informal, place-based, and on-line learning venues that can support and broker effective learning along the lifespan. *Learning Sciences in Informal Environments: People, Places, and Pursuits*[1] refers to lifelong, life-wide, and life-deep learning, and several contributors to this book are playing important roles in strengthening this multidimensional spectrum of learning possibility through partnerships and collaborations. With a focus on more effective partnership practice for out-of-school STEM (science, technology, engineering, and math) learning, **Ron Ottinger** (executive director, STEM Next Opportunity Fund) and **Cary Sneider** (Portland State University) reflect on their efforts and insights over the last decades to leverage limited resources in order to make a bigger impact on learning. **Katherine Prince**, director for Strategic Foresight at KnowledgeWorks, a nonprofit based in Cincinnati, Ohio, draws on her extensive work on trends in the future of learning (including the impact of digital technology) to suggest how museums can play a leadership role in contributing to vibrant, integrated, and connected learning ecosystems. **John H. Falk**, founder and executive director of the Institute for Learning Innovation and Sea Grant Professor Emeritus of Free-Choice Learning, Oregon State University, writes about "partnering with the public." **Elyse Eidman-Aadahl**, chief executive officer of the National Writing Project, provides guidance about creating safe and effective gathering places for learning practitioners that nurture strong collaborations. **Gregg Behr**, chief executive officer of The Grable Foundation in Pittsburgh, shares insights about that city's Remake Learning Network that are complemented by the Children's Museum of Pittsburgh's director **Jane Werner**'s reflections (with colleague **Suzanne McCaffrey**) on her museum's equally catalytic and always dynamic role in forging neighborhood, regional, and national partnerships that support child, family, and parent learning. Finally, **Rafi Santo,** learning scientist in the Learning Sciences Program at Indiana University, draws on his research on the Mozilla Hive Network in New York City to dissect effective behaviors and practices in forming and maintaining strategic partnerships as an organizational practice among a group of museums and youth-serving organizations.

Another partnership profile, from **Peter Ellsworth**, executive director of San Diego's Legler Benbough Foundation, reflects on the importance of—and challenges for—a variety of multi-institutional collaborations as he discusses his foundation's investments in the cultural organizations (mostly museums) in the city's Balboa Park, the site of the 1915/1916 Panama–California Exposition. With significant launching support from the Legler Benbough Foundation, **Peter Comiskey** and the **Balboa Park Cultural Partnership Team** of the Balboa Park Cultural Partnership (and Learning Institute) and **Nik Honeysett** of the Balboa Park Online Collaborative (each boasting substantial foundation and public support) provide partnership profiles of their respective successes and challenges in providing different types of backbone support and services for the park's twenty-four-plus institutions.

The book's "partnership profiles" examine specific partnership activities in nine individual diverse museums—and four multi-institutional networks—around the country. In addition to the two **Balboa Park** multi-institutional examples, the book includes descriptions of the **Florida African American Preservation Heritage Network**, founded by **Althemese P. Barnes**, which pioneered a formal state-wide collaboration focusing on identifying, preserving, and building the capacity of many African American museums and historic sites in that state. A similar state-wide organization, **Virginia Africana**, led by **Audrey Davis**, has evolved in partnership with the Virginia Endowment for the Humanities and the Virginia Association of Museums into its own independent nonprofit entity to support Virginia's diverse network of African American museums and historic sites.

Among the examples of individual museums, Museum Director **Deborah Schwartz** situates and the **Brooklyn Historical Society**'s partnership, inspired by a shared cultural focus on the abolitionist movement, within the museum's long-term strategic plan and community-building efforts. In the **Jewish Museum of Maryland** profile, Museum Director **Marvin Pinkert** and Johns Hopkins University Professor **Lindsay Thompson** inform the story of how the museum's expansion plans have become part of a broader neighborhood revitalization effort. Chapters on two art museums, the **Minneapolis Institute of Arts** (by **Elisabeth Callahan** and **Karleen Gardner**) and **The Phillips Collection** (with contributions by **Dorothy Kosinski** and **Suzanne Wright**) focus on museum engagement with specific neighborhoods, and, in the case of the Phillips, with a formal merger with a state university as well. Under the leadership of **Nancy Stueber**, the **Oregon Museum of Science and Industry** (OMSI) has long made partnership—at many levels—part of its DNA; in the OMSI profile, contributions from **Marcie Benne**, **Lauren Moreno**, and **Kyrie Kellett** add to Stueber's reflections on ways in which partnerships are key components of OMSI's strategic plan. In different ways from the **Children's Museum of Pittsburgh**, but with similar significant impact, the **Children's Museum of Houston** has become trusted a community anchor. Director **Tammie Kahn** provides an illuminating account of the museum's evolution within the greater Houston area. In Albuquerque, New Mexico, **Explora Museum** Executive Director **Joe**

Hastings and Deputy Director and Director of Community Engagement **Kristin Leigh** narrate their journey as a "turning out" museum that makes community listening central to its partnership co-creation practice. In his piece, "Be Our Guest!," Museum Director **John Wetenhall** uses his experiences at The **George Washington University Museum/Textile Museum** to demonstrate how a university-based museum has reinvented its campus and community presence through partnerships.

PARTNERSHIP PERSPECTIVES I

My Partnership Journey

1

MARSHA L. SEMMEL

The Taft Museum:
Partnership as a Minor Chord

MY CONVICTION THAT PARTNERSHIPS are an essential and strategic aspect of museum practice certainly were not a part of my conceptions when I entered the museum field in 1975 as a part-time educator, curator, and communications manager at the Taft Museum in Cincinnati, Ohio. Indeed, I was one of many at the time who sidled into the museum world as a result of a graduate degree in art history without any deep understanding of the history or societal role of museums. Luckily, my graduate training at the University of Cincinnati often forged connections between the works we studied in our textbooks (or on slides during lectures) and the works and exhibitions on display at area museums. Graduate students were also enlisted in several art documentation, research, and exhibition-related projects in the city. There was ample emphasis on the social role of art—as well as the evolution of museums in American culture.

But the social role of the museum within its community, along with the progressive teachings of philosophers like John Dewey, the admonitions and practice of Newark Museum Director John Cotton Dana—who argued in the early twentieth century that a "museum is only as good as it is of use"[1]—and a commitment to broadening the inclusive reach of a museum were not understandings that I brought with me to my first museum job. What I did encounter at the Taft was a strong ethos about education. There was a nationally recognized in-school program that paired repeated in-classroom engagement with elementary school students and teachers

3

in area schools with related, theme-oriented visits to the museum. There was a crackerjack and imaginative docent corps. Additionally, there was openness toward experimentation in the four temporary exhibitions the museum installed each year. There were also occasional partnerships with the other cultural partners that were members of The Fine Arts Fund, established in 1927 by the Taft founders Charles Phelps and Annie Sinton Taft to provide seeds for the ongoing support of the museum and other organizations. But, by and large, partnership was not a core ethos of the museum.

Conner Prairie: Shifting the Lens on Community Collaboration

It wasn't until my 1996 appointment as president and chief executive officer (CEO) of Conner Prairie, in Fishers, Indiana, outside of Indianapolis (after several other positions and a decade-plus service at the National Endowment for the Humanities), that my conviction about the importance of museums engaging in sustained and meaningful partnerships took root. It became clear, during a strategic planning process that involved museum trustees, officials from Earlham College,[2] educators, business people, and museum neighbors, that it made mission and business sense to join forces with different organizations and community members in order for the museum to move successfully into the future—and add greater value to our Indianapolis-area community.

While my stint at the museum was only two years, our strategic planning and programmatic efforts drew on our resources and on multiple voices and a careful study of the changing demographics of the metropolitan region and the needs of the area's audiences. The museum had enjoyed a long and successful partnership with the Cincinnati Symphony, which remained intact. We also looked at other dimensions of community engagement. I participated in Leadership Indianapolis and MAGIC, a regional planning and economic development consortium. We recognized that the museum needed to be far more involved in the educational, civic, and cultural issues of our region, and we began to take more aggressive and intentional steps to adjust our internal culture as well as our programmatic initiatives. We made headway in diversifying our board, working collaboratively with different stakeholders on many fronts, planning for the presentation of as yet untold stories (such as The Underground Railroad) with other program shifts and building new relationships that would re-balance our focus on tourists in favor of addressing local needs.

Moreover, as two of the Conner Prairie board members were executives at DowElanco, a multinational corporation with world headquarters nearby, we created a museum-corporate partnership that enabled Conner Prairie to tap the extraordinary and deep professional development curriculum that the company had created for its vast international staff, without any financial cost to the museum. Both entities agreed that this collaboration added value to each organization, as we each had priorities on diversity, situational leadership, and other leadership and professional development skills. The corporation valued yet additional different voices and perspectives in its training. Corporate staff also volunteered in several museum events, including the raising and completion of a recently acquired historic cabin. This "back-of-house" collaboration yielded positive results in staff skill building and adaptability.

Women of the West: Partnerships Creating Credibility and Demonstrating Value

I left Conner Prairie at the end of 1997 to accept the position as first CEO for a start-up museum, The Women of the West Museum, established in Boulder, Colorado, in 1991 by a husband-wife team, Toni Dewey and Victor Danilov. Dewey had been a successful corporate executive for Motorola—breaking the glass ceiling in the C-suite—and Danilov had a long career as a museum director, including serving as CEO of the Museum of Science and Industry in Chicago. As recent transplants to Boulder, they were struck by the invisibility of women's stories in regional museums and sought to remedy that void by creating a new museum, which, benefiting from recent scholarship, would be devoted to a critical exploration of women's history in the American West.

The museum had a compelling vision but no collections and no physical location. I was hired on the heels of a lengthy, damaging, and contentious siege within Boulder that fulminated over the museum's proposed site as the centerpiece of a new housing development that was situated in an one hundred-year-flood plain. By my recruitment, the site had been resolved and schematics for the museum building developed, but wounds remained. With the help of experienced consultants and a fledgling staff, we determined that partnerships were the only strategy that could demonstrate our public value as a new and untested organization that still faced much community and donor skepticism. If the museum was ever to be successful, it had to begin with establishing relationships not only with potential donors and an anticipated national audience, but with our local community. With a tiny but brave and innovative staff—notably a newly minted history PhD and a newly minted teacher—we undertook a series of community-based relationships and partnerships. These partnerships included an elementary school in the heart of Denver, the local YWCA, the Boulder affordable housing authority, a Denver summer youth arts program, other area museums and libraries, and even a local real estate development company. In each case, we aligned the evolving Women of the West Museum mission with that of the other organization. Each project was co-created with our community partners, including classroom teachers, youth, artists, other community residents, and area libraries and museums. In each, we jointly established project goals, defined a participatory development process, learned to trust each other, and made necessary course corrections along the way. We also hired an experienced museum media hand to help curate a series of online exhibitions, each of which also was the result of a partnership. The first online exhibition, for example, *There Are No Renters Here: Women on the Sod House Frontier*, looked at the experiences of women on the sod house frontier and was a collaboration with the Nebraska Historical Society. The museum began to garner positive press, valuable programmatic experience, new funders, and community champions.

Despite this increased recognition for our local and online programs, the museum struggled to regain trust and obtain major financial backing. Doubts continued to lurk about its ultimate sustainability. In the wake of the tech bubble burst in 2001/2002, the board saw little hope of raising the funds needed to complete the planned one-hundred-thousand square foot building. Of further concern was the ability to provide adequate operating funds should the proposed museum open. Thus, my final months on the project focused on finding a merger partner who would continue to support the Women of the West mission and vision, albeit in a different physical space and within a larger organization. The merger process—the most extreme form of collaboration!—was carefully and methodically planned, beginning with the creation of a merger committee of the board and consultation with a former nonprofit leader who had led her organization through a fairly recent, successful merger process. We then drafted and circulated a request for proposals that yielded three interested prospects. All three were carefully considered, with conversations, site visits, and other deliberations that probed the many dimensions of a different structural relationship. Ultimately, we consummated a formal agreement with the Autry Museum of the American West in Los Angeles, California, confident that that museum was committed to continue and foster the

Women of the West Museum's mission. Terms of the merger included financial commitments, but, more importantly, the respective museum boards funded endowments for two positions, a researcher and a curator, who would be charged with continuing the work of the Women of the West Museum within the Autry's broader mission of capturing the full and inclusive stories of the American West. Another part of the agreement had four Women of the West Museum trustees assuming positions on the Autry board. The process was one of slow and steady courtship, with mutual trust developing, especially among museum leadership and board members, as specific terms took shape.[3]

Institute of Museum and Library Services: Partnerships Move to Center Stage

I returned to Washington, DC, for renewed service in a Federal cultural agency in late December 2002 as the first director of the Office of Strategic Partnerships at the Institute of Museum and Library Services (IMLS), a position I held (along with shorter service in other roles, including deputy for museum services and interim agency director) from 2003 to 2013. Recruited by former Texas State Librarian and IMLS Director Robert Martin, my specific introductory assignment was to build on the work of the previous interim director (and deputy for museum services), Beverly Sheppard, and to deepen the agency's work with public broadcasting. Sheppard had authored *The 21st Century Learner*.[4] This report described the challenges facing American society in the early twenty-first century, noted the rapid rise of new digital technologies, and argued that "Learning across a lifetime, supported throughout our communities, is increasingly essential to a healthy and productive society."[5]

> America must be more than an information society. . . . We must become a nation of learners—individuals, families, communities engaged in learning in our schools and colleges, libraries, museums, archives, workplaces, places of worship and our own living rooms.[6]

This challenge, according to Sheppard, necessitated creating a "new infrastructure" that encompassed diverse content, physical and intellectual access, and a comprehensive delivery system.

> In partnership, museums, libraries, and others can create a flexible learning ecosystem, a community campus of resources for all. They can address the learning divide that threatens our society and explore ways to provide the skills, resources, tools and learning dispositions that all learners need.[7]

Key to Sheppard's argument was collaboration:

> Old boundaries will have to be erased and new collaborations spawned. Our communities are filled with potential partners: public radio and television, community service organizations, the faith community, community colleges and universities—all of which offer both allied and complementary assets to museums and libraries.[8]

This report, and related IMLS grant initiatives, resonated with me as authentic, relevant, and timely.

Although Sheppard had left the agency before my arrival, Martin also endorsed the "21st Century Learner" vision, and he directed me, as one of my first partnership tasks, to work with the Corporation for Public Broadcasting to forge a formal collaboration around what became *The Partnership for a Nation of Learners*.[9] Based on earlier collaborative work between the two organizations, including "Partners in Public Service" initiative at Penn State University in 2000, which funded eight museum/library/broadcasting partnerships, the two entities convened a Partnership for a Nation of Learners Summit in 2003, which brought together leaders of IMLS and Corporation for Public Broadcasting as well as constituents, representatives from other agencies, and other funders. The summit reaffirmed the value of organizational collaboration for public good, with consensus that "our democracy, prosperity, and individual achievement all depend on the ability to learn continually, adapt to change readily, and evaluate information critically."[10] Through a formal memorandum of understanding the partnership was launched officially in 2004, with the announcement of a Community Collaboration Grants program that supported museum/library/broadcasting partnerships that would meet community needs. Twenty collaborations received support, with the partnership also funding a series of professional development opportunities for grantees, national videoconferences and audioconferences, and a shared website.

Joining Forces, Creating Value provides in-depth profiles of six funded community collaboration grantees, with shorter "snapshots" of fourteen others. The publication concludes with a section on "predictive" and "outcome" characteristics of successful partnerships, as well as "lessons learned" gleaned from program grantees, grouped under five headings:

- Align project purpose with institutional mission and community need.
- Take the time to plan.
- Choose partners carefully and get to know them well.

- Build relationships and communicate.
- Recognize that a collaborative whole is stronger than the sum of its parts.

My decade of service at IMLS involved managing many ongoing and new inter-agency partnerships with other government entities as well as establishing new formal relationships with various nongovernmental organizations, including the Salzburg Global Forum, the Arts Education Partnership, the Campaign for Grade-Level Reading, and the John D. and Catherine T. MacArthur Foundation. These collaborations covered a broad scope of mission-related projects, including "Connecting to Collections" (addressing museum and library conservation and preservation needs and priorities), "Museums, Libraries, and 21st Century Skills" (museums and libraries as venues for fostering twenty-first-century learning competencies), "Growing Young Minds: How Museums and Libraries Create Lifelong Learners" (museums and libraries as core partners in successful, community- and home-centered early learning practice), and "Learning Labs" (museums and libraries as effective and welcoming laboratories for youth-focused digital and media production, "making," and learning).

Through the IMLS work on twenty-first-century skills (which built on the important collaborative—but principally school-based—achievements of the Partnership for 21st Century Skills), I got to know the work of Connie Yowell, formerly at the MacArthur Foundation and current CEO of Collective Shift, who launched a multi-million-dollar Digital Media and Learning Initiative (with which IMLS partnered for our 21st Century Learning Labs project). Yowell's focus on youth learning practices in an era of digital and social media explosion led to the funding of significant research and experimental practice, which continue under the auspices of her new organization and through the Connected Learning Alliance and the Educator Innovator website.

Through that association, I learned more about the potential for museums and libraries as positive nodes within dynamic, technologically enriched, learning ecosystems, including the Hive Networks supported by MacArthur, the Mozilla Foundation, and others. I absorbed the groundbreaking research and practice promoted by many scholars, including Mizuko (Mimi) Ito, danah boyd, Nichole Pinkard, and others on the frontiers of these learning networks. Ito, a cultural anthropologist now at University of California, Irvine, published her ethnographic research study of youth digital social media practice in 2009 and her categories of "hanging out," "messing around," and "geeking out" (HOMAGO) influenced the design and programming of the museum/library learning labs, with Chicago Public Library's YOUMedia Center a flagship library site. Nichole Pinkard, associate professor of Interactive Media, Human Computer Interaction, and Education at DePaul University in Chicago, had founded the Digital Youth Network to help underserved youth learners to develop technical, creative, and analytical skills—both in and beyond the classroom and helped recruit and train youth mentors. danah boyd's research on the social network activities of teens further enriched my understanding of the realm of youth learning.

I found the work of John Seely Brown particularly powerful in nurturing my evolving understanding of the networked society—both during my IMLS years and after—and the implications for learners of any age. JSB, as he is known, has long championed new models of learning based on new contexts. *A New Culture of Learning: Cultivating the Imagination for a World of Constant Change*[11] articulates the two elements that comprise these new contexts: The first, "a massive information network that provides almost unlimited access and resources to learn about anything. The second is a bounded and structured environment that allows for unlimited agency to build and experiment with things within those boundaries."[12] With the explosion of new knowledge enabled by big data, the cloud, and other digital affordances, it is no longer adequate to rely a "sage on the stage" or top-down model where experts dispense accumulated knowledge to learners. Learning to ask questions is far more important than acquiring answers. "Expertise is less about having a stockpile of information or facts at one's disposal and increasingly about knowing how to find and evaluate information on a given topic."[13] In their Stanford MediaX Keynote 2017, "Sense-Making in Our Post AlphaGo World: New Mindsets and Lenses May Be Required," JSB and Ann Pendleton-Jullian take this argument further, contending that the accelerating cycle of knowledge obsolescence in "this increasingly fast, radically contingent and hyper-connected world" requires new critical skills, where "reading context may be, at the very least, as important as reading content."[14] Noting that in the "global networked age that is densely interconnected many of our problems are wicked problems," Brown and Pendleton-Jullian contend that "everything is changed by hyper-connectivity."[15] They argue for a "blended ontology" with "imagination as the binding agent"[16] and call for "a kind of distributed community of practice that has a sense of interconnection enough to be able to create something quite new called a networked imagination."[17] Understanding that many museums (and libraries) drawing on the work of

John Dewey and Maria Montessori to drive their educational practice, JSB long acknowledged these organizations' relevance in the contemporary learning environment.

The partnerships forged and continued during my IMLS years emphasized museums and libraries as anchor organizations that preserve and make more accessible diverse representations of cultural heritage, serve as agents for positive community change, and serve as hubs in vibrant formal and informal learning ecosystems. They were about moving museums and libraries from "nice" to "necessary." While I served under the leadership of three different IMLS leaders, another memorable (and long-lasting) "discovery" during Robert Martin's tenure was the work of Mark Moore.

One of director Martin's gifts to incoming senior employees was *Creating Public Value: Strategic Management in Government* by Mark Moore.[18] The volume provides important learning insights about defining public value and the relationships between purpose, organizational structure, the authorizing environment, and audiences to be held in dynamic equilibrium in order to be effective. Although that book focused on government and other municipal organizations, Moore had moved to Harvard's Hauser Center for Nonprofit Organizations and was actively adapting his model to those entities. From my vantage point, key, museum-related "take-aways" from Moore's work are (1) museums have a mandate for demonstrating their public value and (2) success depends on a constant strategic monitoring of a dynamic system in order to attain the state of equilibrium required for organizational sustainability.[19]

In sum, during my time at IMLS, I came to see my strategic partnership role as a kind of bumblebee: "buzzing around" within the museum and library sectors and on the borders, monitoring broader trends and issues, and attempting, through various partnerships, to cross-pollinate various sectors, especially around serving learners' needs and addressing pressing societal and community issues. It was key, in each relationship, to demonstrate how the partnership would further the goals of each entity in service to the public—and, hopefully, to plant the seeds for ongoing collaborative endeavors that addressed broader societal needs.

I also strengthened my experience with—and knowledge of—the core ingredients for effective collaboration, including specific leadership skills, intentional community listening actions, and a responsive and partner-oriented organizational culture. Looming ever larger in the background of all of this work was the exponential growth of digital connectivity and the realities of a dynamic, hyperconnected, global environment.

Post-IMLS to Today: New Ventures, New Knowledge, New Skills

During my time at IMLS, I became connected to a new leadership initiative focused on leaders in science centers and children's museums. Originated by the Noyce Foundation (based in Palo Alto, California) as well as research conducted by the Association of Science and Technology Centers, IMLS invested in the planning for this executive professional development program. As the representative of one of the initial funders, I was invited to observe the capstone activities of what became the year-long Noyce Leadership Institute (NLI) and was privileged, in subsequent years, to serve on occasion as leader-in-residence during the program's periodic week-long "intensives." The institute's tenets included building leader self-awareness and managing change, understanding adaptive leadership, and an "action learning" component that required fellows to identify and implement a real community engagement project at their home institution. It thus interwove the leadership skills required for internal change and external impact.

In mid-2013, when the Noyce Foundation offered me a contract position as a senior advisor to the Institute, I decided to take the plunge. The institute had developed into a powerful, highly regarded global executive development program for senior staff at science centers and related science-oriented organizations. My outward-facing position at the IMLS had built on my CEO and other leadership experiences. I was eager to "give back" the knowledge and experience I had accrued over my career, especially in service to leadership for more effective museum-community engagement and impact. The institute's requirement for each fellow to wrestle with a real, museum-based, strategic community engagement initiative served, in virtually every case, to help the fellows build and flex their partnership "muscles," and, with my decade of partnership experience, this further inspired my enthusiasm.

The NLI "curriculum" also drew heavily on the adaptive leadership work of Ronald Heifetz and Marty Linsky of Harvard University and the change management writings of John Kotter. The abilities to move from the "balcony" to the "dance floor" and back again,[20] and to understand how to establish an understanding of the urgency for change, build a coalition that shares that urgency, and collectively shape the change vision,[21] are essential within a single organization; their importance increases in today's dynamic, interconnected world.

Through my association with NLI and Lynn Luckow, one of its principal advisors, I managed to cross paths with Bob Johansen, another thinker whose work on evolving leadership competencies has been critical to my current understanding about successful partnerships. Johansen, a distinguished fellow at Palo Alto's Institute for the Future, has focused on the leadership skills required for today's hyperconnected, VUCA (volatile, uncertain, complex, and ambiguous) environment. His volume, *Leaders Make the Future: Ten Leadership Skills for an Uncertain World* identifies ten essential leadership skills for today's world, with its rapid change and challenging disruptions in the areas of technology, scientific discovery, mass migrations, and finance. The most important skill, "commons creating," is "the ability to stimulate, grow and nurture shared assets that can benefit other players—and allow competition at a higher level." This includes partnerships but moves beyond a transactional definition of the term to a larger transformational level. "Commons creation is the culmination of all the other skills. Because it is complicated and there are many stakeholders, creating commons is often frustrating but also very satisfying for leaders who can do it."[22] In 2014, Johansen (with Karl Ronn) further elaborated on the benefits of (and urgency for) partnerships in *The Reciprocity Advantage: A New Way to Partner for Innovation and Growth*.[23] They define reciprocity as "the practice of exchanging with others for mutual benefit." Elaborating on the "commons creating" skill of the previous book, Johansen states that successful reciprocity-based partnerships, "in a world of increasing global connectivity," will need to be based on an expanded "radius of trust" and transparency among the partners.[24] In Johansen's latest volume, *The New Leadership Literacies: Thriving in a Future of Extreme Disruption and Distributed Everything*, the skills from the 2009 volume are situated in the all-the-more VUCA world, adding five new "leadership literacies" that include "Leadership for Shape-Shifting Organizations."[25] Johansen asserts that these skills can facilitate the transformation of the negative "VUCA" into the more positive *V*ision, *U*nderstanding, *C*larity, and *A*gility needed in today's world.

Noting that the future is likely to see a continued breakdown in traditional hierarchical organizations, Johansen predicts "Lots of diverse partners will come together in new ways to create new kinds of organizational structures that will be more fluid and less rigid."[26] Such "shape-shifting" organizations will be characterized by fluctuating leadership, fluid hierarchies, and distributed, noncentralized authority. The implications for leadership are profound, with "commons creating" more important than ever. Commons creating "allows assets to be shared and provides mutual-benefit partnering models for innovation."[27]

Similarly, during my NLI affiliation and after the institute shut its doors in 2016, another partnership-related development that has loomed larger throughout the nonprofit and public sectors has been Collective Impact. Although the idea of network thinking, or systems effects, has been around for many years, collective impact, in its most recent incarnation and its many variations, has become a significant development that has considerable implications for museum-related partnerships and broader community-wide collaborations. Coined and amplified in a series of articles in the *Stanford Social Innovation Review* (SSIR), this approach, in brief, builds on the work of such scholars as David Snowden (complexity) and Ronald Heifetz (adaptive leadership). With increased pressure from policy makers, donors, and funders for organizations in the nonprofit and municipal sectors to demonstrate measurable outcomes—and, in many cases, scant evidence that substantial investments have indeed "moved the needle" in dealing effectively with current and persistent societal problems—there has been increased demand for collaborative, system-wide efforts to address those challenges that have no simple, replicable, "playbook" solutions.

In their SSIR articles, John Kania, Mark Kramer, and others have defined "five conditions" of collective impact and explored multiple dimensions, implications, adaptations, and case studies using this approach. Other researchers and practitioners have continued to add to this body of literature, with critiques, potential "potholes," variations, and increasing numbers of tools and resources (on everything from systems mapping to evaluation) available on the FSG website, in SSIR and other journals, and in other sources.[28]

The five conditions are:

- A common agenda, a "shared vision for change including a common understanding of the problem and a joint approach to solving it through agreed upon outcomes";
- Shared measurement, where "participants hold each other accountable";
- Mutually reinforcing activities, "coordinated through a mutually reinforcing plan of action";
- Continuous, consistent, and open communication, supporting trust and shared objectives; and
- Backbone support, "a separate organization(s) with staff and a specific set of skills to serve as the backbone for the entire initiative and coordinate participating organizations and agencies."

Collective impact proponents note that this is not an approach to be applied to every situation and that many issues are much more suitable for less complex forms of partnerships, alliances, and networks. Nonetheless, they argue that this can be an effective method for creating system-wide impact. Many critics support the importance of networks, the need for a systems approach, and the importance of broader, measurable outcomes. Nonetheless, these naysayers have criticized the lack of evidence for the efficacy of the "five conditions," worry about "process fatigue" and insufficient dollars; and point out the hazards of a top-down ("grass tops") approach that "imposes" a problem-solving strategy on a community, rather than developing a plan with community members.

Adaptive leadership, the VUCA world, shape-shifting organizations, collective impact. All have implications for museum partnerships and successful network participation. My recent roles as senior advisor, faculty, and consultant continue to strengthen my convictions about the evolving contexts of leadership, organizational development, strategic positioning, and community engagement and the place of partnership and collaboration.

Partnerships, to be successful, require leadership skills (both internal and external); communications skills, especially listening; flexibility yet focus on a "north star" goal; strategic thinking; dealing with ambiguity; and continuous learning. These skills are highlighted in a number of the chapters in this volume.

Just as I remain convinced that professional growth requires continuous learning, adaptive thinking, and staying abreast of changes in the surrounding environment—whether these are the needs of your community, demographic shifts, trends in learning, evolving forms of evaluation and public value-creation, global warming, or technological innovation—I believe that strategically considering, creating, and leveraging partnerships and collaborations is an essential part of every museum professional's toolbox and will be an increasingly important dimension of institutional success and sustainability.

As a person with deep roots in the liberal arts and the humanities (including an undergraduate program that emphasized multidisciplinary courses), I have long appreciated a piece by historian William Cronon in *The American Scholar*, Vol. 67, No. 4, Autumn 1998. In "'Only Connect' The Goals of a Liberal Education," Cronon shared his list of ten personal qualities that he believed characterized people who embodied the values of a liberal education. The tenth states: "They follow E. M. Forster's injunction from *Howards End*, 'Only connect.'" "More than anything else, being an educated person means being able to see connections that allow one to make sense of the world and act within it in creative ways. Every one of the qualities I have described here—listening, reading, talking, writing, puzzle solving, truth seeking, seeing through other people's eyes, leading, working in a community—is finally about connecting."

Although he was referring to individuals, I believe that Cronon's observations aptly describe an obligation (or opportunity) that is possible for our museums, and one whose benefits can be duly amplified through our partnerships and broader community connections.

My partnership journey is far from over.

Other References

Harwood, R. C. (2014). Putting Community in Collective Impact. *The Collective Impact Forum*. www.fsg.org.

Kania, J., and Kramer, M. (2011). Collective Impact. *Stanford Social Innovation Review*, vol. 9, no. 1 (Winter): pages 36–41.

Kania, J., and Kramer, M. (2013). Embracing Emergence: How Collective Impact Addresses Complexity. *Stanford Social Innovation Review*. Available online: https://ssir.org/articles/entry/social_progress_through_collective_impact (January 21, 2013).

Kania, J., Kramer, M., and Russell, P. (2014). Strategic Philanthropy for a Complex World. *Stanford Social Innovation Review*. Available online: https://ssir.org/up_for_debate/article/strategic_philanthropy. Summer 2014.

Thompson, K. (2014). Collective Impact: Funder, Heal Thyself. *Stanford Social Innovation Review*.

Varda, Danielle M. "Are Backbone Organizations Eroding the Norms that Make Networks Succeed?" https://nonprofitquarterly.org/2018/02/06/backbone-organization.

From a Museum Basement to a City of Learning

Pittsburgh's Remake Learning Network

2

GREGG BEHR

BIOGRAPHY: *IN HIS TWELFTH YEAR as executive director of the Grable Foundation,* **Gregg Behr** *manages a grantmaking portfolio advancing high-quality early childhood education, improved teaching and learning in public schools, and robust out-of-school time support. From 2002 to 2006, Mr. Behr served as president of The Forbes Funds, another Pittsburgh-based foundation that supports nonprofit capacity building, research, and leadership development. Nationally, he is a trustee for GreatNonprofits.org and Grantmakers for Education. In Pittsburgh, he co-chairs Remake Learning. In 2016, the White House recognized Mr. Behr as a Champion of Change for his efforts to advance making and learning; in 2015, he was recognized as one of America's Top 30 Technologists, Transformers, and Trailblazers by the Center for Digital Education; and in 2014, Gregg accepted the Tribeca Disruptive Innovation Award on behalf of Pittsburgh's efforts to reimagine and remake learning.*

FROM OUR ORIGINS as a steel town to today's hub for research and technology, Pittsburgh's story is one of innovation and reinvention. Perhaps it's fitting, then, that the home of Mr. Rogers now helps lead the movement to transform education, drawing from the learning sciences and our region's rich institutional resources. Pittsburgh and members of its Remake Learning Network—a coalition of some 250 schools, libraries, universities, start-ups, museums, and others—have worked for more than a decade to create imaginative, future-focused learning opportunities that prepare kids for tomorrows we can't yet imagine. Our all-hands effort to share knowledge, resources, and talent has influenced thousands of learners, earning praise from the Obama White House, the World Economic Forum, education experts, and national journalists.

> "From hands-on circuitry projects for kindergartners to 'maker spaces' inside local museums, this former steel town has quietly emerged as a national model for supporting fresh approaches to technology-infused education, especially for young children." –Benjamin Herold, writing in *EdWeek*

And in many ways, it was born in a museum.

It started small: a few teachers and technologists meeting over breakfast to talk shop, discussing their respective fields and how they might collaborate. The group grew as our ideas expanded; soon, diners and coffee shops couldn't contain us. That's how we found ourselves at the Children's Museum of Pittsburgh one morning, huddled in a basement theater with a gong we'd borrowed from the city's symphony.

In our own ed-freak version of *The Gong Show*, our group—which by now consisted of teachers, parents, gamers, researchers, roboticists, and museum staff—gave each member three minutes to spell out his or her vision for the future of learning and how their work could help shape it. When one person's time was up, we'd strike the gong and move on. We didn't know it then, but the ideas seeded that day would shape what eventually became the Remake Learning Network. And the organic, playful spirit of those early meetings continues to define our work as a collective of diverse people and institutions who together on children's behalf.

> "Remake Learning is about connecting people in different silos who never would have connected without it." –Professional Development Provider and Remake Learning Network Member

The Remake Learning Network now comprises multiple organizations and partnerships that serve vastly different constituencies. Some members focus on makerspaces, some on technology, some on STEM, and some on something else. The partnerships formed within the Network draw upon and amplify each organization's individual strengths in service of creative learning—an ed-tech firm partners with an advocacy group, for example, to develop a communication app for kindergartners. A group of hip-hop artists partners with an afterschool provider to host poetry workshops. University researchers partner with classroom educators to implement new techniques for teaching fractions. The list goes on and on, and as the Network grows, so too does the number of potential partnerships.

The result is a "city of learning": a place where kids and families can find incredible learning experiences by walking through any number of front doors, whether those doors belong to schools, libraries, community centers, parks, or virtual spaces.

Of the Remake Learning Network's many points of entry, museums are among the most visible. We're fortunate to have a number of world-class institutions here in Pittsburgh, including the Children's Museum, the Senator John Heinz History Center, the Frick Art & Historical Center, and the four museums that comprise the Carnegie Institute: the Museum of Art, the Museum of Natural History, the Science Center, and the Andy Warhol Museum. Given that these museums and others provide immersive, hands-on, multisensory experiences that encourage families and children to challenge themselves and construct meaning, they're uniquely positioned to help students develop twenty-first-century skills such as critical thinking, creativity, and teamwork. And though each museum is an important learning space on its own—with longstanding programs, exhibits, and relationships with communities and schools—their presence in the Remake Learning Network has strengthened both the institutions themselves and the Network as a whole.

Take, for example, the MAKESHOP at the Children's Museum of Pittsburgh. What is today a nationally renowned makerspace grew from a simple conversation at a Remake Learning Network event. In 2010, Museum Director Jane Werner began talking with Jesse Schell, a professor at Carnegie Mellon University's Entertainment Technology Center (ETC) and chief executive officer of game design company Schell Games. Drew Davidson, the ETC's director, soon joined them, and the three discussed how the maker movement and its rapidly advancing tools allowed amateur makers to build almost anything. What might happen, they wondered, if the Children's Museum helped kids do the same?

In a different time or place, their conversation likely wouldn't have led to much, assuming it happened at all. On the surface, their organizations are worlds apart: The ETC is the country's top professional graduate program for interactive entertainment, drawing programmers, artists, and designers from around the world. Founded by Don Marinelli and the late Randy Pausch (of "Last Lecture" fame), the ETC challenges students to create games, programs, and stories using cutting-edge technology and design. Its alumni take positions at Google, Electronic Arts, and other high-tech employers. The Children's Museum, on the other hand, while equally respected in its field, serves a completely different constituency of learners—many of whom can barely walk or talk. Schell Games is one of the country's largest independent game developers, creating mobile apps, virtual reality games, and even theme park attractions. What could the organizations possibly offer each other?

As it turns out, lots. All three have a vested interest in innovative, interdisciplinary teaching and learning. All three create immersive experiences that inspire, educate, and engage. And all three want the best for Pittsburgh's kids.

The organizations, along with the University of Pittsburgh Center for Learning in Out-of-School Environments (UPCLOSE), began working together to develop programs in woodworking, circuitry, sewing, animation, and making. The resulting MAKESHOP married UPCLOSE's academic research; the Children's Museum's mission to spark joy and curiosity; the ETC's focus on technology, art, and design; and Schell Games' expertise in creating interactive experiences. Within four years, the MAKESHOP became a permanent, fully staffed museum feature replete with professional-grade art, building, and programming tools; today, its maker-educators offer events and workshops on a near-daily basis. The MAKESHOP has boosted the Children's Museum's attendance, increased the average age of its visitors, and led to deeper family engagement. According to Werner, "MAKESHOP has really made us think differently about what it means to be a museum and the role of museums in people's lives."

The partnership's benefits are not limited to the museum and its visitors. The more kids visit spaces like the MAKESHOP—spaces where they're encouraged to be curious, creative, and experimental—the more they will gravitate toward places like the ETC and Schell Games. Increasingly, the MAKESHOP impacts educators, too: the museum's Maker Education Boot Camp Program, a four-day professional development experience for classroom teachers and museum professionals, has helped hundreds of educators take the philosophy and practice of making back to their institutions. In fact, of the more than one hundred educators who participated in the 2013/2014 bootcamp, more than 70 percent reported significant or transformative changes in their practice.

This is why the Remake Learning Network exists: to facilitate partnerships that create great opportunities for kids. When they work well, there is no limit to what they can do. Of course, partnerships can also be messy, and networks of partnerships can be chaotic—especially if they are relatively loose and informal. (The Remake Learning Network, for example, has guiding principles but no centralized governing structure or membership requirements.) But if managed properly, flexibility and open-endedness can be a partnership's greatest strength.

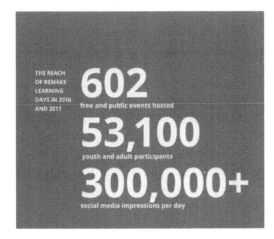

THE REACH OF REMAKE LEARNING DAYS IN 2016 AND 2017

602 free and public events hosted

53,100 youth and adult participants

300,000+ social media impressions per day

Figure 2.1.
Learning together: *A Decade of Collaboration and Innovation Across Greater Pittsburgh and West Virginia*, prepared by the Sprout Fund on behalf of Remake Learning. Learn more at remakelearning.org/learningtogether.

In 2017, the Network celebrated our tenth anniversary, and we used the opportunity to take stock, assess our mission and vision, and rededicate ourselves to the future. Our mission: "Remake Learning is a network that ignites engaging, relevant, and equitable learning practices in support of young people navigating rapid social and technological change." We issued a report, *Learning Together: A Decade of Collaboration and Innovation across Greater Pittsburgh and West Virginia*, which documents our accomplishments. The network now includes more than thirty counties in three states and has engaged 533 organizations and its projects and programs have involved more than fifty-three thousand individuals. Participating organizations include 130 school systems, twenty-seven libraries, eighteen museums, thirty-eight community centers, thirty higher education institutions, 196 nonprofit organizations, sixteen civic and government partners, fifty-four corporate and business partners, and twenty-four funders. We have hosted visitors from around the country and sent delegates to many international events. As we grow and create together, we intend to continue to adapt to the changes in the world—and in the world of learning.

Here are some of the lessons my Network colleagues and I have learned during our decade-plus on the ground.

1. **Staffing is critical.** When partnerships reach a certain size, they become difficult to run from the side of someone's desk. Eventually, you'll need a person whose entire job is to think about the partnership—how it is running, what it is accomplishing, how its

impact might be measured and expanded. The Children's Museum, for example, dedicates several full- and part-time employees exclusively to the MAKESHOP. The Remake Learning Network itself has multiple employees, responsible for managing its working groups, organizing delegations, hosting events, and more.

2. **Do not underestimate the importance of communications and documentation.** This is definitely something I did not appreciate enough early on. Stories in the media are motivating to both the community and the people engaged in the work. They are idea generators. They help you make your case. And they spur competition in constructive, positive ways.

3. **Take advantage of small grants that allow for experimentation.** Some of the Remake Learning Network's most successful projects started with an educator saying, "Hey, I've been talking with an ed-tech company, and we have an idea we'd like to try." The Labs—a program that provides teens with access to equipment, software, and mentors to make movies, build robots, learn photography, and more—began with a small grant. Now it has been expanded across the many branches of Pittsburgh's Carnegie Library. If you're an educator, do not be afraid to ask for grants; if you are a funder, do not be afraid to take risks on new partnerships and ideas.

4. **Build on your strengths.** Recognize what makes your organization uniquely positioned to achieve your vision and think broadly about how other organizations might help you get there.

5. **Read the Remake Learning Playbook.** Full of essays, tips, case studies, and lessons learned, the Playbook distills everything we have learned so far into a simple, engaging read. Visit remakelearning.org/playbook.

6. **Meet people where they are—literally.** Go places. Go to conferences and events beyond your region and sector. Doing so prompts ideas and sparks camaraderie, especially when colleagues are traveling together and spending time with unexpected people from different organizations and professions.

7. **At the same time, be open and inclusive.** Actively invite people to come see your organization and its work.

One final thought: When thinking about partnerships, it's more important than ever to deliberately design for equity. For too long, education has worked for some children, while leaving large groups of others behind. If we are to truly remake education, we must do so for all—skills like creativity, problem-solving, and the ability to communicate and collaborate cannot be reserved for a privileged few. It's up to us to ensure that all children experience the joys of learning, whether it takes place in schools, libraries, museums, or spaces we have not yet invented.

Partnerships as the Great Good Place **3**

ELYSE EIDMAN-AADAHL

*BIOGRAPHY: **Elyse Eidman-Aadahl** is executive director of the National Writing Project, a network of nearly 185 literacy-focused professional learning and research communities located at universities across the United States. Based at the University of California, Berkeley, Eidman-Aadahl's work at the National Writing Project includes leading nationally networked learning and research initiatives for educators working in kindergarten through twelfth grade, university, and out-of-school settings, including the YOUmedia and Intersections networks of libraries and museums.*

Whter I was just beginning my career in education, I had the good fortune to work at a large rural high school with an extraordinary faculty. The year I began, the school was undergoing certification review, and everyone was assigned to one or more evaluation committees. I was assigned to a committee that made a very smart decision to do its work every other Friday at a local watering hole named Sharkey's Cove. (Cue: theme from *Cheers*) With time, that "perfect watering hole" came to host an ongoing intellectual community that was at once public and professional, but also convivial and homey.

Though never mentioned in formal accounts of the school and its work, those regular quasi-faculty meetings, which grew in size and continued for many years, did as much to shape the culture and impact of our common institution at that time as any of our investments in staff development. The informal network of trusting relationships between and among staff across the departments of the school, though barely visible to outsiders, became the foundation for joint action and continuous improvement that distinguished the institution at its best. Much later, after years of research and experience leading networks and partnership programs across the country through my role at the National Writing Project, I've come to better understand the special alchemy that was present at Sharkey's Cove and observe how thoughtful leaders can design for the kind of practitioner-learning that happened there.

Across the many examples of networks and partnerships described in this volume, partnerships and networks are doing more than designing new learning opportunities for the public—they are also creating exciting contexts for learning and leadership development for their own staff. For many practitioners, networks such as Pittsburgh's Remake Learning Network, the Balboa Park Cultural Partnership, the Balboa Park Online Collaborative, and Virginia Africana provide a transformative professional opportunity—the network itself becoming their Sharkey's Cove. Networks that plan for open-ended, ongoing opportunities for the practitioners in their organizations to meet, explore ideas together, and engage in self-directed learning can both pursue the practical goals of their institutional partnerships and unleash learning and leadership development for their staff. In short, the "Third Place" is a natural home for thriving communities of practice, and partnership networks can be the vehicle to create and sustain them.

Partnerships and Networks as the Third Place

At the National Writing Project, a forty-four-year-old network of partnering universities, school systems, and local learning organizations (including libraries and museums), we have been exploring the potential of networks and collaborative structures to create Third Places for practitioner-learning for many years. The notion of the Third Place, or sometimes called Third Space, is drawn from sociologist Ray Oldenburg's *The Great Good Place: Cafes, Coffee Shops, Community Centers, Beauty Parlors, General Stores, Bars, Hangouts, and How They Get You through the Day.*[1] Oldenburg's interest was in these ubiquitous yet rarely studied places in a community—places exactly like Sharkey's Cove. The best of them, he found, were places of conviviality and openness—"where everybody knows your name and they're always glad you came"—where regulars and newbies mixed and democratic possibilities were entertained and expanded. Oldenburg's research spanned the role of coffee houses in the American Revolution to barbershops and beauty parlors in the Civil Rights movement. Following his lead, others have extended the concept to a range of institutions, including the internet, and have linked Third Places both to quality of life in neighborhoods and to our civic fabric.[2]

Key to the quality and functioning of these Great Good Places is their unique positioning as something other than either the private nature of home life or the instrumental nature of our workplaces: public, yet "homey"; professional, yet open and egalitarian; voluntary, yet powered by participant commitment. In short, Third Places are alternative spaces where a different set of rules apply. Similarly, partnership settings that shake up taken-for-granted patterns of workplace activity also create alternative spaces where a different set of rules apply. Partnerships introduce both risk and reward into organizational settings. Managing the balance of these risks and rewards for institutional functioning generally falls to the leaders of an institution who know that rightly addressed, the rewards can outweigh the risks.

Partnerships operate not only in the boardroom, but also on the floor, creating conditions for risk and reward for practitioners, too. For this reason, "the partnership" or network can itself create that Great Good Place that is productive of learning, sustains commitment, and powers action not only for the "institution," but also for the practitioners who work there. This is not to say that practitioners cannot or do not learn on the job in their single institution. Indeed, practice itself provides a context for thousands of daily experiments in action and result. But over time, all successful practitioners adapt to the basic conditions of their specific workplace. As they grow in seniority, much of what they know becomes tacit, embedded in routine actions and ways of working within an organization. When practitioners work together across institutional contexts, the taken-for-granted elements of practice are called into question as staff see colleagues across settings doing similar work with similar values in markedly different ways. For staff too, then, the partnership, collaboration, or learning networks becomes their Sharkey's Cove, the Third Place,[3] a public/professional space outside their home institution where they may be free of instrumental expectations and hierarchies and invited to think freshly about their work.

Building the Third Place into Networks and Partnerships

So how can network leaders build a Great Good Place into their designs for network activity and partnership deliverables? Across our work with the National Writing Project, a network of 185 university-based partnership programs, we've seen that a first step is to take the model and metaphor of the Great Good Place seriously. The second is to put it to use for learning.

To build the space, invest in time: Sharkey's Cove enticed us with its cheesy nautical-themed decor and its welcoming stance toward a group of educators who would sit for hours and not spend much money. But what made Sharkey's Cove our Third Place was the investment of time together, one that was originally provided through the structure of our recertification work. Time was the first investment and is central to the Third Place.

The power of open-ended time in the Third Place is deeply related to the nature of practice itself. Across organizations, time to think is a precious commodity. Whether standing at a station on the museum floor or circulating around a busy classroom, frontline staff spend their days juggling, minute by minute, an almost infinite number of individual interests and demands from learners while simultaneously navigating competing distractions on the floor or in the building. Much like the old vaudeville performer spinning plates on poles who is always running from one plate to another to give it a boost before it falls down, frontline staff find that the pace, complexity, and "always on/always public" nature of practice provides little time for systematic reflection, self-assessment, or deliberate learning. Administrative staff may have more "downtime," but their work too may be pressured by escalating demands, frequent meetings, and never-ending deadlines. Regardless of their position, staff in smaller institutions or educational organizations may find themselves too few in number to constitute a community of practice or get feedback on their work.

Third place thinking reminds us of the need for a regular, consistent, open time for a community of practice to emerge across organizations working in partnership, whether face to face or online.

Frequency may be less important than consistency and predictability. As for the space, workplace amenities or advanced online tool sets may be less important than comfort and conviviality, and in networks of multiple institutions, a kind of neutrality that signals that the space belongs to everyone. For some networks, meeting at a truly "other" space like a co-working or community space may work, but institutions can share hosting as well as long as they can create the right atmosphere and boundaries to allow their own staff to feel as if they are "free" from their own workplace demands. Finally, branding is critical to mark the Third Place as an alternative to more instrumental activities like "meetings" or "task groups." Think of the Science Cafe or Dine & Discuss nights rather than a "partnership planning meeting."

Design for participatory culture: At Sharkey's Cove, we benefited from beginning with participatory work—peer-driven and participant-led. Across our active National Writing Project Third Spaces, we see that the culture is voluntary, yet highly participatory. Standing in contrast with traditional classes or speakers, the expectation is that everyone carries the weight of making something productive happen. Establishing such a culture, particularly across organizations who are just beginning to work in partnership, is generally a first goal for network leaders. Community-building activities where everyone contributes and everyone gains are critical at the start and may include participation in community maintenance activities like hosting, calendar planning, and cleaning up. The pot-luck dinner can be both metaphor and reality.

In such a culture, participants soon find themselves ready for more ambitious learning activities, and, fortunately, there are many collections of peer-driven activities that have been tested and refined over many years. Collections of tools for Open Space Technologies, Action Research, and Ed Camps, as well as toolkits assembled by groups supporting Communities of Practice are broadly available online. Alternatively, groups may decide to pursue common readings or plan a round robin of Ignite Talks, a series of "fast and fun presentations . . . [in which] speakers must build their presentations with 20 slides, each of which is show for 15 seconds" resulting in a quick five-minute presentation.[4] All of these tools and technologies serve to build a common participatory culture that soon becomes associated with Third Space learning.

Bring in the practice: Open learning activities can build a strong and supportive culture among practitioners in a network or partnership setting. This culture, though, may have its strongest impact when it becomes a tool for self-reflection and feedback on practice. Typically, practitioners have few opportunities to observe practitioners in other settings and organizations, let alone the opportunity to see how their approaches and strategies fit within a larger map of activities across a network. Third Spaces are ideal settings for the study of practice because they are removed from the contexts of employee observations and review, so network leaders often find ways to "bring in the practice." Studying the actual artifacts of curriculum, sharing the approaches underlying a museum's interpretation plan, and observing expert practitioners at work—perhaps in very different institutional settings—provide different entry points into learning, one that makes practice concrete and analyzable in a way that "talking about" practice does not.

When treated with appreciation as artifacts of practice, a focus on the "stuff" of practice signals a respect for the day-to-day work of frontline staff. And the stuff is essential to the conversation as much of practice fades after the moment of enactment. Discussions, comments, interactions disappear into the air, leaving only imperfect memories of the day, and after time these memories disappear and distort. Turning a partnership's Great Good Place into a practice-focused space requires routines and activities where practitioners bring, display, and study the artifacts of curriculum, the actual content of exhibits, floor activities, or other educational programs, even recordings of questions and discussions or cross-observation notes. Such work can be electrifying when staff find they get actionable and supportive feedback on their work, drawing on the diverse perspectives and organizational backgrounds of network colleagues.

Such work can also be risky, too. So bringing in the practice requires the community to acknowledge the vulnerability that comes with such sharing. Norms and processes that bring predictable and positive structures to conversations about practice, as well as leadership by experienced members of the community, help communities develop the cultural competence to routinely navigate the risks associated with going public with practice. Groups such as the National School Reform Faculty,[5] whose work centers on facilitating Critical Friends Groups, have published dozens of protocols and provide training in peer-led facilitation.

Third Space thinking invites us to turn problems into inquiries: What happens when . . .? What if I try . . .? To what end?

Turn problems into inquiries: If lists of activities or protocols for interaction seem a far distance from the voluntary, supportive community of the neighborhood bar, the connection is found in how participants use the Third Place to explore questions and topics that matter to them and respond directly to their needs and interests. Third Space thinking invites us to turn problems into inquiries: What happens when . . .? What if I try . . .? To what end? In the manner of action research and practitioner inquiry, the diverse practitioners who network in the Third Place can support each other in taking up desired improvements in practices or institutional processes, trying out action and monitoring the results. In this case, all the investment in learning how to capture and record practice or collect artifacts and data pays off in action learning.

My Sharkey's Cove group benefited from its beginning in processes that yielded data and artifacts from our common institution. We were able to see how each of us and our practice fit into a larger whole, and we could raise questions that were both personally relevant but also related to common interests. Networks and partnerships afford similar opportunities as they collect data, generate activity reports, or circulate evaluation findings. What turns these common activities into Third Space thinking is the invitation for all participants to discuss, frame, and use these materials to advance their own questions about their work and the work of the partnership.

Let learners be leaders: Oldenburg makes much of the mix of "regulars" and newbies in *The Great Good Place*.[6] The proprietor sets the tone, but regulars are essential for giving a place its character and inducting new members into the common culture. The Third Space translation is clear— let learners become leaders. Many would argue that networks should identify a person, perhaps as a staff position, to coordinate and manage their Third Place—the equivalent of the proprietor. But it is the culture of the regulars that will both establish the learning potential of the effort and carry the culture back to their institutions and the perspectives of the institution into the Third Space.

Networks who invest in their regulars to develop skills and experience in facilitating adult learning in professional settings create new pathways for leadership development that provide educators (and other museum staff) with professional and career development without, necessarily, moving out of their departmental setting into management and administration or different museum areas. For many such "lead learners," these are the opportunities that provide the spark that enhances job satisfaction and retention. And even these roles have growth trajectories built-in as lead learners mentor and support newcomers who might become new regulars in the space, working to ensure pathways to leadership for others that keep the culture fresh, responsive, and forward-looking. Stagnant leadership impedes innovation—therefore, turning leadership over to new members is an important skill. Learning that skill in the informal culture of the Third Space can enhance leadership capacity back in the institution itself.

The actual Sharkey's Cove is no more, having been razed in a burst of commercial development. The Sharkey's Cove gang never really found another place, and that was fine. The years together had shaped our attitudes about professional community, learning, and reflection; we carried those new attitudes and ideas into new settings. But sociologists in the tradition of Robert Putnam in *Bowling Alone* nonetheless worry about the loss of too many Sharkey's Coves in our communities.[7] The importance of and need for human connection is still present and an essential part of learning, both online and off. Networks, partnerships, "learning ecosystems," connected learning, and other models that knit together learning institutions and programs to enrich learning opportunities in their areas respond to the importance of connection, so it is natural that they would become places where their most valuable resource—their staff—can learn too.

Partnerships, Not Mergers   4

PETER ELLSWORTH

BIOGRAPHY: PETER ELLSWORTH is the chief executive officer of the Legler Ben-bough Foundation, which was established in 1985 in order to improve the quality of life for San Diegans. During his lifetime, Legler Benbough was a businessman, rancher, civic leader, and philanthropist who contributed to San Diego's civic and cultural life. The Foundation has taken a focused approach funding in only three areas: providing community economic opportunity by supporting, developing, and enhancing the Research and Innovation Economy being developed around the University of California at San Diego and within the university itself; providing cultural opportunity through funding the institutions located in Balboa Park; and providing opportunity in health, education, and welfare through funding of organizations and programs in the Diamond Neighborhoods of San Diego. Balboa Park is the site of the 1915 Panama–California Exposition and one of the largest public cultural and recreational areas in the United States.

Lessons from Balboa Park Collaborations

CREATING COLLABORATIONS (partnerships) has been a principal ob-jective of our foundation for many years. As we worked in each of our specific focus areas, it became increasingly apparent that the parties we were serving could be much more efficient and effective by working together in a variety of ways. In Balboa Park, for example, these partnerships have included the Balboa Park Cultural Partnership and the Balboa Park Online Collaborative.

In the Balboa Park Cultural Partnership, the museums in the park have come together and successfully addressed things like:

- Energy sustainability (at very considerable cost savings);
- Unifying museum content for common marketing both regionally and nationally;
- Creating the Balboa Park Pass to allow more affordable and useful visitation of the museums as a group, while using part of the proceeds for free museum access for underprivileged families;
- Creating forums both for training of museum personnel and communicating to the public (Balboa Park Learning Institute), and;
- Multimuseum events for the public, like the Maker's Faire.

Have they accomplished all that they are capable of? No, I believe there are many other as yet underdeveloped opportunities. The partnership could save money by sharing more back-room expenses or explore exhibits at multiple museums on a common theme to provide an enhanced visitor experience. The proximate location of so many museums in Balboa Park—a feat that could not be duplicated anyplace else—gives the public an opportunity to see one subject from many perspectives. But, despite these as-yet-unrealized options, these organizations have come a long way: from not wanting to even meet when the collaborative began to recently establishing their collective park brand "One Park, One Team."

Balboa Park Online Collaborative was created when technology was just beginning to have a potential impact on museums. We supported the museum directors to come together and explore the opportunities and the challenges posed by technology and its new approach to the visitor experience. The collaborative that was created has:

- Provided the vehicle for the development of a common park website and for individual websites that all relate to each other;
- Provided the vehicle for the technical support of websites and web projects for both individual museum and park-wide, and;
- Provided the vehicle to obtain national recognition and funding that could not otherwise have been obtained due to the collaborative's quite unique scope and number of participating institutions.

As the institutions have come to acknowledge and appreciate the value of technology, and as the number of commercial providers supplying services in the area has increased, the collaborative has shifted its emphasis away from technical support—now available elsewhere—to collaborative efforts to develop a few dramatic and compelling technology-based offerings that deliver the mission message of the institutions in new ways.

What We Have Learned

1. **This is about partnership, not merger.** It is essential that in the development of the concept, design, strategy, and in the process of implementation, that all those who are included feel that they are listened to and valued. This is not about the funders or the big guys telling everyone what to do. *It is about the group.* This can be frustrating because sometimes it is hard to get people to participate and then be held responsible for an outcome that they do not like.

2. **The partnership has to be approached from a community mission perspective.** A principal challenge in elevating the discussion of a potential collaborative to where it needs to be (i.e., what is the benefit to the community from the prospective partnership) is that museums frequently do not see their mission from a community perspective and fail to appreciate that public members on their board are there to represent the public that is paying part of the costs of the institution though tax and other benefits, not just to support the goals and objectives of the particular institution. Great museum leaders are understandably and importantly passionate about the subjects addressed by their institution and the collections that represent those subjects. Usually these leaders' education and experience is almost entirely centered on the content focus of the museum. Consequently, they view their mission from the institution's perspective, a view reinforced by the need of funds to survive and often by the operations and processes of those who provide the funding. In this environment, collaboration with their competitors for funding and other services is, understandably, an unnatural act. For collaborative efforts to be successful, under these circumstances, the leaders have to agree that the collaboration is the best, or the only, way for their particular mission to be successful, and they need to appreciate and accept this as providing significant value to the community that they serve. This cannot be assumed, and time needs to be taken at the beginning of any collaborative, and at every stage of the collaborative endeavor, to be sure that the objectives of the collaboration are understood and accepted by the leaders as directly related to the success of the

institution's mission. Museum leaders need to have the time and opportunity to understand and articulate how a partnership supports their organization's mission before the details of the collaboration can be successfully addressed. Only when one can feel the leader's spirit of "We have to do this" should the specifics of the relationship be established. Working together almost always requires some individual sacrifices and compromises. These things will not easily occur unless the mission-related reasons for making those sacrifices and changes are clearly—and jointly—understood.

3. **The collaborative enterprise takes a lot of time and patience.** The meetings, the private discussions, the telephone calls, and emails to put one of these things together takes an enormous amount of time. Patience is required to deal with the multitude of issues that need to be addressed. Importantly, the discussion is not over when the partnership is created. As the collective effort proceeds, the central issue of why this effort is worth it needs to be revisited on a regular basis. My measure of whether a collaborative effort is successful is whether we are closer to our goals this month or year than we were last month or year. In my experience, trying to measure success in terms of achieving ultimate goals is usually frustrating and not helpful in reaching these goals in the long term. It is a long and sometimes frustrating road, but the results are well worth the effort.

Us versus Them 5
How to Bridge Boundaries to Discover New Partnership Frontiers

CHRIS ERNST

*BIOGRAPHY: BY INTEGRATING deep global experience with applied expertise, **Chris Ernst**, PhD, is uniquely positioned to enable innovation and change in complex, multistakeholder, cross-boundary environments. He has worked with organizations and communities across sectors in most parts of the world from generals and ambassadors in Iraq to the executive director of a leading nonprofit in India to the chief executive officer of a disruptive innovation company in Silicon Valley to the leaders of the world's largest philanthropy. Chris has held leadership roles with the globally top-ranked Center for Creative Leadership, as vice president for organization effectiveness at Juniper Networks in Silicon Valley, and presently, as global head of people and organizational potential at the Bill & Melinda Gates Foundation. As an active researcher, writer, and speaker on global issues, his work is published in top academic journals and outlets such as* HBR, Wall Street Journal, Forbes, *and* MIT Sloan Management Review, *and in authoring two books, including Center for Creative Leadership's best-seller,* Boundary Spanning Leadership. *As a practicing executive, he has served in multiyear expatriate roles in Asia and Europe, led cross-functional and multicultural teams, and designed and facilitated leadership interventions in diverse industry contexts across six continents.*

The Interconnected World

THE WORLD HAS BECOME increasingly boundless and interconnected. Technology has changed the pace and means of interactions. Long-established structures and boundaries are breaking down. New business models, new operating rules, and new partnerships are possible—and expected—in order to engage new audiences, foster innovation, or drive growth.

But rather than enjoying and benefiting from the greater connectivity that is now possible, many leaders are stymied. The technical advances that have dismantled so many physical boundaries may have created a flat world, but they have not led to the innovation and collaboration many expected. The divides and rifts of human relationships remain and seem somehow more intractable. On both large-scale, global dimensions, and in everyday, routine interactions, lines get drawn. Progress stalls, innovation falters, and conflict simmers or flares.

Bridging boundaries between groups is the new and critical work of leadership.

Overriding "Us versus Them"

When leaders think and act in ways that allow employees, contributors, partners, and audiences to override "Us versus Them" reactions, they grow the capacity for effective collaboration within teams and organizations—and across organizations, groups, and communities. When leaders model and facilitate cross-boundary relationships, they open the door to innovative processes, expanded mindsets, greater flexibility, increased inclusion and engagement, and enduring partnerships. They achieve outcomes that are greater than any group could create on their own.

If new approaches are needed to create and sustain vibrant museums and museum communities—and achieve their objectives—attention and care must be given to build relationships, collaborations, and partnerships. This begins by understanding and addressing five boundaries:

1. **Vertical boundaries** are those that cross level, rank, seniority, authority, and power. The separation of groups into layers of top, middle, and entry level—each with corresponding levels of authority—is a ubiquitous feature in nearly all organizations. Even within flatter organizations with less formal organization structures, vertical boundaries remain in some form, even if unspoken, resulting in varying levels of status and respect. In some museums, the vertical "pecking order" pyramid includes the director, chief operations officer, and director of development at a higher level than other departments. Curators may also occupy an elevated niche, although that is changing. Within departments, be they development, marketing, or education, there is usually a clear vertical reporting structure.

2. **Horizontal boundaries** are the walls that separate groups by areas of experience and expertise. Most museums have created separate

functional offices for development or advancement, curatorial, education, operations, marketing, and perhaps information technology support. The negative costs of horizontal boundaries are revealed when one function is favored over another, when the work of one unit or product line threatens the viability of another, or when departments work at cross-purposes.

3. **Demographic boundaries** are found in the space between diverse groups, including the entire range of human diversity from gender and race to education and ideology. Inclusion, equity, and voice are increasingly relevant to decisions about staffing, community, and audience—and the way in which authentic and productive intra-organizational relationships and community connections unfold.

4. **Geographic boundaries** are represented by distance, locations, cultures, regions, and markets. Boundaries of geography create constraints when there is a need for collaboration across different locations. Even for more local museums, demographic changes within their communities and service area may also change the geographies within which museums operate. Museums may be physically bound or locally focused, but draw interest and audiences well beyond a narrow geography. Based on their mission and focus, and increasingly their "reach" via social media and digital resources, museum contributors, collaborators, partners—and audiences—may come from anywhere in the world.

These boundaries often operate as barriers, rooted in identity: our core values, how we define ourselves, and our beliefs about how we fit in. Whether obvious or subtle, they set up groups of "like" and "unlike" people and creating suspicion, distrust, or misunderstanding. People start working at cross-purposes, knowingly or not.

Of course, eliminating boundaries is not an option. Organizations need to involve and work with people who have different values and beliefs, mindsets and expertise, perspectives and priorities. So, what can you do to span boundaries and generate the collaboration needed for innovation, problem-solving, and sustainability? Three strategies, each with two practices and numerous possible tactics, are needed. The process, depicted in Figure 5.1 below, creates a nexus of collaboration between previously divided groups.

Manage Boundaries

The first step to spanning boundaries is, ironically, to create or strengthen them. You must be able to see group boundaries clearly before you can bridge them. Well-meaning leaders often start by introducing groups and focusing on points of similarity in an effort to drive connection and collaboration. But this overlooks the reality of the boundaries that exist, the ways people identify themselves, and the history and experiences they have had. Without a chance to claim their boundaries, individuals and groups will put up defenses or feel disrespected. The "Us versus Them" instinct will override the stated goal of collaboration or inclusion. Instead, leaders can help groups see and value difference in two ways: buffering and reflecting.

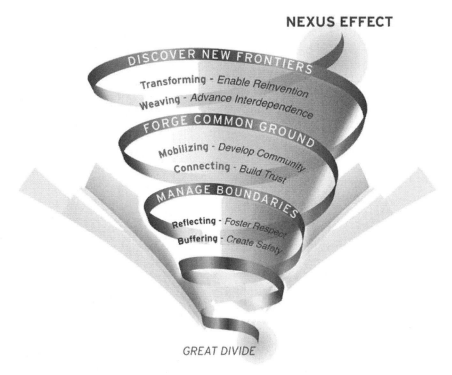

Figure 5.1.   Chris Ernst and Donna Chrobat-Mason. *Boundary Spanning Leadership* (2011). Forging/common/ground.

The practice of buffering is about creating safety. It is about defining boundaries, clarifying identity, and creating purpose within a group. This might be a functional or project team, a demographic group within your organization—or, thinking broadly, it could be your full museum staff and the "other" group is an outside funder or potential partner organization. By "building a buffer," people see clearly who they are and strengthen that identity with others who are familiar and alike in some way. This creates a state of psychological safety and protects the group.

Once groups have achieved a state of safety between them, the next practice, reflecting, involves deeper understanding of boundaries to foster respect. When space for reflecting is created, different groups "look across" the boundary between them, while keeping the boundary intact. They are able to exchange knowledge and see the distinct perspectives of others. Reflecting helps articulate difference but also uncover similarities. Knowledge of the "other" deepens and respect is built.

Forge Common Ground

The next step is to find what is universal and shared, to bring groups together around a shared purpose. The focus is to integrate different groups, building trust, engagement, and shared accountability. The original identities and boundaries do not disappear; rather, they are suspended or reframed as people willingly seek to be part of something larger than themselves. Two practices—connecting and mobilizing—allow people to find and create common ground.

The practice of connecting builds trust by creating a third space, a neutral zone for members of different groups to interact as individuals. They have a chance to connect as individuals and find personal ties or similarities that they would not have readily recognized previously. Connecting involves "stepping outside" of ourselves and "stepping into" a space (mentally and often physically as well) that is neither "mine" nor "yours." New networks and deeper relationships are formed.

The next practice, mobilizing, involves reframing boundaries to create a new community, another sense of belonging and another facet of identity. Through mobilizing, groups "move outside" their group boundary and "move inside" a new, larger boundary. Mindsets expand from "Us versus Them" to "We." The key here is taking action together. Shared work allows a group to set aside differences for a specific goal, purpose, activity, and time.

Discover New Frontiers

A frontier is a place of emergent possibility, the border between the known and unknown. The third step of boundary spanning is to operate in the space where similarities and differences meet to create something new.

Differentiated skills, perspectives, and resources, fueled by an integrated vision and strategy, bring forth what was unseen, unknown, or impossible before. The two practices here are weaving and transforming.

Think of weaving as interlacing multiple strands, representing different groups, perspectives, or expertise. Each strand remains distinct but is combined with others to create a larger whole. The interconnectedness, the interdependence, of the strands is essential to the idea, the design, and the outcome of the new creation. Skilled weavers establish a creative space to draw out and integrate group differences, foster collective learning, and develop interdependence.

Transform

The final practice, transforming, relies on that interdependence for reinvention. Group members are able to cross over the boundaries of others and values, beliefs, and perspective shift in fundamental and transformative ways. The strands of identity become less distinct over time, as they interact and operate as a whole. In this state, people begin to operate outside the known context. Groups begin to let go of established norms and see alternative futures and emergent possibilities.

The outcomes of weaving and transforming—innovative ideas, new solutions, adapting to change, or creating disruption—are often what leaders are looking for when they talk about leveraging diversity, engaging creativity, or becoming more collaborative. But the process and the outcomes fall short without the prior work of managing differences and finding common ground and clear efforts toward interdependence and reinvention.

At this point, you may sense that boundary spanning has value, but can't quite picture it. You may be asking, what does boundary-spanning leadership look like? Consider how a group of thirty-eight leaders from three distinct-but-related fields—libraries, archives, and museums—came together and used the boundary-spanning leadership methodology to advance their shared core mission: to collect, make accessible, and preserve information for today and for future generations.

Example: Boundary-Spanning Experience with Partners

My colleagues from the Center for Creative Leadership, with the Institute of Museum and Library Services and the Educopia Institute, used boundary spanning as the foundation of the Nexus Leading across Boundaries (LAB) project.[1] Industry and association leaders became project partners to evaluate their capacity for collective alignment and transformation, with an emphasis on creating a shared leadership development framework and training. The participants and their organizations faced similar, disruptive challenges, and yet saw themselves as having separate, sometimes competing, priorities and needs. Differences seemed greater than commonalities.

The participants met in 2013 for what would be the first of several in-person sessions over the next few years. Their initial time together began with "managing boundaries" conversations, reinforcing and supporting the uniqueness and differences of each segment (libraries, archives, and museums) but also subgroups (region, specialty, and field). Sharing those perspectives and identities with others, without judging or threat, created awareness and understanding across boundaries. Then, as the work shifted to "forging common ground," individuals had time to connect as individuals and cross-boundary groups worked on small projects or activities together, creating baseline ideas for a leadership competency framework. Lastly, in "discovering new frontiers," energy around the work and what was shared resulted in creative discussions that combined and built on ideas. People were open to multiple perspectives and to critique in ways they would not have been if they had jumped right to the problem solving and planning work.

Boundary spanning was not only part of the group process; it was also integral to the leadership framework the participants developed for their profession. The framework and the training curriculum that followed reflected roles and challenges at various levels and the need to span boundaries, build networks, and collaborate. Through boundary-spanning practices and perspectives, the LAB group and the organizations and professionals who have been involved in the leadership training have sparked new thinking about the "knowledge dissemination professions." Transforming through collaboration and partnership is now possible and exciting for the organizations involved—something that had been unthinkable before.

This example shows how a boundary-spanning experience was facilitated and then embedded into sector-focused effort. It involved outside expertise and funding to jump-start something new. More commonly—and simply—boundary spanning comes from a series of choices and tactics that take place in the context of everyday work. Museum leaders and innovators can apply these ideas to create, strengthen, and sustain relationships and partnerships that will bring their organizations into the future.

Boundary Spanning in Your Own Organization

First, on your own or with a small group, think about the boundaries (vertical, horizontal, stakeholder, demographic, geographic) that are currently most prevalent, most pressing, or most difficult to span. Next, consider the nature of your challenge. What is mission-critical work for the organization? Why is boundary spanning relevant? Then you can begin to question legacy boundaries and start to figure out who should be involved. You might:

- Bring together members of two or more internal groups to create a new project team, aimed at addressing a key need or challenge.
- Consistently use cross-functional teams to navigate strategic change— or re-energize routine work.
- Strengthen or expand an existing external relationship or partnership.
- Explore a new partnership with an organization that is similar to yours, but in a different location—or an organization that is different, but shares your audience or geography.
- Reach out to an organization from a completely different sector to tackle a shared problem.
- Test the waters with a competitor by collaborating on a small-scale project or narrow-scope partnership to explore new, collaborative frontiers together.

As you are considering potential collaborators and partners, start practicing boundary spanning with one or more tactics, based on the six practices. You might begin with you and your staff to experience and model boundary spanning. You could help existing teams or group to be more effective, or begin right away with a new team or partnership. Use the ideas that follow, tailoring them or making up your own tactics, keeping in mind your goal (creating safety, building trust, etc.).

Buffering tactics create safety. How will you define boundaries, clarify identity, and establish purpose?

Key questions:

- Have we asked and answered: Who are we as a defined group?
- Have we defined our purpose or calling? Have we differentiated our work from the work of others in the organization?
- Have we clarified our boundaries so that other groups know where our responsibilities and obligations end and begin?
- Have we created a safe space for the group and individual team members?

Possible tactics:

- Create a statement of purpose or team charter that reflects shared values, who you are, what you do, and how you work.
- Clarify roles and responsibilities within the group. Discuss details of how work gets done, how decisions are made, and norms of communication within your group—and how your group will interact with other groups.
- Have honest conversations about the strengths of the team and its limitations, what it will and will not do.
- Provide time and space for people with shared expertise, interests, or demographics to gather through activities, communities of practice, and affinity groups.
- Celebrate progress and accomplishments as a team.

Reflecting tactics foster respect. How will you help people to understand others, without giving up their own identity, beliefs, positions, or practices?

Key questions:

- Do we encourage learning about others?
- How could we improve or facilitate the exchange of information and viewpoints across organizational lines?
- Do we set a good example, consistently treating others with respect?
- What person, team, region, or culture needs to better understand the group?

Possible tactics:

- Bring in outside views and ideas and give them genuine consideration. Build the habit of asking: How would other departments or divisions think about this? Who else should we ask? Who from that department could we bring in?
- Hold across-level meetings and get to know the people who interact with customers and constituents. They receive information and have perspectives and ideas that you will otherwise miss.
- Invite other groups or leaders in your organization to join your team or project meeting. Bring in customers, contributors, donors, or potential partners.

- Use social media to take in ideas and perspectives unlike your own. Read outside your usual scope and interests, too.
- Create opportunities for people to learn other roles and gain different perspectives. You might have formal job rotations or extended assignments in different roles, but having people shadow a colleague for a few hours over a month is effective, too.
- Get out of your bubble. Accept and extend invitations to social events or activities with colleagues as well as people you do not know well. Encourage others to do the same.

Connecting tactics build trust. How can you suspend your personal or group identity, take a neutral mental stance, and get to know others?

Key questions:

- How does our organization currently create personal connections?
- What structures and systems could encourage connecting?
- How can we harness the power of informal organizational networks?
- What events or opportunities can be created?

Possible tactics:

- Seek and create neutral ground for meetings, conversations, and work sessions. A physical space that is not "owned" by any one group keeps people more relaxed and willing to engage without the trappings of us versus them, mine or yours.
- Find a boundary-spanning partner. When you connect across boundaries with someone, help each other. Having a buddy to navigate into new territory gets you farther, faster.
- Set aside time during face-to-face and virtual meetings to connect personally. Sharing personal updates and having off-task conversation build relationships.
- Use collaborative technology (company intranet, discussion platforms, etc.) to foster cross-boundary sharing and familiarity.
- Get to know people as people. Host dinners or after-work outings; join or create nonwork activities with colleagues (lunchtime yoga? running club? jazz band?).

Mobilizing develops community. How will you tackle shared work?

Key questions:

- How do we develop an inclusive vision and shared goals?
- What would it take to ensure that different groups feel a strong sense of belonging to the organization and its mission?
- How can we work together to make sure that everyone's viewpoint is heard and honored?
- How do we create an environment where people feel accountable to one another and their shared goals?

Possible tactics:

- Have conversations or facilitate activities to talk about values, what matters about the work, and purpose. Make a poster or other tangible reminder of what the group has in common.
- Determine the brand of your boundary-spanning team. Choose a symbol or picture or write a narrative that represents the larger group identity or project purpose.
- Rally around a common threat. Agreeing on the consequences of not succeeding can create focus and energy among diverse people or partners.
- Do not assume people know how to collaborate effectively. Norms and systems for information sharing and decision making are driven by existing boundaries. Give weight to details of how to interact as well as the larger purpose and plans.
- Create a pace or rhythm for ongoing connection, information sharing, and relationships building. Regular meetings—both one-on-ones and group gatherings—are needed to keep progress going and normalize collaboration and connection.

Weaving advances interdependence. How will you to draw out and integrate group differences?

Key questions:

- How do we help individuals from our different groups to integrate their distinctive resources to achieve greater success?

- How can we "work as one" and yet continue to draw from our separate strengths and identities?
- How can we reconcile conflict between groups to uncover new solutions?
- What synergies exist among different groups to foster innovation?

Possible tactics:

- Use innovative staffing solutions, new team configurations, and fresh combinations of task and team. Rotating roles creates new perspectives and expands personal networks.
- Implement simple, small-scale, low-risk projects for boundary-spanning groups to gain experience working together.
- Foster a culture of open debate and constructive conflict. Then decide and act as a single unit, rather than as factions.
- Have a frank conversation about strengths and weaknesses within the partnership. Work to appreciate what the other brings as a great benefit to the partnership, not a sign of incompatibility or a source of frustration or competition.
- Model the collaborative mindset. Frame challenges or assignments as shared problems. Avoid language and behaviors that suggest a problem "belongs to them not us."

Transforming enables reinvention. How will you reimagine the work, the context, and the people?

Key questions:

- Do we want to reinvent who and what we are about as well as how we work together?
- Are we open to being a different group entirely or to establishing something completely new?
- Do we seek collaboration and reinvention across internal and external boundaries?
- How do we marshal wide-ranging expertise and experience to unearth new opportunities and spur new ideas?

Possible tactics:

- With colleagues or potential partners, attend workshops, conferences, and other events that are outside your profession. Encourage others to do likewise.
- Send teams to unexpected places. Send a mixed group (leaders from different functions or partner organizations or employees at various levels or time with the organization, for example) to learn about a business, field, country, or region completely outside your core business.
- Imagine the future together. Give everyone in the organization (and extended network of contributors and partners) a chance to imagine the ideal, transformed organization five years from now.
- Start at the top, but don't keep it there. Senior leaders do need to invest in partner relationships and model collaborative, boundary-spanning behavior. They should also expect boundary spanning to go wide and deep and facilitate and support those efforts.
- Remove and change structures that get in the way of boundary spanning. Review operational systems or tools (talent management systems, approval processes, budget rules) that create unnecessary divisions or reinforce the labels and "Us versus Them" behaviors you are trying to dismantle.

As you likely know from your own experience, it takes more than setting up a cross-functional team or putting people with different perspectives in a room together to foster innovation and solve problems. The "Us versus Them" instinct will easily override the stated goal of collaboration or inclusion. But, wherever boundaries collide, you do have a choice: accept the limiting and counterproductive outcomes of "Us versus Them," or reach for the promise of new possibilities and inspiring results. The places where different groups, ideas, perspectives, history, beliefs, and values intersect are nexus points where innovation, energy, and hope emerge—if given opportunity and a process to do so. Through boundary-spanning leadership, you, your organization, and your partners can create a shared vision and achieve outcomes above and beyond what any could achieve independently.

Partnering with the Public $\qquad$ 6

JOHN H. FALK

BIOGRAPHY: DR. **JOHN H. FALK** *is director of the Institute for Learning Innovation and Emeritus Sea Grant Professor of Free-Choice Learning at Oregon State University. He is a leading expert on free-choice learning: the learning that occurs when people have significant choice and control over the what, where, and when of their learning. His current research focuses on understanding the self-related reasons people utilize free-choice learning settings during their leisure time; studying the community impacts of museums, libraries, zoos, and aquariums; and helping cultural institutions rethink their educational positioning in the twenty-first century. His awards include the NARST: a worldwide organization for improving science teaching and learning through research Distinguished Career Award (2016); Oregon State University, University Outreach and Engagement Vice Provost Award for Excellence, Innovation-Partnerships Award (2016); Council of Scientific Society Presidents Award for Educational Research (2013); and American Alliance of Museums John Cotton Dana Award for Leadership (2010).*

Twenty-First-Century Museums

PARTNERSHIPS ARE INCREASINGLY becoming the modus operandi and lifeblood of twenty-first-century museums. However, to be successful, museums will need to broaden their conceptualization of partnerships. Needed are not merely ongoing and meaningful relationships with other organizations, but, equally if not more importantly, museums need to cultivate ongoing and deep collaborations with the publics that comprise the museum's core audience: partnerships with individuals and partnerships with collections of individuals.

Of course, most museums would claim they already possess such partnerships. They will cite the number of repeat visitors they attract, and how many members they have. *But these are twentieth-century concepts of partnership; audiences are treated as nameless, faceless statistics, not real partners.* How many museums are capable of recognizing their repeat visitors when they walk through the door? How many museum staff are capable of greeting these individuals by name? How many museums actually know their members? How many museums actually know anything about them beyond their giving history and zip code? Why are these individuals actually coming to the museum? What is the passion that animates their current relationship with the museum?

The social and economic landscape of the twenty-first century is rapidly changing. Most significantly for the discussion here are the profound changes in the public's expectations about both the nature and the outcomes of leisure experiences. These changes increasingly demand that museums treat their audiences as true partners, as individuals that they know and care about and whom they treat as co-equals.

Leisure in the Twenty-First Century

Leisure time, more than any other human endeavor, affords people an opportunity to proactively choose to act in ways that comport with their conceptions of well-being; to more or less act in ways consistent with their perceptions of how they would live their life if they had total control.[1] Of course having leisure, at least for most modern-day humans, requires some minimal level of affluence and free time, something that for centuries only the wealthiest fraction of a percent of the population possessed.[2] Although many in the world today continue to grind out a living without measurable leisure time, an ever-increasing percentage of the world's population, particularly within the developed world, has begun to sufficiently escape the grip of poverty to enjoy some amount of leisurely pursuit.

Over the past one hundred plus years, the vast majority of people used leisure as a mechanism for escaping from the physical and mental drudgery and exhaustion of factory work. Classic twentieth-century responses were the escapism fostered by Disney and other theme parks, or a week spent on vacation at the beach or some other resort doing "nothing." Although these leisure diversions are still popular, their market share is declining.[3] As the world of work has become increasingly centered on mental rather than physical labor, more and more of the public's leisure time is being filled with experiences designed to support a range of essentially mental diversions. Rather than simply physically relaxing under a palm tree at the beach, people increasingly see their leisure time as an opportunity to be energized and extended, an opportunity to immerse one's self in new ideas, spaces, and experiences.[4]

In the early years of the twenty-first century, more passive forms of leisure pursuit are being supplanted by activities designed to understand and push the limits of the body, such as whitewater rafting or mountain climbing, or to expand understanding of one's self and the world, such as visits to historic and natural settings, genealogical research, volunteer service experiences, and of course, visits to museums.[5] This broad shift in the perception of leisure is the single greatest contributor to the exponential growth in popularity of museums from a leisure experience that attracted 20 percent of the population annually in the mid-twentieth century to one that currently attracts roughly 60 percent of the population every year.[6] According to leisure researcher Geoff Godbey, "leisure should resemble the best aspects of work: challenges, skills and important relationships."[7] The key is that people perceive that they have some reasonable measure of choice and control over how they spend their time.

All leisure decision making increasingly comes down to a series of value-related, cost-benefit choices in which time plays a crucial role. Whether it is a short trip downtown to visit the shopping mall, a day-long trip to a museum or natural site, or a multiday journey to a domestic or foreign destination that might include a multitude of activities, including shopping, museum-going, and hiking, people weigh the costs and values of the experience and roughly "calculate" how an investment of time in this activity or another will benefit them and their loved ones, actively selecting the option(s) they perceive will afford them maximal satisfaction. What are the characteristics that would make a leisure good or service like museum-going rise above this crowded field? Rather than selecting leisure experiences based merely on their utility, today's increasingly affluent leisure consumers make decisions based on an experience or product's ability to satisfy their perceived personal desires and lifestyles. So complete has been this transformation among the affluent that, today, a majority of the people living in Western Europe, North America, Japan, and Australia have largely exhausted the things they need to purchase or do; instead, they now focus on what they want to purchase or do.[8] As the twenty-first century progresses, the concept of well-being has also shifted. Increasingly people attempt to engage in leisure experiences that promise to make them happier, better partners, parents, or friends, more knowledgeable and competent, experiences that nourish and rejuvenate the spirit and generally give meaning to their lives.[9]

As we move into the third decade of the twenty-first century, five key shifts in the public's leisure expectations have become increasingly important. These five expectations do not always align with the ways museums have historically defined their public role and/or done business. Today's public is seeking ways to:

1. First and foremost, satisfy their individual self-related needs;
2. Personalize/customize their experiences;
3. "Own" experiences (e.g., co-create experiences);
4. Share their experiences with others, but not necessarily those who are immediately in their presence (e.g., social media connections); and
5. Achieve self-actualization (e.g., experiences that build personal identity).

Let me briefly describe further each of these five new leisure expectations.

Self-Related Needs

Visitors come to museums for multiple reasons, but whatever the reason, first and foremost they visit in order to satisfy their own self-related needs.[10] The public's self-related needs, whether defined as the need to discover new and different things, the need to support the learning and satisfaction of others, the need to satisfy a particular intellectual or task-related goal, or some other specific need, are always self-referential and self-reinforcing. As a consequence, visitor self-related needs not only serve to motivate the visit, but also create the trajectory for the entire museum experience. They directly influence virtually every aspect of the visitor's in-museum behavior as well as post-visit meaning making.[11] The public has always used museums this way, but they are becoming increasingly mindful of their visit agendas and increasingly determined to satisfy them.

Personalization/Customization of Experiences

The mass production strategies of the Industrial Age have created a glut of cheap, readily available goods and services. So plentiful have goods and services become that the public can afford to be selective, so selective that they no longer are satisfied with one-size-fits-all solutions. To be successful in the leisure marketplace of the twenty-first century, organizations need to support the public's desire to feel special, to believe that experiences are personal, customized to meet not just anyone's needs, but their needs in particular.[12] In one recent U.S. marketing study, overall 36 percent of consumers said they primarily purchase personalized products or services, with those under forty years of age even more invested. Roughly half of all consumers aged twenty-five to thirty years old said they were primarily attracted to personalized goods and services.[13] Currently, most museums continue to utilize Industrial Age strategies in the development and presentation of their public offerings (e.g., one-size-fits-all exhibitions).

Co-Created Experiences

One outcome of the public's drive for ever-greater customization is the desire by more and more consumers to become directly engaged in defining "personalization." In other words, consumers are no longer satisfied by organization-centric, mass-customization schemes. Instead, informed, networked, empowered, and active consumers increasingly want to be able to directly co-create their own experiences.[14] Currently few museums are positioned, either in terms of staff or content presentation, to accommodate this kind of shift in the locus of value creation. At its extreme, full co-creation would require a museum to be a place where every visitor's experience had at least the potential to be truly unique and unlike that of any other visitor; a place where the visitor exercises as much control over the nature of the experience as does the institution.

Sharing Experiences

People have always wanted to share their experiences with friends and family,[15] but historically time and distance acted as barriers to whom and how effectively one could communicate. The internet and social media have totally transformed person-to-person communication. Today, consumers have instant access to friends and relatives wherever they are. This "instant" person-to-person sharing provides an alternative source of information and perspective with individuals no longer totally dependent on information generated by the organization about programs, services, or quality. As a consequence of these new communication norms, the public is increasingly become more selective in determining those organizations with which they want to have a relationship, basing their views of value (and decisions) on the shared norms of their social network.[16] Museums can and do attempt to influence these socially shared messages of value, but, increasingly, the visitor rather than the organization is in charge.

Self-Actualization and Identity Fulfillment

As the public becomes more educated and more affluent, they are increasingly prioritizing activities that enhance their sense of personal identity.[17] It would make sense that leisure pursuits, where people perceive they have considerable control over time and events, would be excellent settings in which to observe this dynamic at work.[18] This appears to be the case. Leisure researcher John Kelly observed that people use leisure experiences to build and affirm identity.[19] In essence, people use leisure to affirm their self-perceptions through the active selection and participation in activities that extend and build their sense of self. The use of leisure for self-actualization[20] has become the norm.[21] Perhaps the clearest expression of the relationship between identity development and leisure was made by two leisure researchers, Lois Haggard and Dan Williams, who stated, "Through leisure activities we are able to construct situations that provide us with the information that we are who we believe ourselves to be, and provide others with information that will allow them to understand us more accurately."[22] As described by Jay Rounds, museums are currently seen by the public as ideal settings in which to engage in this kind of self-actualization-related, identity-work.[23] This represents a significant niche of opportunity for museums in the leisure market, but museums need to deliver on the promise.

Moving Forward: Some Examples of How Museums Have Begun to Address These Issues

What would museums need to do to partner with the public to accommodate these different needs? The following are just a few of the many examples of how museums are currently beginning to attempt to respond to these twenty-first-century leisure trends, and, in the process, building more robust partnerships with their visitors.

In an effort to put the visitor at the center of the museum's experience, the Art Gallery of Ontario (AGO) conducted extensive research to determine what self-related needs motivated their audiences to visit, as well as why other audiences with similar needs did not visit the AGO. Based on their findings, the AGO literally re-hung and re-interpreted all of their collections in order to directly speak to the needs that motivated visitors to go to the AGO, thus making it less challenging for visitors to satisfy their needs.[24] Building off the same line of research,[25] museums such as the Denver Zoo, Thanksgiving Point Museums, and the Museum of Northwest Art in Washington State have begun reframing the nature and functioning of their institutions' marketing, education programming, docent training, and even shops to better align with visitor expectations and desires.

Technology has given an array of museums the ability to put visitors virtually into the "driver's seat," including allowing them to design and understand their own experiences, explore to their own depth of interest and understanding, and providing mechanisms to extend the visitor experience before and after the museum visit. For example, the Cooper Hewitt Smithsonian National Design Museum created a host of technology-enhancing experiences, including the "super-powered pen." Touching one end of this digital pen to a plus sign on an object label in the museum allows visitors to add the object to their virtual collection. The other end of the pen can be used to draw and design on touch tables located throughout the museum. Collectively, the pen allows visitors to not only "bring home" objects they want to "collect" for future study; it also allows them to leave a mark of their presence at the exhibition and their impressions of it.[26]

Moving beyond customization to co-creation, many science centers have embraced the Maker Movement as a vehicle for more directly supporting co-created visitor experiences. In dedicated makerspaces, museums allow visitors to take control over the content and duration of their experience. Museums provide space, tools, and expert advice; the visitors provide the creativity, labor, and motivation. Collectively, visitors and the museum make things. What is built in these spaces can vary from predefined "starter" projects to virtually anything collectively deemed worthy of building by visitors and the museum. This can involve electronics, wood, fiber, robotics, music, video, or various media associated with the visual arts. These places for co-creation are not limited to building physical objects. Some museums have experimented with MediaLabs, Living Labs, and Digital Spaces, where, respectively, visitors are empowered to design their own animated or live films, conduct biological research, or develop new software tools. In all these contexts, the museum is no longer positioned as the expert purveyor of fixed content; rather, it becomes an enabler and facilitator of others' expertise.

Technology has also been the key to helping visitors move from being passive recipients of experiences to active partners in the dissemination of content and practice. A number of museums have redesigned their websites so that visitors can directly share their experiences with others and bookmark the virtual representations of exhibits. Still others have made it easier for visitors to use their personal mobile devices for collecting interesting information on exhibits and sharing this information with others.[27] A particularly ambitious research effort in Glasgow developed a pilot attempt to build a city-wide museum social network system. The goal was to create a mixed reality system that would support the co-visiting of all museums within Glasgow by both local and remote museum visitors.[28] Although this particular effort ended only with the development of a prototype, it exemplifies what will at some not-too-distant time become commonplace. Digital tools will make it possible for visitors to co-participate in the experience of visiting a museum wherever they reside.

Finally, visitors have long used museums as places for identity-work, but it is only recently that museums have worked to be more proactive partners in supporting these efforts. An increasingly popular approach used by history museums is the use of oral histories as a way to build bridges between the identities of youth and older people. For example, the St. Petersburg Museum of History, a small community museum, trained local, fourteen- to eighteen-year-old African American youth to collect oral histories and then empowered them to capture the memories and stories of elders in the community and then curate into a museum exhibit.[29] Similar efforts have been done by museums as diverse as the Anacostia Community Museum (affiliated with the Smithsonian Institution) in Washington, DC, and the Japanese American National Museum in Los Angeles, California.

The efforts of the Brooklyn Historical Society are arguably at the extreme of these approaches. The museum has combined aspects of self-related need, personalization, co-creation, social communication, and the building of identity in a process of totally redefining its collections policy and exhibition development practices to ensure the active engagement of their audiences and the elimination of the distinction between exhibitions and programs.[30] Rather than thinking of exhibitions as static displays, the museum has re-conceptualized them as meeting places; community spaces in which collections, personal reflection, and public debate, particularly around emotionally charged topics, co-occur. For example, in an exhibition on the role that Brooklyn played in the nineteenth-century abolition movement, the museum partnered with the Weeksville Heritage Center and the Irondale Center at Lafayette Avenue Church to bring documents and personal stories together around this little-known local historical story into the public sphere. Through the creation of multiple platforms for community discourse, the museum helped community members discuss, reflect upon, and share what this history means to present-day life in Brooklyn. Through similar efforts, the museum has opened up its galleries to the local community, blurring the lines between community and museum, visitor and museum professional.

Conclusion

Change is not a nicety, but a necessity; the future is now! Museums cannot comfortably assume that just because they were successful and relevant yesterday, they will be so tomorrow. As we move further into the twenty-first century, and the aforementioned trends become ever more real, only museums that have adapted will prosper. The museums that thrive in this new leisure environment will increasingly be those most committed to building new relationships with their publics, relationships built on trust and shared goals, increasing personalization, new strategies for communication and co-creation, and, most importantly, a strong commitment to the public's needs.

There is no clear road map for how to do this, no cookie-cutter solutions. As suggested previously, many museums are experimenting with new ways to engage and collaborate with their visitors as they strive to accommodate the rapid changes going on in the world. Some of these experiments will work beautifully, others will not. Success in the twenty-first century will be a journey, not a destination. Developing an understanding of how to build lasting and meaningful partnerships with visitors will not be the only thing required for the journey, but, arguably, few will successfully make the journey without this understanding.

Meaningful Partnerships and the Eight "Ates"

7

KATE GOODALL

*BIOGRAPHY: AS CHIEF EXECUTIVE OFFICER of Halcyon, **Kate Goodall** is the driving strategic force behind Halcyon's creative growth. She was instrumental in the development of Halcyon's well-established Halcyon Incubator, the newest creative series Halcyon Stage, and the residency-based Halcyon Arts Lab. Goodall's dedicated passion for arts, sciences, and social impact lends an objective and unstoppable drive for formulating and executing Halcyon's mission of catalyzing emerging creatives across multiple platforms, ideas, and artistic media, striving for a better world. In 2016, Goodall also helped Dr. Sachiko Kuno and Sheila C. Johnson in establishing WE Capital, a consortium of leading businesswomen in the Washington, DC, region that invests in and supports women and women-led companies, inspiring the next generation of female entrepreneurs while providing opportunity for the investors to achieve their investment goals. Prior to establishing Halcyon, Goodall served as chief operations officer of S&R Foundation, where she developed new programs as well as oversaw impactful and capacity-building partnerships. Goodall hails from the museum field and has worked previously at the Association of Science-Technology Centers, American Association of Museums, and the Naval Historical Center, to name a few.*

The Halcyon Story

IN 2013, HALCYON INCUBATOR was a tiny seed of an idea. It began with a large, empty house. Halcyon House was no ordinary building—having been built in 1787 by Benjamin Stoddard, first secretary of the Navy during the American Revolution, and at thirty-thousand square feet, the house is really more of a mansion—but nonetheless we thought of it as a blank canvas. What could we do with this place that is meaningful and impactful? How could it become more than a dusty mausoleum or a wedding venue? How could we use it to empower the next generation of thinkers? How could it be used to make a positive difference in the world? In order to make our dream a reality, we needed to rely on a variety of partners. This perspective tells the Halcyon story and shares some of our learnings as a start-up, especially ways in which we found and leveraged partnerships.

The Beginning: Defining the Vision, Tapping the Wisdom of Others, Launching the Incubator

The idea to create an incubator was not much more unusual then than it is now, but we knew that Halcyon House could be a uniquely inspirational setting, and that inspiration was nothing to be sniffed at. Dr. Sachiko Kuno, the generous donor of Halcyon House and visionary behind the idea, and I set out on a fact-finding mission to map out the existing landscape and answer these preliminary questions—only to find ourselves asking many more. We studied existing incubators and co-working spaces and spoke with luminary organizations in the fields of entrepreneurship, systems change, and international development, including Ashoka, Echoing Green, New Profit, the U.S. State Department, the UN Foundation, Rockefeller, the Case Foundation, Citybridge, and many more.

We discovered many things from these conversations, especially how generously people would share knowledge of what had worked and what had not. This allowed us to ask critical questions, refine ideas quickly, and determine our unique fit as we designed a program with relevance that avoided duplicating existing efforts. Ultimately, these knowledge-sharing sessions helped us to hone in on three big goals:

1. To support the most talented social entrepreneurs from around the world;
2. To "move the needle" on critical twenty-first-century challenges; and
3. To catalyze Washington, DC, as the best place for social entrepreneurs.

We decided that the Halcyon Incubator would have a few defining characteristics:

- **Social Enterprise:** Halcyon would incubate social entrepreneurs, those prioritizing purpose as well as profit, and would measure and transparently report progress toward their goals.

- **Early Stage:** Halcyon had an opportunity to fill a gap. By focusing on the early stages of innovation, Halcyon could provide crucial risk capital to high potential innovators who are traditionally ignored by venture capitalists. We decided to define this as "pre-seed stage."
- **Residency:** In Washington, DC, one of the most expensive cities in the world, the cost of living can be a barrier. Offsetting that cost provides a more level playing field to entrepreneurs, especially those who may not have a parents' basement in which to live or a reliable "safety net." Our program provides both physical and metaphorical "time and space" for people to concentrate fully on launching game-changing ventures. Living together, we would come to discover, provides the added benefit of community, which for these delightfully crazy few is the most consistently reported value of the program.
- **Equity:** Our most hotly debated decision was whether to take equity in the ventures; in other words, would Halcyon financially benefit from successful innovations? This is the norm in many incubators. The Halcyon Incubator differentiated itself once again by opting out of taking equity in any of the enterprises it supports. Despite the potential sustainability this would have lent to the program, we strongly feel this was the correct decision, as taking equity would have created a different selection process and completely changed the incubator's environment and the relationships it has nurtured. In addition to selecting innovators for potential financial success and scalability, we prioritize social impact, kindness, health, and other attributes that would have been diminished by a profit-driven purpose.
- **Diversity:** Despite some initial feedback that we should specialize in one or two sectors to make the concept easier for potential stakeholders, we decided that the advantages of supporting a wide array of business types (healthcare, education, energy, communications, etc.) would make for more collaborative (noncompetitive) cohorts. We believed that we could find the specialized expertise, including mentors and partners, externally. We made it a priority to reach beyond our immediate networks and recruit social entrepreneurs from all walks of life. The resulting incubator has supported entrepreneurs from ages twenty-one to forty-five, from Washington, DC, to Uganda and Singapore. A total of 50 percent of Halcyon's ventures are founded or co-founded by women, and more than 50 percent of the fellows are entrepreneurs of color. This is due to concerted marketing and communications efforts to traditional—and nontraditional—outlets.

As a result, the application ratios continue to mirror the accepted fellow ratios. In addition to the residency (five months to live, for free, at Halcyon), the incubator provides a ten-thousand-dollar stipend to each innovator's venture. Each person receives a field-specific mentor, a separate leadership coach (to help with professional growth, hiring decisions, co-founder issues, etc.), and business, legal, technology, and communications resources to build capacity for these nascent companies.

Finding Partners

In order to provide such a generous package, presently valued at more than ninety thousand dollars of resources and services on average per venture, we needed to find the right partners. In order to attract the best partners, we would have to be able to communicate the value proposition on their terms. Accordingly, each of the partner companies—Deloitte, Arnold & Porter, Amazon Web Services, Sage Communications, and HR Sage— was motivated, to varying degrees, by a combination of five things:

1. A genuine desire to help and generate real social impact as part of the company's culture and corporate social responsibility;
2. A mandate to be innovative and associate with cutting edge projects, usually part of the company's culture;
3. Retention of talented junior staff who are motivated by the social impact of the Halcyon ventures and the company's relationship to the incubator;
4. Recognition of and strategic opportunities for profile-raising at key public and corporate events, in the press or social media, or in co-written publications and reports; and
5. Potential pipeline for future clients, as the Halcyon ventures mature.

We also made a critical hire. Halcyon Incubator's program director, Ryan Ross, designed the selection process and has shepherded each of the ventures; he also manages each of the partner relationships, including regular communications, program integration, evaluation, and renewal. This relationship-building and continued engagement is crucial to any healthy partnership.

The first cohort began in September 2014. As of Spring 2017, cohort six is now almost finished. We select eight ventures per cohort, twice a year, and now receive around 250 applications for every eight spots. We decided that we would be happy with a 25 percent long-term survival rate for our funded ventures (far above industry standard) and have far exceeded that, with an 85 percent survival rate among Halcyon ventures thus far.

As a testament to Halcyon's achievements, the U.S. Small Business Association selected Halcyon as one of the premier growth accelerators nationwide in 2015. Halcyon fellows have won countless awards, including taking top prize at the 2017 Global Entrepreneurship Summit, recently taking three of the spots in the *Forbes* "30 under 30" list of social entrepreneurs, and sweeping the first WeWork "Creator" awards.

Other collective accolades include the Tory Burch fellowship, DC Entrepreneur of the Year Award, the Diana David Spencer fellowship, the Lenosis Family Entrepreneurship Prize, and entry into the first class at the Chobani Incubator. The fellows have gone on to receive catalytic funding from Draper Richards Kaplan, Rockefeller Foundation, Acumen, and more. Even more meaningfully, Halcyon's first forty ventures have raised more than $16.5 million in investment, created over 220 jobs, and impacted over 300,000 people around the world in less than three years. All of this is very much due to our incredible partners' commitment to their work with the Halcyon fellows. The Halcyon team is constantly reflecting upon and refining various aspects of the program to strengthen the parts that work and improve upon the rest. We've gained a deep understanding of the impact investment landscape. We've learned about mentoring, community building, creating an inclusive environment, and building and managing healthy partnerships and collaborations.

My insights about partnerships? *It is essential to be aware of the different stages of a successful partnership life cycle that must be kept in mind when establishing such an engagement. These stages do not follow along in a linear pattern; instead, they overlap and feed into each other, with the process more of a checklist than a road map.*

So expect the process to look less like a straight arrow and more like a curvy line.

The Eight "Ates" to Meaningful Partnerships

1. **Ideate.** Explore your big idea openly and with conviction, ideally with potential partners at an early stage. These future collaborators will feel greater ownership of the project later if they feel "heard"

and have helped contribute from the beginning. Be willing to refine the idea based on their advice, but don't stray too far from your vision. Examine the idea through questions like: What is the problem the project is addressing? What differentiates it and makes it unique? What makes it relevant and current? Who does it serve? Test the concept with those expressing early excitement and also with naysayers. Together, use your passion and this process to form and hone your vision. Set your goals. Make them bold, inspiring, and attainable. A hint: I like goals in sets of three. That number is easy for people to remember, yet still ambitious to achieve.

2. **Investigate.** Talk with lots and lots of people. Do your research on potential partners (both online and through your network). Do not dismiss some "unusual suspects." Know thyself and what you want to achieve: Where do you live within your chosen ecosystem? What is your value and what do you need? Are you spinning off to a new ecosystem, or aiming to dominate an existing one with this new partner? This stage, like others in these pointers, can be described using dating metaphors. You wouldn't want to settle down with the first person who takes you to dinner any more than you would want to partner with the first organization you consider; meet with many. Do not be desperate: it is just as unattractive to a potential business partner as to a potential date. Be selective and aim high. Narrow down potential organizations to one or two and really get to know them; then prepare for the hard questions.

3. **Relate.** This is especially important when refining your top partner choice. What is your organization's culture? Partnerships do not work well between two organizations with drastically different cultures and goals. Be authentic and earnest; you want to attract partners with whom you can work. Partnerships are ultimately about people. Are the elements there for an ongoing and successful relationship with the people, as well as the organization? Are you able to build and nurture the kind of trust that will be an important partnership ingredient? Partnerships do not function well for any extended length of time or in any depth if there is a misalignment here.

4. **Calibrate.** Manage expectations in order to ensure real benefit for both sides. Underpromise, but be ready to overdeliver, and make sure you have the resources to do so. Agree on goals and measurements of success. Will your organization be able to dedicate the proper time and resources to the partnership? If there is a mismatch in terms

of the financial commitment each is making, make sure there is still equal value and that value (in people, time, or other qualitative resources) is clear to both parties. The partnership has to be equally important to each partner; otherwise one may work harder than the other to sustain it. This could build resentment over time. It is vital that the goals and potential of the undertaking are understood and cared about at different levels of the partner organizations. These values can include moving organizational missions forward, seeding new innovation, pushing new boundaries, enhanced marketing, communications, brand awareness, and greater social impact. Make sure you have champions at many levels within each of the partner organizations. Specifically, ensure that a key point person is assigned with monitoring the partnership and communicating back to each partner. Make sure that key decision makers and higher-ups have had the opportunity to meet each other and support the project. They will make the final decisions about continuing the relationship. Make sure that those doing the work—the partner "foot soldiers"—are well-informed throughout the project. Do not forget to nurture them, recognize them, and thank them. This is key, but often forgotten.

5. **Create.** Make it happen! Deliver. Work hard. Do not spread yourself too thin; ensure that you can dedicate the time. Uphold your end of the bargain. Communicate often and be sensitive to the best way to do so. People prefer to receive information in different ways, and can absorb and react with differing frequency, so be ready to adapt to each other's preferred communication style and creative process.

6. **Evaluate.** Align evaluation with original goals. (Indeed, your partnership planning should include attention to defining and measuring outcomes.) Surveys are certainly a useful instrument at this stage. Once you have given thought to the evaluation, construct conversations focusing first on what is working well before you move to what needs attention. Candor is critical here, as is humility, and a nondefensive reception to findings, on both sides. Lay the groundwork for a safe environment, and make sure to listen. In our Deloitte partnership, we took into account feedback from advisors and the fellows, ending up with a Goldilocks approach. Ultimately, we worked with Deloitte to find an ideal solution, balancing a more standard well-scoped consulting engagement with a looser sounding-board approach through constant feedback and tweaks.

7. **Iterate.** Agree on new things to try, what to retain and continue, and on what to stop doing. It is often easy to point to what is not working, but it is sometimes more important to ensure you do not inadvertently stop doing something that is working well. Through numerous interactions with Deloitte leaders, for example, we iterated on strategies for engaging entrepreneurs. One solution that stemmed from these sessions and reflected our constant eye toward evaluation was a jointly created, customizable assessment tool to baseline ventures' and partners' understanding of where the venture stands currently and where it wants to be at the end of the incubator period. With numerous inputs, this tool has proven to be useful to help our incubator's entrepreneurs clarify and tailor their "asks" to partners, while also identifying tradeoffs and key priorities to focus on while they are with Halcyon. As this example illustrates, this iterative stage is where the rubber meets the road, and you move from pilot stage to progress. While it is hard work, it is very exciting and rewarding.

8. **Celebrate.** Very important! Do not forget to stop and celebrate your joint achievements with all of your partners. Shout it from the rooftops whenever you have the opportunity. Recognize small victories as well as the large ones. Give each partner credit at key events. Partner on press opportunities, digital media outlets, and project reports. And for Pete's sake have a party—you have earned it!

Why Museums Must Turn Outward to Find the Right Partners

8

RICHARD C. HARWOOD

BIOGRAPHY: RICHARD C. HARWOOD is founder and president of The Harwood Institute for Public Innovation, a nonpartisan, nonprofit that teaches, coaches, and inspires people and organizations to solve pressing problems and change how communities work together. The institute partners with some of the world's largest nonprofits, and its tools and frameworks have spread to all fifty states in the United States, across Australia and Canada, and have been used by individuals in more than forty countries worldwide.

Little Room to Be Nice but Not Necessary

THE HARTFORD PUBLIC LIBRARY was already working in Asylum Hill, one of the poorest neighborhoods in one of the poorest cities in all of America. But it wanted to have a bigger impact. Matt Poland, its chief executive officer at the time, could have done what so many of us do in these circumstances: gather his staff around a conference table to brainstorm new programs and initiatives and then go implement them. But there were some key questions he was grappling with: How could he and his staff ensure their efforts would be truly relevant and significant to the people of Asylum Hill? Would their efforts actually lead to better positioning the library—more credibility, more funding, more supporters? And could the library, alone, actually make a real dent in the neighborhood's challenges, or would their efforts end up being nice but not necessary?

For museums, like libraries and other cultural institutions, there is little room nowadays to be nice but not necessary.

Poland and his staff took a different path. It started with the recognition that on its own the library could never achieve the relevance or impact that it wanted in Asylum Hill. It would need good partners. Over time, it found them. For instance, the library teamed up with the Hartford Police Department to address public safety issues and build trusting relationships between the police and teenagers. The library brought together neighborhood residents and local media to identify ways to better reflect more of the positive realities of the community. These and other activities led the library staff to shift its internal culture to be more outward looking, which then led to a host of other partnerships—all of which helped the library reposition itself in the community. Poland described the change in the library in this way, "I would describe our role not just as a place for people to come but for being a change agent and an agent of hope in the city of Hartford," He added, "That has worked. I think the change has made a difference in being able to explain that a 21st century public library is more important now than it had been."[1]

The library's specific actions are less important here than the steps it took to re-orient itself to the community and to find the right partners. The library didn't partner with just anyone. It started off by asking a deceptively simple question: *Who should we run with?* Answering this question is easier said than done. While many of us may think we are forging successful partnerships, the hard truth is we are not. Every successful partnership that we fail to forge is a lost opportunity.

The relevance and impact of a museum or any cultural institution depend upon seizing these opportunities.

The Inward Pull

When Tim Henkel was named chief executive officer of the Spokane County United Way in 2007, he and his board felt the United Way must do more than merely raise local dollars and distribute them to other organizations. In their eyes, the organization was failing to make a real difference in the community. Through a series of steps, the United Way decided to refocus on the area's high school dropout challenge. But Henkel had a huge problem on his hands.[2]

It was clear to Henkel that he needed different partners to achieve his new mission. But he felt burdened by an array of agency partners that had come to rely on, even expect, United Way funding year after year. This conundrum of how to get the right partners is one that many organizations, including museums and other cultural institutions, face every day. Yet something often stands in our way of making the hard choices to reset our course. *One of the biggest obstacles is an ingrained inwardness that drives our mindset and practices that lead each of us to behave in ways that literally undermine our hope to be more relevant and impactful.* When it comes to partnerships, this inward pull comes in different forms. Here is just a handful of examples:

- **A fear of ending legacy partners.** You can get locked into legacy partnerships and feel you cannot escape. Many people I have worked with describe themselves as feeling trapped by these long-term partnerships. This was Henkel's challenge; it is one that many museums face. But the reality is that such legacy partners often hold you back and hold you down. Simply put, you need to find ways to end them.
- **The "We all get along!" justification.** Familiarity or ease of working with specific partners is one of the most common and potent drivers of who we work with. Let's face it: we all gravitate toward teaming up with people and groups we know and like. But when familiarity and comfort drives partnerships your museum can forfeit the opportunity to produce impact in the community. It does not have to be this way.
- **Tokenism.** Some partnerships are formed with the idea that you can "check a box" by securing a certain category of person or group around the table. But this can turn into mere tokenism, which often results in a failure to address a real concern, such as whether your museum holds a deep knowledge about a part of town, is genuinely open to engaging different groups, or is willing to try new ideas. Tokenism provides you with a false sense of security; it also sends a signal of business as usual to the community.
- **An assumption about power and credibility.** There are times when you may need certain groups to give your efforts greater credibility or power. But too often we reflexively turn to these groups when we do not need them, or when they in fact tell others that we are merely reaching out to the usual suspects. For museums, which often yearn for such relationships, you can end up with the wrong partners for the wrong reasons—and fail to get the right ones.
- **More partners are always better.** This reflex is based on the belief that bringing more partners to the table will ensure greater credibility, achieve more impact, and bring more resources. But often the reverse is closer to the truth: The more partners you bring on, the more you can end up spending all your time entangled in the managing of partners and process, and taking your eye and resources off the actual work that needs to get done. More is not always better. This

is especially true for museums that can be strapped for time and have limited resources and staffing.

Henkel had to face up to each of these and other inward reflexes, none of which was easy for him. At each turn, he felt the pressure to return to what he knew and what his organization had done in the past. But ultimately, he decided to take an alternate path. He summoned the courage to convene all his partners that ran the forty-five programs he funded, and he asked them to consider how the community could achieve its aspirations around keeping more kids in school and helping them graduate. Through this conversation, the partners uncovered for themselves that making progress in the community was more important than protecting their own turf and funding. They gave Henkel the signal that he could make changes. Over a four-year period, Henkel carefully shifted out of these partnerships and replaced seventeen of the forty-five programs.

What enabled Henkel to take this course, and Poland to choose his direction, were two critical ingredients: a different orientation to the community, and a different set of criteria for selecting partners.

Turn Outward

A friendly warning: The need for a different orientation does not begin with your museum adopting some new technique or process, or by undertaking yet another strategic plan. You do not have to go down that path! Instead, it starts with something much more simple and radical: Making the personal and organizational choice to embrace a mindset to turn outward toward your community and make the community, not your conference room, your reference point for your actions. Take a moment to think about this, because what I am asking you to do is deceptively simple. Beyond the inward reflexes I have already mentioned regarding partnerships, there are all sorts of additional pressures and factors that conspire to keep us turned inward toward our own organization—for example, we become consumed by internal activities such as the implementation of our own programs, protecting our turf, positioning our own group, and seeking credit, even creating new logos. It is not that you do not need to concern yourself with such things; the problem is when these activities become so consuming that we fail to be turned outward to the very communities to which we seek to be relevant and significant.

The very first "change" that Poland and his staff made at the Hartford Public Library was to make an explicit choice to turn outward. This was true for Henkel, too. They and their staffs made a commitment to adopt a new posture—a different mindset—to be outward facing toward the community and not inward facing toward themselves. Without making this choice, they would not have had the community in their line of sight; they could not know what matters to people. And they could not make their work relevant and significant to the community. As I already noted, but which deserves to be underscored, without turning outward these organizations may well have gone down the well-worn path of undertaking another strategic plan that produced good-sounding, well-meaning activities, but that were disconnected from the very community itself. They may have set out new strategies and programs, but without knowing if they actually address things that matter to people. They may have made budget and staff allocations that made internal sense but which, again, failed to align to the world outside their building.

Specifically, when it comes to being turned outward and finding the right partners, you should never start with such questions as: "How can we find all the partners we can?" or "Who in the community can be our partners?" or "How do we develop a program so that we can get one organization or another to be our partner?" Instead, organizations that form the most effective partnerships ensure they first have clarity about the following factors, and only then can they know what kinds of partners they will need.

1. **You hold a deep knowledge about the community's shared aspirations.** Turning outward requires knowing people's shared aspirations and using this knowledge as the North Star for your work. This will root your efforts in what matters to people—what is relevant to their lives. Thus, before forming partnerships, you must consider whether your organization understands people's aspirations for their community, and how your museum can contribute to them.

2. **You understand the stage of community life.** Every community goes through "stages"—The Harwood Institute has identified five of them in all, from "the waiting place," through "impasse," "catalytic," "growth" and, eventually, "sustain and renew." Knowing what stage your community is in will help you calibrate your museum's strategies and efforts so they are effective

and so that you know the types of partners you will need in order to achieve success. This is critical.

3. **You are clear on your purpose in acting.** Once you know people's shared aspirations and the stage of community life, you will want to be clear on what is the purpose of your museum in taking action. All actions can look good, but many are just "activities" that keep you busy. The most effective groups I have worked with are crystal clear on purpose—why are you acting and what impact do you really hope to achieve in the community.

4. **You gauge your own capacity and resources.** Before identifying potential partners, you must take stock of your museum's skills and resources in relationship to the purpose and impact you are seeking to create in the community. Too few groups do this and end up undertaking efforts they do not have the right capacities for. From there, you can assess, "Who else do we need?" and you can identify the skills and resources that you will need from others to begin making a difference. This allows you to narrow the "playing field" of potential partners and be clear about the commitments they need to make as an organization.

Screening Partners

I like to tell people that when they are forging partnerships they should adopt the posture of actively screening for them. When I first say this, people look at me surprised. Screening? Really? There can be a resistance to this notion. After all, I often hear people say, "Don't all community groups want to do good work?" And, "Isn't the notion of screening kind of harsh, or too hard-nosed?" Or, "Who gave us the right to screen others?"

I do not doubt other people's good intentions to do good work, but their intentions and actions oftentimes do not match up. Indeed, good intentions alone will not enable your museum or others to make a real difference in your community. You need to be serious about finding the right partners if you want to be relevant and impactful. To do this, my experience tells me you to have to actively screen for them. You have to be ruthless about this. I ask you, at a time when your museum must be more relevant and impactful, are you willing to take the risk not to do this?

Here's a quick story involving my own work. The Harwood Institute was planning a multicity initiative with the New England Aquarium to support informal science organizations to bring together various community partners to take collective action on local science-related concerns.

In the proposal process, there was request made by the funder to identify the community partners each local community would work with; because the institute and the aquarium were Turned Outward, we knew that task was simply impossible to do. While we could give examples of the types of partners that might participate, only the local communities could figure out who best to join once they held a better sense of people's shared aspirations, the stage of community life, and the purpose for taking action. You cannot screen for the right partners without this knowledge.

The good news is that this grant did come through (though not all of it!), and at the time that I am writing this chapter, the communities are starting to identify their partners.

Whether I am planning one of the institute's initiatives, or helping others think about their own work, my advice is the same. You should actively screen for partners; here is a set of questions you can use:

1. **To what extent are your potential partners turned outward?** Please do not skip this step. It is critical that you find partners that are turned outward, or have a natural inclination to make the community their frame of reference. Otherwise, you will be misaligned, and over time you will expend your museum's scarce time and resources trying to create alignment with partners that may have very little interest in being turned outward. If you want to be relevant and impactful, you need partners with that focus.

2. **How much do your potential partners value community aspirations?** Durable partnerships are built upon a clear sense that what matters to the community matters to the work of the partnership! One way to discern this is when you are talking with a potential partner; listen for what they talk about most. Is it their own organization's programs and positioning, or do they focus more on the health and progress of the community itself? Another way is to reflect back to them what you have learned about the community's aspirations, and see how they respond: Do they see these aspirations as valuable, important to guide new efforts, actionable? Simply put, you do not want partners who do not value what matters to the community.

3. **Do you and your partners hold a sense of common purpose?** A surprising number of partnerships are formed without really exploring this question. When staff of different organizations and groups meet, we all tend to talk about our own programs and budgets and activities—things driven by inward reflexes—but often

not nearly enough about our common purpose in taking action, especially as it relates to community efforts. Your conversation must shift to the following questions: What are we truly trying to achieve in the community? What can we only achieve together? Why is our working together important for the community—and not just for each of us? These questions will help you determine if there is a sense of common purpose of working in the community rooted in something that you can achieve only by working together.

4. **What capacities do your potential partners have—and do they match what you need to produce community impact?** Many partners would like to think they bring the right capacities and resource to the table, but they often fall short. To avoid this scenario, (1) make sure to examine explicitly your potential partner's capacities to determine that they actually are the right partner for the work you need to achieve together, and (2) spend time talking about their other efforts, priorities and projects to test what else the organization is doing, and whether it can even contribute its capacity at the time you need it. It is better to say "no" to a potential partner than to end up with the consequences of the wrong one.

A Matter of "Fit"

The more I have thought about partnerships over the years, the more I have come to the conclusion that they are fundamentally about fit. They are not about seeking perfect alignment or 100 percent agreement about everything; those things will never happen. Indeed, we must not fall prey to getting stuck in a planning loop looking for the perfect partners or situation. Finding the right partner is not about being dead-set on an organization and pursuing it when there are clear warning signals; you must resist succumbing to choosing partners that you know in your gut are wrong for what you are trying to do in the community. None of these options helps anyone—especially the community. Your test must be whether there is enough of a fit with potential partners to get moving.

But here is what you must be prepared to do if you want to find the right partners: Make choices. Think back to Tim Henkel for a moment; he had to make a whole set of choices, which began with whether his organization was even relevant to the community. Then, he had to respond to a cascading set of choices about what would be his new purpose in taking action and who he needed as the right partners to succeed. He had to make choices about how to move forward with his existing partners, and he had to actively choose how to handle the potential fall-out from making changes. Each of us must be intentional and explicit about the choices we face. We must find the clarity and courage to form partnerships that make sense for our community.

Start Small, Then Grow

There is one last point that is worth mentioning here about partnerships. I have already noted that our instinct can be to get as many potential partners around the table as possible. We sometimes hold onto the belief that more partners will give your museum more credibility, more power, more resources, more of everything! There are times when that may be true. But most of the time, it is not. This course of action produces more headaches, more process, more management, endless meetings, less impact within the community, and thus less relevance for your museum.

My advice is that it is (almost) always better to start small. Do not over-stretch. *Focus on the minimum number of partners for the best outcome at the time, and find those partners with the right fit.* Next, get moving. See what emerges. Understand what is working and what is not working. Then you will be better able to gauge what and who else you need—and where you can strategically go after that. It is far easier to grow something good than to shrink something bad.

The Way Forward

Despite the critical importance of partnerships, all too often organizations such as museums approach these choices without a clear orientation and lens for selecting the right partners. We can inadvertently fall back on ingrained inward reflexes that lead us to choose partners for the wrong reasons, resulting in the wrong outcomes. Why undermine our own goals? You want your museum to be as relevant and impactful as possible.

Working with the wrong partners can stifle your ability to innovate. Partnerships of convenience can lead you to misalign efforts that divert scarce museum resources. Managing large, poorly defined partnerships is a recipe for distraction, inefficiency, and little change in the community. Partnerships formed exclusively with the "usual suspects" can send the wrong signal to the community about the depth of your museum's commitment to meaningful change.

The first step you must take in forming successful partnerships is to make the choice to embrace a mindset of being turned outward toward the community. The second is to actively—ruthlessly—screen partners for the right fit. When you do, your community will benefit. And it will help your museum become more relevant and impactful.

This is no time to be nice but not necessary.

Mapping Collaborations

9

DAVID LA PIANA AND MELISSA MENDES CAMPOS

BIOGRAPHIES: DAVID LA PIANA is the founder and managing partner of La Piana Consulting, which in 2018 celebrates its twentieth year providing nonprofits and foundations with management consulting services in strategy and planning, strategic restructuring, leadership and board development, and change management. David has worked with a wide cross-section of nonprofits including AARP, ACLU, the S.D. Bechtel Jr. Foundation, the NAACP Legal Defense Fund, and YMCA USA. He has authored numerous books and articles, including The Nonprofit Strategy Revolution, The Nonprofit Merger Workbooks I and II, *"Merging Wisely"* (Stanford Social Innovation Review, *Spring 2010),* and The Nonprofit Business Plan. *He is also a sought-after speaker and media resource on a variety of topics including nonprofit trends, philanthropy, leadership, and change management. David has an MPA from the University of San Francisco and holds graduate and undergraduate degrees in Comparative Literature from the University of California at Berkeley.*

Melissa Mendes Campos is a partner with La Piana Consulting, where she works with organizations to make sense of complex choices and make strategic decisions. She has engaged with a diverse array of nonprofits and foundations on projects ranging from strategy development and planning to funder initiatives supporting nonprofit collaboration. Past clients include the Blue Shield of California Foundation and the John Muir/Mt. Diablo Community Health Fund. Melissa also advances La Piana's research, writing, and communications to fulfill its commitment to sharing knowledge across the sector. She is a co-author of "Convergence: How Five Trends Will Reshape the Social Sector," and is currently contributing to a Tenth Anniversary edition of The Nonprofit Strategy Revolution: Real-Time Strategic Planning in a Rapid-Response World. *Melissa has a BA in literature from the University of California at Santa Cruz.*

Introduction

L A PIANA CONSULTING is a national nonprofit management consulting firm founded in 1998 by David La Piana with start-up funding from three major foundations. The David and Lucile Packard Foundation, James Irvine Foundation, and William & Flora Hewlett Foundations sought to create a new resource for collaboration and strategic restructuring in the nonprofit sector, and entrusted David and his colleagues with launching Strategic Solutions, a five-year field-building project that helped change the way nonprofits think about and use mergers, joint ventures, and other restructuring activities to strengthen their ability to advance their mission.

The work of the firm was launched on the partners' collective experience of guiding more than sixty mergers, as well as from direct experience. According to La Piana, "During my 16 years as executive director at East Bay Agency for Children, we grew from serving 20 kids to serving 4,000,

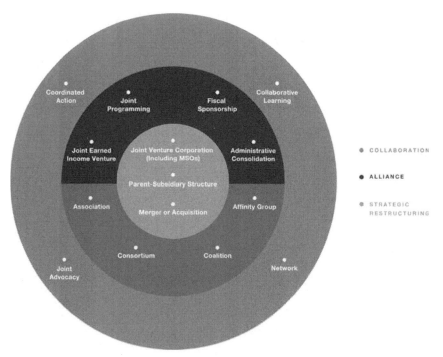

Figure 9.1.   The Collaborative Map, developed by La Piana Consulting, details fifteen ways organizations can join together in pursuit of shared goals. They are visualized in three categories, as shown in the three concentric circles: Collaboration (outer ring), Alliance (middle ring), and Strategic Restructuring (center circle).
La Piana Consulting, Copyright 2018.

and as part of that growth we went through three mergers." Today the agency serves over twenty thousand, again having made merger part of its strategic growth with a fourth merger in 2008.

The firm's Strategic Solutions initiative resulted in a better understanding of nonprofit partnerships ranging from strategic alliances to joint ventures to full-scale mergers. The firm also coined the term "strategic restructuring" to describe this continuum of strategic options, and it produced some of the first literature on the topic in the nonprofit sector. La Piana Consulting has continued to specialize in strategic restructuring consulting services and thought leadership, regularly producing new resources, including the Collaborative Map.

A Note on Definitions

There are many different terms used to describe partnerships between and among nonprofits—and between nonprofits and for-profits, government entities, and unincorporated groups.

The terms shown on the Collaborative Map (Figure 9.1) are among the most common, but not everyone uses these terms in exactly the same way. Such difficulties in terminology are unavoidable, but let us highlight that what is most important when considering a partnership is not what you call it, but what you want to achieve together.

Start with the End in Mind

Regardless of the form a partnership takes, its real value lies in why it has been formed, how it takes action, and what it serves to accomplish. For example, if an organization is seeking a temporary partnership to address a time-limited challenge or opportunity, one of the four forms of collaboration will be best. If it is looking for a more formal relationship that is mutually beneficial at an administrative and/or programmatic level but need not involve a change in corporate entity, one of the eight forms of alliance should be considered. And if a permanent change across the entire organization is desired in service of the mission, one of the three types of strategic restructuring will likely hold the greatest potential.

There is little merit in collaboration merely for collaboration's sake. Collaborative strategy is about working better together.

The following typology distinguishes among collaboration, alliance, and strategic restructuring, and provides reasons and situations for each type.

Four Types of Collaboration

Collaboration does not require a change to the corporate structure of the partner organizations.

Using collaboration, organizations may build relationships in which there is coordinated action, joint advocacy, collaborative learning, or networking.

- Coordinated action is when two or more organizations coordinate their planning or service provision, co-sponsor an event, pool resources to purchase an asset both could use, or solicit better pricing on assets they will purchase and use independently, etcetera.
- Joint advocacy can be aimed at changing policies locally, regionally, or nationally.
- Collaborative learning can happen through community convenings, coordination and sharing of training opportunities, or learning communities.
- Networks are collections of individuals and organizations (often self-organizing) working together to create social change.

Why Collaboration?

- Coordinated action is useful for pooling expertise or resources for a time-limited effort.
- Joint advocacy can provide a stronger collective voice around a shared cause or issue.
- Collaborative learning allows for the sharing of collective wisdom and knowledge and creates opportunities for learning through feedback and reflection.
- Networks can bring diverse strengths, collective power, and shared learning to social issues requiring sustained, coordinated action.
- All forms of collaboration can build a foundation for deeper and more integrated partnerships.

Eight Types of Alliance

Alliances may involve some level of formal agreement and/or require sharing or transfer of decision-making power. However, the organizations involved are not called upon to make changes to their corporate structure.

The Collaborative Map shows alliances as falling into two categories:

1. Those that involve doing some part of your nuts-and-bolts business together (e.g., programming, administration, or revenue generation); and
2. Those that are really more about working together to have an impact on the field (e.g., advancement of a social change agenda or capacity building among like organizations).

The first category includes:

- **Administrative consolidation:** a strategic alliance that entails the sharing, exchanging, or contracting of administrative functions to increase the operational efficiency of one or more of the partner organizations.
- **Fiscal sponsorship:** the practice of a nonprofit organization offering its legal and tax-exempt status to unincorporated groups engaged in activities related to the organization's mission. It typically involves a fee-based contractual agreement, and the fiscal sponsor often provides some administrative support to the project.
- **Joint programming:** a strategic alliance in which organizations come together to launch and manage one or more programs to further shared goals.
- **Joint earned income activity:** when one or more organizations come together to launch or manage a revenue-generating activity that benefits all partners (e.g., a combined capital campaign or social entrepreneurial venture).

The second category includes:

- **Affinity groups:** bring together nonprofit professionals for networking, peer support, and professional growth. Often convened by associations or management support organizations, affinity groups may be organized by issue, identity, individual role, organizational function, stage in one's career, geographic focus, or some combination of these. In some cases, affinity groups may be formalized through the creation of a separate organization.
- **Coalitions, consortiums, and associations:** groups of organizations, individuals, and/or government entities that choose to pool their resources and work toward a common goal. Coalitions typically

share a specific political or social change goal, whereas consortiums and associations typically serve and represent the interests of those involved (though this distinction is not universal).

Why an Alliance?

- Administrative consolidation provides the recipient a more robust level of administrative services than it can muster on its own and generates contract revenue for the provider of those services.
- Fiscal sponsorship gives the sponsored project or organization access the financial and infrastructural advantages of the sponsoring 501(c)(3), enabling it to focus on program delivery.
- Joint programming leverages the skill sets of each organization to more effectively provide services or programs than either could provide on its own, for the ultimate benefit of clients/customers/ audiences. For example, it can aid in expanding a program into a new geographic area.
- Joint earned income ventures allow partners to share benefits (and risks) of a revenue-generating social venture.
- Affinity groups foster networking and shared learning among groups and/or individuals with common interests.
- Coalitions, consortia, and associations can support collective power in advocacy, purchasing, standard-setting, and enforcement, as well as other areas.

Three Types of Strategic Restructuring

The hallmark of strategic restructuring is the change in corporate relationship and structure between the partnering organizations.

Forms of strategic restructuring include the following:

- Joint venture corporations consolidate some portion of the administrative, programmatic, or advocacy functions of two or more organizations within a jointly controlled corporation (i.e., the partner organizations share governance of the new organization). For example, a management service organization is a specific type of joint venture that creates a new organization to integrate administrative functions.
- Parent-subsidiary structure is an integration of some or all administrative functions and programmatic services of participating organizations. Although the visibility and identity of the original organizations often

remain intact in a parent-subsidiary relationship, some organizations may consolidate to the point where they look and function much like a merged entity.

- Merger or acquisition entails the integration of all programmatic and administrative functions of one or more organizations. Note: The Financial Accounting Standards Board requires an "accounting" determination of either a merger or acquisition, as described in the following.
  - □ A merger occurs when two or more organizations are dissolved into a newly created corporation that includes some or all of the resources, administrative infrastructure, and programs of the original organizations.
  - □ An acquisition occurs when one corporation is dissolved (acquired corporation) with all activities and resources transferred into the surviving (acquirer) corporation.

Why Strategic Restructuring?

- Joint venture corporations allow partners to combine their skills and expertise in a specific program area while keeping their other respective programs separate.
- Parent-subsidiary structures enable partners to consolidate administrative and program areas, but each maintains its own corporate entity. This form of partnership can be useful in situations (often temporary) in which the non-transferability of a license, certification, or contract makes merger not feasible.
- Mergers or acquisitions allow for the creation of a single administrative infrastructure, eliminating the redundancy of functions, and for the integration of programmatic activities, which can result not only in reduced duplication of services, but also enhanced service offerings as well as expanded reach to new geographies and constituencies.

While every partnership is different, the Collaborative Map describes some of the characteristic benefits of fifteen different forms of collaboration. Those identified as "Collaboration" do not involve a deep level of integration and may (but need not) be informal or limited in duration. Such partnerships can be effective for pooling expertise or resources, amplifying a policy message around a shared cause, sharing knowledge, and leveraging the power of networks. Partnerships identified in the Collaborative Map as "Alliance," include more formal and often longer-term agreements that can result in organizational efficiencies, program improvements, and joint revenue-generating opportunities, just to name a few. The most permanent and highly integrated form of partnership includes mergers and maintains the category "Strategic Restructuring." These partnerships deliver many of the same benefits as those already described, albeit to a greater degree and on a more lasting and permanent basis.

Strategic Restructuring and Strategic Planning

The La Piana Consulting firm has an equally active strategic planning portfolio, branded as the Real-Time Strategic Planning (RTSP) approach to strategy development. Helping organizations identify, negotiate, and implement effective integrated partnerships complements this work, and vice versa, because strategic restructuring is, itself, a strategy. Often this involves asking organizations to consider their competitors, which could be the same as their potential collaborator. The RTSP process can help nonprofits weigh the potential of collaborative strategies, just as it can be a valuable undertaking for new partnerships or merged organizations to envision their future ahead.

Some Museum Examples

The range of collaborative options used by nonprofits demonstrates that there are solutions to meet a variety of needs, and organizations of all sizes and in all subsectors can benefit. Among museums, one of the more common collaborative strategies we have observed is administrative (or "back office") consolidation. One such partnership, the Chattanooga Museums Collaboration, was recognized as one of eight finalists for the inaugural Collaboration Prize in 2009. A joint effort among the Tennessee Aquarium, Creative Discovery Museum, and Hunter Museum of American Art, this agreement to share administrative resources resulted in operational efficiencies and cost savings, and it also served as a springboard for collaboration in exhibitions, programming, and fundraising.[1]

Museum mergers in which our firm has been involved include the 2011 consolidation of the Honolulu Academy of Arts and The Contemporary Museum to become the Honolulu Museum of Art[2] and the merger of Children's Museum of Winston-Salem and SciWorks to become Kaleideum in 2016.[3] Today, the Honolulu Museum of Art is the state's leading arts institution and the city's vibrant center for visual and performing arts, and Kaleideum combines the arts, literacy, and STEM education into an integrated approach to child learning.

Conclusion

It is important not to be overwhelmed by this menu of options. The first step for any organization is to get clear about their goals for partnership, well before getting attached to a particular type of partnership or approaching a potential partner. Collaboration is not always the right answer, but collaborative strategies like those captured in the Collaborative Map can be very effective for enhancing mission impact and sustainability. It is just one of many important tools in a nonprofit's toolbox and one we try to help organizations wield more effectively.

Growing a Strategic Partnership Mindset within a New Museum

10

Staff Perspectives on the Office of Strategic Partnerships at the Smithsonian Institution's National Museum of African American History and Culture

MARSHA L. SEMMEL, FROM INTERVIEWS WITH NICOLE BRYNER, MARION MCGEE, ALLISON PRABHU, AND AUNTANESHIA STAVELOZ

BIOGRAPHIES: NICOLE BRYNER is a museum program specialist in the National Museum of African American History and Culture's (NMAAHC) Office of Strategic Partnerships (OSP), which works to advance the African American Museum and African diaspora field through collaborations that focus on professional development, capacity building, and organizational sustainability. Nicole's portfolio includes international programs (including the Slave Wrecks Project), convenings, and partnerships with national networked groups. Before joining NMAAHC in 2014, Nicole worked in the chairman's office at the National Endowment for the Arts, and prior to that she was a museum/theater educator at Ford's Theatre, the Folger Shakespeare Library, and the Shakespeare Theatre Company. She has an MSEd from Bank Street College of Education's Leadership in Museum Education Program and a BS in theater from Franklin & Marshall College.

Marion "Missy" McGee is a program specialist in the OSP of the NMAAHC. She is responsible for the design, implementation, and evaluation of key collaborative initiatives, and multistate programs for the only national museum Congressionally mandated to strengthen and elevate the profile of African American museums, Historically Black Colleges and Universities (HBCM), and other institutions promoting the study or appreciation of African American history and African diaspora cultural heritage in the United States. Her areas of expertise include long-term strategic planning and prudent financial management through participatory leadership. She is a servant leader who believes in creative problem-solving through the embrace of failure, experimentation, and innovation. Marion is serving her second term on the Association of African American Museums (AAAM) Board of Directors where she most recently chaired the 2017 national program committee for the organization's annual conference.

Allison Prabhu is a supervisory program manager in the OSP at the Smithsonian's NMAAHC. Ms. Prabhu oversees many of OSP's partnerships with national organizations, as well as OSP's work in South America and the Caribbean. She also leads the team's internal strategic planning process. Allison has a breadth of experience in the private and federal sectors, spanning a spectrum of disciplines including exhibit content design and development, research, grants management, project management, operations, and strategic collaboration. Prior to joining the Smithsonian, Allison worked in strategic partnerships at the Federal Institute of Museum and Library Services.

Auntaneshia Staveloz boasts a twenty-year career in museums and is the supervisory program manager for the OSP at the Smithsonian NMAAHC. Her office is a unique department within Smithsonian, dedicated to professional development and institutional capacity building to support the sustainability and growth of African American and African diaspora museums through collaborative initiatives with networked organizations. Prior to her tenure at the Smithsonian, Staveloz worked with the American Alliance of Museums, and currently serves as an executive board member for the AAAM.

Introduction

THE NMAAHC WAS ESTABLISHED as the nineteenth Smithsonian Institution museum by 2003 legislation that identified collaboration as a core attribute of the museum in fulfilling its mission. The

> purpose of the Museum shall be to provide for collaboration between the Museum and other museums, historically black colleges and universities, historical societies, educational institutions, and other organizations that promote the study or appreciation of African American life, art, history, or culture, including collaboration concerning development of cooperative programs and exhibitions; identification, management, and care of collections; and training of museum professionals.[1]

Although the museum's building on the National Mall did not open until September 2016, many of its functions were up and running well before that time. In response to the legislative mandate NMAAHC leadership established the Office of Community and Constituent Services (CCS) in 2012 under the leadership of Dr. Deborah L. Mack, a recognized scholar who had considerable museum experience. CCS was responsible for identifying opportunities for strategic partnerships and ensuring alignment with the museum's mission and vision as related to its collaborative role. Between 2012 and 2016, the office grew from two people to its current eight full-time and two contract professionals. Over this time, the office developed and piloted a number of initiatives; convened representatives from other NMAAHC and Smithsonian departments, scholars in African American history and culture, museum professionals from African American and other museums, and representatives from relevant professional associations; supported other professional museum gatherings; and conducted relevant audience and sector research. In October 2016, CCS was officially renamed the Office of Strategic Partnerships (OSP).

This chapter focuses on the evolution of the CCS/OSP office, and its approach to collaborations, principally through the reflections of several mid-level staff members who were recruited from 2014 through 2016. What does it feel like—if you are not in the driver's seat—to help establish and define a new department devoted to collaborations, especially within a new museum that in itself is defining its role and position within the much larger entity of the Smithsonian Institution?

The chapter reflects a January 2018 conversation with four members of the OSP staff and concludes with some of their subsequent individual observations. Our conversation covered many topics relating to the office, its foci, its evolution, and its place within NMAAHC, the Smithsonian overall, and the museum field as a whole. Some of the material in this chapter also draws on a report prepared for the NMAAHC OSP in 2017, by DeJesus and Associates, a museum consulting firm based in Washington, DC.

An Evolving Identity

Since its establishment, the CCS/OSP office has continued to hone and evolve its focus and activities. This is in response to assessing the outcomes of its most promising partnerships, continued reflection with the broader constituent universe (as cited in the legislation), and the evolution and the maturation of the entire museum. OSP staff, therefore, have many lessons to share about establishing a new strategic partnership function. These lessons apply to strategic partner selection, partnership relationship building, negotiating partnership terms and agreements, and effective internal and external communication and representation. They also speak to the type of partnership "mindset" and skills that support effective collaborations.

These staff noted that when Dr. Mack took command of the CCS, she was not only defining the office and its work; she was also playing a role in many other museum areas, including exhibitions, curatorial, and visitor engagement. As such, she was a key member of the museum's executive team. Even before the office took on new staff, Dr. Mack was forging collaborations. These pilot projects aligned with key museum focus areas (local, regional, national, and international) and often drew on Dr. Mack's existing professional relationships as well as those of other NMAAHC staff. Many relied on Dr. Mack's deep knowledge of—and experience in—the museum and scholarly field, her extensive professional network, the respect with which she was held within the museum and academic sector, and her strong and strategic leadership abilities. Each pilot was carefully developed in accordance with the museum's legislative mandate, and each involved the museum providing major support (finances, resources) to the partner entity. The projects, like several other museum initiatives, such as "Save African-American Treasures" and various temporary exhibitions, were occurring in different Smithsonian venues and other sites well before the museum's September 2016 official opening.

This collaborative focus was a deliberate strategy of museum director Lonnie Bunch and his senior team. In a lecture delivered to an international convening of a committee of the International Council of Museums in October 2015, for example, Bunch cited five leadership principles for creating sustainable museums, among them, "Embrace the need to build alliances that provide long-term strategic relationships. This helps you to do more with less. At NMAAHC, the CCS was designed to fill voids and reach into communities and local museums." In addition, because the museum was "built on the shoulders" of others, particularly other African American museums around the country, Bunch recognized that the museum was one more node, an albeit important one, in a longstanding network of related sites and institutions. He did not want that message lost as the new museum took shape.

The early CCS partnerships coalesced around professional development, convening, and capacity building. By the end of the 2015 fiscal year, CCS had collaborated with more than thirty organizational partners on more than twenty-five different programs. The partnerships included intra-Smithsonian collaborations, such as a 2014 joint Smithsonian "grand challenges" award to Anacostia Community Museum, NMAAHC, and the Center for Folklife and Cultural Heritage to explore how the African diaspora could be incorporated in Smithsonian exhibitions and public programming. An example at the state and regional level was the CCS work with the Southeastern Museums Conference to establish the John Kinard Scholarship that funded two members of the AAAM to attend the Jekyll Island Management Institute, a program for mid-career museum professionals. The office's strong national partnerships included the AAAM, where CCS supported AAAM professional development and capacity building trainings through the annual conference and connecting members to other national resources. With Historically Black Colleges and Universities, the CCS supported museum internships at pilot sites that occurred at the campus museum or another local museum. Finally, an example of an early international partnership was the African Slave Wrecks Project, a long-term collaborative among seven core partners in the United States and Africa designed to combine research, training, capacity building, and education to build new scholarship and knowledge about the study of the global slave trade. The CCS coordinated and funded a five-day conservation workshop for African-based project participants.

During these early years, as Dr. Mack began to staff up the office, there was a shared awareness of the experimental and path-breaking nature of the work. For some of the relationships, staff worked with Smithsonian administrators to forge new protocols and formats that would accommodate the partnership activities—and still conform to existing Smithsonian procedures. The risk-taking was exciting, ambitious, and occasionally stressful. All in all, staff noted that, in this period, CCS was "building the plane as it was flying it."

Partnership Characteristics

As diverse as these foundational partnerships were, they shared the following characteristics:

- **Strategic:** Each fulfilled the overarching collaborative mandate of the founding legislation;
- **Iterative:** Partnerships tended to begin as pilots and move through a process of assessing results and incorporating lessons learned for next stages of the collaboration—or for new relationships;
- **Connective and multi-leveled:** Many partnerships reflected the museum's broad geographic focus, the diversity of the sector, and the willingness to explore different types of projects. A consistent theme, however, was a focus on connecting multiple institutions (some of which had never worked together) and leveraging programming formats designed to expand each partnership's reach and impact.

This work has resulted in the creation of new collaborative relationships, increased awareness and trust between NMAAHC and partners, and an understanding that the many different segments of the African American history and culture world are part of a "much larger educational enterprise," according to OSP staff.

In the early months, honing the focus, experimenting with various formats and partners, and continually responding to the needs and opportunities from beyond the museum (other museums, Historically Black Colleges and Universities, professional organizations) and within the museum (the Slave Wrecks project) could be confusing and overwhelming to fellow NMAAHC colleagues, who were deep into their own departmental work as all prepared for the museum's grand opening. Intra-museum communication—and firmly defining the OSP role within NMAAHC—could be challenging. For many staffers, there was not a clear understanding of the OSP's purview and scope, in some measure due to the flurry of its activities and experiments, in some because no other Smithsonian museum had a similar office, and in others simply due to the pressing department-focused demands experienced by all museum staff. Ironically, even the "Lift Every Voice" campaign, described below, had a challenging time finding its own voice, recognition, and presence within the museum.

OSP Coming Together

A seminal moment in the OSP's history occurred when CCS/OSP was responsible for coordinating the "Lift Every Voice" global initiative in conjunction with the museum's 2016 opening. The goal was to provide "an opportunity to showcase and honor the work of all institutions and individuals preserving, honoring and sharing the many stories of African American and African Diaspora people and their contributions to the American story."[2] Museums, libraries, community centers, overseas embassies, and other organizations were invited to "use the occasion of the museum's opening to 'Lift Your Voice' and tell the nation about the great work you are doing to celebrate African American History and Culture in your hometown. Co-brand your event/activity with the museum and show how your organization exists as part of a national story." The downloadable guide suggested ways to create a local opening ceremony "watch parties," other signature events, and social media engagement. As the initiative concluded, there were more than twelve hundred domestic and global partners in twenty-two countries.

"Lift Every Voice" included a robust intra-Smithsonian partnership with the Smithsonian Institution's Traveling Exhibition Service (SITES), which worked with the CCS to create and circulate—nationally and internationally—a poster exhibition that featured information about NMAAHC and its collections.

Three additional events have helped the OSP establish a firmer, better understood, and broadly recognized position with the NMAAHC. First, the opening of the museum, despite huge crowds and all manner of adjustments, has provided a new sense of stability and organizational "settling in" that has supported clarification of each department's role in the museum.

Second, the OSP has itself attained a new level of maturity. A key milestone was the launch of the OSP website in August 2017.[3] The website debuted in advance of the 2017 annual meeting of the AAAM, and it represented a distillation and clarification of the OSP goals, purpose, and priorities. It has been enormously helpful in clarifying the OSP's work to colleagues throughout the museum and the Smithsonian, and to professionals throughout the field.

The site contains the OSP's "identity statement":

The Office of Strategic Partnerships leverages the Museum's research and programmatic initiatives to act as a catalyst, empowering and advancing the work of museums and related cultural heritage organizations dedicated to African American and Diaspora history by

- *Collaborating with regional, national, and global networks to connect needs to resources*
- *Promoting organizational sustainability*
- *Cultivating and supporting museum professionals*

It includes such Frequently Asked Questions as, "Who are your partners?" "What types of organizations do you serve?" and "Do you have opportunities for museum professionals?" In addition, it links to sections on professional development opportunities, internships and fellowships, and a "collaborate with us" form that enables interested parties to make more specific connections to the office. The site is further clear about what the OSP does *not* do or support.[4]

Thus, by the time of the August 2017 annual meeting of the AAAM in Washington, DC, the OSP role had crystallized its identity, based on its many pilot experiences, even as all agreed that it would still be fluid, flexible, and open to the consideration of future partnership opportunities.

The third factor in fostering greater understanding of the OSP, especially within the museum and the broader Smithsonian, was its role in supporting the AAAM conference, the largest in the professional association's thirty-nine-year history, and one that capitalized on the opening of the museum and its many resources.

OSP staff noted that this organizing and coordinating role made the office and its purpose, functions, and value more visible to other NMAAHC staff and changed intra-museum perceptions and visibility. Colleagues had a deeper understanding and recognition of the role and value of the OSP, although OSP staff acknowledged that there is still some distance to go. As Nicole Bryner noted, "Our hosting AAAM really helped us in the museum:

we 'showed, not told.' We worked closely and effectively with the museum's project management and special events teams. This helped us in the museum and with the field." Marion McGee added, "Yes, even though the museum as a whole operated for five years on the principle of 'believing before seeing,' with OSP, it's been 'show, don't tell.' AAAM demonstrated what capacity we had. Before, some departments didn't understand what we did; after AAAM, they understood us better—the full scope of what we do." In other words, the AAAM conference and the OSP website have helped museum colleagues see that OSP's role has been more than transactional and begin to understand its potential, transformative impact throughout the broader field.

OSP staff were further encouraged by the recent "Smithsonian 2022" strategic plan[5] and its emphasis on "One Smithsonian." The plan's first goal emphasizes greater collaboration across all parts of the institution.

Significantly, the NMAAHC OSP is the only one of the nineteen Smithsonian Institution units that has a specific office devoted to strategic partnerships, and this fact has caused OSP staff to have to explain and clarify its role in many inter-museum meetings. One of the most successful NMAAHC–OSP–Smithsonian Institution partnerships has been with SITES, the Smithsonian's Traveling Exhibition Service. In addition to "Lift Every Voice," SITES has worked with OSP on the 2017 Museums of the Caribbean conference; the Smithsonian's central administration ("the Castle") which funded other Smithsonian Institution units to mount commemorative programs and projects in conjunction with NMAAHC opening; and other U.S. embassies overseas.

As OSP staff discussed the impact of the OSP within the Smithsonian, they noted their participation in a number of cross-unit programs and projects. Bryner is participating a Smithsonian Institution–wide leadership program, which involves a temporary work placement in the Sparks Lab at the National Museum of American History. A mid-February 2018 meeting, hosted by Smithsonian Organization and Audience Research and with the goal of "furthering seamless collaboration across units," explicitly cited the OSP's cross-unit work and experience with implementing complex, multi-unit Smithsonian events. Nevertheless, despite significant progress, staff thought that there is still "far to go." One noted that the role of OSP "in the field is clear," but not well understood within the Smithsonian as a whole. "There is interest in OSP work, but there are hurdles. We are not about diversifying the entire museum workforce or dealing with potentially controversial topics. Our focus is different."

Staff recognized the critical roles played by Director Bunch and OSP Director Mack in establishing the supporting the work of the office. They also praised Dr. Mack's supporting their own leadership development.

While all recognized that, with her stellar reputation and manifold connections, Dr. Mack was—and is—critical to OSP's work, staff noted that as they move projects beyond the "pilot" stage and into more established and sustained relationships, she has decentralized and delegated the work, enabling different OSP staff to take leading roles, and give more recognition and authority to members of the team.

At its current stage, the overall number of partnerships has been reduced, whereas several have deepened or expanded. For example, Interpretive Workshops with the National Association of Interpretation have evolved, with the NMAAHC-OSP partnership still including the Southeastern Museums Conference and the National Association of Interpretation but eligible participation expand beyond AAAM members to include other museum professionals who are addressing the interpretation of African American history and other "difficult histories." With its three-year history, the partnership now includes the non-NMAAHC partners taking increasing ownership of the collaboration.

While each partnership is in a different stage, OSP staff noted that with the pilot efforts, largely funded by NMAAHC, providing proof-of-concept, the museum is looking for more equity in the relationships: shared responsibilities; more partner investment of time, money, and other resources; and more reciprocity. "At first, we offered professional development and scholarships opportunities at no cost. Now pretty much all projects require some fee. We still underwrite, but there's got to be some investment by the partner. The prospective partner needs to put some of its 'skin in the game.'"

In addition, with its more clearly defined priorities, staff noted that they have more ability to say "no" to partnership requests that are not fitting the OSP's goals. In many cases, if the request doesn't fit the OSP priorities (determined through the website's "Collaborate with Us" form), the office can provide links to other resources that are more in line and appropriate with nature of request. As a result of its history with so many related organizations, staff have been able to serve as a clearinghouse and direct inquiries to appropriate offices, programs, and resources within the museum, the Smithsonian, and the country.

Partnership Pointers: Protocols and Process

Allison Prabhu: While we believe that some sort of agreement in writing (whether or not money exchanges hands) is critical to establishing agreed upon parameters, we are wedded, understandably, to the government protocols mandated by the Smithsonian.

The components that we generally include in our formal Statements of Work include the following:

- Description of both (or many) institutions/organizations involved.
- The justification for the partnerships or project. Here we are clear about the "why" of the project, how it fits within our mission, and what need is being addressed.
- An outline of what tasks/deliverables we expect from our partners. We often include within that list what our office will contribute and areas where we expect to work together.
- A timeline for the deliverables.

OSP Values

As staff discussed their values, they noted that, unlike some of their Smithsonian colleagues, they do not see themselves as the experts and ultimate authorities: "We value listening and learning from our partners. We don't dictate. We try to meet people where they are, not where they expect us to be."What are the distinguishing principals held by the members of the OSP team? And what have team members learned?

Marion McGee: "We privilege teamwork, collaboration, shared opportunities, respecting our respective work styles. . . . It can be a challenge for us to work within the overall SI system, which does not necessarily practice our values."

Allison Prabhu noted that her "lessons learned" include the importance "flexibility, risk-taking, handling ambiguity, starting with smaller pilots, evaluating them, and either evolving them or ending them." Staveloz, Bryner, Prabhu, and McGree agreed that it is also a challenge to find time for reflection. "We need to bake insights from our partnerships and our process into our work." And all agreed that there had been much progress, "even though there's a long way to go."

See the text boxes for more detailed reflections by four individuals who are part of the OSP team.

Auntaneshia Staveloz, Supervisory Program Manager

The Office of Strategic Partnerships (OSP) at the National Museum of African American History and Culture was born out the museum's promise to elevate the existence and presence of its sister African American and African diaspora museums and cultural institutions from across the globe. These institutions played key roles in the journey they led up to the opening of the National

Museum on the Smithsonian Mall. It is because of many of these longstanding institutions that the National Museum of African American History and Culture was possible. Several African American museums were the museum's biggest supporters and critics. The collective feelings of support from sister organizations came with the satisfaction of long overdue acknowledgment and legitimacy of contributions made by African and African diaspora people. Criticism came from longstanding institutions who were telling these stories and preserving the history and culture of a people with limited resources, fearing a takeover and monopoly over potential funneling of funding away from these existing institutions. The OSP became the proof of a commitment to Lift as We Climb—elevating all who are committed to the work of preserving and sharing the history and artifacts of black culture.

The OSP dedicates its entire department resources to impact change in the field of African American and African diaspora museums, resulting in equitable visibility, credibility, and organizationally sustainable institutions. A challenge surrounding the department's work is its inability to fit into a traditional box of museum practice. All museums are structured to work with its general publics—families, private citizens, school, and other groups. The publics of the OSP are institutions of similar mission and purpose. The OSP focus is vested in the development of professionals within sister organizations and the organizational sustainability of those organizations. The OSP has a motto of "we can show you better than we can tell you what we do." Our intentional ways of working with partners value the process of the work as much as the content. How we go about our work and collegiality of purpose is just as much part of the process as the output. The department is gaining a cohort of supporters of people who are beginning to understand the nuances of our work and its intersection with the broad range of disciplines across the museum. Increasingly, the OSP is called upon to provide strategic insights on how colleagues are organizing their work with both the process and product in mind.

Allison Prabhu, Supervisory Program Manager

My experience thus far as part of the leadership team of the Office of Strategic Partnerships has provided me a tremendous opportunity for professional growth. I feel fortunate to be learning from Dr. Deborah Mack, who is an exemplary strategic leader and visionary. The greatest lesson I have learned, and continue to learn, is to simultaneously see all potential partners, projects, and initiatives as concrete action-items for the present as well as building blocks of a greater future vision. It is easy to get caught up in the day-to-day work without stepping back to reflect on how the work is building toward something greater. The key to doing this with success as a trusted collaborator is to listen carefully, be flexible, and learn from both success and failure. It cannot be done in a vacuum. This kind of work requires internal team members and external partners who bring diverse experiences, skill sets, and perspectives.

Marion McGee, Museum Partnership Specialist

I joined the staff of National Museum of African American History and Culture (NMAAHC) on May 16, 2016, as one the newest members of the Office of Strategic Partnerships (OSP) team. Our unit's unique purpose enables us to lead the effort in positioning NMAAHC as one of the most collaborative institutions within the nineteen Smithsonian units, while providing direct support for the museum's congressional mandate, to strengthen and elevate organizations that promote the study or appreciation of African American history and culture.

OSP has fostered both an internal and external culture of collaboration that has enabled us to cultivate a greater level of trust, communication, and participation among our constituents and partners, such as the Museums Association of the Caribbean, the Association of African American Museums (AAAM), and the TyPA Fundacion. The OSP continues to reap the benefits of employing participatory approaches in order to catalyze sustained change. During my tenure in OSP, I have witnessed the positive impact that piloting innovative programming through mutual partnerships can have on the Smithsonian's work culture as well as the larger museum field.

Our department's 2017 coordination of the AAAM Annual Meeting and Conference within NMAAHC's inaugural year, for example, demonstrated OSP's ability to leverage the attention and goodwill of NMAAHC's global alliances to attract the largest cohort of conference participants in the history of AAAM, while also marking the first nation-wide convening of museums hosted by NMAAHC. The "Lift Every Voice" campaign also helped demonstrate the value of OSP's work for our NMAAHC colleagues, as well as other Smithsonian staff.

OSP's successful partnership development efforts rely greatly on the embrace of innovation and experimentation, which requires some level of comfort with ambiguity. Our ability to continue leading strategic growth, both within NMAAHC and the museum field writ large, will depend on our level of responsiveness to change and the rising challenges of shifting from a "start-up" to a sustainable, future-focused organization. Given the tremendous amount of change happening throughout the field, museums and associated networks must seek new approaches to remain relevant in a technologically advanced era, while becoming more responsive to an increasingly more diverse workforce of multigenerational museum professionals. My hope is that OSP's value to NMAAHC will be recognized in both intrinsic and instrumental ways such that our unit's culture of collaboration does not remain the exception, but steadily becomes a genuine characteristic of the entire museum's culture.

Nicole Bryner, Museum Programs Specialist

When I first began working at the Smithsonian, my preconceived notions of the institution mirrored what most museum professionals see: a seat of authority, of vast resources, simultaneously a model for best practices and an unreachable icon. This was the Show. It comes as no surprise that in reality, the Smithsonian is just as complex and flawed as any museum, and that the trick of doing outward-facing work like we do at National Museum of African American History and Culture's Office of Strategic Partnerships (OSP) is to strike a balance between harnessing the resources and prominence of the Smithsonian while overcoming its reputation as a big fish in its own inaccessible pond.

Having done this work for nearly four years, there are three key takeaways I have found that guide me as I think about how we collaborate:

1. Our approach to collaboration happens at all levels. OSP is very clear about what we value in partnerships: truly listening to partners, meeting their stated needs (rather than what we decide their needs are), developing shared investment and buy-in, encouraging sustainability and vitality, and reflecting and evaluating at every step. The key to these values is that they guide not only why and what we do, but *how* we do it. Our collaborations with each other, our collaborations within the museum and the larger Smithsonian, our external collaborations all are informed by what we have identified as best practices for partnerships, and we would be far less effective if we did not live by this approach in all things.

2. As mentioned, the Smithsonian does not have a reputation as a two-way street. The most important thing we can communicate to potential partners is that we do not have all the answers, and we cannot decide what is best for them. We need to meet them where they are, and listen, and then do our best to connect them to the resources that meet *their* stated need. It would be much easier to have cookie-cutter programming and require our constituents to fit themselves into our predetermined boxes, but it would lessen our impact considerably.

3. The paradox of strategic partnerships: the better we are at empowering and lifting the field, the less credit we will get for doing so. By working primarily with network organizations, and promoting an ethos of sustainability and replicability in our partnerships, it is our goal to create an environment wherein our constituents will have the capacity to grow and thrive independently. Because of the nature of our work, its impact will not always be clearly linked back to us; indeed, in some ways our goal is to be one of many collaborators contributing to this collective impact. Understanding how to articulate our impact (and making peace with sharing the credit for it broadly) is something I continue to explore and grapple with, but I think unlocking it will make our work that much stronger and vital.

Partnerships for STEM beyond the School Day

11

RON OTTINGER AND DR. CARY SNEIDER

BIOGRAPHIES: *A NATIONAL LEADER and expert in STEM learning,* **Ron Ottinger** *is known for his expertise in informal and out-of-school time (OST) STEM education and in building collaborations among schools, science centers, communities, and afterschool programs that increase STEM learning opportunities for young people. Ron is executive director of STEM Next and serves as co-chair of the national STEM Funders Network. Additionally, Ron is the co-chair for the National STEM Learning Ecosystem Initiative. As the executive editor of STEM Ready America, Ron convened the nation's leading STEM experts presenting bold and persuasive evidence—as well as real-world examples of effective practices, programs, and partnerships on how science, technology, engineering, and mathematics knowledge and skills are preparing young people to be successful in school today and the workforce tomorrow. For the past nine years, he led the Noyce Foundation which for a quarter-century was dedicated to helping young people become curious, thoughtful, and engaged learners. Prior to joining Noyce, Ron served for fourteen years as national associate director of the nonprofit AVID Center. He was elected to three terms on the San Diego City Schools' Board of Education from 1992 to 2004, during a period of major reform of the school system and was the longest-running board president.*

Cary Sneider is a visiting scholar at Portland State University in Portland, Oregon, and a consultant on STEM education for charitable foundations that focus on environmental and informal education. He is also a member of the National Assessment Governing Board, which sets policy for the National Assessment of Educational Progress, also known as "The Nation's Report Card." He contributed to A Framework for K–12 Science Education and served as the lead for engineering on the writing team for the Next Generation Science Standards. His previous appointments include vice president for programs at the Museum of Science in Boston, director of astronomy and physics education at Lawrence Hall of Science in Berkeley, California, and science teacher in Maine, California, Costa Rica, and the Federated States of Micronesia. He earned a BA degree in astronomy from Harvard College and a PhD degree in science education from the University of California at Berkeley.

HOW DOES A SMALL FAMILY FOUNDATION make a big impact? The short answer is by selecting a focused goal with high potential for national impact, a strong desire to partner with other organizations, a commitment to research, and persistence for a decade or longer. This chapter will focus on promoting partnership through philanthropy, both as a systematic planned process and a readiness to take advantage of serendipitous opportunities. In order to lay the groundwork for the story, we will start by explaining who we are, and what we were attempting to accomplish through partnerships.

Introduction

The Noyce Foundation was created in 1990 to honor the memory and legacy of Dr. Robert N. Noyce, co-founder of Intel and inventor of the integrated circuit, which fueled the personal computer revolution and gave Silicon Valley its name. While the foundation had substantial resources, the endowment was only about 1 percent of the large well-known foundations such as Carnegie, Ford, and Gates that were already supporting STEM education mostly in kindergarten to twelfth grade and higher education systems. When I joined the foundation as executive director in 2006, the trustees had decided that the foundation's special niche would be STEM education beyond the school day, such as afterschool, summer camps, and visits to science centers. Our goal would be to increase the number and quality of STEM experiences that would spark curiosity, interest, and engagement—especially among girls, children of color, and low-income youth who traditionally have been turned off to science—leading to a higher percentage of STEM-literate adults, and an increase in young people who choose to enter STEM professions.

The decision to focus on STEM in outside-of-school-time (OST), was stimulated in large part by the increasing pressure of high-stakes testing in mathematics and reading that was squeezing out science from formal schooling, especially in elementary school—a perception that was later supported by rigorous research.[1] The imperative to increase test scores was also beginning to invade afterschool programs, with a large infusion of funding for 21st Century Community Learning Centers, which was established by Congress as part of the No Child Left Behind legislation to provide opportunities for low-income students to continue working on core academic subjects after the school day, along with some enrichment opportunities.

We were influenced in our decision to emphasize the affective outcomes of interest and engagement in STEM by a research study conducted by Dr. Robert Tai and his team at the University of Virginia that had just been published in the journal *Science*.[2] The correlational study was based on a sample of 24,599 eighth graders, who were followed until age twenty-five. Not surprisingly, early math scores were significant predictors of who would eventually pursue STEM fields in college. However, an even stronger predictor was the response to an eighth-grade survey question, "What kind of work do you expect to be doing when you are thirty years old?" Youth who expressed interest in science-related careers when they were in the eighth grade were 1.9 times more likely to go into the life sciences, and 3.4 times more likely to go into physical sciences or engineering than those who had non-science career expectations. The finding that interest and engagement in middle school has profound impacts on choice of career later in life has subsequently been reinforced by additional research findings.[3]

STEM in OST was clearly an opportunity for a small foundation to fill a niche that had great potential for national impact, where few others had provided leadership or adequate funding. The trustees set the goal—to greatly expand high-quality STEM programming beyond the school day for all youth—within the constraints of the Foundation's resources. It was my job as executive director to figure out how to achieve the goal. In 2006 after interviews with National Science Foundation informal science staff, afterschool leaders, and foundation colleagues, I proposed the following four-point strategy[4]:

1. **Field Building.** Partner with organizations and networks that were already providing experiences for youth outside of school, but not necessarily in the area of STEM, to incentivize and help them develop the infrastructure needed to scale up quality STEM programs nationwide. The foundation would fund capacity building, not programs.
2. **Research.** Work with researchers interested in developing methods of measuring program quality and affective outcomes of OST STEM programs to identify the most effective approaches that should be scaled up and determine if we were moving the needle.

3. **Leadership.** Engage with leaders of youth organizations to help them build the capacity of their organizations to develop high-quality STEM programs. Work with leaders of museums and science centers and encourage them to expand their services to youth of greatest need outside of their four walls within their communities. Partner with like-minded private foundation, corporate, and public agency colleagues to leverage Noyce Foundation funds.

4. **Pathways.** Start by expanding the pipeline of youth interested and engaged in STEM at the entrance to the pipeline and find ways to sustain their interest and engagement over time with a continuum of programs and connections to STEM pathways in high schools, community colleges, and universities.

In the beginning the Noyce Foundation trustees debated the wisdom of such a high-risk strategy. Unlike the school system, which was already organized with the primary goal to educate children, the wide diversity of programs for children and youth that operate outside the schools had a broad range of goals. Some focused on building character. Other goals were to keep children safe during the hours after school when their parents were still at work, and to provide recreation opportunities. While many science centers offered summer camps and afterschool programs, these were mostly available to the children of relatively affluent parents. Although some scholarships were available, such programs were not widely available to children from low-income communities. And although many afterschool programs offered math and some science, these were typically "homework help" sessions—not the sort of stimulating hands on programs that the Noyce trustees had in mind. Yet another challenge was that most facilitators of afterschool and summer programs had little or no training as teachers, let alone science and engineering teachers. There were also few educational researchers who focused on STEM in OST, as the overwhelming majority of science education research concerned learning in school.[5] In a word, there was no recognizable "field" of STEM education in OST, and no leadership with enough financial support to get the ball rolling.

Nonetheless, the trustees committed to this strategy. To assist in implementation, Dr. Alan Friedman, a Noyce trustee and former executive director of the New York Hall of Science, suggested that we bring on Dr. Cary Sneider as the foundation's STEM consultant. Other consultants were also brought on from time to time, and all of the trustees were generous with their time, ideas, and extensive contacts within the STEM community.

STEM Today

Now that a decade of field building has passed, I think it is fair to say that there is a strong and growing field that has become known as STEM outside of school time (STEM in OST) that is supported by researchers and practitioners in a wide range of organizations, with financial support from a variety of sources, including local, state, and national government agencies, businesses, and private foundations. While I cannot claim that the Noyce Foundation (now STEM Next Opportunity Fund) can take all the credit for this vibrant community of tens of thousands of afterschool educators and millions of children, we certainly played a pivotal role.

In order to provide a broad overview of the field, we recently collaborated with one of our key partners, the Charles Stewart Mott Foundation, to publish STEMReadyAmerica.org, a series of thirteen articles by over forty co-authors that provides highlights of this vibrant field as it is today. This chapter will focus on how our four strategies played out through specific tactics over the past decade. Although most of these tactics cut across two or more of the strategies, we present them here in the context of the four main strategies to illustrate how they helped us achieve our broader goals.

Field Building

Our overall strategy for building the field of STEM in OST was to partner with organizations that were already providing experiences for youth in OST, but not necessarily in the area of STEM, to incentivize and help them develop the infrastructure needed to scale up quality STEM programs nationwide. In order to implement this strategy, we developed the following tactics, each of which we believe to be critical in building the field.

Think of our grant recipients as partners and colleagues.

For a great majority of government, corporate, or foundation program officers, the role of grantor and grantee is quite distinct. Grantors provide the funds and are responsible to read evaluations and project reports to ensure that the funds are well spent, whereas grantees expect considerable independence in carrying out the projects that they have proposed, within the constraints of their grant agreements. Not so with the Noyce Foundation. *We considered our grantees to be colleagues and partners in building the field of STEM in OST.* In many cases that meant monthly phone calls by me and our small staff and consultants, and a lot of travel to organizations' headquarters and field operations. When I took part in a meeting or workshop being conducted by one of our grantees, I was not there to check up on them; I was there to participate as a partner and critical friend, asking probing questions and making connections. When special expertise would be helpful and requested, I would do my best to identify the right consultant to help out. A great advantage of this approach was that mid-course corrections could be made easily in response to changing conditions, and we learned what works and where the challenges lay alongside our grantees.

Select Partners Thoughtfully

An important decision at the start of this work was not to issue requests for proposals, like the National Science Foundation and many other foundations. Instead, we spoke to field leaders and funder colleagues who led us to the pivotal individuals and organizations that had the capacity to create quality programs for children and youth, that were open to including STEM in their offerings, and willing to partner with STEM-rich institutions, such as science-technology centers. Potential grantees were invited to submit short concept papers for improving STEM education outside of school settings. Those who submitted promising concept papers were asked to submit full proposals with budgets. For example, our first major grantee in this work was the National 4-H Council, which is the guiding body for the 4-H national movement. 4-H was the largest national youth development with a focus on science, and the Council was ready and willing to partner with us to implement the tactic that helped us rapidly scale up quality STEM in OST to millions of youth in a short time—leveraging existing youth organization structures.

Leverage Existing Organizations

4-H is one of the largest youth organizations in the United States, serving more than six million children a year, served by a hierarchy of state and county officers and more than 300,000 local volunteers. A series of grants from the Noyce Foundation to the National 4-H Council over the period 2007 to 2013 made it possible for 4-H to include substantial hands-on STEM programming for more than a million children and youth each year. The effort also provided a number of valuable lessons about how best to work with such large organizations. Lessons included the importance of developing curricula appropriate to the organization, of providing extensive professional development to a largely volunteer adult workforce, of developing uniform methods of collecting data to determine how many youths are involved and for what duration, and of evaluating the quality and effectiveness of the programs from several different perspectives. Subsequently we provided similar kinds of support to Boys and Girls Clubs of America, Y-USA, and Girls Inc.

Provide Long-Term Support

Another important difference from traditional philanthropy was that rather than seeding projects with one or two time-limited grants and moving on, we supported most of our grantees over several years, starting with relatively small narrowly defined grants, and ramping up as the organization's capacity and scope of the project grew. For example, our first grant to 4-H was to develop a national strategic plan and an initial model curriculum, which was about renewable energy. Subsequent grants included professional development for how to use the materials, marketing activities to get more youth interested in STEM through 4-H clubs, resources to help with local fundraising, the creation of a website as the number of STEM curricula and other resources grew, and an evaluation program that would provide data for assessing program quality and youth responses. Our goal was not just to provide programs that were confined to a grant period, but to build the commitment and capacity of the National 4-H Council to provide ongoing support for STEM in OST as a fundamental service to the nation's youth.

Encourage Sustainability Through Partnerships

As with all our grantees, we strongly encouraged the National 4-H Council to seek other partners, both for financial and in-kind support for their STEM initiative. For example, the National Association of Rocketry (NAR) provided an infusion of adult leaders and youth interested in model rocketry to join with 4-H clubs at a local level. In return, 4-H provided more venues for the NAR to expand its model rocketry activities. By the time our grant funding ended, the National 4-H Council had developed relationships with more than a dozen partners. With 4-H and other grantees, we also encouraged sustainability by diversifying sources of funding. One approach has been to provide grants with a match requirement. In some cases, we have provided funding to hire a person with professional development expertise. And by maintaining contacts with executive directors and program officers from sister foundations, we have provided introductions and recommendations that have helped our grantees multiply their funding streams for STEM.

Research

Building a field requires more than funding programs. It is also necessary to develop a research base with methods and tools to learn from initial efforts. Consequently, we partnered with university and other researchers interested in developing methods of measuring program quality and affective outcomes of OST STEM programs. We wanted to identify the most effective approaches that should be scaled up and determine if we were moving the needle.

Develop Measures of Quality and Impact

It is one thing to decide to provide high-quality STEM programs to youth, and quite another to determine which programs have sufficiently high quality to be worth scaling up. It is not sufficient for field builders to say, "we'll know it when we see it." As a result, one of our first grantees was Dr. Gil Noam, founder and director of the PEAR Institute—Partnership in Education and Resilience at Harvard University's McLean Hospital in Belmont, Massachusetts. Dr. Noam had a strong track record as a rigorous researcher with a commitment to child and youth development and education. He had developed a measure of quality STEM programs in afterschool with support from the National Science Foundation. The observation instrument, called Dimensions of Success (DOS),[6] was a valid and reliable instrument for an observer to judge program quality along twelve dimensions, organized in four domains: (a) features of the learning organization, (b) activity engagement, (c) STEM knowledge and practices, and (d) youth development in STEM. We funded the PEAR Institute's use of the instrument in a number of contexts, including one study that showed the tool could provide reliable measures of program quality whether used by professional evaluators or locally trained program leaders. A complement to the DOS tool enables a program leader to choose a logical course of action based on the results of the observations. At last report more than forty-five organizations—including many funded by the Noyce Foundation or STEM Next—have been trained in the use of DOS to evaluate and improve their programs.

Work with Teams of Practitioners and Researchers

We also supported PEAR to develop and validate an instrument for measuring youth outcomes, called the Common Instrument Suite, in collaboration with leaders of our other grant programs for youth. Developing a tool for measuring youth outcomes in OST is a major challenge as STEM programs vary so much. Initially we funded PEAR to provide an online database of existing assessment tools suitable for use outside of school time.[7] While the ATIS (Assessment Tools in Informal Science) database has been useful to individual program evaluators, it did not make it possible to compare different programs. Because each program had its own evaluator, each study was self-contained and provided little useful data to the broader field. In 2011 we brought together the directors and evaluators of our major youth programs to meet with Dr. Noam to decide which of the instruments from the ATIS website could be used to evaluate all of our grantees' programs. As practitioners, our grantees understood that it was not feasible to have children and youth answer a long survey, so none of the existing instruments on the list met the need. The result was a collaboration that led to the development of the Common Instrument Suite, which is a very short but reliable survey to determine how a program affected youth interest and engagement, identity formation, career awareness, and twenty-first-century skills in a STEM program. At last report more than 250 organizations were using the Common Instrument Suite or one of its variations, both to evaluate the effectiveness of their programs and to share with PEAR to conduct fundamental research. With more than seventy thousand data points at last count, PEAR is able to make generalizable statements about the most successful programs and is able to provide data to individual program evaluators about how their program stacks up against a national sample. This innovation alone has helped to transform individual isolated programs into a field for collaborative research.

Search for Root Causes

The decline of interest in STEM among middle school students has been known for some time, but there have been few ideas for how to reverse it.[8] To answer that important question, the Noyce Foundation supported *Synergies*, a four-year project conducted by John Falk and Lynn Dierking at Oregon State University to trace changes in middle school students' interests in STEM, and the effectiveness of interventions to see if the commonly observed decline in science interest at that age level can be reversed. Among the findings:

- Because the research followed the same youth for four years, rather than sampling different youth at different times, we see that not all youth have the same levels and trajectories of interest over time. In fact, most of the overall decline in STEM interest observed was attributable to about a quarter of youth whose STEM interest sharply declined between sixth and seventh grade. The interest of another 40 percent remained stable, and for about a third, science and math interest remained high and technology interest actually significantly increased. In other words, traditional efforts to address declining youth STEM interest appear to make the assumption that interest can be developed or supported with one-size-fits-all solution, such as changing how science is taught in classrooms.[9]

The researchers conclude by pointing to the value of STEM in OST as a means of providing additional pathways to engage youth and enable them to pursue their changing STEM interests.

Leadership

A growing field needs a network of connected leaders who share a broad vision, and who have the capabilities to build the capacity of their organizations to develop high-quality STEM programs. Equally important are leaders of museums, science centers, and other science-rich institutions who can work in collaboration with community organizations to expand STEM programs for youth of greatest need within their communities. We have developed several tactics to implement the leadership strategy.

Incentivize a culture of collaboration: As the number of large youth organizations committed to implementing quality STEM programs grew, it became clear that they had much to learn from each other. So one of our more recent projects is Imagine Science, a collaboration among the chief executive officers of Boys and Girls Clubs of America, Girls Inc., National 4-H Council, and Y-USA. The four organizations already collectively serve more than eighteen million youth annually, at more than 100,000 locations nationwide. Each organization individually has committed to expanding the reach of hands-on STEM learning opportunities to underrepresented youth nationwide, and collectively they came together to share resources, expertise, and a mission of reaching the most underserved youth in their local communities through the Imagine Science initiative. It is the first-ever formal national joint-operations effort that aspires to design and implement informal STEM programming for youth in communities in every state in the nation. Through Imagine Science, all four partners combined their resources, including hands-on STEM curricula designed especially for OST, experienced training and technical assistance staff, and outcomes and data management, as well as fundraising expertise and tools.

Leverage existing networks of leaders: One of our strongest national partners is the Charles Stewart Mott Foundation, which began more than a decade ago to establish Statewide Afterschool Networks of partners to focus on policy and improve the quality of afterschool and summer programming for youth in each state. The connection with STEM was slow to get started because the foundation's leaders did not want to require their state leaders to focus on one aspect of programming at the expense of others. Then, in 2010, Jeff Buehler, the program coordinator for the Missouri state network, proposed Project Liftoff to expand STEM in OST in Missouri as well as in surrounding Midwestern state networks. As a result of these initial pilot efforts, the Mott Foundation's executive, board, and youth programs leadership formed a national partnership with the Noyce Foundation, and now STEM Next Opportunity Fund, to support statewide STEM system building in thirty-two state networks.

Establish STEM collaborations among OST professional organizations: Starting in 2011 the Noyce Foundation initiated support for the three major national organizations of afterschool and summer education: the National Afterschool Association (NAA), the National Summer Learning Association (NSLA), and the Afterschool Alliance (AA). Rather than invite proposals from each of these organizations separately, the Noyce Foundation worked with consultant Judy Nee, former president and chief executive officer of the NAA, to engage all three of these organizations in working together to make STEM a part of their conferences, provide advocacy for support of STEM by Congress, and reach out to affiliates. A series of grants to these organizations has enabled each of them to further develop their unique capabilities to promote STEM nationwide and develop STEM leaders. For example, a grant to the NAA is developing a system of digital badges, signifying increased capabilities of frontline OST facilitators. Support for the NSLA has enabled the organization to develop research briefs on how summer STEM programs can help close the achievement gap and focus on STEM summer policy in states. A grant to the Afterschool Alliance supports the STEM Hub, a consortium of sixteen national organizations working together to develop new funding streams and advocate for STEM through evidence and messaging. A key component of the STEM Hub is a Messaging Toolkit,[10] created by the Frameworks Institute, a nonprofit research organization that the Noyce Foundation has supported to create messages that are effective with a broad range of stakeholders.

Develop a network of connected leaders at museums and science centers: The Noyce Leadership Institute has been our means of working directly with executives in museums and science centers to help them develop a shared vision and increase their capacity to manage change, focus outward to their broader community, engage peers, and form key partnerships. From 2008 to 2015, 123 Noyce Fellows and ninety-four sponsors participated in Noyce Leadership Institute. These individuals represent ninety-five institutions from twenty-one nations. The active phase of the Noyce Leadership Fellowship concluded with the seventh and final cohort in 2015. Currently, the alumni network continues to engage in shared learning opportunities and many science centers in the United States are actively engaged in our national initiatives, including the Mott statewide afterschool networks, the Every Hour Counts urban intermediary network, and the national STEM Learning Ecosystem initiative.

Share philanthropic leadership: One of our guidelines is not just to form new partnerships, but to also be a productive thought and funding partner with other private, corporate, and public agency funders. Strong partnerships are two-way streets, in which each partner has an equal opportunity to define success, offer lessons learned, and provide a pathway for getting from where we are to where we want to be. The Noyce Foundation (and now STEM Next Opportunity Fund) is a member of the STEM Funder's Network, a confederation of twenty-four private and corporate foundations with the common field building goal of improving STEM education nationwide in and out of school. Along with Gerald Solomon, executive director of the Samueli Foundation, I co-led the STEM Funders Network for the initial six years. One of the collaborative initiatives of the STEM Funders Network is the development of STEM Learning Ecosystems, which are collaborations among formal and informal educators with support from local businesses, libraries, universities, science centers, and other partners, with the goal of creating more effective models of engaging youth and fostering student learning. Almost half of the STEM Funder Network member private foundations and corporations are encouraging the development of STEM Learning Ecosystems in fifty-six locations, including major cities, states, regions, and rural communities.

Pathways

The Noyce trustees were keenly aware that generating initial interest is not sufficient. In order to sustain interest, youth need a continuum of meaningful STEM experiences over many years. This recognition has helped to guide both our selection of partners to fund, conversations with our grantees, and efforts to communicate with the broader field.

Selection of Partners

Although the focus of our funding efforts has been on upper elementary and middle school youth, as that period of life is so important in forming lifelong interests and self-perceptions, we have been encouraging grantees to extend a continuum of programming into high school, higher education, and careers. As examples, Jobs For the Future created the Possible Futures-Possible Selves middle grades career awareness curriculum that works in school day and afterschool settings; Techbridge Girls brings back youth who have "graduated" from the program as mentors to new recruits; and Boys and Girls Clubs of America has created a STEM Ready Youth continuum and aspires to prepare over two thousand low-income youth for STEM majors in college and careers.

Communication

One of the most recent projects of STEM Next Opportunity Fund is to support a series of case studies on family engagement in STEM. Techbridge Girls founder and former executive director, Linda Kekelis, and researcher Karen Sammet, who has led projects for Google and others, are leading the project. Their scan of the literature found a number of research studies that point to the important role played by families in encouraging children and youth to develop STEM interests and see themselves as capable STEM learners. Fathers are particularly critical in encouraging or discouraging their daughters from pursuing early STEM interests in elementary grades. The STEM Next website is providing an open channel to this research by hosting blogs about how informal educators can involve families in helping youth and adult family members develop STEM interests across the age spectrum.

Conclusion

As the field of STEM in OST has taken root, many of these threads, initially separate, have intertwined, and now form a woven fabric. Some of these connections have already been mentioned in this chapter, such as the collaboration of major national youth development organizations in a consortium that is called Imagine Science. But there are others as well. Many of the museum and science center leaders who became Noyce

Fellows through the Noyce Leadership Institute are now leading STEM Ecosystems that are being supported by the STEM Funders Network. The Mott State Afterschool Network leaders are interacting with many of the leaders of large youth development organizations, STEM Learning Ecosystems, and Every Hour Counts urban intermediaries in their states. And the research tools that have been developed by the PEAR Institute have become "industry standards" and helpful tools to a great many of our grantees to monitor and improve program quality, and to provide valid and reliable youth assessments and evaluations that are required by a majority of funders.

One of the most gratifying collaborations among our grantees has been a research study carried out by the PEAR Institute and the Institute for Measurement, Methodology, Analysis, & Policy at Texas Tech University in collaboration with the Mott Foundation and STEM Next Opportunity Fund.[11] The purpose of the study was to examine outcomes of informal STEM learning in a range of settings. The study included sixteen hundred children and youth in grades four to twelve enrolled in 160 programs in eleven Mott statewide afterschool networks. The researchers conducted observations of program quality using the Dimensions of Success instrument and youth assessments using the Common Instrument Suite measure of STEM-related attitudes and twenty-first-century skills. Analysis of student self-reported changes showed that participation in a STEM afterschool program increased positive attitudes toward STEM:

- 78 percent of students said they are more interested in STEM.
- 73 percent of students said they had a more positive STEM identity.
- 80 percent of students said their STEM career knowledge increased.

Not only did participation in STEM afterschool programs influence how students think about STEM, more than 70 percent of students across all states reported positive gains in twenty-first-century skills, including perseverance and critical thinking. Programs that received the highest ratings on the Dimensions of Success observation tool had youth participants that reported the most positive STEM-related outcomes, particularly for students' self-reported change in STEM career interest, STEM career knowledge, and STEM identity, lending strong empirical support to the link between quality STEM programs and positive outcomes for youth.

As this chapter has intended to show, the Noyce Foundation, and its legacy successor the STEM Next Opportunity Fund, has worked with dozens of national organizations and networks, more than fifty private and public funder colleagues, and hundreds of individual leaders to build the field of STEM in OST across the nation. If there is a single overarching strategy that encompasses our approach, it has been the idea that through partnerships we can accomplish far more than we could ever accomplish working in isolation. The idea is captured in the following quote from Ban Ki-moon, who was Secretary General of the United Nations from 2007 to 2016.

> One of the main lessons I have learned during my five years as Secretary-General is that broad partnerships are the key to solving broad challenges. When governments, the United Nations, businesses, philanthropies and civil society work hand-in-hand, we can achieve great things.[12]

Museums Can Take a Lead in Cultivating Vibrant Learning Ecosystems

12

KATHERINE PRINCE

*BIOGRAPHY: ONE OF THE UNITED STATES' foremost educational futurists, **Katherine Prince** leads KnowledgeWorks' exploration of the future of learning. As senior director of strategic foresight, she speaks and writes about the trends shaping education over the next decade and helps education stakeholders strategize about how to become active agents of change in shaping the future. Before joining KnowledgeWorks in 2006, Katherine supported large-scale changes in working practice at Britain's Open University and helped U.S. federal agencies and other clients increase service quality by incorporating a customer perspective into their organizational planning. Katherine holds a BA in English from Ohio Wesleyan University, an MA in English from the University of Iowa, and an MBA from The Open University. She earned a certificate in foresight from the University of Houston and is a member of the Association of Professional Futurists.*

Partners in Code

WHEN WE LOOK TO THE FUTURE, we have the opportunity to ask provocative questions about what could be. Those questions can help us challenge current assumptions, identify new ways of addressing pressing challenges, and reach for exciting visions. In considering future possibilities for museums and partnerships, we might ask questions such as:

- What if the health of a museum were measured by the strength of its relationships with varied partners?
- What if museums were recognized for playing an integral role in lifelong learning ecosystems?

- What if public funding for museums and other community-based learning venues was viewed as being an integral part of the investment in public education?

Would you want those things to happen? Resist them? What positive and negative implications might there be?

Such questions might seem unusual in light of today's realities. But the ecosystem approach that they reflect might be essential for museums' long-term strategies and learners' future readiness.

That is because we are entering a new era, one that colleagues and I describe as an era of partners in code.[1] Our economy, our institutions, and our societal structures are shifting at an accelerating pace. Central to this shift are exponential advances in digital technologies, enabling people to develop new uses for, and relationships with, machines that are increasingly wearable, connected, and smart. We are partnering with the code inside our computers, smartphones, cars, thermostats, home assistants, and toys in small and large ways that affect daily life, work, and learning. We can expect to do so more and more over the next decade and beyond.

Given the exponential rate of change, this new era of partners in code is ushering in unprecedented levels of complexity. That complexity can make it difficult to detect important shifts, much less to consider how we might respond to them. It can also raise deep questions about how museums and other organizations approach and support learning, and what we want the outcomes to be. In light of some of the shifts on the horizon, today's understanding of what education systems and other learning organizations aim to accomplish seems insufficient for the emerging era. To align with new possibilities on the horizon, we need to redefine how education stakeholders think of and approach readiness for further learning, work, and life and foster interconnected learning ecosystems that aim to help all learners thrive.

In regard to redefining readiness, as the rise of smart machines continues over the coming decades, we can expect them to increasingly perform not just routine, noncognitive tasks, but also many of the nonroutine, cognitive tasks that currently comprise much knowledge-based work. Smart machines' increasing sophistication will raise questions about the role of people in the workplace. Smart machines could augment human work, making many jobs safer, easier, and more interesting; they could also replace human contributions in some or many settings.[2]

To complicate matters further, a decline in full-time employment is also changing work and readiness. The relative ease of coordinating work across many people and places is leading to more contingent or project-based work and is spurring the spread of taskification, or the breaking down of jobs into discrete tasks that can be managed using platforms. Tenure in full-time jobs has been decreasing, with the average employee in the United States holding 11.7 jobs during their lifetime.[3] The company Intuit projects that over 40 percent of the U.S. workforce could be involved in the contingent economy as early as 2020.[4]

Together, the rise of smart machines and the decline of full-time employment are surfacing two critical uncertainties related to the future of readiness: a) the degree to which people might experience technological displacement in the workplace by 2040; and b) the extent to which the societal response will be either coordinated, supporting people in navigating the changing employment landscape, or more laissez-faire, leaving individuals to rely on their own resources or on pockets of support to which they may have access (see Figure 12.1). At the very least, we can expect

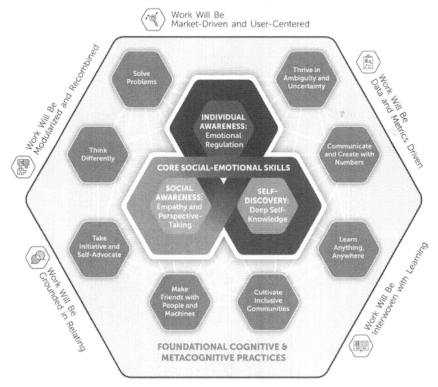

Figure 12.1.   A New Foundation for Readiness
KnowledgeWorks Foundation, Copyright 2017.

that people will need to reskill and upskill more and more often over the course of their careers. We can also project that fewer people will find themselves climbing career ladders, with more people laying career mosaics comprised of many kinds of work.

To help people prepare to thrive in face of such uncertainties and increasing complexity, we think that museums and other learning organizations need to emphasize a new foundation for readiness grounded in the following core social-emotional skills.

- **Deep self-knowledge** will help people develop visions for their lives and continue to discover their own personal and professional strengths, weaknesses, passions, and emotional patterns.
- **Individual awareness** will help people recognize and regulate their emotions; understand the triggers that spark them; and shift to more desired, productive emotional states when needed.
- **Social awareness** will help people recognize others' emotions and perspectives, enabling them to build relationships in support of learning, collaboration, and innovation and foster inclusive work environments.

Layered atop those core social-emotional skills, cognitive and metacognitive practices such as thinking differently, solving problems, cultivating inclusive communities, communicating and creating with numbers, and learning how to keep learning promise to help people prepare for life and work in the era of partners in code. Academic and context-specific skills will continue to have an important place, but these key skills and practices will provide a foundation on which individuals can build as they adapt to changing circumstances and craft the trajectories of their lives.

Such a new foundation for readiness seems to demand a new educational focus on feeling and relating. We need to know how to leverage our emotion system in order to bring our uniquely human capacities to smart machine partnerships. Put another way, helping people develop fully as human beings promises to go farthest in helping us thrive in the era of partners in code.

With their focus on free-choice and interest-driven learning and their relative freedom from regulation and accountability, museums are well positioned to respond to this renewed focus on feeling and relating and to support the development of foundational readiness skills and practices. The kinds of learning and engagement that can happen in and through museums can help people extend their ways of thinking and knowing, grapple with quandaries, and broaden their cultural, historical, and social perspectives. More specific opportunities for museums to respond to the era of partners in code include:

- Prioritizing support for social-emotional skill development.
- Partnering with kindergarten through twelfth grade schools, postsecondary and higher education institutions, and other organizations to raise awareness and exchange practice about effective approaches to doing so.
- Cultivating learning experiences that help people engage with ambiguity and uncertainty.
- Supporting people in developing creativity, cognitive diversity, and flexible thinking.
- Helping people nurture aspirational visions for their lives and reflect on how their experiences relate to their passions, purpose, aspirations, and goals.

While many museums already support learning in such ways, museums could help lead the way toward creating more personalized and relevant learning for learners of all ages by partnering with other organizations to foster interconnected learning ecosystems that make such learning far more widespread than it is today. In our view, a learning ecosystem is a network of relationships among educators and other learning agents, learners, resources, and assets in a specific social, economic, and geographic context. *To be vibrant and equitable, learning ecosystems require deep partnerships across a diverse array of digital, blended, and place-based learning providers, reflecting the resources and needs of particular geographies as well as individual learners' needs.*[5] Such learning ecosystems extend far beyond traditional kindergarten through twelfth grade schools and postsecondary and higher education institutions to include museums, zoos, science centers, libraries, parks, and other cultural and community-based institutions.

Vibrant and equitable learning ecosystems could contribute to the development of a more flexible learning infrastructure than is common today, supporting increased learner agency and inspiring all learners to develop to their fullest potential. But their emergence is not a given, especially in light of the persistent inequities in our current education system. There is a very real danger that vibrant ecosystems might exist only for those people with the resources to supplement or customize their learning journeys beyond the offerings of traditional schools, colleges, and universities. Instead of becoming more vibrant and interconnected, future learning ecosystems could increasingly become more fractured, leaving many learners without such resources falling behind.[6] As museums and other learning organizations respond to the opportunities and challenges presented by the new era of partners in code, they need to partner to cultivate learning oases and to avoid learning deserts.

Beyond the benefits for individuals and communities, fostering interconnected learning ecosystems promises to be a key strategy for organizational resilience.[7] As social, economic, political, and environmental factors shift, standalone organizations could become increasingly susceptible to system shocks, and funding sources could shift if tax bases get disrupted or funders' priorities change. In face of such challenges, contributing to interconnected learning ecosystems can help museums strengthen their contributions to learning while also supporting both organizational and community vitality.

Indeed, museums could serve as leaders in expanding stakeholders' visions for what is possible for learning and where, how, and when it occurs. Because they engage people of every age group and with many motivations and consider all people to be learners, museums can draw on their distinctive strengths and experience when cultivating vibrant learning ecosystems. For example, they could:

- Illuminate new possibilities for educating the whole person by normalizing lifelong, life-wide learning, helping to expand society's definition of who is a learner and helping others embrace the full range of when and where learning occurs.
- Collaborate with partners to envision what community-based, personalized learning ecosystems might look like and to find new opportunities to knit together current systems and organizations in support of those visions.
- Curate learning challenges and pathways that encourage pervasive access to interactive, personalized, self-paced learning.
- Create or extend staff roles that focus on helping learners navigate and complete learning options and develop key future-ready skills.
- Build networks with other organizations and use technologies such as matchmaking platforms, or other new forms of infrastructure, to help learners connect with the place-based experiences and build linkages among them.
- Design accessible ways for learners to find and take part in such offerings and networks to help ensure that everyone has the opportunity to participate.

- Advocate for new funding streams that expand access to public funds and support lifelong learning and create more flexibility within existing funding streams.
- Advocate for education metrics that align with desired practices, knowing that even modest changes could incentivize ecosystem-wide changes and increase access to free-choice learning.
- Practice inclusive design that seeks intentionally to engage communities around disparities and to encourage grassroots decision making.
- Engage audiences in conversations about their goals and aspirations and lead efforts to broaden society's and education institutions' views of success.
- Be at the forefront of the conversation about how to measure, verify, and credential learning that takes place outside of traditional classrooms and at different times of life.
- Advocate for the importance of local education solutions and approaches that response to learners' and communities' needs.[8]

While such practices might seem daunting, some museums are beginning to contribute to the creation of vibrant learning ecosystems today.

In one example, SURGE Columbus, a six-organization collaborative of museums, libraries, and media organizations, aims "to empower teens to discover and pursue their learning interests outside of school by connecting them with mentors, digital and cultural resources, and each other." The collaborative works to create a "learning ecology" that helps teens "develop their skills in critical thinking, civic engagement, media literacy, media production, and creative expression" and become "creative citizens who can think on their feet in order to actively participate in civil discourse, compete in the global economy, and develop 21st-century learning skills."[9] One of the spaces, the Columbus Museum of Art's Teen Open Studio, invites young people to drop in to create with traditional and new technologies, following their interests as they explore different media and projects. Teens from over thirty high schools in central Ohio use that space.[10] Through such engagement, SURGE Columbus is working to create an inviting and open afterschool learning ecosystem that teens can navigate coherently.

In another example, the Grand Rapids Public Museum School in Michigan opened as a middle school in 2015 in the former site of the Grand Rapids Public Museum and in 2017 won a ten-million-dollar grant from the XQ Institute's Super School Project to expand into high school. Being located next door to the museum's current building, the school's students and community members will have access to its artifacts, expanding their use from 30 to 75 percent. The increased use of collections is due to increased student interaction and access. The school will also use the surrounding community as a classroom. In addition to emphasizing place-based education, this public school reflects partnerships among Grand Rapids Public Schools, Grand Rapids Public Museum, Grand Valley State University, Kendall College of Art and Design, the City of Grand Rapids, and Downtown Grand Rapids, Inc.[11] In effect, it is designing school to extend over a learning ecosystem centered on its location and making extensive use of a museum's assets and expertise.

Lastly, the nonprofit Balboa Park Cultural Partnership brings together thirty arts, science, and cultural institutions in Balboa Park, San Diego, to collaborate toward greater organizational efficiency, innovation, and excellence. Its vision is "to serve as a national model for exceptional collaboration, innovative education, and transformative arts, science, and cultural experiences."[12] Among the partnership's programs, the Learning Institute encourages professional learning and exchange among staff and volunteers of arts, science, and cultural institutions.[13] Not only is the Balboa Park Cultural Partnership fostering an ecosystem approach among its member institutions, its support of professional learning is also building capacity among a broader ecosystem of institutions.

It can be fun to imagine how an intentional focus on cultivating vibrant learning ecosystems might help museums meet organizational goals, support future-ready learning for children and adults, and contribute to community vitality. It is also urgent to shift our thinking beyond managing discrete organizations toward fostering deep partnerships. In this complex and rapidly changing time when what it means to be ready for further learning, work, and life is shifting profoundly, we need brave leadership that will help people see and realize new possibilities for learning. Museums can help lead the way toward the future of learning.

Seeking Synergy   13
Strategic Partnership Development as Organizational Practice in Informal Education Organizations

RAFI SANTO

BIOGRAPHY: RAFI SANTO, PhD, is a learning scientist based at New York University focused on the intersection of digital culture, education, and institutional change. Centering his work within research-practice partnerships, he has studied, collaborated with, and facilitated a range of organizational networks related to digital learning, computing, and technology in education. Within informal education, he has focused on organizational change and the design of innovation networks around digital learning, focusing on both regional networks including the Mozilla Hive NYC Learning Network, a collective of seventy informal education organizations, as well as national networks, such as the Digital Learning Challenge community supported by the Susan Crown Exchange. In work in kindergarten through twelfth grade schooling, he has partnered with the CS for All National Consortium to support school districts to develop values-driven strategic plans around universal computing education initiatives. He is co-author of a four-volume collection on digital making from MIT Press called Interconnections: Understanding Systems through Digital Design. *His work has been supported by the Spencer Foundation, the MacArthur Foundation, the Mozilla Foundation, the Susan Crown Exchange, and the National Science Foundation.*

Strategic Partnership Development

A MUSEUM SPREADS ITS CITIZEN SCIENCE program to a half-dozen community recreation centers across its city. A community-based organization with a focus on socioemotional learning leverages a network of local expert organizations in maker education to help it develop its own makerspace. A library system increases its teen program offerings in areas like fashion, game design, and film-making by connecting local branches to specialized educational nonprofits. In these examples and so many others, informal education organizations utilize partnerships to "punch above their weight." Through collaboration across organizations, they are able to reach more young people, increase their internal capacity, spread their pedagogical practices, and expand the range of learning opportunities available to their youth. Yet while partnerships within education are now often an everyday part of organizational life, the processes of carrying them out and forming them cannot be taken for granted. A critical aspect of partnerships in informal education organizations needs to be explored—the dynamics surrounding *strategic partnership development.*

The findings shared here are rooted in almost five years of engagement in a research-practice partnership with the Hive NYC Learning Network, a collective of over seventy informal learning organizations based in New York City. As a network actively oriented toward using cross-organizational partnerships to explore the role and potential of emergent digital technologies for youth learning, Hive NYC was a rich context to investigate questions of how such partnerships come about. Two broad categories of phenomena associated with strategic partnership development are explored here.

The first category contains antecedents to the process of partnership development—factors that either directly instigated a process of exploring a potential partnership or were in some way preceding conditions to this process. Following this, the second category outlines facilitating actions—actions taken by informal learning organizations once the process of exploring a potential partnership was underway. These facilitating actions move the process forward toward either the formalization of a partnership or the decision to not pursue partnership. As informal education organizations increasingly look to partnerships for a variety of strategic purposes, the frameworks offered here might help organizations better understand the dynamics involved in partnership formation so that they may reflect on the partnership process.

Context—Hive Research Lab and Hive NYC Learning Network

This study took place within the context of a larger research-practice partnership between a university-based research group called Hive Research Lab and the Hive NYC Learning Network. Largely a project of the Mozilla Foundation,[1] Hive Learning Networks are regional collectives of educational stakeholders, principally youth-serving informal learning organizations, including museums, libraries, nonprofit and community-based organizations, as well as some institutions of higher education and industry partners. They are oriented toward promoting digital literacy, equity and inclusion with regards to technology and digital culture, pedagogical approaches that focus on interest-driven learning, and generally positioning youth as producers as opposed to only consumers of media and technology. Hives aim to achieve these ends through the creation of strong collectives of informal learning organizations supported by catalytic funding and network participation structures. Mozilla Foundation, largely known for its relationship to the popular open-source web browser Firefox but having also been a supporter of digital literacy initiatives, has acted as the network steward that supported these activities in many cities. Between 2010 and 2017, it actively developed Hives in New York, Chicago, Kansas City, Chattanooga, Austin, and Toronto, with some amount of support for others in various other locations. In New York, museum Hive participants included the Museum of Modern Art, the American Museum of Natural History, the Rubin Museum of Art, the Bronx Museum, the New York Hall of Science, the Museum of the Moving Image, the Brooklyn Museum, the Smithsonian's Cooper-Hewitt National Design Museum, and the Wildlife Conservation Society.

Elyse Eidmann-Adahl, director of the National Writing Project, once characterized Hives as both "Networks for Learning" and "Networks that Learn." On the one hand, a Hive acted as an ecosystem of youth-facing learning opportunities that span a city in order to support interest-driven learning pathways around digital media (the "Network for Learning"); on the other, as a "Network that Learns," participant organizations learned together how best to support such youth learning.[2,3] In this way, the "network" was seen simultaneously as a something experienced by both young people and institutions.

The partnership between Hive NYC and Hive Research Lab focused on simultaneously supporting the network to advance its goals of being a strong learning context for both the youth and organizations within it, as well as producing more broadly applicable research useful to both practitioners and scholars beyond the network. One key area of study for the research group focused on how partnerships played a role in the process of organizational learning, and the framework and examples presented in this chapter is one that emerged from this line of inquiry.[4]

Notes

1. While it is not in the scope of this chapter to explore the institutional history of Hive Learning Networks as an initiative, it is important to note that the key actors involved in their founding were connected to and supported by the MacArthur Foundation, with the Social Science Research Council acting as the founding steward in New York and DePaul University's Digital Youth Network acting as the founding steward in Chicago. Mozilla became the steward in New York in October 2011 and in Chicago in July 2013, and ended its stewardship

of those and other Hive Networks at the end of 2017. In one location, Pittsburgh, an existing network, the Kids+Creativity Network, later known as the Remake Learning Network, was briefly branded as and received support from the MacArthur Foundation to become a Hive network.

2. Ching, D. 2016. "'Now I Can Actually Do What I Want': Social Learning Ecologies Supporting Youth Pathways in Digital Media Making." Doctoral dissertation. New York University, New York.

3. Ching, D., Santo, R., Hoadley, C., and Peppler, K. 2015. *On-Ramps, Lane Changes, Detours and Destinations: Building Connected Learning Pathways in Hive NYC through Brokering Future Learning Opportunities*. New York: Hive Research Lab. http://bit.ly/brokering.

4. The foundation for this analysis is qualitative data from one-hour interviews with twenty-four informal learning organizations within the Hive NYC Learning Network that took place during 2014 and 2015. The interviews focused on accounts shared by member organizations related to how they engaged in forming new partnerships. These included the contexts in which partnerships formed, activities organizations engaged in during this process, considerations they made during decisions about whether to engage in a partnership, what a partnership might focus on, and what steps they took to solidify such partnerships. The data from interviews was also augmented by fieldwork within network contexts like meet-ups, community calls, holiday parties, conferences, and the community's online listserv between 2012 and 2016. These contexts were especially relevant to the question of strategic partnership development as these were often spaces that facilitated such activities, a theme that will be addressed in the findings.

In analyzing the data, I aimed to address the question of what factors and practices were salient to the process of strategic partnership development. While the broader study of organizational learning this analysis was situated in was driven by existing cultural-historical theories of learning (Engeström, 1987), for this particular analysis I used a grounded theory approach to deriving emergent themes from the data (Glaser, 2017).The analysis resulted in two sets of thematically driven factors and/or actions: a) antecedents to the process of partnership development—factors that either directly instigated a process of exploring a potential partnership, or were in some way preceding conditions to this process; and b) facilitating actions—actions taken by informal learning organizations once the process of exploring a potential partnership was underway in order to move forward toward either the formalization of a partnership or the decision to not pursue partnership.

The Role of Strategic Partnerships in Informal Education Organizations

These findings contribute to a small but growing literature on the nature of partnerships in informal education organizations. While there is a fair amount known about how informal education organizations partner with schools,[1] partnerships within informal education organizations are less frequently explored. Prior work on the Hive NYC Network has explored the ways that such partnerships can support different kinds of goals and needs, especially with regards to the process of developing and spreading new programs, technologies, or educational initiatives.[2] A study examining ninety-four formal partnerships among organizations in the Hive NYC Network found that the roles these organizations played for one another fell into one of three broad categories—providing *expertise*, providing *networks*, and providing *resources*.

Expertise-related roles included designing new curricula or programs, playing an advisory role on a project, helping to facilitate a program, providing strategic planning assistance, or conducting evaluations or research. *Network-related roles* included activities such as recruiting youth, providing access to a network of educators associated with one's organization, or providing access to a distribution network such as an online portal with a wide audience. *Resource-related roles* within partnerships included providing physical space and facilities, specialized technology or equipment, and intellectual property.

By configuring these roles in a variety of ways, informal education organizations could develop new initiatives, refine existing ones, reach new audiences of both youth and educators, increase their own capacity in a variety of new pedagogical specializations, and provide new and distinctive learning opportunities for youth.

Developing Strategic Partnerships

Collaboration among Hive members was a strong network value, and members were regularly engaged in the process of developing new partnerships. The process of strategic partnership development was often talked about as being "in conversation" with another organization—going through a process of determining whether formal collaboration might be possible or beneficial. At times this process could be very directed and time-bound. Two actors from separate organizations connect at a network meet-up and sense that there could be some potential in working together. They exchange information and bring their respective teams into a series of phone calls or meetings taking place over the course of weeks where the organizations share their current work and brainstorm possible ways of working together; they either find clear next steps or one or both of the actors concludes that there is no immediate possibility or desire to partner.

In other cases, being "in conversation" might be interwoven within the fabric of a longer and more organic relationship. Two organizations may have been generally familiar with one another for some time and had more informal relationships of knowledge-sharing, giving advice, and making introductions for one another. A leadership change in one organization prompts a re-evaluation of what the relationship could look like, and inspired by this internal shift at one organization, the two actors, long familiar with the range of one another's work, meet to discuss potential collaborations.

The following sections look at two sets of factors: *antecedents* to strategic partnership development processes and *facilitating actions* taken within existing ones that were meant to move the process along either toward formalization of the partnership or a decision to not pursue a partnership.

Antecedents to Strategic Partnership Development

Prior to directly engaging in the kinds of deliberation, ideation, and negotiation that characterize the later stages of developing a partnership, a number of *antecedents* help spark this process. There are seven antecedents to strategic partnership development found in the data, which often were intertwined: *affinity, exploratory stance, trusted brokerage, coercive pressure, network participation, working in the open,* and *open signaling.*

Affinity: A common precursor to strategic partnership development was *affinity* among employees within organizations. That is, an individual staff member might have a general admiration, sense of shared values, and appreciation for the work of another actor, be it a specific individual, an organization more broadly, or both.

Ricardo, an employee at the Science Exploration Center, in describing talks that he and his colleagues were in with TECHform, a technology-oriented youth development organization, shared a general admiration of the organization's leadership ("Jim is a really brilliant individual") and appreciation of their pedagogical approach ("I really love to see what the students are learning. There's an application to it."), and he generally saw a strong alignment of values. Hive members regularly shared such sentiments as "oh, we've wanted to find a project to work on together for ages now" when sharing stories about how formal partnerships came about. This pointed to the reality that sometimes the process of initiating a partnership exploration process was motivated, at least to some degree, by affinity, with an intuition that some possible way of working together would be found upon sharing more about current work underway and strategic priorities.

Exploratory Stance: A second precursor is *exploratory stance.* That is, an organization is in a place where it is generally assessing potential directions or next steps it might take and is open to meeting with and engaging in discussions around potential partnerships with other organizations as part of the process of better defining its own strategy.

In one interview, an employee from Ludo Learning Lab, when discussing a number of meetings it was having with potential collaborators, framed its organization as being in a moment where it had a "general stance of experimentation," saying that

> we were super interested in just partnering with another Hive organization. It came at a time for our organization where we were looking for new projects but we weren't really sure which direction to head into.

Having an exploratory stance can act as a precursor and motivation for engaging in strategic partnership development and is distinct in that there may not necessarily some highly specified strategy or project being advanced through this process, at least initially. Rather, such activities might be seen as a "strategy to develop strategy" and can contribute to larger process of clarifying potential new directions and possible futures for an organization.

Trusted Brokerage: A third precursor identified is *trusted brokerage*. Essentially, an intermediary familiar with two actors previously unconnected or loosely connected sees some potential for collaboration and makes an introduction that facilitates actions linked to strategic partnership development.

In one interview, a participant mentioned a person that regularly played this role of being a trusted broker for her organization when asked about how a specific partnership came about.

> Kara actually suggested that they [talk to us]. So often Kara has kind of been a catalyst in that. She's done a ton of brokering on our behalf. She knows us really well as an organization.

The broker here is familiar with this organization (in this case, she was a former employee), and, presumably, had similar familiarity, at least to some degree, with the other organization as well.

In another instance shared by the same participant, she pointed to a different organization that regularly acted as a trusted broker:

> They just really frequently introduce us to organizations who are looking to take advantage of our expertise. They're kind of playing the role of convener in the games and learning space.

Organizations acting as trusted brokers are not necessarily only looking out for the specific organizations they are connecting, but are also potentially acting more broadly as stewards of a particular part of a sector, a role where promoting the success of individual organization through brokering is part of a larger field-strengthening orientation.

Additionally, while trusted brokerage may be initiated by the brokers themselves, it can also be instigated by an actor either generally seeking collaborators to fill a certain need (e.g., "Do you know anyone that has experience integrating scientific inquiry and coding?") or more specifically looking to connect with a particular organization (e.g., "Can you introduce me to the folks at SciCode?"). In these cases, trusted brokerage can be the result of self-advocacy or search activities for the organization seeking partners.

Coercive Pressure: One precursor previously identified in literature on institutional theory is *coercive pressure*.[3] As Small[4] notes, coercive pressure can mediate the formation of social ties between organizations and "stem(s) from larger authorities that mandate or establish regulations resulting in inter-organizational ties or the exchange of resources across organizations." The phenomenon is somewhat similar to trusted brokerage in that it involves an outside actor mediating the process of strategic partnership development in some way.

Coercive pressure manifested in the research study in a number of ways. Some resembled the mechanisms of trusted brokerage, whereby a third actor actively connects two previously unconnected actors, seeing some way that these two actors might benefit or that by aligning their strategies the benefit that might accrue to the broader field. The distinction here is that the connection may be less mediated by trust, though trust may be present, and more by the power and position of the actor making the connection.

One place where coercive pressure was salient within Hive, less targeted to a specific organization, was criteria for Hive grants. Many Requests for Proposals required multiple organizational actors to participate in funded projects. A Request for Proposal from the Hive Digital Media and Learning Fund, for example, stated for some types of grants that "Partnership with another member of the Network is strongly encouraged. Partnerships with groups outside the Network will also be considered." Other funding competitions simply stated, "Partnership with at least one other group in the Network is required," and for projects involving at least three partners, two from the Hive network were required.

Participants responded to such coercive pressures in various ways. Generally, they were as part of the natural landscape of organizational life. In one case, a Hive member reported that he initially bristled when some powerful actor recommended that his organization engage in a partnership with another group, but he eventually came to appreciate the specialized expertise that the recommended organization brought to their partnership and the unlikeliness that they would have worked together independent of such pressure. Others resisted such direct recommendations and proposed alternative relationships with organizations they trusted and with whom they had more experience that would fulfill the same function. Many study participants described a phenomenon they deemed "shotgun marriages," wherein two organizations end up partnering because some powerful actor either had a direct or indirect influence. In these cases, partnerships were either formed quickly, often without much deliberation or specification, and, potentially, without the depth that might allow the relationship to more effectively leverage respective organizational resources and navigate emergent challenges.

Network Participation: One of the most salient preconditions of partnership formation is *network participation*, when an organization's staff participates in contexts created by broader networks of actors. In Hive NYC, the network's managers created a range of participation structures, including monthly meet-ups, community calls, working groups, and member-led professional development opportunities where member organizations would gather in person. They also created such online contexts as a community listserv, blog, directory, project portfolio, and Slack channel where members were able to participate. Finally, the network stewards would often coordinate and encourage participation in broader field-level gatherings such as conferences or symposia, and travel funds were often made available for participation in these events. In all of these contexts, relationships would form and information would circulate among network members that would support the process of strategic partnership development.

Within these kinds of network structures, the nature and design of the experience would often support larger processes of strategic partnership formation. Promoting the often-stated view that the most valuable conversations "happen in the hallway," many of the in-person meet-ups were structured to ensure that member organizations had time to informally connect with one another. At the same time, these network contexts often contained more formal mechanisms for supporting strategic partnership development: presentations and share-outs about specific organizational practices or models, small and large group conversations that focused on common issues, and even formal activities where organizations were invited to share current strategic challenges. These activities helped to make more transparent how participants might leverage each other's expertise, resources and networks for strategic partnerships.

Working in the Open: Linked to modes of work found in open source culture, *working in the open* is a set of work practices and program development that values transparency, an experimental stance, and open contribution and collaboration by large communities.[5] "Working open" covers a range of organizational approaches to innovation and scaling work that emphasize:

1. *Public storytelling and context setting,* where a project will regularly use public and semi-public channels to share about an initiative that promotes discoverability;
2. *Rapid prototyping "in the wild,"* where early stage project ideas will be tested in public contexts;
3. *Enabling community contribution,* or specifically designing a project's division of labor in a way that allows new actors to get involved;
4. *Public reflection and documentation,* or documenting learnings and having a trail of accessible artifacts that are created and share along the way; and, finally
5. *Creating remixable work products,* ones that can easily, and legally, be adapted and reconfigured by others that wish to build on them.

While these practices are ones that emerged from a technology culture associated with Free/Open Source Software, in Hive NYC they took place across both digital and in-person contexts, with sharing about projects happening in the context of in-person meet ups as much as on blog posts. The values of collaboration, transparency, and collective impact that guided these practices were more important than the range of digital tools. Taken together, practices of working in the open were often precursors to partnership development, setting the foundation for a given organization or project to be discovered and for potential collaborators to understand how they might contribute.

Open Signaling: A final antecedent found in the data was that of *open signaling*—mechanisms for making clear within semi-public contexts an interest in forming partnerships with other actors. Often, such signaling occurred in contexts that were developed by the Hive NYC network stewards, such as within the community's online listserv or in face-to-face meet-ups or community calls. Sometimes these contexts included explicit opportunities where organizations collectively engaged in activities designed to promote open signaling around particular needs. In other cases, a specific organization might share out about an early stage project and indicate its interest in finding partners that might be willing to act as testing or adoption sites, as in the instance of an organization developing an SMS-based tool meant to facilitate communication between educators and teens that was looking to find organizations interested in using and giving feedback on an early stage prototype of the technology.

Within the open signaling practices observed, actors indicated different needs and interests that varied in terms of their specificity. In one case, an organization posted to the Hive listserv with the subject line "Looking for a Partner?" and within the post outlined broadly what it could offer potential partners ("approximately 200 scientists on staff who can be accessed for guest talks, collaborative design work and one-on-one mentoring," "the ability to implement short-term or long-term programs in which science-interested youth can explore particular topics") and what needs it was looking to have filled through partnerships ("access to youth from under-represented communities," "creative approaches to engaging youth in science"). That approach was quite broad, with many potential avenues that interested collaborators could pursue through understanding the general needs of the posting organization.

A second example indicates a more targeted approach. Posting to the Hive listserv with the subject line "Looking to Finalize List of Partners," an organization indicated interest in finding additional implementation sites that would receive professional development and then run a technology-enabled environmental activism program developed by the organization. It outlined a specific scope of work that partners would undertake, a description of the program to be implemented, and the nature of the support the organization would provide.

Other, even more formal, mechanisms of open signaling included organizations publicly announcing a new initiative seeking network partners and providing a short-form "interest application" to be completed by potential partners.

Generally, the presence of open signaling indicated a degree of trust between organizations in the network and indexed strong norms around collaboration. While these behaviors did not replace the more intensive facilitating processes explored in the next section, open signaling helped support such facilitation.

Facilitating Actions within Strategic Partnership Development

Once the process of coming together to discuss a potential partnership was underway, there were a number of facilitating actions that moved the process of strategic partnership development forward toward project formalization, definition of roles, and procurement and provision of resources. This section describes four of these: *establishing identity, seeking synergy, framing value,* and *assessing capacity.*

Establishing Identity: The first facilitating action was the practice of *establishing identity,* through which organizations made more transparent their respective capacities, assets, interests, and needs. Participants framed this practice as "getting to know" another organization, "self-framing," and "defining resources." Within a discussion, this practice might look like a combination of telling the organization's broad story and orientation with a more detailed outlining of current initiatives and programs.

One participant noted that within such conversations he might share something along the lines of "We've been doing a lot of X and not as much Y, but are really looking to do less X," aiming not only to share what the organization has done and currently did, but also making clear the kind of work it wanted to do in the future. Thus, the process of establishing identity in this context was both retrospective and prospective. The potential partner could therefore prime the other(s) to see whether it could help the inquiring organization move in its desired strategic direction.

The process of establishing identity could also be condensed or even skipped over entirely if the actors involved had, through other mechanisms, become deeply familiar with one another and had a clear sense of the potential opportunities that might be pursued together.

Seeking Synergy: The centerpiece of strategic partnership development is arguably the process of seeking synergy. All preceding actions lead up to and support this process of establishing concrete possibilities for collaboration. Participants talked about this practice in terms of "brainstorming," "shooting around ideas," and "seeking reciprocity," essentially determining what needs might be filled or possibilities pursued through creative re-combination of distinctive assets that organizations bring to the table.

In one instance, a participant described details related to potential collaborations recently identified with another organization. Her organization had been developing media production tools focused on teaching about intellectual property and fair use through remixing existing video. The organization they were in discussion with had access to a broad array of intellectual property that was in the public domain and thus not legally restricted in how others use it. She described the potential synergy between their organizations in this way:

> *Lisa:* [Our executive director] met with them and he talked with them and they loved the project and they love what it's about. And what we want to do is work on creating basically a conduit where people can import directly from the Internet Archives into the Message Mixer.
>
> *Researcher:* Which means that you don't need to worry about fair use.
>
> *Lisa:* Yeah. . . . [It's] public domain. It also cuts out a major technical barrier for a lot of educators because a lot of people [are] like, "How do I download a video? How do I upload a video?" [And] it solves a problem with the fair use issue in terms of how you acquire media, . . . So we don't have to worry about that. It makes it easier for our students. It makes it easier for educators. It also helps to, I think, raise the function of what their organization can do and what they're there for. So that funnel would be huge.

She pointed to a number of problems that might be solved by creating a partnership between the two organizations. For her organization, both technical literacy challenges concerning how to download and upload media could be avoided, and legal challenges associated with potentially using copyrighted intellectual property become less of a concern through access to an archive of media in the public domain. For the potential partner, she described how it created beneficial application and use of its assets ("raises the function of what their organization can do and what they're there for"). Both organizations would receive benefits and be able, through a potential collaboration, to solve problems inherent within their contexts. The process of seeking synergy helped identify problems inherent in the daily work of the organizations and resolve those problems through focusing on a shared goal.

At the same time, not all processes of seeking synergy end up with clear ways of moving forward together. In one case, a participant shared a process of partnership development that ended up with little to show for it, largely because it was not clear exactly what benefit could come from collaborating.

> We both had similar ideas, we both had similar philosophies. And we both had distribution [channels], we both had content, we both felt like we could make stuff, and it was this process of trying to figure out who did

what. . . . It was just hard to figure out how the puzzle pieces fit together. Nothing ever came of it, it was unfortunate. We wanted to partner, it was just unclear enough how to do it.

Even having affinity in place—what seemed like respect and admiration for one another's work ("similar philosophies"), and a desire to partner— the process of seeking synergy was not successful. What kinds of problems each of the organizations could solve for one another remained elusive. Another instance pointed to a similar dynamic, with a participant, Ricardo, describing meetings with a potential partner:

> We were at TECHform two weeks ago. It's Jim, Sam—big thinkers shooting out ideas, and then me just jotting down a lot of notes and just, "Okay. How can we logistically make sense of all of this?" . . . Sam's really a big thinker. . . . But sometimes, it can get too excessive. "Okay. What are we doing? You sound like you said a really great idea, but–?" . . . . What usually happens is that– . . . "Oh, you're a great organization, and I'm a great organization. You guys do cool stuff." And then list your stuff, and then, that's it. Nothing ever comes of it. "Oh, we would love to do that because you guys are doing that." You say, "Alright," and then you walk out of the meeting like, "Nothing happened. What's the next step?"

Essentially, Ricardo is describing how the process can start with affinity, move into a more substantive set of discussions around strategic partnership development with identities being established, but the process stalls there, with possibilities being generated but a lack of concretizing something that is in the realm of possibility for both organizations.

These examples reveal that the process of seeking synergy is tentative and fragile, and there are many reasons that alignment might not be reached. There simply might not be an obvious way to work together, or there might not be adequate resources of staff time or funding. Additionally, while one group might wonder why "nothing happened," even though many ideas were generated, it is possible that the other organization might not have found the concepts for collaboration sufficiently compelling. Finally, the prospective partner might question the level of expertise or capacity that becomes visible during the process of inter-organizational familiarization.

Framing Value: Interwoven with the process of seeking synergy is *framing value* of potential partnership projects—a process of showing other actors why it might be beneficial to work together, even if its value is not immediately apparent. One participant described this action:

[Our executive director] likens a lot of [the process] to his political background where you're trying to talk about mutual benefits. And a lot of it depends on flattering the other person. . . . It's a matter of how are you constructing the message in a way that is endearing and alluring to the person that you're talking to.

She shared a number of examples of how this has played out within the process of strategic partnership development within her organization:

So we are in talks with WebDex, right? We're talking about issues around fair use in interacting with content that exists that is out there and finding a proactive way to make it relevant and talk about it, remixing it, using it for education, all those things. That's kind of the frame that we're putting around it for WebDex. And then we're also of course talking about the fact that our population is demographically very diverse and tends to not be kids who are engaging with media in this way. When we go and talk to the Engaged Network, which is a marketing firm that would help us . . . to spread the tool and get more users to adopt it, get more school districts to adopt it, that conversation has more to do with making it sound like an interesting challenge to them because it's a little bit more complicated than just sending out a tweet. . . . And that is a challenge that's interesting to them. . . . And then the social educational benefits on top of that are also appealing.

For each of the potential partners, she described how her organization constructed particular narratives and arguments for why it would be of value to engage in a partnership. For WebDex, she used the frame of making their content "relevant" through "remix" and use within an educational setting. This enabled the other organization to understand why a partnership would help solve one of their challenges. For the Engaged Network, she talked about appealing to the unique and complex nature of "get[ting] more school districts to adopt" its tool, and how that is distinct from what they might usually be doing in marketing campaigns. For both potential partners, she emphasized appealing to the pro-social and mission driven aspect of working with her organization. All of these helped frame the value of a possible collaboration.

Assessing Capacity: A final facilitating action was *assessing capacity*—actions taken that help determine a potential partner's expertise, capabilities, work style, and interactional fluidity. Participants shared how evaluating a potential partner's capacity was ongoing throughout the entire process of strategic partnership development. Assessing capacity could include evaluating the kinds of ideas around collaboration that a potential partner put forward, observing the ways the potential partner structured and engaged within a conversation, learning more about a partner's approach to tasks, or other, more formal actions such as reading responses to formal Requests for Partnership.

One participant talked about how, at the end of the phone call with a potential partner, he would often suggest that one of the actors write a follow-up email detailing the possible collaborations that had been discussed, including agreed-upon next steps, such as sending promised supporting documentation or scheduling the next phone call or meeting. He shared that when a potential partner does not follow through on such a commitment or inaccurately captures the next steps, doubts surface about the relationship's viability.

In another case, an organization had a promising conversation with another and decided to move forward on a collaborative funding proposal. The process of proposal writing, however, provided serious warning signs:

> It was a proposal that we were going to submit. . . . If the other partner isn't basically pulling their weight and being as helpful as they possibly can be in the proposal writing process, if they are not consistently checking in, that is something—OK, so this is what's it's like to start a proposal process and it's not going to go well during programming. So we should just stuff the whole thing, and we did.

This process helped evaluate the capacity of the potential partner and resulted in a decision to abandon plans to work together.

Such actions can help develop—or damage irrevocably—trust between new partners. They shed light on such questions as: How does the other organization work? Can I rely on them? How do they react if things don't go as planned? Questions like these are answered in large and small ways throughout the process of strategic partnership development, and continue, of course, in more substantive ways within formal partnerships that are born out of that process.

Conclusion

The process of strategic partnership development is explored in this chapter as observed in the context of a network of informal education organizations. The different factors discussed, antecedents to and actions taken within partnership exploration, can contribute to the broader organizational practice of strategic partnership development. Rather than reducing such processes to the most explicit and formal moments of interactions between organizations, empirical analysis has attempted to show the ways that these actions span both long and short timescales. Broader practices of network participation are ongoing and occur along longer timescales, but they can often facilitate more intensive moments of seeking synergy between two organizations. At the same time, more micro-level dynamics that happen in the course of a conversation among potential partners, such as the ways one actor is able to frame value, or fails to, can play important roles in the process of partnership development.

The findings suggest that there are certain actions organizations, including museums, can take to become more effective in forming partnerships. Putting resources into participating in networks and publicly documenting work creates the conditions necessary for other actors to understand how they might partner with another organization. Forming a strong social network that deeply understands its work makes it more likely that an organization ends up benefiting from trusted brokerage. And within the process of exploring a given partnership, attending intentionally to how those involved are able to establish identity, frame value, seek synergy, and assess capacity will likely result in more robust and mutually beneficial partnerships. When done well, strategic partnership development can play a critical role in resolving internal challenges and advancing strategic priorities through transforming and expanding an organizational ecosystem by figuring out potential ways that assets another organization brings to the table might be leveraged. These partnerships can also increase the broader community impact of collaborative efforts. With today's increased emphasis on broad learning ecosystems and recognition that partnership development can lead to formal collaborations that support the design, improvement, and spread of educational projects, insights into the factors that drive partnerships can provide useful cues along the way to success.

Other References

Barron, B., Gomez, K., Pinkard, N., and Martin, C. K. 2014. *The Digital Youth Network: Cultivating Digital Media Citizenship in Urban Communities*. Cambridge, MA: MIT Press.

Bevan, B., with Dillon, J., Hein, G. E., Macdonald, M., Michalchik, V., Miller, D., Root, D., Rudder, L., Xanthoudaki, M., and Yoon, S. 2010. *Making Science Matter: collaborations between informal science education organizations and schools. A CAISE Inquiry Group Report*. Washington, DC: Center for Advancement of Informal Science Education (CAISE).

Bodily, S. J., Augustine, C., and Zakaras, L. 2008. *Revitalizing Arts Education through Community-Wide Coordination*. Santa Monica, CA: RAND Corporation.

Ching, D. 2016. "'Now I Can Actually do What I Want': Social Learning Ecologies Supporting Youth Pathways in Digital Media Making." Doctoral dissertation. New York University, New York.

Ching, D., Santo, R., Hoadley, C., and Peppler, K. (2015). *On-Ramps, Lane Changes, Detours and Destinations: Building Connected Learning Pathways in Hive NYC through Brokering Future Learning Opportunities.* New York: Hive Research Lab. http://bit.ly/brokering.

Ching, D., Santo, R., Hoadley, C., and Peppler, K. (2016). "Not Just a Blip in Someone's Life: Integrating Brokering Practices into Out-of-School Programming as a Means of Supporting Youth Futures." *On the Horizon,* 24(3), 296–312.

DiMaggio, P., and Powell, W. W. (1983). "The Iron Cage Revisited: Collective Rationality and Institutional Isomorphism in Organizational Fields." *American Sociological Review,* 48(2), 147–60.

Engeström, Y. (1987). *Learning by Expanding: An Activity-Theoretical Approach to Developmental Research.* Helsinki: Orienta-Konsultit.

Glaser, B. (2017). *Discovery of Grounded Theory: Strategies for Qualitative Research.* New York: Routledge.

James Irvine Foundation. (2005). *Museums after School: How Museums Are Reaching Kids, Partnering with Schools, and Making a Difference.* San Francisco, CA: James Irvine Foundation.

Pinkard, N., Barron, B., and Martin, C. (2008, June). "Digital Youth Network: Fusing School and After-School Contexts to Develop Youth's New Media Literacies." In *Proceedings of the 8th International Conference for the Learning Sciences,* 3, 113–14.

Russell, J. L., Knutson, K., and Crowley, K. (2012). "Informal Learning Organizations as Part of an Educational Ecology: Lessons from Collaboration across the Formal-Informal Divide." *Journal of Educational Change,* 14(3), 259–81.

Santo, R. (2017). "Working Open in the Hive: How Informal Education Organizations Learn, Collaborate and Innovate in Networks." Doctoral dissertation. Indiana University, Bloomington, IN.

The People's University   **14**

MARSHA L. SEMMEL, FROM INTERVIEWS WITH
FELTON THOMAS, JR.

*BIOGRAPHY: FELTON THOMAS, JR., is the immediate past president of the
Public Library Association and was appointed director of the Cleveland (Ohio)
Public Library (CPL) in January 2009. Prior to accepting the position of director
of CPL, Felton served as director of Regional Branch Services for the Las Vegas–
Clark County (Nevada) Library District and President of the Nevada Library
Association. He has served on the PLA Board of Directors since 2012, and he was
named to the Aspen Institute's Task Force on Learning and the Internet in 2014.
His awards and accomplishments include being named a "Mover and Shaker" by
Library Journal and being selected as White House Champion of Change for
Making in 2016.*

Introduction

FELTON THOMAS, JR., has been the chief executive officer of the
Cleveland Public Library since January 2009. He brought years
of library and leadership experience to Cleveland, including his
participation in the Urban Libraries Council's Executive Leadership Institute and the Institute of Museum and Library Services/Salzburg Global
Forum's 2011 international symposium, *Libraries and Museums in an Era
of Participatory Culture.*[1] According to Thomas, those experiences helped
hone his skills in leading organizational change; promoting self-awareness,
understanding and the importance of public value; and commitment to the
broader, deeper role that public libraries could play in community learning
and revitalization, as well as individual growth and well-being.

Upon arriving in Cleveland, Thomas found daunting community statistics, with especially high rates of crime and poverty. Yet he also found "a fantastic city that had all of the infrastructure necessary to create the city of the future."[2] Cleveland Public Library first opened as a "Public School Library" for the Cleveland Board of Education in 1869. It was the first large public library to allow people to select their own books directly from its bookshelves.[3] As the third largest public research library in the country after New York City and Boston, the Cleveland Public Library had manifested, throughout its long history, its ongoing commitment to the city's poor.

Thomas' passion for public libraries stems from his youth. Thomas saw the public library as the safest place in his neighborhood as he was growing up in Las Vegas. At age thirteen, he became the youngest employee in Las Vegas–Clark County Library District history when a librarian noticed his enthusiasm and encouraged him to become a page. For Thomas, the library is a core community anchor, and the Cleveland post "was the perfect place for [my] philosophy—the library as social activist."

Creating Change: Organizational Culture and New Partnerships

Although he saw the Cleveland Public Library's potential, Thomas had to initially confront sobering financial statistics and some cultural challenges upon his arrival in 2009. A seventy-two-million-dollar annual budget had been reduced to fifty-three million dollars. The staff of one thousand had been downsized to seven hundred. Library hours had been cut. Thomas was determined to shift the organization's mindset from despairing about current cutbacks to moving forward with the vision of a library for the future. His plan would not happen overnight and required many actions and steps internally and externally, with new partnerships playing essential roles.

For Thomas, a critical first step involved recognizing the power of the library's original mission and values dedicated to public service and education (see Figure 14.1). The current mission and values would need to be updated in order to present a relevant vision for the library for today and tomorrow. He positioned the library as a "community-deficit fighter," launching initiatives aimed at addressing community needs in the areas of technology, education, and economic development.

Within the library, fulfilling this vision required a substantial organizational culture change. An early example was the community's need for an organization to address the summer meals gap for needy school children. When Thomas proposed that the library collaborate with a local food bank to address this need, some of the staff protested, "We are librarians, not lunch ladies." Yet Thomas was resolute. He formulated, practiced, and continually communicated three core values that became expectations for each library staff member. The values were:

1. We all sacrifice;
2. We all operate with integrity (we do what we say we'll do); and
3. We respect everyone, in and out of our organization.

There was a salary freeze and more cuts, and Thomas included himself in each of these "sacrifices." Among the challenges, libraries—and librarians—are not always comfortable with change. In order for the organization to survive, however, and for the betterment of the city of Cleveland, Thomas had to lead significant change. For many staff, it was a long and difficult process to abandon some old practices and move into new programmatic and partnership territory. Thomas had to note repeatedly that the library's survival "depends on our doing things differently."

"As a leader, you can never over-communicate," he states. Given the fact that the library's financial support is determined by the voter's approval of a property tax levy every five years, it has regular opportunities to learn what the citizenry of Cleveland thinks about the library's public value. In 2013, the voters registered 76 percent approval, the highest level in the library's history; in 2017, the voters again registered high approval. In time, staff expectations shifted in alignment with the new vision, and the budget was adjusted to reflect these broader community priorities. The focus became service to the community. As different community needs surfaced, Thomas and his staff asked, "Do we have the capacity to do address this need? Can we do it well? Should we take this on?"

As Thomas continued to make his mark, he prioritized re-introducing the library to multiple communities where it had lost some of its previous strong connections. "Since the early 1900s," Thomas noted that "the Cleveland Public Library had purchased books in native languages. We found that material, we purchased new material, and we brought reading materials to other sites, like the Cleveland Clinic."[4]

We used to host parties for new refugees. We restarted that practice with a program that invited new immigrants to "cook something and come and share your culture."

The library's 2012 strategic plan notes:

> Whenever the Library isolated itself from the community it is mandated to serve, the Library weakened itself. Whenever the Library stopped taking risks, the Library stunted its own progress. Whenever the Library rested on its laurels, the Library caused its relevance to be call into question. . . . This Strategic Plan is a direct challenge to complacency.[5]

The library's vision:

> Cleveland Public Library will be the driving force behind a powerful culture of learning that will inspire Clevelanders from all walks of life to continually learn, share and seek out new knowledge in ways that are beneficial to themselves, their community and the world.

The mission became "We are the 'People's University,' the center of learning for a diverse and inclusive community."

The Role of Partnerships

From his earliest days at the Cleveland Public Library, Thomas has envisioned partnership as an essential strategic priority. The early collaboration over summer meals with the Greater Cleveland Food Bank has grown in many ways. The Food Bank's mission is "to ensure that everyone in our communities has the nutritious food they need every day." The food bank is the largest hunger relief organization in northeast Ohio, having provided fifty million meals in 2016 to hungry people in Cuyahoga, Ashtabula, Geauga, Lake, Ashland, and Richland counties.[6] The libraries continue to distribute free meals to youth, with more than 150,000 meals provided in 2016. That year, a new program began with libraries providing produce to community members. One branch library distributed more than 250 bags of produce to patrons in two hours. As an indication of his dedication to the community-minded work of the food bank, Thomas is now president of its board of directors. "Legal Aid at the Library" is an ongoing partnership with the Legal Aid Society. The society hosts free legal advice clinics at library branches throughout the city, providing first come, first served legal assistance to people with civil legal issues.

Through a partnership with Cleveland Department of Public Health, some library branches serve as sites for people to receive immunizations.

Other relationships have been forged with the Cleveland Indians, the Cleveland Metropolitan School District, Starting Point for Child Care and Early Education, United Way of Greater Cleveland, Landscape Art Neighborhood Development Studio, and the National Aeronautics and Space Association.

In the cultural realm, the library has worked with the Cleveland Museum of Natural History, the Cleveland Museum of Art, the Great Lakes Theater, the Cleveland Playhouse, the Cleveland Metroparks Zoo, and the Great Lakes Science Center.

The work with the Museum of Natural History provides an informative example. Many of these relationships are part of the People's University, one of the library's major initiatives. When Thomas arrived in Cleveland in 2009, there had been a group of museum professionals who worked with a consultant to create a city-wide museum pass program, not unlike other similar museum-library programs in other communities where passes were available for checkout at the various libraries. The group could not figure out how to make the program work financially, could not overcome organizational differences and individual perspectives, and in the end it never happened.

In 2013, Thomas was approached by the relatively new director of the Cleveland Museum of Natural History, Evelyn Gates, about reviving the pass program. They began with a small pilot program. At a branch library near the museum, the partners worked together to create a kit that included four free passes for families to visit the museum along with a copy of a children's book *Going to a Museum (A World of Field Trips)*, by Rebecca Rissman. The pilot proved successful, and the program has spread to eight libraries. It has achieved its goal: more than 50 percent of the families who check out the kit use the passes to visit the museum. The library has since been approached by the Cleveland Symphony and the Cleveland Museum of Art to experiment with similar endeavors.

The People's University

One of Thomas' discoveries was the library's longstanding tag line, "the People's University." This fit perfectly with his belief that the successful future for the library depended on translating the core values of the past into services and programs that were the most creative, useful, and inspiring for the future. What did it mean to be the "People's University" for the Cleveland residents of today? For Thomas, it meant becoming the "pre-eminent out-of-school learning institution in the nation."[7] Accordingly, this is now the library's driving mission, and Thomas has understood that success necessitated authentic and sustained partnerships.

The People's University is the library's "North Star," with a soft launch in early 2017. Progress continues, with the passage of a November 2017 library levy on the Cleveland ballot passing with the support of 69 percent of voters. After more research, further conversations with potential partners and community members, the library is rebranding the project as the "People's Academy." It has launched with a pilot class on digital photography taught at the library by faculty from the Cleveland Art Museum, with class participants having the option to earn a digital badge credential for their participation.

"The entire People's University concept is built on partnerships. There is a specific graphic with the learner at the center and the various entities encircling the learner as the center of a networked world." (Figure 14.1) The key criterion: "Can our partner encircle the learner in a way that will enable the learner to be successful?" The library's partners include the Great Lakes Science Center, the Cleveland Museum of Art, Cuyahoga Community College of Cleveland State University, and Ohio Means Jobs of Cleveland–Cuyahoga County. As this concept has developed, each learner is at the center of a network of learning opportunities, and the Cleveland Public Library is at the center of the learning ecosystem, serving as a hub where learners can discover and connect to various resources and expertise. In addition, the library provides opportunities for individuals with specific expertise to become "teachers" themselves, sharing their knowledge and passion with others in the community.

Partnership Elements

What are the formal elements of the People's University collaborations? The library completes a Memorandum of Understanding with the various partner entities, which spells out shared goals and aspirations. It works with the partners to determine the "sweet spots" of a relationship for each, and how a collaboration can serve the goals of each organization. The partnership with Ohio Means Jobs, for example, works as follows: "People want jobs. Ohio Means Jobs provides help in such skills as resume writing. Through the partnership with Ohio Means Jobs, people enrolled in the People's University will have the opportunity, in Ohio Means Jobs sites in our public libraries, to receive training and learn about specific jobs. Libraries will provide financial literacy training and job obtainment skills."

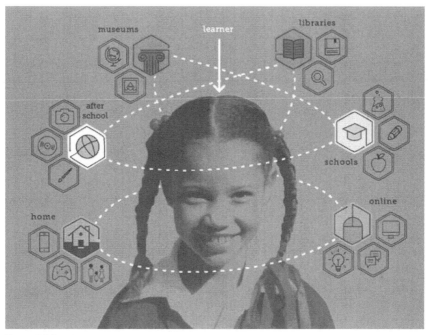

Figure 14.1.

What Is the Potential of Museum/ Library Partnerships?

Thomas offered the following thoughts about what libraries have to offer to museums: "Libraries are open to everyone, and free to everyone. They are outward facing, used to giving everything away for free, and know how to work inside communities. Partnerships come naturally to them. Many museums are more inward facing, addressing a smaller, niche, user base. The cultural organizations of Cleveland's University Circle, for example, literally face each other, 'turning their backs' on the surrounding community. These organizations need to address critiques about their elitism, especially since, increasingly, funders, community leaders, senior staff and board members are encouraging museums to address issues of equity and access, to invite and include visitors who look more like their neighborhood communities. Working with libraries can support this goal, even if organizations like the Cleveland Museum of Art (CMA) have a free admissions policy. The Museum of Art has been an enthusiastic participant in the People's University."

What museums have to offer to libraries: "Museums have valuable content, and content expertise. They can enhance the art track that is part of the People's University, for example. In addition, their reputations and stature can bring a certain amount of gravitas to library programs. The Cleveland Museum of Art is one of the best museums in the country, and it's terrific that it is working so enthusiastically with us, and the Cleveland Museum of Natural History is a welcomed partner with its $150 million expansion and renovation."

What is Thomas' advice for fostering a partnership mindset within a museum staff? "My advice is to continually communicate the importance of having all eyes on the 'prize,' which, in my view, is consumer betterment and community betterment. Staff needs to understand the larger context for each partnership and what our ultimate goals are. When we began our work with the Food Bank, some librarians were quick to note that they were not 'lunch ladies,' considering the food distribution duties as outside the parameter of their jobs. When I talked about the level of poverty in Cleveland, the number of children who went hungry every day, and the role that the library could have in ameliorating this problem, the tide began to turn. The staff needs to understand the goals for each partnership, the hoped-for 'north star,' and the CEO needs to set the tone and consistently support this approach. It takes constant and consistent communication."

Six Keys to Successful Partnerships

In a recent address to the Greater Cleveland Food Bank, "Together We Are Better," Thomas summarized his partnership approach in "Six Keys to Successful Partnerships":

- **Shared purpose:** Make sure each organization has shared goals and the same understanding of what needs to be achieved.
- **Shared power:** Each organization has something different to bring to the table, be it financial support or a large network. Partners realizing—and truly believing—that each of these components are valuable will help lead to shared power.
- **Shared view of interdependence:** This entails realizing that the shared purpose cannot be met without the work of each organization.
- **Mutual respect and trust:** These two features need to be held not only in the beginning of collaboration but throughout the process.

Part of this is making sure each organization does what they said they would do.

- **Shared control:** The previous steps help build up to shared control. This means making sure resources are shared in an efficient manner to accomplish the goal of the relationship.
- **Shared indicators of progress:** Having a conversation with the organizations about whether the purpose is being achieved is crucial. Checking up on progress and finding out what works and does not work will help better realize the overall goal.

Conclusion

Felton Thomas' belief that librarianship is all about "making the world a better place" and his dedicated service as a community deficit fighter have paid off in the years that he has been at the helm of the Cleveland Public Library System. He continues to work with partners to promote learning, including digital literacy, workforce development, and quality of life through the library's multiple initiatives and relationships. Today, the Cleveland Public Library's finances have stabilized, circulation continues to rise, and the library is counted among the top ten libraries in the nation. More importantly, the community sees the library as relevant to their lives. Strategic and sustained partnerships have been essential throughout.

PARTNERSHIP PROFILES II

From "They" to "We": A Study in Collaboration   **15**

BALBOA PARK CULTURAL PARTNERSHIP TEAM UNDER LEADERSHIP OF PETER COMISKEY, WITH CONTRIBUTIONS FROM KRISTEN N. MIHALKO

BIOGRAPHY: ***Peter Comiskey*** *has been the executive director of the Balboa Park Cultural Partnership since 2013. Previously, he served as executive director of California's Downtown Anaheim, and executive director of the MUZEO Museum and Cultural Center in Anaheim. He was managing director of Explore USA from 2002 to 2005. Kristin N. Mihalko is senior manager, programs, and special events for the Balboa Park Cultural Partnership. She has worked at Balboa Park since 2014. Previously, Mihalko worked in different positions at the Armed Services YMCA of San Diego and the San Diego YMCA.*

Balboa Park and the Balboa Park Cultural Partnership

K NOWN AS THE "JEWEL OF SAN DIEGO," Balboa Park is a natural and cultural destination with lush gardens, captivating museums, and iconic architecture. More than a century old, the park spans twelve hundred acres and is home to more than eighty-five nonprofit organizations. This multifaceted area hosts seventeen diverse museums, numerous performing arts venues, sixty-five miles of hiking trails, a public golf course, multiple fitness centers, and the San Diego Zoo. While many believe New York's Central Park holds the title of largest urban park, it is Balboa Park that is the nation's largest urban park. In fact, the ever-changing Balboa Park Cultural District attracts twelve million visitors each year. Researchers estimate that 6.7 million of them experience a Balboa Park Cultural Partnership (BPCP) member organization, with 57.4 percent being area residents and 42.6 percent being nonresidents.[1]

Each of the many organizations that make up Balboa Park is its own entity, with its own management structure, goals, programmatic focus, and staff or volunteers. Bringing these groups together can be a daunting task. As we've seen in the Balboa Park Learning Institute (BPLI), however, there is more that unites the organizations of Balboa Park than divides them. We are all looking to bring visitors—whether residents or tourists—to take part in our learning and recreational offerings. We all want to provide one-of-a-kind experiences that people will remember for years to come. We all hope that people will participate in more than one park activity, and return time and time again, because no matter what someone has experienced in Balboa Park, there is still more to explore.

In 2003, thirteen organizations came together with the goal of uniting the nonprofits of Balboa Park. The Balboa Park Cultural Partnership (BPCP) was established with the financial support of the Legler Benbough Foundation as a way to leverage the individual goals of the park's nonprofit organizations within the greater needs of the park as a whole and for the publics they serve. Prior to BPCP, institutions in the park saw themselves as direct competitors. There was little incentive for collaboration. The "carrot" provided by the Legler Benbough Foundation's investment spurred a different orientation and the beginning of a new way of doing business. BPCP was formed as a nonprofit membership organization and began with intensive strategic planning by the executive leadership of Balboa Park's cultural institutions and a community council of civic, corporate, governmental, and philanthropic representatives. BPCP's initial purpose was to catalyze collaboration among the park's cultural institutions by engaging the leadership of the different organizations to bring together their collective resources and collections in order to create a shared, park-wide vision. BPCP offered a new central point of access for external stakeholders (including visitors) to the institutions and an opportunity for them to be represented by a single, unified voice.

By the end of 2013, all of the organizations in the park that could be a BPCP member were part of the collaborative. Developing strategies for streamlining operations, negotiating joint contracts with outside vendors, and finding cost-efficient ways to purchase in bulk were important components of the organization's early behind-the-scenes work. By increasing communication across organizations, improving professional practices, incubating important programs—including the Balboa Park Online Collaborative—the BPCP set the stage for a more public-facing role in the park. The work took time, trust-building, and commitment from the organizations, with a few challenges and setbacks, but the BPCP eventually crystallized into the effective organization it is today. The BPCP now represents thirty organizations, including museums, performing arts groups and theaters, cultural centers, gardens, and the San Diego Zoo. Its vision "is for Balboa Park to serve as a national model for exceptional collaboration, innovative education, and transformative arts, science and cultural experiences."[2] The current strategic outcomes sought by the BPCP are[3]:

1. Increase the economic and environmental sustainability of our members and Balboa Park.
2. Optimize the visitor experience and opportunity for lifelong learning in Balboa Park.
3. Strengthen the visibility, voice, and leadership of the partnership.
4. Develop the partnership's organizational strength and capacity for success, and become an employer, service provider, and investment of choice.

The guiding principles of the BPCP are to create and enhance opportunities for collaboration and networking within park organizations; however, in recent years, the focus has been on advocacy and collaboration. In 2014, through a collaborative process of working with park organizations, BPCP successfully launched the Explorer program, the first-ever annual pass that provides unlimited general admission to all seventeen museums in the park for a year, which also provides added benefits to all BPCP member organizations. The collaborative worked together to provide up to thirty thousand Explorer passes to underserved and economically disadvantaged communities and to our large military community in San Diego. To date, BPCP's Sustainability Program brought ten buildings in the park to LEED certification and continues to provide professional development and networking opportunities through Green Teams and Facility Directors meetings throughout the park. BPCP's Learning Institute, among other projects, has overseen two National Science Foundation grants including the "Art of Science Learning," both a local and national program that tackled significant societal and community issues by combining the creativity of the arts with STEM to solve real-world problems, and the InforMath Collaborative, a project among three museums in the park and San Diego State University's Center for Research in Mathematics and Science Education to investigate research questions pertaining to mathematics and informal education. In May of 2017, BPCP led a consortium of arts organizations in arts advocacy for the City of San Diego. All of these projects were important testaments to collaboration. However, in order to fully understand how BPCP explores, incubates, adapts, evaluates, and launches a collaborative program, this chapter focuses on one specific project, the "Guest Experience Initiative."

The Balboa Park Learning Institute

While BPCP focuses on advocacy and collaboration as guiding principles, the BPLI is a means of delivering a variety of education initiatives that strengthen the staff and volunteer infrastructure of the park through professional development. The BPLI was launched in October 2008 with a three-year, $500,000 21st Century Museum Professionals matching grant from the Institute of Museum and Library Services (IMLS). From 2008 to 2011, more than 5,577 professionals participated in more than 193 programs on such subjects as audience engagement (including "Evaluating the Balboa Park Experience"), environmental sustainability, leadership and management, human resources, collections care and emergency/disaster preparedness, and development and fundraising.

"Evaluating the Balboa Park Experience" was the BPLI's first ten-month professional development program, which combined a new way of understanding audience experience in terms of motivation, perceived benefits, and behavior patterns as well as the importance of evaluation and audience research. Beginning March 2010, this project involved twenty cross-functional staff members from twelve Balboa Park museums and the Balboa Park Visitor's Center. Over the years, the BPLI created other programs, including Mix Up Meet Up, an informal networking program that randomly matches up a participant with another park colleague once a month for three months, and the Smith Leadership Symposium, an annual conference in Balboa Park that hosts industry thought-leaders who discuss trending and relevant topics for the audience of arts, science, and culture professionals.

The Smith Leadership Symposium is made possible by an endowment from the Smith Family in memory of Robert "Bob" Smith, a San Diego civic and business leader who provided strategic planning consulting for many park organizations including the San Diego Natural History Museum, the Zoological Society of San Diego, and the BPCP. The BPLI has also received financial support through The Parker Foundation, Legler Benbough Foundation, the James Irvine Foundation, and the City of San Diego's Commission for Arts and Culture. Over the years, the focus of BPLI has shifted to the Smith Leadership Symposium and other advocacy efforts within the San Diego area as the priority for professional development programming has waned within the Balboa Park organizations due to budgetary constraints. The various programs BPLI has created over the years give unique snapshots of the relevant issues that Balboa Park organizations have wanted to address, and how both budgets and leadership stresses can make particular programming more fragile.

The BPLI's Guest Experience Initiative

Balboa Park is home to more than thirty-five hundred paid staff and more than seven thousand volunteers. For this reason, a project like the Guest Experience Initiative, designed to orient staff and volunteers from many organizations throughout the park to serve as ambassadors for all park visitors was a massive, if appropriate, undertaking. This initiative, supported by IMLS funding, was designed to integrate guidance from outside professionals about best practices of customer service and audience engagement with the contributions and feedback from employees and volunteers. Its goal was to create and test a training framework that could be used in an ongoing way to orient employees and volunteers in a consistent and in-depth manner.

Much like visitors to a theme park, Balboa Park users perceive the park as a single entity and expect consistent guest experiences throughout. Our challenge was to create this unified experience despite the many unrelated park entities, each group and organization possessing varying missions, management types, goals, and operating structures. Until the BPLI undertook the Guest Experience Initiative, more often than not a visitor would arrive at a museum and be unable to ascertain such basic information as the location of the nearest park restroom. Further, someone who might want information on current exhibits or potential linkages among Balboa Park museum exhibitions and collections might ask a museum's frontline team member but would not necessarily receive an informed answer. Due to these disconnects, park guests might miss out on experiences that corresponded to their interests, or, worse yet, find themselves confused frustrated and simply leave. Aware of these concerns, BPLI took on this issue with a shared commitment to change the culture of guest experience, with our dedicated staff, a thoughtfully conceived process, and a funding partner who was willing to support the effort. The National Leadership Grant from the IMLS enabled BPLI construct and implement a multiyear collaborative learning project.

During the initiative, thirty-three staff members from seventeen organizations in the park attended twenty-one workshops and invested up to seventy-five hours per participant as they explored ways to enhance the visitor experience. Program participants included frontline staff members (those at the front desk) and also educators and public program managers. The goal was to empower these participants to help shape the course of the future orientation program, which would be offered for staff and volunteers.

This project was divided into two phases. The first phase (October through December 2013) focused on assessments, tours, visitor interactions, and special presentations by speakers from both inside and outside the park. For example, Stephanie Weaver, author and founder of *Experienceology*, presented and facilitated activities around her "8 Steps to Great Visitor Experiences," which examines the physical, emotional, and intellectual comfort of a visitor. Participants reviewed and refreshed their knowledge of the park and its many institutions, modeled the visitor experience, and practiced customer service skills. Local and national guest speakers guided participants on behind-the-scenes park tours. Participants also learned about the history of Balboa Park and took part in improvisational activities and organizational assessments.

During the second program's phase (January through May 2014) the participants honed in on their problem-solving, communication, and collaboration skills through a design-thinking workshop. The workshop led to the development of a customer service skills training module and a new park orientation. Participants in the program thus became more knowledgeable about the park as a whole, became better customer service representatives for their own organizations, and developed the materials for other park staff and volunteers. This was the case regardless of the role they played within their institution.

An evaluation of the Guest Experience Initiative by an outside research firm concluded that "participants found the experience to be a very positive and enriching one. By the end, participants had a deeper and richer understanding of customer service and recognized that a guest's visit to their institution is part of a larger Balboa Park experience. Eighty-three percent described their attitude towards customer service as more positive, and 94 percent believed their experience had a positive effect on their work performance." As a result of this collaborative, co-creation process, participants collectively developed four Balboa Park customer service values: to be responsive, engaging, knowledgeable, and innovative. These would frame the future Guest Experience curriculum that would be taught to others.

One of our principal insights after the initial cohort of Guest Experience Initiative participants was that it is crucial that subsequent groups will need to participate fully in the program in order to garner the most benefit. Those that have the most invested will see the most gain. Therefore, we recognized that we needed to create user-friendly ways of translating the insights and awareness of the benefits of participation from the first cohort of program developers to future participants. In keeping with our first-phase learnings about effective pedagogy, we also believed that the program required participatory components that would provide plentiful opportunities for hands-on learning. Our solution to this challenge was an experiment using online interactive learning as part of the training. The module's elements included video interviews with several of the executive directors of the nonprofits in the park, a landmark scavenger hunt tour through the park, a virtual tour with a park ranger, an interactive map and quizzes that assessed the learner's way finding knowledge, and historic information on the park's buildings. The orientation module's segments conclude by checking learning comprehension through a short quiz, assessing participant knowledge on items as simple (but important) as "where is the closest restaurant or restroom from a particular location" or "where is the best place to park depending on where I'd like to visit?"

The Learning Institute met with eighteen organizations and sixty-one of their team members to share the value of online learning and how the Orientation and Guest Experience Training would benefit their team members. However, we did not require BPCP member organizations to register their staff or volunteers. Since April 2016, more than two hundred individuals have taken the Balboa Park Orientation and Guest Experience Training through the online system. Many volunteer coordinators in the park have found the orientation to be a valuable asset in onboarding their new volunteers and often choose to participate as a group. Overall, one of the most rewarding outcomes of the program has been that participants gain a deeper and richer understanding of customer service and recognize that a guest's visit to their institution is part of a larger Balboa Park experience. They embrace the idea of being part of something larger than just their own organization, a concept we call "One Park—One Team." For the first time, park team members have an opportunity to work together toward a common goal. Visitors to the park now have a more interconnected journey—one where they have informed staff and volunteers who can provide them with consistent in-depth information, and also one where team members in the park also feel more connected to one another.

One Park—One Team

The greatest success of BPLI's Guest Experience Initiative is the goodwill it has created through the concept of "One Park—One Team." This ability to work more closely together has fostered closer professional and volunteer relationships among team members in the park. Many of the organizations realize that in order to maximize capacity within their institution, there are real benefits in joining forces with other park entities. For example, the Learning Institute oversaw the InforMath Collaborative, a National Science Foundation grant that includes three Balboa Park museums, the Reuben Fleet Science Center, Mingei International Museum, and the Museum of Photographic Arts, along with San Diego State University's Center for Research in Mathematics and Science Education. Through this project, the three museums created a relationship that has spawned additional partnerships, including exhibition and programmatic opportunities. The Fleet Science Center and Museum of Photographic Arts, for example, have worked closely together on creating collaborative STEAM programming, bridging the gap between science and art.

It is throughout these realized partnerships—and others that continue to emerge—that the concept of "One Park—One Team" flourishes in Balboa Park. We will always be an amalgam of organizations managed by different entities, with different governance structures. But the BPCP and the BPLI have helped to nurture a shared identity, better public experiences, more effective marketing and access, back-of-house efficiencies, and, overall, a common spirit.

The Balboa Park Online Collaborative: 16
Partnering in Digital Resource Creation

NIK HONEYSETT

BIOGRAPHY: NIK HONEYSETT is the chief executive officer of the Balboa Park Online Collaborative (BPOC), a San Diego–based, nonprofit consultancy that provides technology support and development services, and business and digital strategy for the cultural sector. Previously, he was head of administration at the Getty Museum. He is a former American Alliance of Museums board member and sits on the boards of Museum Computer Network and Guru, a technology start-up providing mobile experiences for the cultural, attraction, and sports sectors. He is a frequent speaker on issues of organizational and digital strategy, and is on the adjunct faculty for Johns Hopkins and the Getty Leadership Institute teaching digital strategy and technology management.

History of the Balboa Park Online Collaborative (BPOC)

BALBOA PARK is a twelve hundred-acre urban cultural park about half a mile northeast of downtown San Diego. In addition to open space areas, gardens, and trail paths, it contains museums, theaters, recreational facilities, restaurants, and a zoo. Placed in reserve in 1835, the park's site is one of the oldest in the United States dedicated to public recreational use.

Founded in 2008 to serve seventeen organizations in Balboa Park, the BPOC collaborates and leverages its size to help museums, art, science, and cultural organizations make cost-effective, sustainable, and strategic technology decisions with a range of technical support, digital production services, and digital strategy. While the BPOC supports the broader museum community, it focuses on the cultural organizations within the park where their physical proximity and physical partnership efforts present a solid foundation for digital collaboration.

BPOC is the brainchild of the Legler Benbough Foundation, a charitable foundation established in 1985 to promote philanthropist Legler Benbough's interest in helping improve the quality of life for San Diegans. In addition to myriad discrete funding projects across San Diego, the foundation has been responsible for supporting key projects, initiatives, and collaborative efforts in Balboa Park. One such initiative is the Balboa Park Cultural Partnership, the core governance structure in the park upon which many collaborations sit. Initially formed to support city advocacy, the Balboa Park Cultural Partnership is a recognition of the strength of a single unified voice. The partnership focuses on developing a collaborative culture on matters of mutual interest in addition to advocacy, marketing, sustainability, and specific initiatives including the Explorer Pass, a single-entry ticket for park museums.

BPOC's name and inception came in response to multiple requests to the Legler Benbough foundation for grant money to develop or update institutional websites, a significant trend in the early 2000s as museums began to understand the necessity and value of a web presence to promote their activities and programming. Recognizing that multiple institutions wanted the same service and assistance, the foundation engaged an expert in museum technology to meet with the park directors to see what kind of collaborative opportunities might be developed. The meetings were extensive and revealed a significant lack of technology literacy and understanding surrounding the potential of technology and its relevance to new and emerging audiences. As discussions progressed, there was particular concern that any unified technology plan should not result in a "loss of control" on behalf of the institutions, an undercurrent that continues through to today. After significant discussions, the foundation proposed a plan to create the BPOC (in reference to collaborative efforts around building websites) as a private operating foundation within the Legler Benbough Foundation with the express understanding that the park directors were in full support, were willing to participate in BPOC's products and services, and were willing to advise on the direction of the enterprise. The foundation allocated three million dollars over three years, and the park directors hired the founding executive director.

Over the next three years, BPOC invested the allocated funds across infrastructure, training, digital production, and digitization. Today, based on that initial investment and current fixed assets, Balboa Park has a high-bandwidth fiber network, a data center, free public access Wi-Fi stretching across two hundred acres of the park's central mesa, free-standing networked visitor touchscreen kiosks, a wayfinding visitor app, a multi-institutional digital asset management system, and a single website (balboapark.org) representing everything that is Balboa Park. This website receives 2.6 million digital visits a year.

In 2012, BPOC and the Legler Benbough Foundation agreed on a transition to its own standalone public charity operating under the 509(a)(1) and 170(b)(1)(a) IRS determinations, an advance ruling that came into effect on December 2017.

Evolution of the Balboa Park Online Collaborative

The early days of BPOC focused on setting up core infrastructure assets, constituting a period of investment and growth with particular attention to campus-wide training and efforts that communicated the value of technology and its potential to attract and engage audiences. This period of investment and growth was instrumental in attracting talented museum technologists to Balboa Park who created innovative uses of technology and modeled key infrastructure solutions, as well as drew national attention to BPOC projects and development efforts. Within a short period of time BPOC became known as a center for innovation and infrastructure know-how, garnering recognition and awards and a reputation for sharing knowledge and expertise to the museum technology community.

During these earlier years, BPOC worked hard to expand its relationship with all thirty cultural organizations in the park by adding contract-based information technology support to its service menu, in addition to discrete web and interactive projects, training, digitization, and infrastructure. This initial model was somewhat self-sustaining: as more museums invested in more technology, the requirement to support that technology increased. Through foundation, individual, and federal funding, the technical capability of the park increased to where it is today. The growth phase has now largely been replaced by a maintenance phase. While there are still technology investments to be made, these are less significant as they represent incremental improvements or upgrades across a more technically literate and more mature cultural community.

Structure and Business Model

Today, BPOC has its own fiduciary board and employs ten full-time employees and a stable of freelancers, providing a suite of services and products for park institutions that, by necessity, are offered on an à-la-carte basis. Services are split into four areas, in response to institutional needs:

1. **Information technology services:** critical technology services, ranging from phones and networking, to storage and backup. These services are usually provided on an annual contract basis, but can be provided on a tiered support level for bespoke projects or unanticipated requirements.
2. **Creative projects:** digital development projects for web, mobile, or in-gallery experiences that also include systems integration, collection data management, and digital asset management.
3. **Digital marketing:** contract-based support for web content, email marketing, and social media, that also includes photography, videography, and digital media production.
4. **Digital strategy:** strategic consulting to enable institutional digital initiatives; because this initiative is not reliant on physical proximity, client work is performed on a national level.

The à-la-carte model reflects the diversity in size of clients and the belief that not all institutions require all levels and types of technology support at the same time. BPOC's local client list ranges from volunteer-only institutions to mid- and larger-size institutions. Some of the larger institutions employ an information technology manager or full-time technology staff for their own desktop support, but still contract out basic services such as phones or higher-skilled services such as server administration or ad hoc digital development.

One of the most compelling reasons for collaborative technology is connectivity. BPOC's original investment in laying high-bandwidth fiber throughout the park has paid dividends as institutions rely more and more on high-bandwidth access to support their operational needs. The park's high-bandwidth data line is managed and leased out by BPOC across all the institutions at an unmatched price when compared to nationally recognized telecommunications companies. In certain circumstances, BPOC's data line is the only option. Combined with BPOC's server and storage offerings, services such as offsite storage and backup can be offered at highly competitive rates, particularly compared against cloud storage services where data transfer represents a significant part of the cost. A major component of this high-speed network is the Wi-Fi that BPOC has installed across the central mesa and high-trafficked areas. This is free to the public and available as subnetworks for institutions to conduct their business, such as staff Wi-Fi, mobile ticket sales, or other networked requirements. All institutions support this infrastructure through monthly fees, which is extremely economical because the cost is shared across all cultural institutions.

Challenges Associated with the Collaborative

Based on the original intent to ensure park institutions have a voice in the operations and strategic direction of BPOC, its bylaws require a majority of board members to be from park institutions. This approach has both positive and negative ramifications. While it does ensure that the best interests of the park institutions are a primary concern, it can sometimes put board members in the difficult position of making a decision at odds with their institution. This presents them with the dilemma of choosing between loyalty to their own institution or to the larger BPOC entity.

Despite the original intent that all institutions would support BPOC, this has not occurred. In some cases, economical concerns have tipped the balance toward financial efficiency over park-wide collaboration. Some of the larger organizations now find it less costly to provide in-house information technology support despite the many benefits afforded by BPOC. There is no contractual requirement for park institutions to use BPOC's services; hence, BPOC charges a competitive rate. Our challenge is that this rate includes overhead costs that cover park-wide initiatives on behalf of all park institutions, such as the unified website, balboapark.org, and unified social media. These services are regarded as "essential to the visitor experience," but attempts to have them supported in their own right by every institution, such as through direct subscription, have been unsuccessful. "Essential" has its price.

As organizational digital literacy and technological competencies in the park have increased, so have the expectations. Institutions are becoming savvier, with ever more complex technology-based projects that are demanding increasing levels of skill, expertise, and service. However, BPOC was established from the outset as a subsidized service provider, and the initial and continued generosity of the Legler Benbough Foundation has set an expectation that technology is cheap or even free. BPOC's fortunate ability to secure both federal and foundation grants to deliver technology projects has worked to cement the notion of low-cost accessibility and service. These expectations—of increasingly sophisticated expertise, and low cost, subsidized service provision—have been working against each other, with BPOC caught in the middle trying to support a small community with technology services that are being commoditized more and more every day, forcing increasingly tighter margins. For example, BPOC provides website development and hosting, as building a website used to be a fairly technical and demanding endeavor. However, now anyone with a credit card can create a very sophisticated and sleek website. Hosting, too, is now a highly commoditized product available at a fraction of the cost that BPOC can provide it for.

Opportunities

The key opportunities for BPOC, and indeed any technology collaboration of this nature, are efforts that leverage the close physical proximity of the institutions, while creating a product or service that directly benefits the visitor community as a whole, or that truly benefit the client group. The high-speed network and Wi-Fi, unified website, and shared social media that BPOC provides are clear examples of these services. Other opportunities include bringing in high-end and sophisticated applications to distribute them out to the institutions over our shared network, affording small and volunteer institutions access to technology that would normally be financially prohibitive. A good park-based example is our digital asset management program, which has many potential front-of-house and back-of-house benefits within institutions and across the park. Fulfilling this potential, however, can present challenges in aligning and coordinating the timing of institutional requirements and priorities. There are many other areas where campus-wide applications could be brought in, but there is some reluctance on the part of park institutions to "play" in a shared application environment that houses sensitive data such as financials and visitor and, particularly, donor information.

Balboa Park has every major museum type—and topic—within a few hundred acres: living collections, transportation, air and space, natural history, anthropology, history, historic house, art, photography, sports, and military. It is, by definition, an encyclopedic destination, something akin to the Washington Mall, but with a Southern California climate. Add in our collaborative environment and growing technological infrastructure, and it becomes the ideal place to flesh out technology ideas and prototypes. In the early 1990s, the San Diego Museum of Art launched one of the first museum interactive touchscreens, and the park continued that legacy as one of the first cultural spaces to experiment with beacon technology, and, more recently, augmented reality and the piloting of telepresence devices as a way of providing remote fieldtrips for Title One schools. The latter project highlights another benefit of collaborative endeavor: the ability to secure grants from federal, city, and foundation sources, with funders looking for greater returns on investment and more substantial institutional and public (in this case, educational) impact.

Vision, Goals, and Legacy

Collaboration is a key value and important force within Balboa Park, but with thirty cultural institutions it has had mixed success, particularly for initiatives that require full participation. Some institutions prefer to "wait and see" before making a commitment. Partial collaboration can be costlier and less effective than no collaboration, and any group looking to partner needs to understand that compromise and an "all-in" approach where each individual entity has "skin in the game" is the ideal. Recent changes in government administration have certainly focused the need for better collaborative efforts with respect to advocacy, but for BPOC, whose domain is technology, collaboration is often a moving target. What was once a specialized service is now a commodity that puts great pressure on BPOC to quickly adapt in an evolving environment.

There is no question that on a technology infrastructure level, BPOC has provided the park with a robust foundation on which many technology initiatives, both back- and front-of-house, can sit. In our information-rich environment, high-bandwidth and Wi-Fi are simply the cost of doing business, and from a collaborative standpoint, BPOC has been able to leverage technology to promote further collaboration, and more importantly, dependency between park institutions through projects like the Explorer Pass.

As BPOC approaches its tenth year, it is interesting to review its success relative to the *adoption curve* (Figure 16.1) which is a recognized trend indicator governing market acceptance, particularly for technology, and also seen as a predictor for how long certain technologies and services might take to be fully adopted by park institutions.

Looking at the various technologies and services that BPOC has developed, the most mature is the data and internet service, which should fully capture the laggards by 2018, an almost ten-year cycle from when the service first began. The timeline of information technology contract services and collection, and digital asset management systems adoption,

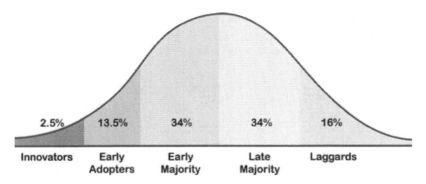

Figure 16.1.
Balboa Park Online Collaborative

confirms this ten-year, full-adoption cycle, and as the park institutions move into comprehensive online collections presentation, where BPOC hopes to provide a compelling encyclopedic view of park collections, it will be a few years before the late majority and hopefully the laggards are appropriately represented.

The park has no ultimate arbiter for decision making, so the environment truly is one of collaboration where initiatives and shared progress happen through consensus building and the gradual alignment of priorities. In this situation, the adoption curve presents a compelling predictive tool of how long collaborative endeavor can take, and clearly communicates what BPOC has come to understand with respect to sustainable collaboration: *collaboration is complex and time consuming.*

As a corollary, at BPOC's inception, the founding director issued smartphones to the museum directors to help them understand "mobile." Now we have the broad realization that a mobile-friendly website is no longer enough. More people are visiting our websites on a mobile device than a desktop, audiences want to consume content and have experiences wherever they are whenever they want, and a fully responsive website speaks as much about the museum as the quality of the galleries, exhibitions, and the professionalism of staff. A ten-year conversation that will continue.

In Pursuit of Freedom
A Partnership Grows in Brooklyn

17

DEBORAH SCHWARTZ, WITH INTRODUCTION BY MARSHA L. SEMMEL

BIOGRAPHY: DEBORAH SCHWARTZ is president of the Brooklyn Historical Society (BHS), a nationally renowned urban history center, founded in 1863. Since 2006 Schwartz has been responsible for BHS's increasing activity, including its award-winning Oral History Initiatives and Education programs. Schwartz has made partnerships a hallmark of her work, including long-term partnerships with the Brooklyn Navy Yard and Weeksville Heritage Center. In 2017, BHS launched a new satellite museum in DUMBO that focuses on the history of the Brooklyn Waterfront. Schwartz has taught in New York University's Museum Studies Program and at Bank Street College of Education. She has taught workshops on museum leadership in China and the Ukraine. From 2002 to 2006 she served as the Edward John Noble Foundation Deputy Director for Education at the Museum of Modern Art. In 2002, she curated the critically acclaimed exhibition Art Inside Out for the Children's Museum of Manhattan. From 1983 to 2000 Schwartz worked at the Brooklyn Museum, where she served as vice director for education and program development. She has published numerous articles on education and community building in museums.

Introduction

WHEN DEBORAH SCHWARTZ BECAME the director of the BHS in 2006, the museum was in a state of stress, financial and otherwise, that provided substantial challenges—and new opportunities. Schwartz requested and practiced transparency as a fundamental tenet in planning and communication from her first moment, especially with her Board of Trustees. That principle has remained a guidepost for relationship building. In addition, Schwartz understood that fixing the museum's financial situation had to "go hand-in-hand with strategic planning and a vision for the future that [she] needed to sell locally, regionally, and nationally." In the ensuing visioning process, the BHS affirmed its commitment to represent all the communities of Brooklyn, which, as Schwartz notes, would be among the largest four cities in the United States if considered as a separate entity, with more than 175 languages spoken.

The resulting mission statement—"Brooklyn Historical Society connects the past to the present and makes the vibrant history of Brooklyn tangible, relevant, and meaningful for today's diverse communities and for generations to come"—has guided the society's activities for almost a decade.

Importantly, in order to fulfill that mission, Schwartz and her board and staff recognized that they needed to venture out beyond their national landmarked building on Pierrepont Street that has been the museum's home since 1881. "We couldn't achieve our vision without partnerships," notes Schwartz. "We began partner[ing] with other institutions on educational programs, public programs, and oral history projects. We created a whole host of new relationships throughout the Borough."

These relationships, with community groups including the Vietnam War veterans, the Brooklyn Navy Yard, Brooklyn Movement Center, Greenwood Cemetery, and many other institutions, have borne fruit and have affected every part of BHS. This is the story of one of these partnerships as told by Deborah Schwartz.

Birth of the Project

In 2008, BHS, Weeksville Heritage Center, and the Irondale Ensemble Project banded together to create a multifaceted project about the history of the abolitionist movement in Brooklyn. The project reached the public's eye in 2014 and continued to roll out in phases over nearly a decade.

The project, now known as *In Pursuit of Freedom* (IPoF), was prompted initially by a call for proposals put forward by the Downtown Brooklyn Partnership, a public-private partnership with funds made available by the City of New York. Projects sought were to address the little known and little understood history of abolition in the Borough of Brooklyn.

For years, BHS and the Weeksville Heritage Center had collaborated on projects, including a project in 1993 prompted by a racially fraught incident in Crown Heights, called the "Crown Heights History Project." Pam Green, executive director of Weeksville, and the then-director of the BHS, had begun to know each other and were excited about the prospect of collaboration given the institutions' shared mission and values.

At the same time, Irondale Theater Ensemble, a bold activist theater company, had recently moved from Manhattan and relocated in Fort Greene, Brooklyn. I had known their executive director, Terry Greiss, for years, and was endlessly impressed by his commitment to education and community engagement. It took a matter of days for these three uniquely positioned organizations to agree on the potential mutually beneficial project, eventually leading to the successful submission of a proposal that included the following components:

- A series of permanent historical markers and multimedia walking tours that would take place throughout the borough, spotlighting people and places significant to the history of abolition;
- Interpretive exhibitions at the BHS, Weeksville Heritage Center, and the Irondale Center;
- A content-rich website to tell the story of the history of abolition in Brooklyn, introduce the walking tours, preview interpretive installations, and present archival documents, images, maps, and other resources to the public;
- An educational curriculum built on the excellent work already available through all three organizations, expanded to provide school children throughout New York City with primary source documents, images, maps, and new resources about Brooklyn's role in the struggle for freedom in the nineteenth century;
- An original theater production drawing upon the story of abolition in Brooklyn, revealing provocative questions and issues about social relations and moral choices that continue to challenge contemporary society;
- A two-day scholarly symposium and a series of college courses to engage the postsecondary community with new scholarship, and provide opportunities to bring some of the new research to local colleges through courses about urban history, religion and social change, and the history of minorities; and
- A commemorative art installation by an internationally renowned artist at Willoughby Square Park in downtown Brooklyn.

The project unfolded publicly in 2012 when Irondale produced an original theatrical performance called *Color between the Lines*; the website launched in 2013, as did a curriculum, and the BHS exhibition *Brooklyn Abolitionists*/IPoF opened in 2014. Weeksville opened its chapter of IPoF:

Weeksville/Transforming Community, an interactive media exhibition, in 2017.

A project that spanned almost a decade from planning, to research, to public program, this partnership by definition required dedication, focus, and ongoing passion. This chapter provides some insights about the partnership and its continuing legacy.

Ambitious Projects Change with Time

A good project team needs to know when to change course, and how to keep funders and stakeholders informed. Financial constraints and evolving intelligence that is unknowable at the beginning of a project will naturally have an impact on what can be achieved. Decision making about these inevitable changes must be established early on as part of the partnership, or misunderstandings and miscommunications run the risk of undermining trust. Trust and transparency are essential ingredients to a successful partnership.

As IPoF evolved, some components of the project took different forms than the initial concept. A symposium evolved into a series of public programs, with the team realizing that the project was far more powerful as public history serving a broad audience, rather than delivering program that might be skewed to academics and scholars. As a result, for example, we decided to have Pulitzer Prize–winning historian Eric Foner participate in a discussion with BHS Director of Public History Julie Golia, in which they analyzed the Emancipation Proclamation, based upon a question and answer session with a general audience of adults and high school students.

The historic markers never came to fruition because of bureaucratic roadblocks and excessive cost. And the public monument in Willoughby Square Park will launch at some future date, when the park that has been designated to house it actually gets built! It is no small feat that everything else from the originally outlined project came to public light with notably positive outcomes.

Picking the Right Partners Is Where the Story Begins

The best partnerships bring together people and institutions with complementary skills and expertise. The missions of the three institutions, described below, are complementary and distinctive. Recognizing that each of the organizations brought unique expertise and focus to the partnership was an important part of IPoF's success.

BHS, founded in 1863, is a nationally recognized urban history center dedicated to preserving and encouraging the study of Brooklyn's extraordinary four-hundred-year history. BHS connects the past to the present and makes the vibrant history of Brooklyn tangible, relevant, and meaningful for today's diverse communities, and for generations to come.

Weeksville Heritage Center is a multidisciplinary cultural center dedicated to preserving the history of the nineteenth-century African American community of Weeksville and beyond. Using a contemporary lens, the center activates this unique history through the presentation of innovative, vanguard, and experimental programs. Weeksville advances its mission through history, preservation, visual and performing arts, ecology, and the built environment.

The **Irondale Ensemble Project** was founded as an experimental/research theater to further investigate the performance and education techniques developed at the Long Wharf Theatre in the late 1970s. It exists today as a company dedicated to the exploring the emerging themes in our society with a permanent ensemble of artists that has developed a distinctive body of work and practices. Irondale creates and presents theater, performance, and education programs that challenge traditional assumptions about art, and help us to better understand today's world.

Identifying Individual Team Members and Their Work

In my view, the heart of a successful partnership project is well-chosen staff with well-defined tasks. With limited resources, it is wise to bring a team together in which each team member provides a distinct and well-defined role and expertise. Team members need clear understanding about who has the authority to make decisions (and the scope of their decision-making power) and about who speaks for the project. These roles should be deliberately considered and carefully defined. If the team members have clear and well-defined roles, the goals of the project are far more likely to be met.

IPoF required tremendous coordination, which included biweekly meetings of the project director and the executive directors of the three institutions. The project director, initially situated at BHS, eventually had an elaborate schedule in which she rotated physically among the three partner institutions in order build substantial relationships with all members of the team. Large meetings of all of the staff hired to work on the project plus the curatorial and education teams of the partnering institutions occurred on a monthly basis, and included fifteen to twenty participants. Keeping track of decision making required great effort. We would marvel at the work that got done, but just as often we were painfully aware that we had not brought a decision to closure or achieved the outcomes we hoped to accomplish. A strong and well-organized project manager was an essential member of the team. This member of the team needed to be superbly well organized, savvy about budgets and workflow, understand the complexity of exhibition development, and preferably grounded in a knowledge of New York City history. In the course of the project, no fewer than three project managers came and went. It was not an easy job.

Long-Term Partnerships Require Patience, Trust, and Mutual Respect

Without patience, trust, and mutual respect, colleagues can easily fall sway to frustration. It is far too easy to look for ways to explain problems as the result of someone else's shortcomings. Over many years of work together, Terry Greiss, executive director of Irondale Ensemble Project, Pam Green, president of Weeksville Heritage Center, and I came to know each other well. We built friendships, shared frustrations, and became each other's confidants. If I were to start a project like this one again, however, I would put much more effort into making sure that all members of the team had opportunities to break bread together, to get to know and trust each other personally, and to spend time cultivating a shared vision for the project. Meeting agendas and to-do lists are necessary, but they are not a substitute for genuine and personal relationships that can kick in when a project hits inevitable bumps in the road.

Budgets for Partnership Projects Must Be Clear and Transparent

Full disclosure about time spent by staff managing complex projects must be accounted for and fully agreed upon from the beginning of a partnership.

IPoF operated over a six-year period with a total budget of $4.3 million. Given the size of the project, fundraising was a huge effort for the partnership. IPoF was sufficiently ambitious and well-defined to garner funds from the Institute of Museum and Library Services, National Endowment for the Humanities, the U.S. Department of Education, the NYC Economic Development Corporation, the Nathan Cummings Foundation, and other funders. BHS took on the role of fiduciary agent for the project, as we were the largest of the three institutions, and therefore most able to manage the funds as they came in, deal with cash flow, retroactive pay schedules, and rigorous reporting requirements from the federal government. A project with multiple funders, public and private, required complex reporting and frequent rethinking about the allocation of funds. Financial challenges are certainly a regular occurrence in the not-for-profit world, but partnerships add layers of financial burden and accountability. It is easy to underestimate the amount of time and energy required to manage the finances of a project funded through multiple sources with varying reporting and matching requirements.

Within the IPoF team, the added burden to BHS's finance department was generally underestimated. Additional administrative staff should have been accounted for in the project but were not. Beyond the internal stress of the project, the lessons about partnerships should extend to funders who should be encouraged to recognize the added strain of collaborative partnerships, and should make funds available for administrative staff, recognizing the complexity of the administrative, communications, and financial work required to create a healthy, successful partnership.

Projects with Grand Ambitions Call for Moments of Celebration

With a partnership like IPoF, that had so many moving parts, taking the time to acknowledge the impressive achievements of the project team often got lost. Moments to celebrate came intermittently and were crucial in recognizing the accomplishments of a hard-working (and occasionally exhausted) team. There was opening night of *Color between the Lines*, the opening of the exhibition *Brooklyn Abolitionists*/IPoF at BHS, and most recently, the opening of *Weeksville/Transforming Community*. Each project richly deserved a celebration, not only to welcome in the public, but to pause and reflect on the labors and accomplishments of a staff that had come together, in many cases above and beyond their daily work responsibilities, to create programs and products that had lasting impact on the partner institutions and on the public, who experienced the results.

Legacy of a Partnership

Of the many triumphs found in the IPoF, perhaps nothing is more rewarding than the epilogue—the ongoing relationships and the potential for additional work together. New projects in and among the three institutions continue to unfold. In 2015, BHS and Weeksville partnered on a project called *Voices of Crown Heights*. As described on the BHS website, "Through oral history interviews, a web-based listening portal and curated digital exhibit, listening stations, podcasts, public conversations and listening sessions, *Voices of Crown Heights* seeks to immerse diverse audiences in unheard voices of the past and present that challenge a singular linear narrative of Crown Height's History." Weeksville, now under the leadership of Tia Powell Harris, promises to continue to engage in serious ventures dedicated to the history of Brooklyn and the communities we serve.

Irondale and BHS continue to feature *Color between the Lines* in various educational programs, most recently in 2016 and 2018, a national Summer Teacher Institute called *Freedom for One, Freedom for All? Abolition and Woman Suffrage 1830s–1920s*, held in partnership with the Museum of the City of New York, and funded by the National Endowment for the Humanities.

With each new configuration of work together, the lessons of IPoF inform the future. In many respects, the project leaves the partners with a series of lessons that we keep in our heads and delight in sharing with others who take on the commitments of partnership in creating work that is bigger than the sum of its parts.

Lessons Learned and Ingredients for Successful Collaboration

- Establish goals collectively.
- Get to know one another. Break bread together.
- Establish clear and reasonable expectations.
- Establish the who and how of decision making.
- Understand each other's skill sets.
- Be clear about timelines and responsibilities for getting a project done.
- Be transparent about everything, especially money.
- If something goes wrong, take time to clear the air; listen to a range of takes on a problem and how to solve it. Make collective decisions about how to fix a problem and make sure decisions are well communicated.
- Make sure everyone involved in the partnership is getting ample recognition for their work—in public and behind the scenes.
- Celebrate what you have accomplished.
- Find opportunities to build upon a partnership. Do not squander the relationships built over time.

A Note from Deborah Schwartz

Postscript and Thanks: None of what I have described in this chapter could have happened without the collaboration and friendship of Pam Green and Terry Greiss. There is also a host of colleagues whose efforts were essential to IPoF. The list is too long to name, but they are all acknowledged on the website, http://pursuitoffreedom.org/about/project/. After Pam Green left Weeksville in 2013, her replacement, Tia Powell Harris, helped to further bring IPoF to fruition. Prithi Kanakamedala was the project historian, and Kate Fermoile was the ultimate project manager.

Additionally, in an effort to give my readers a sense of the project's scope and scale, I would like to acknowledge the funders of this partnership: IPoF was funded by New York City Mayor Michael Bloomberg, the New York City Department of Cultural Affairs; the New York City Economic Development Corporation; the U.S. Department of Education Underground Railroad Educational and Cultural Program; the National Endowment for the Humanities; the Nathan Cummings Foundation; and the New York State Council on the Humanities; with additional funds provided by The Bay and Paul Foundations, New York Community Trust, and Verizon Foundation.

IPoF educational materials were developed with additional funds provided by the U.S. Department of Education Underground Railroad Educational and Cultural Program; the National Grid Foundation; Con Edison; Members of the New York State Senate and Assembly; New York City Council Members; and a grant from the Association for the Study of African American Life and History, made possible by the Department of the Interior, National Park Service.

Habla Español? 18

TAMMIE KAHN

BIOGRAPHY: TAMMIE KAHN has served as the executive director of the Children's Museum of Houston (CMH) since 1995 and is responsible for the museum's direction, management, long-term planning, and expansion, which has doubled the learning space of the museum and created an Institute for Family Learning that focuses on improving a child's math, science, and literacy skills. The CMH is consistently ranked among the best children's museums in the United States. Kahn serves as an appointee of President Barack Obama to the National Museum and Library Services Board. She is past president of the Houston Museum District Association, and she has served on the boards of the Association of Children's Museums, the Institute for Learning Innovation, the Greater Houston Collaborative for Children, the South Main Center Association, El Centro de Corazon, Talento Bilingue de Houston, and the Houston Holocaust Museum, and also on the Advisory Boards of Friends of Hermann Park and the Zoological Society of Houston. She holds a BS from the University of Texas at Austin and an MBA from the University of Houston. Prior to her role at the CMH, she was associate director of the Museum of Fine Arts, Houston.

Introduction

IN FALL OF 1992, the CMH moved into its highly publicized, long-awaited building in the Houston Museum District. The most prominent exterior feature of the Robert Venturi design was the front entry loggia supported by thirteen large sculptures that looked like giant paper doll cut-outs. Originally envisioned to resemble a "comic book" in appearance, CMH board members requested the kid sculptures be painted to represent the ethnic kaleidoscope of Houston's diverse population.

Thirteen different Merle Norman cosmetics foundation colors were used to ensure a realistic spectrum of skin tones for the kids. The museum thus made a quality landmark architectural statement along the front block of its entry that celebrated and welcomed all people.

Our Partners in the Beginning

First-year attendance immediately surpassed projections, and the museum's pride was rightfully justified. Its ethnically diverse board and staff were pleased to see the ethnically diverse audience streaming into the new building. Imagine our surprise when we heard from the leaders of organizations like the Houston Area Urban League and the Houston Independent School District that they did not consider the museum accessible to a large portion of Houston's children: the one-third who were growing up in families living below the poverty line. The museum's traditional weekly "free attendance" times, Title One school tours, and seemingly robust outreach programs were not sufficient to have beneficial impact for these families. Most of this audience had no idea that a children's museum existed, and their advocates told us this population did not grasp the museum's potential value to their families. It became clear that the museum was not fulfilling its mission to ignite a lifelong love of learning in *all* children.

Houston's disproportionately high child poverty rate resulted from identifiable root causes: a dramatic absorption of people from Central America, Mexico, Asia, and Africa beginning in the late 1980s; a relocation of Americans leaving low-opportunity regions such as the Rust Belt; and historical discrimination that has left large areas of Houston without basic access to quality child development, quality public education, public transportation, affordable housing, healthy food choices, and medical care. Houston became the Ellis Island of the late twentieth century, drawing more than ten thousand new residents each month seeking the American Dream. There was no social safety net and few resources provided from government entities. Rather than organized systems, there was an informal network of independent agencies within low-resourced neighborhoods struggling to keep up with service demand. These agencies, in some cases more trusted than effective or efficient in their neighborhoods, were the partners we needed in order to reach this one-third of Houston's families.

Habla Español?

Our first overtures to ten agencies were not received enthusiastically. Our partnership criteria had led us to choose some of the larger, established service agencies that had stable funding streams, reputations based on demonstrated results in the community, professional staff, and locations in one of two primary geographic service areas for Spanish-speaking immigrant populations. We arranged meetings with anyone who would see us. We started by being honest about our intentions, and why we sought the group as our partner. *We soon discovered that chief executive officer–to–chief executive officer agreements were, in many cases, simply polite formalities. "Bigger" did not necessarily mean "effective" when it came to serving the community.*

The agencies were sufficiently decentralized so that the real power to embed the museum in a meaningful way rested with the frontline staff. Communication between chief executive officers was required, but the museum needed our own program staff to be ready to promote, receive, and respond to the suggestions of agencies' program staff. We were transparent about our "credibility gap" in the low-income communities. We needed partners to "vouch for us" to their constituents to help us establish a trusted brand among the people served by the partners we sought. Accordingly, we showered these staff members with free tickets and monthly English/Spanish calendars that promoted all the great museum happenings that changed weekly in order to ensure all Houstonians felt welcomed attending the CMH. Even with the promise of unlimited free tickets, our would-be partners were skeptical. How would their low-income constituents be treated in such a place? Would we embarrass the parents, of whom more than 50 percent were deemed illiterate? Did any of our staff speak Spanish? These prospective partners assured us that their constituents were too poor, worked too many jobs, and had such poor transportation that they would not use the free tickets. How could a small organization like the CMH bring something needed to the table? But they agreed to try. We agreed that our Spanish-speaking staff would go door to door in their neighborhoods with door knockers (hanging flyers hung on doorknobs), make personal pitches at community meetings inviting participants to attend the museum, and find transportation money so the agencies could bring their constituents to the museum in groups.

A Houston city council member well known in immigrant communities conducted more than thirty focus groups. Overwhelming positive feedback from these focus groups gave us the bargaining position to approach our partners from a position of strength. Not only did we begin to understand our value—immigrants often expressed a much higher appreciation of and desire to attend museums than U.S.-born citizens—but they also shared their aspirations for their children and recognized, without our prompting, that we could have important impact. One woman wrote in Spanish, "I've left everything I love in my home country to give my children a better future. Tell me what I should do for them and I will do it." That one sentence written by one woman in 1996 forever changed the trajectory of our organization.

Commitment to Provide What People Want

Once we established our first several partnerships, word quickly traveled through our network to other agencies that asked for the same support. In the first twelve months of establishing our initial partnerships, we added forty-six more agency partners and began to retool our onsite parenting and child development programs for delivery in community sites outside of our original two areas. We prioritized hiring Spanish-fluent educators, and also committed to using the Spanish language in all museum public relations, gallery labels, and activity guides. A total of 45 percent of all gallery and box office staff were fluent in Spanish. We were busy recruiting partner agencies no matter their size, and we said "yes" to any agency who reached out to us. We had determined that an agency's size and reputation among the funding community did not mean that the community it served equally valued it. Nor was it a guarantee of passionate, effective leadership.

Sustainability of Commitment

Our board was adamant that one-third of the city's population needed our attention and endorsed our partnership efforts. We had no additional funding, however, because the museum was focused on retiring some building debt and raising endowment monies. Our quickly growing community partner network with the growth of community program sites, seemed impossible to sustain and contradicted the image of our big, bright landmark building. Foundation and corporate leaders repeatedly asked, "What can you do inside of that wonderful new building? Aren't you diluting your already thin operational budget to focus outside of the museum walls? Isn't it better for all children to have a museum-based experience even if it's only one time?" To answer these questions, we used testimonials from our partners and their constituents, and we pointed to the quickly increasing attendance numbers driven by free ticket redemptions. Within two years more than 30 percent of our total annual attendance was due to our growing partner ticket distribution network, resulting in visitors who not only better reflected Houston's ethnicity but also the socio-economic distribution of its families.

With the increased communication between our program staff, partner agency staff, and the constituents whom we were co-serving, the museum better understood how to redevelop and message in-community programming with consequent better adoption by low-income, immigrant families. In the third year of building our partner networks, with our increasing reputation as a "boots on the ground" program provider, we began to attract major funding partners interested in reaching the neighborhoods we were serving. Our city's largest independent school district (ISD) asked us to develop and deliver "summer learning loss" curricula and activities that would be disseminated through our growing partner network. A major corporation looking for a signature project funded our three-year development of a parent engagement program empowering parents to engage in weekly at-home activities that supported their children's school learning. This experience deepened our relationship with the Houston Independent School District (HISD), taught us how to work within the cultures of individual schools, and required us to adopt measurement tools that ultimately led us to evaluation methods that used outcome-focused logic models. A total of 25 percent of the CMH's annual operating budget was allocated to in-community efforts, enabling us to hire a manager of outreach programs to grow the agency partnership network and to hire staff dedicated exclusively to delivery of offsite programs that we had tested first at the museum. Board-level connections enabled us to partner with local universities to co-develop programming and guide our evaluation efforts. This credibility allowed the museum to pursue the largest formal networks in Houston as our next partners, including the Houston Public Library, the YMCA (the largest provider of out of school care in Harris County), HISD, and more than fifteen other area ISDs.

Partnership Examples Involving the Houston Children's Museum

Family Literacy Involvement Program (FLIP)
Partners: Houston Public Library, University of Texas Medical School/ Children's Learning Institute, with initial funding from the Institute for Museum and Library Services and subsequent annual funding from local contributors.

FLIP was developed to empower families to take an active role in their children's learning and support their children's development of early literacy skills. FLIP is a free resource for any Houston Public Library (HPL) cardholder. A total of 250 unique FLIP Kits exist, the majority of which are available in English and Spanish, with select kits also available in Vietnamese and Chinese. Each kit is designed for a specific age range (infants, toddlers, preschool, kindergarten/first grade, and second/third grade) and contains a book and all supplies parents need to engage in a related literacy-oriented craft activity with their child. While the book is returned to HPL, the family keeps the craft project. There are multiple copies of each kit; currently, twenty-four hundred kits are in circulation through thirty HPL branches (including the library branch on site at the museum) and fifty Houston ISD schools. Ten years following FLIP's launch, the museum continues to bolster the kits by adding new titles each year and through the efforts of a dedicated, three-person team who clean and replenish kits on a weekly basis. Ongoing evaluation is provided by the Children's Learning Institute at the University of Texas Medical School, which co-developed the project's learning goals and the evaluation protocol. The initial funder investment of $1 million is supported by the museum's $145,000 of annual fundraising. Circulation exceeds thirteen thousand each year. Evaluation has indicated a significant gain in literacy skills when the kits are used as compared to the outcomes of simply reading a book.

YMCA-Based A'STEAM (Afterschool Science, Technology, Engineering, Art/Design, and Math)

Partners: *YMCA Greater Houston, with initial funding from YMCA sources and subsequent annual funding from co-funded sources.*

This program was designed in 2012 to maximize efficient use of both the CMH's and the YMCA's resources to deliver STEAM programs for low-income children in afterschool care sites at thirty YMCAs. The museum provides curriculum, all program supplies, and professional development and training for YMCA staff. The museum also evaluates the children's learning outcomes. This program was expanded in 2015 and 2016 to include literacy-focused programming and summer learning loss programming, and was ultimately expanded to 108 YMCA locations, thus ensuring year-round out-of-school opportunities for every YMCA serving low-income children in the greater Houston area. The YMCA benefits by having the museum responsible for training and evaluating YMCA staff to deliver content that can be unfamiliar to them. The museum's proven, extensive staff training for its own para-professional gallery staff was adapted by the museum for YMCA staff to ensure optimal learning outcomes for the children in their care. The museum's evaluation expertise with out-of-school learning is essential in providing results that continue to secure funders' commitments. More than forty-one thousand children are served annually. Evaluation conducted for third- and fifth-grade participants saw a mean increase in their post-test scores increase by 25 percent on STEM content measures.

Parent Stars

Partners: More than 220 HISD and surrounding ISD schools annually, with funding sources available to schools for parent engagement.

Parent Stars evolved from one of the museum's earliest ISD partnerships. With a growing emphasis by area ISDs on serving pre-kindergarten and kindergarten-aged children, effective parent engagement programming became a mandate. The museum's programs are geared to help parents of Title 1 pre-kindergarten through sixth-grade-aged children understand how their children learn, as well as the expectations placed on the students by the school. Museum staff engage parents in programming that helps them to continue effective museum-style learning at home with their children. Parents are also encouraged to return to the museum with their families as often as possible using free admission tickets. Parent Stars is a collection of twelve themed workshops and corresponding bilingual activity books, as well as after-hours school fieldtrips to the museum for families and faculty. The CMH works with faculty from each school to tailor content of and number of workshops to the particular needs of the participating classes. More than seventy-five thousand participate in Parent Stars annually, with schools seeing measurable improvement in parent engagement, students' performance, and overall participation in school.

Staff Skills and Dispositions

None of this work would be possible without our committed museum staff. Our outreach team is multidisciplined, and each member respects others' unique talents and responsibilities. We have salespeople making contact with our partners, a person who runs a kind of "call center" to take the incoming queries, and marketing and graphic people to churn out digital and hard copy materials that encourage parents to participate in activities and encourage our Open Doors partners to actively distribute our free passes and other critical communications pieces to their constituents.

First and foremost, we hire people with at least five to seven years of classroom teaching experience, and, ideally, a high comfort level connecting to children in nonschool settings such as camps and out-of-school programs. To support them, we have a team of twenty para-professionals with teaching experience but not necessarily teaching degrees.

We look for people who have a personal connection through their own experiences with kids growing up in poorly resourced communities, and who understand that such children have unlimited potential. Spanish speakers are particularly important in reaching the largest ethnic segment in our service area.

Finally, we need people who have limitless energy and who can focus on our overall learning goals while juggling and managing complex logistical details. We expect accountability, and we do measure the results of their efforts. Our team must be dedicated to providing their absolute best—whatever "the best" means for that child in that circumstance on that particular day. If a child needs a different array of resources, or a different level of support from home base, the museum staff member should immediately identify, or at least brainstorm, how to make that happen. The rest of us—from myself to CMH interns—are here at their disposal. Nothing comes before our service to those who place their trust in us. We want to reach the greatest possible number of children with excellent programs that have measurable outcomes.

Tum Hindi me baat kar sakte ho? Kya aap Urdu boltay hai?

During the twenty years that the CMH has prioritized building external partnerships, the Houston Standard Metropolitan Statistical Area has grown 64 percent to a total of 5.8 million people. In the City of Houston there is no ethnic majority, although the largest group is Latino, predicted to make up more than 50 percent of the population before 2020. Houston is home to the United States' second-largest Vietnamese population, the second-largest Nigerian population, and was, by the mid-2010s, declared the location of the largest number of refugees entering the United States. The 30 percent of children living in poverty remains among the highest in the nation in an urban setting. Without a state personal income tax, and despite attempts by some local foundations to encourage collective impact action for improving early childhood learning opportunities, there is more to be done than there are sources of identified funding. Families living in poverty are still assisted primarily by independent not-for-profit agencies addressing community needs that are perceived by all stakeholders to vary from neighborhood to neighborhood.

Today every Houstonian lives within two miles of an agency that distributes free admission tickets to the museum. Our partner network is more than 870 organizations in Harris County, with an additional fifty agencies in an adjoining county. Our partners include faith-based agencies, schools, libraries, out-of-school providers, food pantries, subsidized housing locations, and government officials. A team of twenty-five educators accumulated so much mileage last year driving to partner sites to deliver programs that they could have driven around the Earth's circumference three times. We provide direct delivery of our service to two hundred partner sites monthly. We will add Hindi and Urdu in the coming year as an institutional language, just as we did Spanish in the early 1990s. We serve 350,000 annually onsite at no charge and almost that many at no charge through in-community programming. Our brand is so valued that when the mayor of Houston hired a consultant to conduct dozens of town hall meetings in low-income and immigrant communities, the only organization whose name was mentioned, unaided, in every meeting as an organization that benefited their families and was also a welcoming place for them was the CMH.

Partnerships in Transforming a Neighborhood and Learning Landscape

19

SUZANNE MCCAFFREY AND JANE WERNER

BIOGRAPHIES: SUZANNE MCCAFFREY is the director of new media at Children's Museum of Pittsburgh, where she oversees web-based and digital communication streams through the museum's websites, social media, digital platforms, and video production. She seeks to create interactive "moments" for museum visitors, educators, and donors that incorporate their voices and extend their connection to the museum experience. As a marketing professional for more than two decades, McCaffrey has managed many website creation and redesign projects, interactive experiences, video projects, social media campaigns, and writing projects ranging from books to ad campaigns, annual reports, and exhibit copy. In addition to the Children's Museum, she has held marketing and writing positions with the University of Pittsburgh, Big Brothers & Big Sisters of Greater Pittsburgh, and the Physicians Committee for Responsible Medicine.

Jane Werner's thirty-four years of museum experience includes twenty-six years at The Children's Museum of Pittsburgh where she served as program director, deputy director, and currently executive director. Werner leads the team responsible for all aspects of the museum's mission and vision, exhibits, public programming, funding, and operations. The Children's Museum of Pittsburgh expanded in November 2004 after the completion of a twenty-nine-million-dollar capital campaign. Attendance grew from 80,000 to currently 300,000. The project was the recipient of the 2006 American Institute of Architects National Award and National Trust for Historic Preservation Award. The museum received the 2009 National Medal from the Institute of Museum and Library Services for its work in the community, and in 2011 the Children's Museum of Pittsburgh was named one of the top ten children's museums by Parents Magazine.

Introduction

PITTSBURGH SITS AT THE confluence of three rivers—the Allegheny, Monongahela, and Ohio—and with a modest city footprint, is considered a mid-sized U.S. city. But its neighborliness, not its lack of sprawl, were what once inspired children's television pioneer and Pittsburgh-native Fred Rogers to call Pittsburgh one of America's "biggest small towns."

The city's North Side, once known as Allegheny City, was a thriving, prosperous area through the first half of the twentieth century, home to industries such as iron, glass, rope, and flour. After World War II, the area suffered a significant decline due to the postwar expansion of highways and suburbs, uprooting many residents and spurring others to move.[1] Allegheny Commons, the central crossroads of the North Side, once boasted a central market, town hall, park, and the Carnegie Library of Allegheny, one of the first Free Libraries created by industrialist Andrew Carnegie. But in the redevelopment of the 1960s, buildings in the Commons were torn down, replaced by a shopping mall, parking garage, and apartment buildings. This sixty-million-dollar answer to suburbia blocked direct access to North Side neighborhoods from downtown Pittsburgh. Business in the area slumped, and when the steel industry collapsed in the 1970s and 1980s, the North Side and the entire city of Pittsburgh fell into decline.[2]

The story of the Children's Museum is over forty years old. It starts with volunteers from the Junior League who thought Pittsburgh needed a children's museum and continues with both volunteers and professionals, working together, to create something different and special as a cultural institution in an underserved community.

The museum opened its doors in 1983 at the heart of the city's North Side, occupying the basement of the historic Old Post Office Building. Its founding was spurred by the Junior League of Pittsburgh and a number of civic-minded foundations that saw the value in supporting cultural infrastructure even as the city's industrial identity struggled. One of the museum's earliest, and arguably most important, mentors was Fred Rogers, who produced his iconic children's television program in Pittsburgh.

Support for an interactive, family-centric institution was strong and the Children's Museum grew, expanding into its entire building in 1985. By 1998, the museum saw more than 100,000 visitors each year and was exceeding capacity, despite the North Side being challenged by poverty and urban decay. With a pressing need to grow, the museum committed to its location and chose to expand its existing facility rather than relocate to the suburbs. A plan was conceived that allowed the museum to serve a larger audience, address the needs of other local child-based organizations, and eventually transform the former city center into a cultural campus for children and families.

Growing a New Museum Model

The museum defines itself as a cultural rather than an educational organization. We have more than a passing interest in education, but culture is where we find ourselves located literally and figuratively. As a cultural organization we can work in the community with various subject matters, experiment with many topics, and both succeed and fail in spectacular fashion. Over the years, we've woven learning and research into our practice to codify the impact of the Children's Museum of Pittsburgh in the community. In the past fifteen years, we've worked with the University of Pittsburgh's Center for Learning in Out of School Environments (UP-CLOSE) and our own Learning and Research Department to understand how the visitor learns in our cultural environment. This work deepens our interactions with our audience and our understanding of the power of our exhibits, programs, and work in the community.

We launched our twenty-nine-million-dollar expansion project in 2000, aiming to nearly quadruple our size to eighty thousand square feet by joining the current building and the vacant Buhl Planetarium building next door with a third, contemporary building.

The project was committed to four core ideas:

1. **Creating interactive exhibits based on a guiding philosophy of *Play with Real Stuff*:** New exhibits were built by our staff and informed by research on how families learn in a museum setting, conducted through a new partnership with the UPCLOSE.
2. **Partnering with other child-focused organizations:** The museum devoted more than thirty thousand square feet of space to rent to organizations who work with or on behalf of children, creating an "incubator" environment where staff work side by side, share resources and ideas, and champion missions related to children and education, the arts, social services, and advocacy. The museum's current partners are The Saturday Light Brigade, a family radio program; Reading Is Fundamental Pittsburgh, a literacy program; Allies for Children, a child advocacy organization; two pre-kindergarten/Head Start classrooms of Pittsburgh Public Schools; and UPCLOSE.

3. **Fostering design excellence:** The project received the Honor Award for Architecture from the American Institute of Architects, while the museum received the Rudy Bruner Award for Urban Excellence and the National Preservation Honor Award from the National Trust for Historic Preservation. The museum also worked with artists to commission and incorporate interactive art works throughout the building.
4. **Building in a green and sustainable manner:** The building received silver LEED certification for green building practices, one of the first museums in the country to pursue this status.

The expanded Children's Museum opened on time and under budget in 2004. This was the first step toward realizing the dream of a cultural campus for children and families.

Reviving Neighborhood Charms

Soon after its expansion, the Children's Museum had its first opportunity to stretch the traditional role of a museum and actively work to enhance the quality of place in its immediate neighborhood. It partnered with the City of Pittsburgh, the Andy Warhol Museum, and the Northside Leadership Conference to help revive a theater that would occupy the former home of the Carnegie Music Hall in an adjacent historic landmark building.

Through a nonprofit created to oversee the project, a $2.5 million renovation was conceived. The museum served as the lead fundraiser and the design and construction manager, and provided leadership, accounting services, and parking for the venue once it opened. The New Hazlett Theater was completed in September 2006 and today is a thriving cultural asset offering a variety of performances and community services. It is also an active participant in planning the future of Allegheny Commons.

This success furthered the idea that the North Side's cultural assets— "charms" forming a "bracelet" of creativity and connection—can be catalysts for positive change in the community. Using the "rising tide lifts all boats" philosophy, cultural institutions that take an active role in promoting community welfare not only help the community but ensure their own long-term success and potentially fulfill their missions more effectively.

The Charm Bracelet Project was launched in 2006, with the Children's Museum in a leadership role and the goal of inspiring neighboring cultural institutions to collaborate on creative projects related to community life.

More than thirty-five projects were funded over three years, with the stipulation that each involved a large institution partnering with a smaller one, to the benefit of both. For example, the National Aviary, Carnegie Science Center, and Andy Warhol Museum created projects with small North Side organizations such as Artists Image Resources, Venture Outdoors, and Young Men and Women's African American Heritage Association. A wide variety of projects were pursued—from public art and performance to community events to outdoor recreation projects. Neighbors were engaged in activities such as kayaking lessons, book making, cross-generational interviews, and screen printing.

At the Charm Bracelet Project's completion in 2011, the majority of "charms" remained thriving institutions, while some of the funded projects have led to future collaborations and long-term initiatives that continue to this day.

Polishing a New "Diamond"

In conjunction with the Charm Bracelet Project, the museum set its sights on reinvigorating a long-neglected city-owned park right outside its doors starting in 2007. The park, formerly known as Ober Park as well as Diamond Square due to its rhombus shape, had once been prominent as the central crossroads of the North Side. But the park was transformed into a concrete, sunken plaza as a result of the urban planning of the 1960s, and eventually fell into disrepair.

The museum envisioned returning the park to a central meeting place, serving both residents and visitors. It held discussions, tours, and creative activities with current North Side residents, community groups, and city officials and learned that all parties desired a multiuse space that honored the site's history. The museum embarked on raising more than $6.5 million to fund the project, and served as design and construction manager for it.

Completed in 2012, Buhl Community Park is now a vibrant, accessible place for the whole community to meet, lunch, walk their dogs, even get married. A misting sculpture by artist Ned Kahn, known as *Cloud Arbor*, is a whimsical feature that sends out a cloud of mist every few minutes, cooling the summer heat and thrilling children. Museum visitors use the park to extend their visits, and programs such as the lunchtime Solar Concert Series and the annual Maker Faire Pittsburgh attract even more people to enjoy the park.

Taking Museum Experiences Out of House

By 2011, the Children's Museum had taken several steps toward creating the cultural campus it envisioned. But a new exhibit gave it the opportunity to reach beyond its doors and bring innovative museum experiences to an even wider and more diverse audience.

That year, the museum opened MAKESHOP, a permanent, eighteen-hundred-square-foot exhibit space dedicated to making and tinkering, and a space where informal learning opportunities and research-based understanding could converge around the worlds of digital and physical creating and invention. The space was developed as an experiment, in partnership with Carnegie Mellon University's Entertainment Technology Center and UPCLOSE. The museum's research partnership with UPCLOSE allowed the space to support vital learning research about how making supports twenty-first-century learning, creativity, communication, and family learning.

Since MAKESHOP opened, the museum has emerged as a national leader at the forefront of making and learning, with research and resources to disseminate to museum and educational audiences. Through annual educator boot camps and trainings, in-depth teacher residencies, and major convening events for the museum and library field, the museum has helped translate making across a variety of learning contexts. The MAKESHOP initiative has allowed the museum to help others establish makerspaces in schools, museums, community centers, universities, libraries, and beyond. Some notable projects include the following.

Making Spaces: In 2015, the Children's Museum's efforts in the field of making garnered the interest of crowd-funding force Kickstarter and a new partnership was formed. Together, they developed a national model for schools to use crowd-funding campaigns to fund and create school-based makerspaces. In the pilot phase, seven Pittsburgh region schools raised more than $108,000 from five hundred donors to spur the creation of new makerspaces.

The museum is now sharing the model with more institutions by leading "Making Spaces," a national strategy funded by Google to sustainably integrate making in up to one hundred schools annually across the country. The Children's Museum worked with partner Maker Education Initiative to convene ten museums, libraries, and nonprofit educational spaces nationwide to serve as hubs that each help five to ten schools launch crowd-funding campaigns to raise funds for their makerspaces. The museum provides maker education expertise and guidance to help each school hone their approach to implementing maker education.

Hosanna House: Hosanna House is a multipurpose community center in Wilkinsburg, a low-income borough east of Pittsburgh that has absorbed more than its share of social and economic dislocation over the past twenty-five years. The center serves more than thirty-five thousand children and families a year with child care services, a preschool program, afterschool programs, sports programs, community development, and a summer camp. Despite outreach programs in place at the Children's Museum, families from Wilkinsburg and other low-income communities of Pittsburgh have not traditionally visited the museum with regularity for reasons such as cost, distance, and lack of awareness. At the same time, the museum's research around its maker programs revealed that racially and economically diverse children and families are less likely to participate and engage in making activities due to lack of access, awareness, and educator/adult support.

Starting in 2016, the museum worked with Hosanna House to transform an underutilized space in its facility into a "community museum" with a makerspace and creative arts studio. The museum placed exhibit components there for families to enjoy and ultimately created a makerspace, which is now providing making activities for hundreds of preschool children, afterschool students, and summer camp youth. Hosanna House staff are trained at the museum's Maker Educator Boot Camp to facilitate the activities and a Museum Teaching Artist also serves in residence. To encourage a deeper relationship, the museum also provided ninety Hosanna House families the opportunity to become museum members at no cost.

ACTION Housing—MyPlace Lofts: Over the past two years, the Children's Museum has worked with ACTION Housing, the leading provider of quality affordable housing and related services in western Pennsylvania, to create a program and space that gives vulnerable young adults who have aged out of the foster care system the opportunity to build life and career skills with hands-on learning and making. The museum launched a makerspace, similar to the museum's MAKESHOP, in ACTION-Housing's MyPlace Lofts for at-risk young adults living there. Youth work with museum staff to gain career skills in technology, sewing, woodworking, and engineering, while building life skills such as creativity and persistence.

Since the project launched, roughly 50 percent of MyPlace Lofts residents participate in weekly sessions with museum staff, and also use the space independently to work on projects. Participating residents have gravitated toward projects such as woodworking, jewelry making, and sewing.

A community that is supportive and beginning to sustain itself has grown around the makerspace. Residents share resources, encourage one another, and teach peers new skills and techniques. One resident, after learning that the others did not know how to crochet, led the group in an impromptu crochet class and crocheting is now a regular activity in the space.

This year, the museum began sessions focusing on practical projects that will prepare residents for their next living situation. For example, "DIY Apartment" teaches residents how to use skills they have gained from the program to furnish future apartments on a budget.

Participants have shown tremendous interest in entrepreneurship and taken part in several museum events throughout the year, such as 21+ MAKEnights, Maker Faire Pittsburgh, and various community events. These events not only allow residents to sell what they've made, but build relationships, share expertise, and gain skills.

The Museum Lab

As one of the final steps in creating the largest cultural campus for children and families in the United States, the Children's Museum is currently pursuing the renovation of the nearby, city-owned Carnegie Library of Allegheny that stands between it and the New Hazlett Theater. When it opened in 1889, this building was the second Carnegie Library in the United States. In 2006, lightning struck the building's clock tower and the library chose to vacate the site and relocate to another location a few blocks away.

The museum has launched a campaign to raise more than eighteen million dollars to transform this beautiful, yet neglected, historic building into the Museum Lab, a National Center for Excellence in Education. The Museum Lab will be a multiuse facility where informal and formal educators will come together to test and study ideas to transform education. This endeavor will further the museum's already proven success in leading collaborative learning efforts and creating replicable models in education— hands-on, open-ended experiences using old and new technologies.

Manchester Academic Charter School, a North Side school, will relocate its grades six to eight to the building and participate as an onsite learning cohort. Likewise, partner organizations from the Children's Museum's 2004 expansion will find more space in the building, including UPCLOSE, The Saturday Light Brigade, Reading is Fundamental, and Allies for Children. The Lab will also serve as one of the educational centers for Pittsburgh's Remake Learning movement; provide training programs for formal and informal educators; and offer public programs for all ages to learn skills such as design, construction, and engineering.

The first phase of the Museum Lab is on track for completion at the beginning of 2019. At its completion, the project will deliver not only a new facility, but new programs and new opportunities for partnership and collaboration for the benefit of children and families. The project has an estimated economic impact of over $2.4 million in total value added per year from employee compensation, property-type income, and indirect business taxes.[3]

A Partnership Mindset: Our Board, Staff, and Approach

None of this could have happened without the support of our board of trustees and the hard-working talents of our committed staff.

The board supports the museum's vision. We are blessed with a dedicated thirty-person board who provides just the right amount of support to allow staff to try out ideas and concepts; who pursues funding for big, audacious ideas; and who are constantly asking good and provocative questions. We are going against all of the "best practices" manuals on board governance by doing away with term limits and it seems to suit us well. We do have three-year terms, which allow people to make a graceful exit, but for those who have grown with the museum, we keep them close by re-electing them every three years. The board members share one thing in common: they are interested in a financially conservative museum that fulfills its mission progressively and with verve. The board looks for those traits when recruiting new members to their ranks. They also look for kind people.

Our staff is essential to our success. It takes people—talented, professional, smart, and kind people—to create fresh and joyful experiences at the Children's Museum of Pittsburgh. We have people with all of those attributes in abundance. We tend to take on projects that are unifying rather than divisive. Our "Love and Forgiveness" exhibit was revelatory, and our current project on "Kindness" is timely. Working on these projects together has created an atmosphere of respect for each other's point of view. Maybe this is the effect of living and working in the same city where Fred Rogers' created Mister Rogers' Neighborhood. Maybe we like each other just the way we are. Maybe we all just have the same sense of humor. Or maybe we realize how lucky we are to be working in the field of children's museums.

We tend to start projects with small experiments that have potential to be big ideas. Most of those small experiments are funded by a "New Ideas Fund." We find this fund essential for innovation and growth. The successful Hazlett Theater, MAKESHOP, Making Spaces, the New Media and Business Development departments, and a few failed experiments were initially bankrolled by this fund. Each small experiment has an initial investment of between five thousand to fifteen thousand dollars from the fund. By testing out ideas, we can make bigger bets on the ideas that seem most promising.

The New Ideas Fund was created through a grant from a local foundation ten years ago. We have long since used the initial funding of $250,000 and have kept it going by budgeting it every year as part of our annual budgeting process. It is a sacred line item. In the last analysis, we determined that for every dollar spent from the New Ideas Fund, we either earned or raised an additional seven dollars. No investment can promise that kind of return. And it keeps us fresh and relevant by investing in the talents of our staff.

There is something to be said, however, for maintaining partnerships. Partnerships are easy to make but difficult to maintain. It comes down to the people involved in the partnerships. Like any relationship, partnerships have their ups and downs. The issues of finances, time, and the change in personnel all play a part in the strength or weakness of the partnership.

- Being clear at every step of the partnership about finances is essential. Money issues can kill a project before it gets off the ground. Share business plans, budgets, grant proposals. Be an open book, literally.
- Spend time on the partnership before a project is ever conceived. Get to know the organization and the people who run it before there is even an idea of what the two organizations could do together. Open the museum up to the partner organization before you have funding. Build goodwill. The old adage *good things take time* plays a key role in a strong partnership. It's tough to write an organization into a grant if there has been little time spent in trying to understand its strengths and weaknesses.
- People come and go in organizations. Sometimes the change in personnel can kill a great project, while sometimes the change in personnel can strengthen the project. In both cases, the leaders of the organizations should try to get to know each other well and be clear about why the project exists.

Conclusion

For almost twenty years, the Children's Museum has evolved into an agent of change in our community by aligning our goals in supportive partnerships with other entities and communities. Through this work, we have redefined the role of our museum. Pittsburgh's North Side has turned a significant corner in recent years, attracting other projects that are making it a thriving and desirable district. The hermetic mall at the center of Allegheny Commons has undergone a dramatic transformation, bustling with new technology companies, start-ups, and restaurants. Pittsburgh recently announced plans to revive the streets that once bisected Allegheny Commons and bring local traffic into, rather than around, many of these assets.

The Children's Museum's dream of a cultural campus for children, which seemed like an audacious idea back in 2000, is now closer than ever to being realized. From its earliest days, key partnerships and collaborations have helped the museum bring the campus from a dream to a blueprint to a its soon-to-be expanded footprint. By creating a center conceived and built for the benefit of children and families, Pittsburgh's North Side continues a steady, positive trajectory toward a remarkable evolution.

The opportunities to go beyond the museum's doors and its neighborhood continue as well. The museum will embark on a multiyear project with Pittsburgh Public Schools to improve early childhood learning for economically disadvantaged and racially diverse children. The project will start by further integrating the museum's resources, exhibits, and programs into the school's formal curriculum, seeking what works with the Pittsburgh Public Schools demographic. The museum will research and apply its findings on learning design and environmental design from two Head Start classrooms in our building to help design four early childhood classes and an infant and toddler room for a low-income refugee population residing in Pittsburgh's Northview Heights community. The classrooms, along with a Family Support Center, will serve as anchors for many young families for whom English is a second language. This project is another way that the museum is looking for new ways to not only positively impact families in the Pittsburgh community, but further influence field-wide conversations about learning theory, practice, and policy.

A Museum Turns Outward $\qquad$ **20**

MARSHA L. SEMMEL, FROM INTERVIEWS WITH JOE HASTINGS
AND KRISTIN LEIGH

*BIOGRAPHIES: **JOE HASTINGS** is the executive director of Explora, a hands-on learning center in Albuquerque, New Mexico. He works with a talented staff of over one hundred educators, exhibit builders, high school interns, and volunteers to create opportunities for inspirational discovery and the joy of learning through interactive experiences in art, science, and technology. Hastings worked for thirteen years at the Exploratorium, San Francisco, in various roles including director of the Center for Museum Partnerships. Hastings is a 2009 Noyce Leadership Fellow and serves on the boards of the Association of Children's Museums, Twirl Taos, and the Informal Learning Leadership Collaborative. Hastings previously served as a board member of the Association of Technology and Science Centers, Amarillo Habitat for Humanity, and Taos Youth Soccer League. He also served as an advisor to the Donald W. Reynolds Foundation, which invested over $150 million in children's discovery learning networks in Arkansas, Oklahoma, and Nevada.*

__Kristin Leigh__ is the deputy director and director of community engagement at Explora in Albuquerque, New Mexico, where she has worked since 2001. Leigh began her time at Explora supervising the education group, where she worked on the development of inquiry science programs for students of all ages, professional development workshops for teachers and bench scientists, a teen intern program, and a variety of afterschool and weekend family programs. Leigh holds a master's in education degree in science curriculum and instruction from Arizona State University. Passionate about her community, Leigh has volunteered with a number of Albuquerque organizations, including Cuidando los Niños, Partnership for Community Action, and Alice King Community School. She was named Albuquerque Business First's 2014 Woman of Influence in the Nonprofit Sector and received the Association *of Science-Technology Centers' 2016 Roy L. Shafer Leading Edge Award for Leadership. Leigh is an alumni fellow of the Noyce Leadership Institute (NLI).*

Introduction

EXPLORA SCIENCE CENTER opened in downtown Albuquerque's First Plaza Galleria in 1993. The museum moved to the Sheraton Old Town, and then to Winrock Center. In 1995, Explora merged with the Albuquerque Children's Museum and became Explora Science Center and Children's Museum.[1] The museum opened its current location in December 2003. From its beginnings, the museum has been dedicated to education and learning, emphasizing a hands-on, inquiry-based approach to science. The museum has a longtime focus on underserved audiences, including those at the lower rungs of the economic scale, and has provided services to children and families throughout the state from its earliest years. New Mexico, with a total population of 2.1 million has among the highest levels of poverty, including child poverty, in the United States. Joe Hastings became chief executive officer of Explora in November 2012, after stints at the Exploratorium in San Francisco and as director of the Don Harris Discovery Center in Amarillo, Texas. Hastings' various roles at the Exploratorium in his thirteen years there included the directorship of the Center for Museum Partnerships. In Amarillo, he focused on strategically repositioning the museum as a community gathering place, welcoming to families, and playing a critical role in school science education.

During his tenure at Explora, Hastings has combined a focus on stabilizing the museum's financial position with steering the museum through a series of strategic planning processes, with a special focus on ways in which the already-popular museum could become more deeply engaged in community issues—and make an even greater difference in the lives of the children and families of New Mexico. A member of the second cohort of the NLI, a global program for leaders in science and technology centers, children's museums, and other science-based public-serving organizations, Hastings has leveraged the NLI's focus on the self-aware leader, adaptable leadership, and civic engagement in his work at Explora. Partnership has been a cardinal principle in the museum's playbook.

Hastings' senior executive partner in this work is Kristin Leigh, deputy director and director of community engagement, who has worked at the museum since 2001. A former science classroom teacher, Leigh is also an alumna of the NLI and is a recipient of the Association of Science Technology Center's Roy L. Shafer Leading Edge Award (2016).

From the beginning of their work together, the Hastings/Leigh team aimed to deepen the strong community-focused work of Explora, and some of their efforts drew on the NLI experiences and the NLI's requirement that all fellows develop a museum-based community engagement strategic initiative that formed the "action learning" part of their fellowship year. During Hastings' stint at NLI, the program's community engagement resources included a presentation by Richard Harwood, founder of the Harwood Institute for Public Innovation.[2] Harwood's method, involving "turning outward" in order to learn a community's aspirations, assessing a community's readiness for change, and authentically listening to community members' expression of needs, resonated with Hastings. Through NLI, Hastings and Leigh also were introduced to the work of sociologist Peter Block, his insights into community formation and fragmentation, and approaches to restoring a sense of belonging, integration, and positive change.[3] Another component of the NLI program involved a site visit to Market Creek, a highly diverse, once violence-ridden San Diego neighborhood that has been transformed through a long-term commitment of the Jacobs Foundation and the work of various community organizers in revitalizing the neighborhood. Fellows learned firsthand about the importance of bringing community members together through a variety of strategies, including "living room conversations," potluck dinners, and leveraging the various gifts and talents of community members to create positive community-oriented resources, including a shopping center, library, cultural center and gallery, performance spaces, and festivals.[4]

Each of these approaches emphasized the importance of developing trust, committing for the "long haul," eschewing "one-off" efforts, and moving slowly and in response to authentic community needs. Through the process, the museum needs to understand and determine how its mission and resources can most effectively address specific community problems and challenges.

Hastings and Leigh were not starting from scratch. The community-focused efforts of Explora's founding director, Paul Tatter, and his successor, Patrick Lopez, had earned the museum a coveted National Medal of Community Service, and White House recognition, from the Institute of Museum and Library Services (IMLS) in 2010. The museum was serving families, teachers, and children around the state, but always from the museum's perspective of needs that had to be met. Hastings and Leigh sensed there was more work to be done with some populations who were not yet connected to Explora, in order for the organization to become a highly relevant community resource and anchor institution.

In moving Explora deeper into its community engagement focus, and seeking to connect in deeper ways with hitherto underserved area populations, Hastings and Leigh worked with consultant Bill Booth, former director of COSI Toledo, who helped them implement certain elements of the Harwood "turning outward" practices. In the process, Hastings and Leigh have transformed the nature of their partnership work—and the museum's place in the community. The museum's "lessons learned" from these new collaborations have transformed Explora's mission, vision, strategy, and long-term goals and spawned strengthened relationships with key public and private stakeholders at the local and state levels.

Partnership Examples

Nurse-Family Partnership of the University of New Mexico's Center for Development and Disability: This program is a free, voluntary program that brings new mothers together with nurse home visitors. It involves a specially trained nurse visiting the mother-to-be regularly throughout her pregnancy and continuing until the child turns two years old. As Hastings and Leigh strove to practice a new community engagement approach, they began by focusing on groups with whom they had at least one loose connection—a name that could be dropped in the hopes of securing an invitation to a meeting. This included the neighborhood associations bordering Explora and groups with which specific Explora staff had affiliations.

Upbeat and determined, Leigh telephoned a number of community organizations, asking them to consider letting Leigh attend a meeting, bring snacks, and use an hour to facilitate a listening session. Not too many organizations returned her calls. Leigh says of that time, "Responding to my calls, emails, and invitations was fairly low on people's to-do lists, and this provided a moment of insight into how difficult this work might be and how far Explora would have to come. Once conversations began, however, word began to travel." Leigh felt as if they had a breakthrough on the day the phone rang and the voice on the other end, a nurse with the Nurse-Family Partnership program, said, "I hear you're holding conversations with groups around town, and we'd really love if you would come listen to our first-time moms." Leigh attended a meeting with the young Latina mothers and their home-visiting nurses. As she tells it, "There I was, a blond, blue-eyed, non-Spanish speaker in a mostly Latina group of

women. At first, they were pretty quiet. Turnout was lower than anticipated. One young mother's car seat had been stolen from her vehicle the
night before, preventing her from transporting her infant to our meeting.
Other moms couldn't find childcare, and I will always remember passing
around the babies of the moms who came anyway, taking turns cuddling
while we talked." Despite the slow start, Leigh's authenticity and humility
came through, and she learned, through the conversation, about the specific challenges faced by these young mothers, many with big educational
and professional aspirations, yet facing great challenges without childcare,
transportation, or other basic services. Through the conversations, Leigh
understood the need for more accessible, high-quality early childhood
care, along with one of the mothers' most critical, short-term needs—a
place to bring their young infants and toddlers while they were preparing
for the GED exam. Nurse-Family Partnership became a Community Partner Member Organization, and the home visiting nurses began delivering
no-cost museum memberships to the new parents, along with advice for
ways in which to utilize Explora best. The partnership has endured for
more than four years, with the monthly moms' meeting often taking place
in Explora meeting rooms and frequent first birthday celebrations, Easter
egg hunts, and more taking place at Explora with the NFP client families.

New Mexico Autism Society (NMAS): This partnership began
when Explora held a community listening session with families associated
with the NMAS. As an Autism Society blog posted by Sarah Baca (May
26, 2015) noted, at the session, "staff from Explora learned a lot about the
aspirations and concerns of these families and immediately recognized ways
to improve access to science-rich learning experiences." The development
of a variety of tools and programs for these families—including social
stories, visual schedules, noise-cancelling headphones—were prototyped
by members of the Autism Society before moving to implementation. A
total of 258 families from the Autism Society received no-cost memberships to Explora, which helped them access the new resources and provide
important feedback for their improvement. The current tracked use rate
of Explora's new sensory-friendly materials, which can be checked out
from the admissions desk, is at about seven uses per month. Additionally, the Sensory-Friendly Resources page of the Explora website receives
about eighty hits per week. Twenty students with autism attended science
summer camp at Explora in 2017, participating in camp programs co-
developed by Explora and NMAS. Sensory-friendly hours now take place
regularly at Explora, and over fifty Explora staff have received training on
working with families affected by autism.

Partnership for Community Action (PCA) in Albuquerque's South Valley: This organization has been dedicated, since 1990, to building strong and healthy communities in Albuquerque's South Valley and across New Mexico. "PCA focuses on critical community issues like education, economic sustainability, wellness and immigrant rights. Through raising awareness and advocacy opportunities, we support people and families to become strong leaders in their neighborhoods and in New Mexico."[5] During a listening session with immigrant mothers served by PCA, Explora heard a deep commitment to providing children with educational opportunities, despite many barriers to access. Explora welcomed PCA's families with memberships, and staff from both organizations worked together to design a bilingual afterschool engineering club, providing the families of PCA with a dedicated resource available in their neighborhood. Leigh describes a recent site visit to the program, called Explora Ingeniería:

> I saw 12 kids and 8 parents, all doing engineering activities facilitated in Spanish. With them were Andres, an Explora educator, and Jose Luis, an engineer from Sandia National Laboratories. Andres was working with a group of kids, who were stomping a modified bike pump to launch rockets they had designed, then running back to re-engineer their rocket's fins and re-test them. Cheers or groans announced how each modification fared. Nearby, a little brother was on mama's lap, experimenting with balance. Every time the mother placed an object on a wire, it fell off, and the little one laughed. Then, he'd try. Jose Luis gave the boy extra paper clips to add weight and help balance the object. When the boy succeeded, he snuggled into his mom's neck with a satisfied giggle. The mom chatted in Spanish with Jose Luis about how he became an engineer in order to provide for his family.

The club has been so relevant for participating families that PCA is helping raise funds to create a second program in another community.

The School for the Blind and Visually Impaired: This partnership began when museum staff encountered therapists from the School for the Blind and Visually Impaired bringing toddlers to the museum so that the youngsters could practice using their canes. It has evolved into the museum working on a deeper, more sustained level with those occupational therapists who specialize in working with two- and three-year-olds. Now, these practitioners regularly contribute to Explora's exhibition development workshops in order to advise on all dimensions of accessibility, from physical layout to exhibits graphics.

Explora Today and Tomorrow

In 2013 as this new orientation to community partnerships began, Explora renamed its community engagement program to reflect the changing nature of the relationships, from a previously more unidirectional approach to one based on program co-creation. "Helping Hands," which implied the "stronger" museum organization helping a "weaker" community group, became the "Community Partner Membership Program." In July 2014, the museum was honored with a Noyce Foundation Bright Lights Award, recognizing museums "that have done an outstanding job of systemic engagement with their local communities."

The consistent and ongoing practice of "turning outward" has led the museum to increased local and national fundraising success. Leigh notes, "We're talking with people all the time, and now we co-apply for large-scale, more systemic grants. For example, we went to United Way of Central New Mexico for our work with the Autism Society, and having NMAS as a co-applicant strengthened our proposal."

In 2017, Explora received one of ten National Leadership Grants from IMLS for a partnership with the New Mexico State Library, Central New Mexico Community College, the University of New Mexico Cariño Toy Lending Library, the New Mexico Public Broadcasting Station, and the Bernalillo Count Early Childhood Accountability Partnership "to create and support STEM Charging Stations for Young Children and Families." IMLS wrote in its review of the project,

> This proposal comes from recommendations from national and local reports on STEM (Science, Technology, Engineering, and Math) best practices, coupled with listening sessions and a track record of collaboration with the partners. This is a rare example within the applicant pool of a true community anchor proposal.

The project, building on years of the museum's collaboration-building work, is focused on addressing the achievement gap between low-income children and their more economically advantaged peers. It aligns with Explora's new strategic plan and future directions. Leigh says,

> We are thrilled to be working with such important partners on this two-year project to address critical issues for young children in our state. As part of Explora's Cradle through Career STEM Learning Strategic Focus, this project will bring local STEM organizations together to give our youngest learners the best chance for future successes in life, school, and career.

The museum has honed, codified, and internalized its partnership strategy into three steps: (a) Listen. (b) Welcome. (c) Co-create. These steps are adjusted for each potential partnership group, but they have proved effective and resilient. They reflect the Explora leaders' realization that community members do not necessarily readily comprehend museum motives in partnering, may be wary of museum professionals, and may not believe that the museum could help them address their specific needs. In short, there are some basic issues of understanding and trust. Hastings and Leigh stressed that, in community listening sessions, it is important to hear from the prospective partner's stakeholders first. Begin with a question like "What kind of community do WE want?" Leigh noted, "It has been important for us to use the 'we' pronoun. After all, the museum is part of the community and shares responsibility for creating the changes to which we aspire." Hastings and Leigh differentiated their approach from traditional focus groups, where organizations get individuals' reactions and views on specific aspects of the museum's work. Similarly, Explora's sustained, co-created initiatives are quite different from traditional museum outreach.

What have been the implications of this changed orientation to community engagement for museum staff and members of the Board of Directors? Hastings acknowledged that there was some initial staff wariness when he arrived, with some thinking that his "turning outward" focus reflected diminished respect for staff knowledge and experience. Now, the tide has changed. As Leigh put it,

> As we have developed new community relationships, many staff have risen to the occasion, and not only the "usual suspects," like program staff. People from various museum departments have assumed key roles, and we've discovered—and used—previously unknown staff talents and interests. Developing community partnerships requires unique skills that not everyone has, but staff from many different working groups have been successful at it, and many other staff members have been involved in listening, welcoming, and co-creating with new partners.

Hastings noted that, initially, Board members were focused more on addressing the museum's pressing financial challenges than engaging community members in listening sessions. For some board members, a benefit of these sessions, according to Hastings, was their comparatively low cost, as well as a belief that this practice presented few risks, with many potential benefits. As the museum's role in the community deepened through the burgeoning partnerships, some board members were heartened by the positive "buzz" they began to hear within their respective networks. In

Explora's most recent strategic planning process, insights from community partners—in addition to presentations by local and national authorities on such topics as early childhood, teen learning, and workforce skill development—served to shape the museum's plans and further define its broadened community focus. The board is also diversifying its ranks; the director of the PCA is now a member of the Explora board.

Explora documented its most recent use of its community partnership process, for its latest strategic plan, in a "shared aspirations" document that synthesizes the results of a series of fifteen community listening sessions that the museum held between January 2014 and June 2016. The sessions

> provided data to help us better understand our community and its rhythms. The fifteen listening sessions, involving more than 150 people, taught us much about the aspirations, concerns, and challenges shared by members of the Albuquerque community and created a framework around which Explora can engage more deeply and serve as a relevant community anchor and change agent.[6]

The fifteen community organizations participating in this many-month process included the New Mexico Montessori Network, the New Mexico Asian Family Center's Vietnamese Families Group, the International District Healthy Communities Council, the Wells Park Neighborhood Association, the Sawmill Community Land Trust, and several other local and state-wide groups.

These listening sessions yielded seven shared community aspirations, summarized as desires for:

1. An inclusive, accessible community;
2. A child-centered community;
3. A community with abundant educational opportunities;
4. A community with plentiful, high-quality early childhood education;
5. A safe community;
6. A community with less poverty and more jobs; and
7. A community with well-planned neighborhoods.

Each aspiration has a summary statement and accompanying individual participant comments. These listening sessions, capturing the community's hopes, challenges, and concerns, helped the museum create the framework that is driving its future. The museum's recent experiences, its deep and growing relationships with many state and local leaders and community members and their needs and priorities, and the insights from each of the focused partnerships have also been key. The new strategic focus, Cradle through Career STEM Learning, creates a set of priorities and goals for "early explorers," aged zero to four years ("engage"); "young scientists," aged five to twelve years ("educate"), and "future science leaders," aged thirteen years to adulthood ("employ"). This focus will drive the museum's future programmatic offerings and physical plant. Each piece relies on partnerships as core elements. For example, plans for an early learning center for "early explorers" include office space for other early learning partners and "wrap-around" services as well as a Central New Mexico Community College Lab School for pre-service early childhood professionals. The "young scientists" museum will be the home and backbone organization for STEM-NM, New Mexico's official STEM Learning Ecosystem, and the home and fiscal sponsor of the New Mexico Out-of-School Time Network. The planned STEM education and workforce development center will include partnerships with Air Force Research Laboratory, the University of New Mexico STEM Outreach and Diversity Office, and others, and will connect students with work opportunities in local STEM businesses.

As the museum's partnership approach has gained currency in the museum sector, Explora has become a site for field-wide professional development. In April 2017, the museum hosted representatives from five museums from around the country to discuss and demonstrate its community listening work, giving these museum professionals some real-time experience with this approach.

The museum has distilled a list of traits for museum professionals entering into co-created museum/community partnerships:

- Ability to "take" whatever you hear, without being defensive.
- Ability to steer the conversation away from the museum, keeping it focused on the broader community.
- Comfort in a listening role.
- Humility.
- An ability to focus on learning, rather than assuming knowledge.
- An ability to be open to the "wisdom of the community."

As the museum moves into its next era, Explora's three-part community engagement process: "listen, welcome, and co-create" has been critical to expanding its support, re-orienting its programs and services, and rethinking its physical expansion. According to Director Hastings,

The process of turning outward has transformed how people in the community talk about Explora. People are connecting with us all the time.
People are stepping forward to help solve OUR problems. We really
know our visitors. Our visitation is at an all-time high at more than
300,000 per year. Our membership use rates are more than six times per
year. Two city council members are on our board. Other community
leaders have become advocates for the museum.

Leigh chimes in about another challenge:

The sheer amount of new work this engagement strategy has created.
Now, Explora is the go-to for lots of people, with lots of ideas for how
to make change. When we ask, what might we try that could make a difference?, lots of people have ideas. Our senior staff recently started listing
our current projects and initiatives on a white board in the director's office, and we stopped when we hit about 80 different items. This amazing
growth has forced us to rethink our program management capacity, leading to hiring project management experts to provide training for Explora
staff, hiring two project managers to supervise implementation of certain
large-scale efforts, and re-arranging the senior leadership team to better
distribute leadership of these efforts and leave room for new growth. New
challenges, yes. But it's been worth it.

Growing a Network of Small Cultural Organizations

21

Florida African American Heritage Preservation Network and Virginia Africana

MARSHA L. SEMMEL, WITH CONTRIBUTIONS FROM
ALTHEMESE P. BARNES, AUDREY DAVIS, AND PHYLLIS FORD

BIOGRAPHIES: ALTHEMESE P. BARNES was born in Tallahassee, Florida, one of ten children, to Mose and Mary Pemberton. Her parents were tenant farmers and later farm owners. The family relocated to the city in the early 1930s. Althemese experienced some of both worlds through visits with her ancestors back to the home roots and life in the city. Though her parents were not high school educated, it was a rule that education and religion were the pillars for which each child would aspire, and they did, matriculating at Florida A&M University. Althemese graduated in 1965 and 1970. She was choral director at Lincoln High School and state employee until retirement in 1995, established the first African American community museum in the historic Riley House, and organized the Florida African American Heritage Preservation Network (FAAHPN) in 2001. President Barack Obama appointed her to the Institute of Museum and Library Services (IMLS) Board in December 2012.

Audrey Davis is director of the Alexandria Black History Museum in Alexandria, Virginia. Davis is a past president of the Virginia Association of Museums and is one of the founders and the director of Virginia Africana: The Network of Museum, History and Preservation Professionals. Davis is currently vice president of the Alexandria Historical Society and is a board member for Living Legends of Alexandria, Preservation Virginia, and the National Women's History Museum. In 2016, The Washington Business Journal listed Davis as number two on their top one hundred list of Washington Power players.

Phyllis Ford is director of The Laurel Grove School Museum, a one-room school established in 1881 to educate African American students in Franconia, Virginia. She has a BA degree in business administration from Bluefield State University, Bluefield, West Virginia, and an MBA from Trinity University,

Washington, DC. Ford is vice president of Virginia Africana Associates, a network of museums, historic sites, cultural organizations, and individuals devoted to Virginia African American history and heritage and whose collections are available to the public. She is president of the Laurel Grove School Association and treasurer of the Fairfax County, Virginia, History Commission.

Introduction

THIS CASE STUDY examines a pioneer statewide network of African American cultural heritage sites, based in central Florida, and its evolution and accomplishments. It also includes a profile of Virginia Africana, one of three other statewide networks associated with African American history and culture sites that have emerged in recent years.

The Florida African American Heritage Preservation Network

The FAAHPN was created in 2001 by Althemese Barnes. Barnes, the founding director of Tallahassee's John Gilmore Riley Center and Museum for African American History, had retired in 1995 after a career in Florida state government, including serving in the Departments of Education and Labor as an employment counselor, civil rights administrator, and program specialist. She had also been state secretary of the Florida chapter of the National Association for the Advancement of Colored People (NAACP).

Her government positions had given Barnes inside knowledge of state programs, policies, and processes—knowledge that would serve her well in her "encore" career in the history and cultural sector. Barnes had always been interested in African American history and had volunteered in two community-based historic preservation projects in Tallahassee: the historic cemetery of Greenwood that had been established by a group of black citizens in 1937, and the John Gilmore Riley Foundation, steward of the home of John Gilmore Riley, an educator born in 1857, who became Leon County's first African American principal and occupied that position for thirty-three years. Barnes helped lead successful campaigns to preserve, and then restore, these two sites. These projects gave Barnes a practical, hands-on education in the principles, best practices, and issues around historic preservation—as well as mechanisms for successful civic engagement.

In the case of the cemetery, Barnes' coordinated public relations campaign helped leverage city challenge grant funds that facilitated raising additional private money for the initial cleanup. In the case of the foundation, its Board, on which Barnes sat, wanted the home to be a place to preserve and promote black history. Accordingly, Barnes stepped up, and, upon leaving state government, became the first Riley House director in 1996, after a majority of the original foundation trustees had died or were in too poor health and unable to implement the intended purpose. To prepare for her new role, she completed a museum certificate program in museum management at Florida State University.

As Barnes delved deeper into the world of historic preservation, including researching various state historic preservation funding programs, she realized that few of these funds had supported sites relating to Florida's African American history. Moreover, there was scant documentation, and no directory, of these sites. Using her work as an education equity coordinator, as well as her NAACP position that provided Barnes with access to people in Florida communities with similar interests in African American heritage and education, Barnes reached out to other equity coordinators and members of the statewide NAACP network. In 1997, she convened a meeting in Tallahassee attracting almost one hundred people who were connected in some way to African American history and preservation. Afterwards, seven individuals (including Barnes) who had met for the first time at the convening—Sandra Rooks-Pinellas of the African American Museum in Clearwater; Clifton Lewis of the L.B. Brown House in Bartow; Sharon Coon, Arts and Cultural Program Consultant in Jacksonville; Patricia Whatley, of the Tajiri Arts Museum in Sanford; Martha Bireda, Blanchard House Museum, Punta Gorda; and Dr. Dorothy Jenkins Fields of the South Florida Black Archive and Museum—agreed to stay in contact. As they got to know each other, group members identified shared challenges.

The most formidable issues were money, especially operating funds, and training, as most sites were led by grassroots individuals with passion and commitment but scant museum or historic preservation knowledge. Most had started museums with their retirement dollars. With her familiarity with legislative policies and procedures and knowledge of various state programs—including state and local grant funding sources—and buoyed by her successful advocacy efforts on behalf of the two Tallahassee sites, Barnes was able to play a pivotal role in mobilizing the group around the common mission of preserving African American history around the state.

At a subsequent convening in Tallahassee in 1999, the group decided to move toward establishing as a formal entity, the FAAHPN, and committed to making the conference a semi-annual occurrence. By 2001, the network was receiving some grants from local foundations, including a $150,000 donation from the Elizabeth Ordway Dunn Foundation to help seed the network. It was presented at a second conference that was hosted by the Jacksonville network site. Barnes notes, this fund "gave the organization the first financial base to begin extensive outreach, make an official filing as a State of Florida Corporation, develop its mission, goals and objectives and publish its first organizational brochure."There were seven original members. Today, the network has twenty-eight active museums and a total of thirty-two museums in the directory that receive some form of network support. Early on, priorities included introducing network executive directors and staff to the state funding opportunities with the Florida Department of State and encouraging and assisting members to seek grants. Equally important was training in "museum best practices" including museum administration and management.[1] These seed monies further enabled the network to reach out to other organizations throughout the state, gain recognition, and raise the visibility, overall, of the many important, yet hitherto unrecognized, African American heritage sites in Florida. Barnes noted,

> It was this movement that can be credited with bringing recognition of the value and benefit of Black contributions and accomplishments to the attention of the State Historic Preservation Office and other institutions as a source that needed to be made a more significant part of planned initiatives. It was a movement that evolved from . . . those seven museum operators who had not known each other initially but who stepped forward to assume leadership roles in preserving the history of their communities. [Like me], . . . they were motivated and inspired with the possibilities and took a leap of faith to see how the common goal of greater inclusion could be better reached [by] working together.

The network motto was "a rising tide lifts all boats."

Building Shared Awareness

Upon organizing, network museums worked to sharpen their awareness of grants that were available through local and state sources to support programs and operations. An initial training session, held in Tallahassee, provided network directors with resource development skills, including grant writing. Several members took advantage of this opportunity and subsequent training sessions, and have been successful in receiving grants from various sources, including the state's Community Redevelopment Agency, Florida Department of State, the Florida Humanities Council, and their local arts and culture agencies. Some served as grant review panelists, and many have presented at local, state, and national conferences about their work.

In 2009, Barnes secured a $350,000 legislative appropriation for the network. With the exception of a single year, this appropriation has continued, and increased. Individual museums have successfully received public and private support for operations, infrastructure, and capital campaigns. The network trustees determined that the funds raised for the network could only be used for general operating assistance, including interns, exhibit design and fabrication support, technology support, consultants, and office and museum supplies and equipment. The network pursues other funding sources for building acquisition, restoration, historic preservation construction, and capital campaigns.

Federal Support and Recognition

As the network coalesced, the Florida African American Historic Preservation Network was able to leverage national support, taking advantage of a new federal program, managed by the Office of Museum Services at the Institute of Museum and Library Services (IMLS), that was created as part of the 2003 legislation that established the National Museum of African American History and Culture at the Smithsonian Institution. Working with leaders in the African American museum sector, IMLS had established Museum Grants for African American History and Culture to support projects that improve the operations, care of collections, and development of professional management at African American museums.

These grants, from $5,000 to $150,000, are offered to museums with a primary purpose and focus on African American life, art, history, and/or culture, encompassing the period of slavery, the era of Reconstruction, the Harlem Renaissance, the civil rights movement, and other periods of the African American diaspora. Nonprofit organizations whose primary purpose is to support museums identified above and Historically Black Colleges or Universities are also eligible to apply.[2] The program made its first grants in 2006, and the network was among the first awardees with the maximum grant of $150,000.

IMLS grants to the network in 2006 and 2008 helped support The Florida African American Museum Exchange, a network initiative that was designed to build the institutional capacity and sustainability of African American museums throughout the state of Florida. Responding to a needs survey supported by IMLS, "Riley Center selected 10 network directors to receive technical support and training in grant-writing, web site development and computer training, partnership building, site upgrading and presence, and strategies to enhance cultural events and exhibitions."[3] In the first year of the project, museum directors participated in three four-day training sessions at different Florida locations. There was also an "each one-teach one" peer-to-peer mentoring component, where directors, upon returning to their home site, were expected to share their learnings with the director of another site. The project also included museum internships for five graduate students, new computers and training in their use for nineteen museums, archival product information for collections care, and support for museum directors to attend other professional conferences, as well as a formal presentation at the 2008 annual meeting of the national Association of African American Museums.[4] Phase two of the project (funded by the 2008 IMLS grant) involved seven museum directors receiving training in collections care, document preservation, and collections management; the cataloguing efforts were placed on the FAAHPN website. In addition, the network created a "Museum Core Competencies Manual" that was distributed widely among museum professionals in the network and at regional meetings.

A 2012 IMLS award supported an internship program and archive for the John Gilmore Riley Center and Museum at Tallahassee Community College, focusing on leadership skill development, coalition and collaborative partnership building, technology, team training, and technical skills. This archive (and the formal partnership with the college) has been a model for other Florida museums.

These investments by a federal cultural agency provided national recognition to the pioneering work of the Florida network. It gave additional impetus to state funders to provide support, and, importantly, it raised the skill and knowledge level of many other museum professionals in Florida's African American sites. Many other Florida-based organizations have subsequently applied for, and received, their own IMLS grants. The program officer who manages the IMLS African American History and Culture Grant program noted, in December 2017, that more grant applications for this funding category routinely come from Florida than from any other state.

Partnership with the National Museum of African American History and Culture

As the Florida network was ramping up, so was the Smithsonian Institution's National Museum of African American History and Culture. A milestone in the Florida project's history was a visit, in September 2009, by Lonnie Bunch, director of the emerging national museum, and his senior colleague John Franklin. Bunch and Franklin toured the African American sites throughout the state, and held a post-tour debriefing meeting with Barnes, other Riley staff and network representatives, and a Leon County commissioner. The tour and meeting familiarized the Washington, DC–based leaders with the network and also discussed ways in which the network could support the important, pre-opening, outreach activities of the National Museum. At the meeting's conclusion, Bunch expressed his belief that the Florida network might well serve as a national model. Two years later, in 2011, Barnes and her colleagues marshaled considerable local support to co-host the annual meeting of the Association of African American Museums in Tallahassee, a first Florida venue for this conference.

The Network as Hub

As it grew, the network created an organizational structure housed at the Riley Foundation Office that included a central administrative office responsible for planning, coordinating and assuring implementation of meeting scheduling and notices, creating marketing and promotional materials, and identifying sources and resources to support network projects, programs, and activities. This office also serves as the connective hub for network members and affiliates. Principal staff include the executive director, and, in 2017, an assistant coordinator position that supports the network administration and management. The administrative budget is lean, with the majority of legislative and other funds going to network sites in the form of noncompetitive general operating grants.

The central office oversees all network policies, procedures, and activities, including:

1. Raising and administering funds;
2. Planning and implementing conferences and convenings, including a minimum of two meetings per year and one conference every other year;
3. Registering new museums based on established standards and criteria;
4. Ensuring the upkeep of the website for network marketing; and
5. Nurturing expansion and sustainability of the network, and mentoring for growth and sustainability as a concept and program.

The network's website is managed by a former intern. There are three regional liaisons—North, Central, and South Florida—with each being the executive director of a network museum, who receives a modest stipend to assist with immediate needs within their region. The liaisons are also members of the conference committee, who are chosen based on their demonstration of leadership, interest, and expressed desire to serve in these capacities. Other, non-museum-related individuals are accepted as affiliate members where there is a demonstration of interest in African American history and culture programs. These individuals receive newsletters from member sites, notices of special exhibits, invitations to meetings, opportunities to outreach to the network museums in their respective communities for research, and other support.

As it has evolved, the network has produced several seminal new resources, such as its *Museum Management—Guide to Core Competencies*, *Florida Black Heritage Trail Guide*, a mobile app, and traveling exhibitions and programs that have demonstrated its tangible value to museums, historic sites, and audiences around the state. These models have also had national impact. In addition, the network continues to focus its activities in the following areas.

Convenings. Two FAAHPN member workshops are conducted annually to highlight current practice in museum leadership, partnerships, scholarship, and museology. Meeting locations rotate among member museums across the state, in order to enable members to showcase current work. The meeting itself also provides some economic benefit to the host community.

Additional Professional Development. In addition to the convenings, the network provides multiple opportunities that keep members abreast of "best practices." These include collaborative programming, such as an exhibit exchange program and a speakers' bureau, shared research, and an active use of social media. Professional development has also addressed research skills, interpreting material culture, and the creation and dissemination of marketing and promotional tools.

Building Technological Capacity

Technological capacity has been a core network priority. Initial funding helped purchase computers for nineteen museums, the first computer ownership for most of the organizations. In 2010 the network coordinated a one-day computer training session for its members at Tallahassee Community College. As technology has advanced, funds secured through the state legislative process have provided interns to museums to keep websites updated via web development and management, social media, and other digital marketing and promotion strategies.

Research: The network, and its members, has forged numerous partnerships with community colleges and universities. These partnerships have enhanced public sites' knowledge of recent research and incorporation of scholarship into their interpretative programs. For example, the network has involved faculty and students in academic public history departments in members' community oral history projects. University students have also participated in public living history programs, provided primary research assistance based on local collections, and assisted in developing publicity and marketing campaigns. Often, research is conducted across the regions with members connecting on topics that lead to new scholarship or material culture discoveries. Florida is a long state, with sixty-seven counties and with many historical plantations that often moved enslaved families across the state within the existing slave system. Other population shifts occurred during the great migration from south to north. These movements have had the effect of dispersing African American history and culture across the state, adding to the complexity and depth of research (including documents and artifacts) that is being discovered and interpreted throughout the network.

Internships: This program, implemented through partnerships with sixteen area colleges and universities, has supported many interns over the two decades of the network's work. It provides "hands-on" practice as well as professional development in public history, museology, historic preservation, and conservation, important facets of successful trajectories in museum-related careers. It has helped build a pipeline of new museum professionals. Several former interns have obtained advanced degrees and are directors or leaders in museums, colleges and universities, and other independent capacities in Florida and across the United States. An important additional impact has been the expertise and substantial institutional benefits that interns have provided, and continue to provide, to network members.

Heritage Tourism: The network has established many collaborations with tour companies, conventions and visitors bureaus, and other entities throughout the state to pursue municipal tourism grants and to collectively market network sites as tourist destinations, especially in response to increased and widespread tourist interest in African American cultural heritage sites. Accordingly, the network, through a special appropriation put forth by a Florida legislator in 2015/2016, developed the FAAHPN mobile app linked to GPS mapping technologies. The app continues to be updated using legislative appropriated funds administered under the Florida Department of State, Division of Cultural Affairs. In 2007, the network provided the content for the first produced *Florida Black Heritage Trail Guide*, which detailed African American landmarks through the state. Under the auspices of Dr. Janet Snyder Matthews, then State Historic Preservation Officer (SHPO) for the Department of State, the network received a grant of fifty thousand dollars to contribute its research and historic intellectual property to the guide. It was printed and published by VISIT FLORIDA. The network was also designated as African American and Diaspora expert for the Florida Department of State's VIVA Florida anniversary, receiving a grant to produce a signature artwork (by artist-in-residence for the John Gilmore Riley Center/Museum Eluster Richardson), and an exhibit for the occasion, which "promoted twelve thousand years of Florida's people, places, and cultural achievements."[5] Included in the programming was a traveling speakers' bureau and exhibit that circulated to five network museums across the state. In 2017, the network was contacted by Villages for Veterans, a national nonprofit dedicated to helping severely wounded veterans to help identify black soldiers killed during the Vietnam War, and has continued to work with this organization, helping to name heretofore unidentified Florida Vietnam veterans.

Moving Beyond Florida: The "Cast the Net" Project

In 2014, the IMLS awarded a two-year, $150,000 "Cast the Net" grant to the FAAHPN to support knowledge sharing with the states of Georgia, Virginia, and North Carolina. The project's goal is to "increase the identification, documentation, and preservation of African-American history and culture" by bringing together representatives from four states to explore whether there are shareable models of state-based collaboratives focusing on African American history and culture. The partnering organizations included the Georgia African American Historic Preservation Network, the North Carolina African American Heritage Commission, and Virginia Africana. The grant included participation in the Florida convenings as well as statewide meetings in each of the three target states to provide onsite training and technical assistance. The goal was to enable these state-wide organizations to build their capacity for serving as viable educational and training hubs for the many African American historic sites and organizations within their boundaries. In addition, the project sought to shed light

Virginia Africana Associates

One of the "Cast the Net"–funded convenings occurred in Hampton, Virginia, under the auspices of its statewide endeavor, Virginia Africana Associates (VAA). Virginia Africana (VA) began in 2006, when the Institute for Museum and Library Services funded a grant to the Legacy Museum in Lynchburg, Virginia, to support the creation of the Central Virginia African American Network.[1] In October 2008, an exploratory meeting was held at the Sixth Mt. Zion Church in Richmond to explore "the feasibility and the viability of creating a statewide network of African American Museums and Historic Sites." The meeting included representatives from the Virginia Foundation for the Humanities (VFH) and the Virginia Association of Museums (VAM). A steering committee continued the planning, and, in March 2011, at the conclusion of the VAM's annual conference in Portsmouth, Virginia, the inaugural statewide meeting of the Virginia African American Museums and Historic Sites Network occurred, with more than one hundred participating attendees. The network was an outgrowth of the Central Virginia Museums Network. In conjunction with the VAM annual meeting, and preceding the African American network's first statewide meeting, the VFH sponsored a double session, "Interpreting African American History: Challenges and Opportunities for Museums & Historic Sites." The panelists, representing museum leaders and scholars, discussed the potential of these sites. According to a VFH summary,

> The panel addressed the fact that African American museums and historic sites, as well as museums offering substantial African American programming, face unique challenges of historical interpretation. They can also be powerful reservoirs of local memory, uncovering and documenting untold stories in the effort to overcome an established historical narrative that excludes or provides only token acknowledgment of African American history. These institutions are uniquely positioned to join two streams of knowledge, uniting deeply-rooted traditional or community-based knowledge with academic research.[2]

Subsequent statewide meetings occurred in 2011 and 2012, that latter at Norfolk State University in conjunction with a symposium, *1619: The Making of America*.

By 2013, the network was renamed VA, with a financial structure created under the auspices of the VFH. According to its "Brief History,"

> VA functioned as a voluntary organization with oversight and administrative support from VFH for the purpose of promoting Virginia's African American history and heritage. Membership was open to any museum, historical site, historical organization, or historian in Virginia with a focus on African Americans.

VFH had established a fairly robust program in African American history and culture. "Our guiding belief is that African American history is not separate from the mainstream Virginia story. It is integral to any fruitful understanding of life in the Commonwealth."[3] In 2000, for example, VFH created the African-American Historic Sites Database "to add long-neglected depth and nuance to Virginia's story and to explore the complexity of African-American history and culture beyond the major themes of slavery and civil rights." According to the Federation of State Humanities Councils,[4] the purpose of VA was to connect hundreds of individuals and sites around the state "in a common endeavor to interpret the lives and achievements of African Americans in every geographic region of the state and to share and shape these separate stories into a collective, statewide narrative."[5] From the outset, VA was "open to museums, historians & historic sites, cultural organizations, educators and individuals whose focus and collections are devoted to Virginia's African American history and heritage."

From 2013 through early 2016, VA held annual conferences; sponsored professional development sessions for social studies teachers, supervisors, and librarians; focused on conservation and preservation issues; and continued to strengthen connections across the formal and informal museum and historic site sectors.

In January 2016, at a meeting at Sixth Mount Zion Baptist Church, the VA's Advisory Council proposed and made the decision to become an autonomous body "with capabilities to pursue funding opportunities."[6] The VA leaders determined that the program could move forward with more effectiveness and efficiency if it stood on its own. Accordingly, in February 2016, VA began functioning as an independent nonprofit entity, VAA. Bylaws were approved by the following month, with the selection of an initial, seven-person board, including officers Audrey P. Davis, president; Phyllis Walker Ford, vice president; Marian Veney Ashton, secretary; and Benjamin C. Ross, treasurer. The organization's mission:

> VAA seeks to promote African American history and culture by sharing best practices and development opportunities, advocating for the preservation and protection of African American heritage within the state, and providing network support. Incorporated in the Commonwealth of Virginia, May 5, 2016, Virginia Africana Associates conducts meetings, workshops, and symposia, both independently and in association allied organizations, such as the Virginia Association of Museums and the Virginia Foundation for the Humanities, which played a key role in its founding.[7]

VA is currently finalizing a strategic plan, with a board strategic planning retreat scheduled for 2018. In addition to its Facebook presence, VAA publishes *Horizon*, a quarterly newsletter, and hosts an annual meeting. As befits a relatively new organizational structure, network members are still working on solidifying relationships, developing trust, sharing information, and establishing the value of the enterprise to potential outside supporters. There are still strong links to the VFH and the VAM, with deepening connections to the national Association of African American Museums and other regional programs.

In August 2017, VA sponsored two sessions at the annual meeting of the Association of African American Museums held in Washington, DC, the biggest gathering ever for Association of African American Museums. At VAA's October 2017 annual meeting, with the theme *Tools of the Trade*, members came together in Alexandria, Virginia, to provide updates on current projects, news of funding opportunities, a discussion of Confederate-related monuments, and participate in a forum on "Where do we go from here?" Significantly supporting the potential for the power of the network to advance the goals of individual institutions, VAA board member and historian Dr. Lauranett Lee emphasized that the most promising current statewide funding opportunities will reward collaborative efforts, such as a 2019 commemoration of the founding of the four hundredth anniversary of the founding of Hampton, Virginia. An update on the "Cast the Net" project by Marion Ashton of the A. T. Johnson Museum also focused on the benefits of collaboration. At the conference, Ashton stated, "Our organization was born out of love for history and for Virginia. We are working together to cement our footprint." She reminded attendees that, although all are volunteers in the growing network, "We are all ambassadors [for VAA] wherever we go."

The conference also featured a keynote address by John Franklin, cultural historian and senior manager at the Smithsonian National Museum of African American History, on current challenges in interpreting African American history and culture.

Its current leaders recognize that the road to success will be long and not without its challenges. The Florida network's example of its multiyear development is instructive. It was several years between the initial state-wide convening and the significant support that eventually came its way. Eventually, according to Phyllis Ford, the hope for the VA network is to create and expand, as has the Florida network, its presence as a strong voice for advocacy, catalyst for state and federal funding, and source of capacity building for the many diverse (often small) African American sites and repositories within the state of Virginia. This would include supporting continued documentation of all of the relevant sites within the state, and stronger professional and infrastructure development in the areas of interpretation, governance, collections management, websites, computers, and other technologies. The group also hopes to promote shared programming and intergenerational partnerships. The challenges, according to Ford, include marshaling people's time and energy. While there is much support for the network's goals, most members have full-time jobs; people have to stretch to carve out time for the hard work of network building.[8] Nonetheless, there is a strong spirit of "this is the time," and VAA continues to move forward. Events planned for 2018 include participation in the annual VAM meeting in Norfolk, presenting a session on "Truth Telling at Historic Sites," conducting a workshop in April 2018 on the Preservation of African American Cemeteries at the Reynolds Homestead at the Rock Spring Plantation in Critz, Virginia, and planning for its annual conference in Richmond, the state capitol, in October 2018.

Current VAA President Audrey Davis addressed the challenges facing VAA in this way:

> Speaking for myself and the current board members of VAA, we feel our biggest challenges are in succession planning as we need younger members to carry on our mission. We also need to build better communication with our membership, strengthen our fundraising and improve our visibility within the museum, preservation and history communities. We have made excellent progress, but much still needs to be done through capacity building. Grants submitted in 2018 to the National Trust for Historic Preservation and to the Association of African American Museums, if received, will aid in this process. The future is bright for VAA. Our Board is dedicated to our mission of preserving African American heritage in Virginia, via best practices, advocacy and dedication to preservation.[9]

Notes

1. This and subsequent information has been informed by "From Virginia Africana to Virginia Africana Associates, Inc.—A Brief History," produced by VAA President Audrey Davis and shared with the author.
2. Virginia Foundation for the Humanities. Date Unknown. "African American Museums and Historic Sites Network Inaugural Meeting."
3. Virginia Humanities. 2018. "Programs—Cultures & Communities—African American Programs." http://www.virginiahumanities.org/programs/.
4. Federation of State Humanities Councils. 2018. "Program: Virginia Africana." http://www.statehumanities.org/program/virginia-africana/.
5. Federation of State Humanities Councils. 2018. "Program: Virginia Africana." http://www.statehumanities.org/program/virginia-africana/.
6. See Note #1 above.
7. Virginia Africana. 2018. "Facebook Page—About Us." https://www.facebook.com/pg/vaafricana/about.
8. Author's personal conversation with Phyllis Ford on October 10, 2017.
9. Personal correspondence with Audrey Davis on February 12, 2018.

on how different states might learn from each other. Are there lessons from the Florida model, for example, that could be used in the admittedly unique context of the other states and that could be adapted to the different states' organizational and governance structures?

As part of the project, the Florida network made available its many products, including its museum core competencies manual and other resources. Accordingly, the May 2017 FAAHPN Conference, commemorating the network's twentieth anniversary, occurred in Tallahassee and brought the "Cast the Net" partners from Georgia, North Carolina, and

Virginia to the state to interact with Florida network leaders and focus on the value of cooperative planning, building organizational capacity, knowledge building, and strategies for sustaining both the networks and the African American sites themselves.

Summing Up

From its inaugural conference in 1997 to the present, FAAHPN has championed the importance of conveying a full and inclusive narrative of Florida's history that must be accessible to all, regardless of race, gender, or age. By developing a portfolio of technical assistance and capacity-building opportunities, training and professional development, public programming, exhibitions, and research to participating partners and stakeholders in organizations across the state, the network has made Florida's rich African American heritage more visible and accessible. It has, therefore, enabled a far more comprehensive public experience of Florida's entire culture and heritage. Network programs have engaged scholars, researchers, students and teachers, and diverse public audiences, including residents and tourists. Moreover, network achievements have had an impact on several nonminority museums, which have increased their inclusion of African American history in their programming. Network members and network-facilitated relationships have supported initiatives at the local, state, and federal levels, particularly in heritage tourism and historic preservation that have highlighted and deepened knowledge of, according to Barnes, "the contributions, achievements, landmarks and legacies, inspired by generations of African Americans." Barnes still holds true to the principles that have guided her during the past two decades: "Live your situation for the best and highest good of all involved and in a way that lifts and supports the whole." "Believe in it, then fight for it." And, "Note that it needs to be done, but if it is not, then do it." She is also mindful of the future:

> To succeed in our increasingly fast-paced, technology-saturated, society it is important and of value to embrace new models of operation and collaboration. We must marry fresh concepts into our missions as stewards of the stories and treasures. Historical and Cultural entrepreneurship is at the forefront of 21st century museum programs and initiatives. To survive, we must leverage together our greatest strengths—and that is being recognized as the keepers of historical truth and authenticity. This is a powerful position, with great opportunity and responsibility. The challenge is to develop and implement promising new ideas, best practices, and models to connect diverse audiences, connecting and executing together.

Conclusion

In some ways, the Florida network was ahead of its time, in its recognizing the power of a network to benefit all of its members and in taking on the ambitious work of organizing diverse entities with common interests to gain visibility, recognition, and, as Barnes notes, to practice the maxim that "a rising tide lifts all boats." The FAAHPN has brought diverse organizations together to create new museum-focused and public resources that serve the needs of individual sites and provide value to Florida residents and tourists. It has increased professionalization of member organizations and strengthened their capacity and stature. It has helped to train a new generation of potential historical and cultural professionals. Finally, even as the network has built the fundraising capacity of different museums, it has provided, for funders, a more efficient way to invest increasingly stretched funds for greater impact. As important has been the network's ability to make a compelling and continued case to funders for the type of infrastructure and operational support that is often the most difficult to obtain.

Many challenges remain, however. As Barnes notes, this is an era of dynamic and constant change. Therefore, an effective network must be flexible enough to grow, learn, and experiment, while concurrently maintaining the strong and trusted relationships that are required for its strength and continuity. Even as a network needs to retain the organizations that have formed its core, it needs to be able to welcome new members and adapt to their needs and points of view. Whether in Florida or Virginia, these networks must continue to build strategically on the power of collaboration through leveraging sufficient resources for their own operations as well as adding value to each of the individual members. This requires both continuing to build and sustain the trust of the network members as well as articulating and evolving, as necessary, the purpose, goals, and priorities of the network in order to match those of the member sites as well as of external stakeholders and supporters. With many of these organizations beginning decades ago as grass roots, volunteer-led, community efforts, another challenge involves accommodating generational shifts, changing business models, and changing funding trends. In the case of Florida, the hard work of the founder, coupled with the energy and commitment of the group of founding directors, has paid off handsomely in shared learning, increased resources, strategic and savvy partnerships (with state government, universities, the state tourism industry, etc.), and public benefit. As the founding generation begins to exit the stage, it will mark a critical turning point for the organization. In the case of Virginia Africana

Associates, as a relatively new independent entity it needs to muster the energies and commitment of its members, deepen its visibility throughout the state with key stakeholders, promote the benefits of collaboration, and continue to trumpet its achievements—while recognizing that it is running a marathon, not a sprint.

Be Our Guest!   **22**

JOHN WETENHALL

BIOGRAPHY: JOHN WETENHALL is founding director of the new George Washington University (GW) Museum and serves on the faculty of George Washington's graduate program in museum studies. Previously, as executive director of The John and Mable Ringling Museum of Art he led a $150 million capital and endowment program that re-established the estate as a prominent cultural attraction in southwest Florida. He also participated in major renovations at the Cheekwood Museum of Art in Nashville and the Birmingham Museum of Art, having additionally held positions as president of the Carnegie Museums of Pittsburgh and as interim director of The Miami Art Museum (now Perez). He is an art historian, trained at Williams (MA) and Stanford (PhD), with an MBA from Vanderbilt. He has served on the boards of the American Alliance of Museums (AAM), the International Council of Museums—US chapter (ICOM–US) and the Association of Academic Museums and Galleries, and has received the lifetime achievement award from the Florida Association of Museums. The substance of this chapter owes special recognition to museum educators Lauren Shenfeld, Tom Goehner, and Lori Kartchner, as well as Ana Dimen Kiss and Martin Kret, who have coordinated logistics on behalf of our dedicated museum team. Provost Forrest Maltzman championed the priority for student and faculty engagement, supported by Deputy Provost Terry Murphy.

I AM HOPING TO SHARE with you a fairly simple proposition: a way to expand a museum's programming without adding more staff or increasing expenses. At a basic level, the recipe requires little more than finding program partners who might benefit from a public place and access to the museum's culturally curious audience. Easy enough, but in practice there is a bit more: expanding definitions of "mission" to broaden the field of potential partners; embracing different forms of programs beyond the basic

staple of lectures, especially given the demographics of diverse communities and the interests of digitally raised younger audiences; and prioritizing
educational programming over the urge to raise money from rental events.
If you find that last proposition a bit of challenge, then you understand that
however straightforward this premise of partnership may be, it requires an
adjustment to values that may run counter to today's more popular mandate to run the nonprofit "more like a business."

Establishing an alternative model for programming is really about
nothing more than embracing a few guiding principles that could apply
at virtually any museum. Thinking about empty, unscheduled space in an
auditorium or multipurpose room as a waste of precious mission, and thus
proposing to find new uses, could happen just about anywhere. On the
other hand, given the tradition of tethering educational programs close to
the permanent collection or current exhibitions, a few leaps of faith may be
required as well. Allow me to walk you through our path of discovery—a
trial-and-error process born from the necessity of a museum merger—in
the hope that from our unusual circumstances, the applicability of our
principles might emerge.

Our Challenge

First, an observation. University museums distinguish themselves from
governmental and private museums in one special way: their largest contributors do not get recognized as donors. For all the names inscribed
on plaques in galleries, mounted over doors, or etched on donor walls,
the largest contribution in annual operating funds normally comes from
tuition-paying students. Our quest for discovering new means of collaboration emerged from this recognition, knowing that a new museum on
the campus of GW could only be as strong as its presence in the minds of
students, and by extension, faculty, staff, and alumni.

Location matters, too. In Washington, DC—home of the Smithsonian Institution's nineteen public museums and nine research centers,
the National Gallery of Art, and a host of worthy private and university
museums—any notion that a small campus museum, however new and
different, can consistently compete for audience, funding, and scholarly
resources would seem, to put it kindly, overambitious. Common sense
suggests that leveraging resources with others to co-organize exhibitions,
share expertise, cross-promote venues, and expand public programs would
generate far more public and scholarly interest than a small museum staff
could possibly generate on its own. Additionally, our Foggy Bottom

neighborhood is rich with intriguing neighbors: the World Bank, International Monetary Fund, State Department, federal offices, and, within a few miles, embassies from around the world. It is an environment for which strategic planning hardly requires more than a city map.

Our new museum was formed from two simultaneous, yet independent initiatives. One was an affiliation between the George Washington University (GW) and The Textile Museum (TM) of Washington, DC. The TM was founded in 1925 as an independent museum to collect and display oriental carpets, a mission that expanded over decades to encompass handmade textiles spanning the globe across Asia, Africa, Central and South America, and Eastern Europe, as well as the Middle East. Over generations, its collection had grown to approach twenty thousand pieces crammed in nearly every available bedroom, closet, pantry, and bathroom throughout its historic estate on Embassy Row. The museum had earned a reputation as a "little engine that could," generating scholarly exhibitions of distinction with beautifully designed catalogues of international appeal. On the other hand, the original buildings were aging, audiences dwindling, and financial conditions eroding over time. Facing millions in expensive building upgrades, The TM found a shelter from its looming financial storm just two miles down the road at GW.

The deal was as follows: the university agreed to construct a new museum in the center of its Foggy Bottom campus in the heart of Washington, DC, as well as to build a collection care and storage facility on GW's satellite campus in Ashburn, Virginia. In turn, The TM agreed to make a permanent "loan" of its collection to the university, contribute to construction, and sell its mansion and gardens in DC's upscale Kalorama neighborhood, with proceeds and all remaining financial assets committed to an endowment that would underwrite the textile-based activities of the new museum. Legal semantics aside, it was a merger.

At the same time, GW was in conversation with a noted collector of maps, documents, and memorabilia relating to the founding of Washington, DC—real estate developer Albert H. Small—to establish a Center for National Capital Area Studies in a charming old building at the heart of campus. Mr. Small contributed funds to renovate the Historic Woodhull House, dating back to 1855, into a permanent home for the display of his collection and a center for scholarly research. This project became an anchor for the new museum building, to be connected by an architectural bridge. So, GW found itself with old and new buildings hosting local and global collections, smack in the center of campus—a seeming embodiment of the strategic catchphrase, "think global, act local."

There is one more element. Over decades GW had built a distinguished reputation for training museum professionals, primarily through its master's degree programs in museum studies and museum education. Each program offers hands-on learning opportunities, internships, special projects, and advanced courses through affiliations with the Smithsonian Institution and a host of other local museums, schools, and cultural centers. Added onto the variety of academic programs offered by the university's Columbian College of Arts and Sciences (which subsequently grew through the acquisition of the Corcoran School of Art in 2014), the new museum came with an implicit mandate to serve a broader academic community as justification for GW's considerable investment.

Idiosyncrasies notwithstanding, as we planned to open this new museum we found ourselves in a position starkly similar to that of many museums today: having to do more with less. Despite a new facility nearly twice the size of the old TM, and a collecting focus now expanded with historical artifacts, the professional staff had not grown in number at all. The TM had actually lost a few positions, leaving the new museum with no more discretionary funding for educational programs than the staff could access at the former site. We were to "grow into" our new facility: double the gallery space, two facilities about forty-five minutes apart by car, and visions of audience expansion—all on essentially the same staff size and programmatic budget of the old museum. Daunting as this may have seemed, I doubt that these expectations would feel foreign to just about any museum professional today who labors under expectations of perpetual annual growth, even as resources seem evermore limited.

Looking more closely, we also faced a confluence of old and new. The TM brought an established membership base of well-educated, worldly textile enthusiasts with an appetite for traditional programs such as lectures, workshops, family days, and exhibition openings. The GW offered younger, more diverse audiences, an academic mission, and an urban location in the heart of Washington's international affairs community. This too seemed to present a microcosm of a profession-wide challenge: How do you expand and diversify audiences without losing the core loyalists who have sustained your museum for decades?

Legacy

Based on nothing more than survival instinct, we adopted an initial premise of "do no harm" to existing programs. At a time when the beloved mansion and gardens on S Street were to be closed and put up for sale—all to benefit a move to a new location in an unknown academic context—educational programs became a means of preserving the past: maintain the participation of existing audiences, sustain relationships with speakers in the scholarly community, and offer something to members during the transitional phase after the old museum closed and before the new one opened. Our transitional goal was to offer the same number of programs offsite as we had on S Street, simply moving "Rug & Textile Saturday Mornings," "Ask a Curator/Ask a Conservator," and special lectures to offsite locations, in addition to adding some extra excursions to local and regional museums, private collections, and related cultural venues. Logistics were difficult and annoyed some long-time members, but the basic programming proved easy—our staff had done that for years. So we succeeded in maintaining a full calendar, even while closed, simply by changing as little as possible.

As one might expect, attendance waned a little, as the inconvenience of new locations took the easy blame. *But more thoughtful analysis indicated a longer, more corrosive trend, and one not much different than experienced by museums across our field: a gradually aging and diminishing audience, well-educated and generally enthusiastic, but not demographically reflective of the population at large.* There was more to this than just the gradual erosion of a stagnating community: the very format of traditional programs contained inherent limitations. The concept that each program would be "curated" by an educator who carefully selected a speaker, placed the program on a printed calendar, and advertised to fill a room with eager listeners presented a model that was somewhat slow, expensive, and limited. Every speaker required unique logistics costing time and money: airfare, hotel, and VIP treatment while in town. Lead times were long: speakers had to be booked months in advance to meet publication deadlines for the quarterly newsletter, followed up by costly advertising and invitations. The educator was on the hook to fill the room or risk offending the speaker and wasting the museum's resources. Think of it like this: add up the expenses needed for each program, plus a cash equivalent of educators' time in preparing the event, then divide by the number of people who show up. It equates to handing each person that sum of money—ten, fifty, or one hundred dollars each. Worth it? Maybe, but there's no denying that the model is time-consuming, expensive, risky, and limited to the amount of such programs that a person can organize in the course of a programming season.

There is, however, one substantial and reassuring virtue to this time-honored model: the educator controls the event, choosing the subject matter and booking the expert of choice, thus guaranteeing a certain level of "quality" or programmatic "integrity" to support the educational reputation of the museum. There is great comfort in this. And lest you think we abandoned this tried-and-true reliance on the museum lecture as we moved into our new facility, I must tell you we did not. We kept programming lectures as always, but did so with the realization that they offered little hope of expanding the audience we had committed to preserve. To attract new and more inclusive audiences, we would need a new model—especially one that could scale up with what limited resources of time, money, and labor we could muster.

Listening

On May 19, 2013, two weeks before my first day of work and two years before the new museum would open, a student newspaper, richly named *The Hatchett*, published a tirade against the museum I had come to direct. Headlined by an announcement of cost overruns (caused by site conditions imposed by an aging old classroom building next door), the article voiced opposition by the Student Association and observed that "museums have been scorned this year." A former association president criticized building a new museum, demanding instead more space for students to gather and socialize. A candidate for the student assembly ran a sarcastic campaign to build museums all over campus.

Alerted to these headwinds of student sentiment, we ventured into the storm. With introductions made by a student-advocate, we met with the heads of student government and leaders from a variety of student associations. We learned that the university hosted hundreds of student-led organizations, many of which represented international students or groups defined by ethnic or racial diversity. For a museum with global collections, this could become a dream audience. We invited representatives of student groups to some "listening sessions" to understand their needs and expectations. *What we heard, simmering under the discontent that the student newspaper had revealed, was a frustration finding places to meet, either for affinity groups or just informally for students to gather, study, or relax.* Even more frustrating, some groups were being charged usage fees for space. No wonder students could be a bit testy about a new museum—especially around the time tuition bills came due.

Faculty seemed the next logical group for outreach, and a few listening sessions revealed many of the same frustrations. The university had no faculty club, and we learned that there were few places or occasions for interdepartmental gatherings, notwithstanding the administration's advocacy for "cross-disciplinary" initiatives. Internal charges applied to faculty events as well as those for students, dissuading many entrepreneurial professors from initiating programs beyond the classrooms controlled by their own departments. While some departments and schools had built impressive public programs that brought celebrities, scholars, and policy makers to the central DC campus, faculty members without institutionalized program budgets seemed to have trouble reaching new audiences or the general public.

Guiding Principles

Our modest effort to listen to potential new audiences had yielded a glaring opportunity: the crying need for program space expressed by student and faculty groups. To address this, though, we would have to adopt some guiding principles to push ourselves beyond the comfort of our own status quo. We needed help letting go of old assumptions as well as new concepts to generate alternative means of engaging audiences. Over time, using language that varied, we came to recognize three basic tenets:

1. *Trade Perfection for Energy:* We would forgo the ideal of programmatic perfection—just the right speaker for a collection-centric topic—so that we could energize our spaces with new audiences and diverse approaches to programming.
2. *Every Hour Our Room Is Empty, We Fall Short of Our Mission:* We would treat down-time as failure, believing it better to host mission-peripheral programs rather than safeguarding the sanctity of a darkened, empty space.
3. *Invite Friends to Invite Their Friends:* By targeting existing groups to bring their programs and participants to us, we would circumvent the museum's perpetual and expensive obligation to recruit audiences for each and every program.

At face value, this was nothing more than a simple hosting model, but in museum practice, it required a loosening of curatorial control, trust in potential partners, and a willingness to pursue the benefits of continual usage by abandoning the security of knowing that "our people" controlled everything.

What we were seeking, through these simple maxims, was a way to develop a sustainable model for inclusive engagement around our old menu of legacy programs. This required changing the relationship of educators to these new programming objectives. Let me offer an analogy. The traditional model pursued for decades by the old TM put educators in a position similar to the pilots of an airplane. Advertise a destination (topic/speaker). Fill seats for every flight (audience). Fly passengers around and land them somewhere else, or in our case, having facilitated an educational journey through a lecture or program, the experience of learning equates to going somewhere, to traveling. Our alternative model moved our educators from the cockpit to the control tower: find planes looking for a place to land and guide them onto our runway—the more the better. Keep them coming.

Expansion

When you start to embrace these principles, two things happen. First, the concept of "mission" begins to broaden. Interpreting a global collection of textiles, assembled primarily for their aesthetic merits, widens from connoisseurship and art historical context to broad topics relating to international customs, global diversity, and cultural literacy. Maps and documents that articulate the founding of an urban center become licenses to explore the values of a nation. Collections and exhibitions become departure points for dialogues on policy, politics, historical analysis, societal interactions, law, ethics, race, ethnicity, and other reflections on the human condition—widely and inclusively interpreted—not just ends in themselves, however worthy and inspiring those aesthetic or historical ends may be. In fairness, lest I overstate causal relationships, we had needed to broaden the context of how we interpreted collections anyway to engage new audiences and increase relevance. What partnerships contributed was a rapid, flexible, experimental platform to accelerate this transition at a scale and pace beyond the capacity of our payroll to afford.

As mission widens, the roster of potential partners begins to expand—and does so dramatically. On campus, the expected partnership with the art history program became, in practice, less fruitful than alliances with the Elliott School of International Affairs, GW's Sustainability Collaborative, and departments throughout the Columbian College of Arts & Sciences. Do not fear: art historians, collectors, and practicing artists did not lose their place at the podium. We just scheduled many, many more activities around them. Students benefited, too. Freed from the prerequisite need to interpret works on gallery walls, the population of potential partners exploded across culturally defined student groups, performance-based clubs, religious associations, and more.

The breadth of collaboration on campus started to spread off campus as well. Embassies asked to utilize our central programming space for cultural gatherings: a lecture by the Cultural Minister of China; an open house to sample Turkish food, music, costumes, and dance; a demonstration visit by Peruvian weavers; and sponsorship of a major exhibition by the Japanese Embassy on behalf of Okinawa, delegations from which were flown to Washington to perform, lead workshops, and share stories (see Figures 22.1 and 22.2). Museum associations and professional groups booked programs, as did individual thought-leaders seeking audiences to test their ideas about museums or to launch a new book. International organizations—the International Monetary Fund, World Bank, State Department—partnered on occasions for co-sponsored programs, receptions, or tours. College alumni groups booked special evenings or lunches, as did other museums, professional associations, and governmental agencies.

As more diverse groups, both on campus and off, learned of availability, the kinds of organizations who called and the purposes for which they wanted to "partner" started to test how broadly even we could define "mission-related." The Med School, Athletics Department, Division of Finance, Council of Deans, and many more lodged requests to use our space. The Smithsonian's National Museum of American History wanted to hold their senior staff retreat in our museum; the Fulbright Scholars asked us to host their regional reception; the American Bar Association called, as did

Figure 22.1.   Student China Tour, 2017
Photo by Zachary Marin / The George Washington University

many others for quasi-museum-based events. Rather than turn some of these groups away on "mission"-based reasons, we decided instead to impose a "fee"—not money, but either a commitment for the group to take a docent-led tour or, as appropriate, agreement to hear a brief speech by the director or a senior museum leader about our new museum's aspirations, upcoming shows and programs, and how our guests might participate in future. In other words, we co-opted other groups' events to generate gallery tours and "friend-raisers" for us.

As we widened the boundaries of mission and broadened the roster of potential program partners, we found that the formats of programs expanded as well. Younger, more diverse audiences decreased demand for the lectern in favor of discussion-based gatherings with audience members as active participants, their own expression considered as vital as the wisdom bestowed by the learned voice at the microphone. We found that students and faculty often enjoyed opportunities to meet classmates or colleagues. Even with lectures, we learned to seat people at tables, sometimes with food and drink available (or bring your own lunch), to balance knowledge with the inherent need for human interaction. Dialogue began to compete with monologue, the formal content of many programs shortened, and shared experiences became as valuable as the individualized process of "learning." Performing arts groups contributed concerts, jam sessions, poetry recitals, play readings, ethnic dances, choral music, fashion shows, and documentary films. We also discovered an excellent way to plan "student nights," "international student nights," and similar fare: have students plan these for us. I am quite certain that they did a far better job anticipating the needs and desires of their colleagues than our team of experts could possibly have calculated. We even assembled a "student corps" of tour guides, encouraged to invent their own interactive collection-based experiences, as an alternative to (not replacement for) our accomplished, dedicated, and valuable volunteer docents.

Looking even more broadly, there is a place where my analogy of an airport control tower is particularly apt, where there is a vast array of mission-related content flying around in search of places to land: on the internet. I must confess that our museum has only very modestly, in a slow and rudimentary manner, scratched the surface of this gold mine of educational treasure. The Fashion Institute of Technology generously allowed us to simulcast their all-day symposium on international costume live from New York. We found real-time lectures on the internet—many live-streamed from overseas—but have yet to marshal the time and energy to fully scour the relevant interviews, symposia, massive open online courses,

Figure 22.2.   Bingata Workshop
Photo courtesy of the George Washington University Museum and The Textile Museum

and videos available. I have no doubt, however, that in the future museums will be increasingly "curating" digital content from partners across
the globe to program their educational spaces—perhaps not unlike operas,
plays, and ballets are fed live to movie theaters today.

Logistics

It helps to have flexible space. Tables with wheels, light enough chairs to
stack and move, and a staff member ready and able to set up a room provide the flexibility necessary to accommodate varying needs for different
educational and social purposes. We equipped our new "multipurpose"
room with a built-in projector and two large monitors wired to cable
television and the internet, so that between programs we could stream
content or even just tune into a music channel for ambience. Some basic
configurations seemed to accommodate most events: lecture-style seating
in rows, tables and chairs for interactive events, and more open arrange-
ments for receptions and social gatherings. It is probably true that at a certain size, fixed auditorium seating may offer better sightlines and perhaps

more capacity, but I suspect we make up in frequency what we may lose in occasional high volume.

The museum opens a bit later than average, 11 am, so that we do not have to close until 7 pm on certain evenings. This allows scheduling after-work groups without incurring the costs of overtime. As for after-hours events, we discourage them by gladly charging exorbitant prices. You would be surprised how many would-be nighttime functions find a way to fit into normal museum hours. This also reduces overtime and helps to protect staff from one of our greatest concerns: burn-out. Requests for space are sorted at weekly facilities meetings so that the logistics of set-up, food requirements, extra security, and other special needs can be established well in advance. We decline the opportunity to host weddings and politely welcome planners of corporate rentals, except for exhibition sponsors, to seek venues elsewhere.

When it comes to scheduling our own legacy programs, we found that establishing templates provides both consistency and flexibility. We established "DC Mondays" and "Textiles at Twelve" every Thursday to offer hour-long informal programs each week. As we find community-based speakers, professors, student projects, videos, performers, and the like, we direct them into these two time-slots: Mondays at noon for Washington history, Thursdays for textiles. Saturday mornings are reserved for rug connoisseurs. We have also produced evening lecture series—same time, same evening of the week, and one printed schedule per theme. Series are better than one-offs because they allow us to build steady audiences, relieving some of the cost and stress of marketing every program individually. They also make unscheduled hours of our public spaces more predictable, maximizing flexibility for university and community groups.

There are a few unpublished priorities that guide us when sorting conflicting requests. Normally, "first come, first served" avoids pitting one group against another. When seeking programs from others, we prefer public programs over private gatherings, and the university community over outside organizations. Events that complement our collections or programs receive special attention, especially if we could potentially develop them into a recurring series (the local Haji Baba club meets here on Saturdays to talk about oriental rugs). But we rarely turn away other proposals, except those for purely social events, parties, or family celebrations. Most of this is no more than common sense, albeit hard work requiring organization, judgment, communication, and tact.

Counter-Intuitions

Accomplished museum professionals have asked me, but what about quality? How can you guarantee content will meet "museum standards"? At face value, I must admit, we cannot. But, then again, when could we? When did our selection of speakers guarantee their brilliance before? Who hasn't programmed a snore-fest or two? All programs come with risk, even those we organize ourselves. What we came to realize is that there is really a better question: Quality compared to what? The very best educational programs ever produced? Then partner-based programming may not be for you. But then how should we consider the space we would otherwise leave unused during most hours the museum is open? Isn't the real alternative not an inspiring oration, but an empty room? Dark. Locked. Irrelevant.

> Accomplished museum professionals have asked me, but what about quality? How can you guarantee content will meet "museum standards"? What we came to realize is that there is really a better question: Quality compared to what?

One could argue that some of these partner groups may not be enough "on mission" to warrant free use of museum space. Perhaps, but we can look at this another way. How much money do we really lose? Yes, we might instead reserve such space for a corporate event or wedding party to vie against restaurants, clubs, and places of worship, but is that really why we exist? Even if a few dollars raised were to buy another lecturer's ticket to town, or rent a bus for another school trip (a very worthy use of funds), are we really better off spending our staff time competing in the hospitality business? Here is a better question: How much might we have spent in advertising to attract to our museum the individual members of groups who asked to use our space? How many ads, billboards, and posters?

This is not as easy as I try to make it sound. Accommodating mission peripheral groups blurs the distinct roles and professional expertise that tend to separate marketing and education functions, potentially leading to internal friction even as we increase the energy levels apparent in our public spaces. Even more challenging, the concept of giving away museum space for free clashes against assumptions that we museum professionals hold tightly and that human nature tells us we must preserve. When we fail to maximize the revenue-generating potential of our programming rooms, we appear, in a business sense, to underutilize resources. To do otherwise, we must prioritize mission over money and affirm our belief in the very purposes that our museums were established in the first place: to serve the public good.

Letting go of programmatic control may tax our instincts even further. We tell ourselves that releasing programming to the custody of partners places at risk the very reputation of our hallowed institution and the standards of "quality" we hold so dear. In practice, co-sponsored activities probably decrease reputational exposure by sharing the risk between museum and partner. But I would submit that the concern is more about evading something else that can be frighteningly difficult for highly trained professionals: placing faith in other people. Fear of the unknown. When we take down the fences we have built around our comfortable spheres of influence, we discover ranges of programmatic possibilities beyond our former reach: New topics and novel formats; activating senses with food and tactile demonstrations; artistic encounters with drama, music, and dance; speakers we may never have dreamed to invite; documentaries, simulcasts, and unlimited content from the world wide web; and access to audiences we had not an earthly clue how to reach. In our experience, we found that partners will surprise far more on the upside than they will ever disappoint. Their contributions can be expansive, revelatory, and uplifting. For whatever could go wrong, the real mistake, at least in our view, would be not to try.

Results

When you are surrounded by change, it can be difficult to comprehend the extent of your own transformation. Our partnerships were nothing more than an extension of existing relationships and a commitment to serve the needs of groups we had not yet met: understand each partner's purpose; offer space, promotion, and logistical support to host an event; open ourselves to diverse proposals; and accept variety and surprise as a means of energizing the routine of normal museum practice. Over time, we hardly noticed what was happening all around us.

About a year after opening, just as we seemed to be establishing a positive reputation for inclusive programs, I received a few notes of "concern" from influential intermediaries who wanted us to engage a certain performing arts group. Apparently, we needed help with our "unimaginative programming" because we did "nothing but lectures." Pondering how our programming strength had been contorted into a weakness, I recalled the slogan of a long-time Dutch friend from the world of business consulting, "facts are our friends." So, we set about the manual labor of counting our programs compared to those of the old TM. They had quadrupled, from around fifty educational events per year to well over two hundred. Legacy programs from the old TM had doubled, thanks in part to the volume generated by weekly "Textiles as Twelve." We also categorized the kinds of offerings we had assembled: workshops, offsite trips, gallery talks, films, festivals, consultations, and, yes, performing arts. As it happens, lectures accounted for less than 50 percent and total performances numbered thirty-nine.

Our friends at the *Hatchett* student newspaper had changed their position by March of 2015, now hailing the new museum as a "cultural center and student hub," detailing how museum-based classes were getting students jobs. Partners themselves became extensions of our public relations. Museums, especially, proved eager to announce our exhibitions and educational programs, as we did theirs, offering our members and core supporters suggestions worthy of their interests while we appeared on a host of other institutions' e-blasts and listservs. And no, they did not steal our donors nor did we theirs.

For me, the most compelling testimonial to the benefits of our approach came when we assembled two simple lists of partners: one from within the university community, the other off campus. I had no idea, nor adequate means of communicating, how many different groups we had engaged: university boards and alumni groups, as well as GW colleges, divisions, and institutes representing curricula ranging from African studies to heart and vascular health to Chinese culture to classics to languages and religious studies, and so much more. Administrative offices from across campus participated: Diversity, Procurement, Research, International Programs, Admissions, etcetera. Student organizations represented Mexico, the Philippines, Turkey, Black Graduate Students, Carlos Slim Scholars, in addition to Indian Bhangra dance companies, acapella singers, jazz bands, student radio, ballroom dancers, theater groups . . . you get the idea.

Beyond the confines of campus, the list expands further: nearly twenty embassies; international nongovernmental organizations, federal offices, Library of Congress, National Endowment for the Arts, and the Peace Corps; museum groups from across the country as well as local partners including Dumbarton Oaks, Hillwood, the Anacostia Museum, the Washington DC Historical Society, and the Smithsonian; museum associations, business groups, craft guilds, textile makers, and other artist groups from as far as South America, South Africa, and Bhutan; the International Conference on Oriental Carpets; and the usual array of local schools and senior living residences. The National Endowment for the Humanities held its fiftieth anniversary dinner under a tent in the courtyard behind the museum and the Corcoran Museum's Women's Committee held their annual gala there as well. The list goes on, toward far more kinds of organizations than any of us could possibly have conceived a strategy to reach.

The surprise of these lists, to me, is that so many of our partners had come to us on their own, by word of mouth. At first, we had to meet people, one-on-one, to recruit speakers, performers, and their constituents. As people discovered benefits of our venue—access to a museum audience, including students and faculty; museum promotion to support theirs; a flexible space with audiovisual support; no-hassle scheduling, a welcoming staff, and no extra charges—we met more potential partners. Then partners referred others so that, over time, our quest for programs gradually became a task of managing requests. Our control tower had become operational; planes want to land on our runway, such that now, at the time of this writing some two and a half years after opening, we finally have scheduling problems and have to turn groups away. We sometimes feel more busy than effective and know we have more to learn. We need to refine our model, target special needs, launch new series, and broaden our impact. Staff and budget have grown, but not nearly enough to meet our aspirations nor serve the various audiences we would so much like to reach, but this is really not about resources, after all.

Looking back, trying genuinely to understand the actual steps that led to our transformation, I realize that what we truly developed was not a system to follow, nor a philosophy to expound, but a simple human and humane skill that we had to discover within ourselves: the ability to trust others.

The Jewish Museum of Maryland   23
Catalyzing Neighborhood Revitalization

MARSHA L. SEMMEL, FROM INTERVIEWS WITH MARVIN PINKERT
AND LINDSAY THOMPSON

BIOGRAPHIES: *MARVIN PINKERT is executive director of the Jewish Museum of Maryland, located in the historic Jonestown neighborhood of Baltimore. Appointed in 2012, he is just the third individual to hold that post. A native of Chicago's South Side, Pinkert was his extended family's tour guide for the Museum of Science and Industry by age seven. After earning degrees at Brandeis (BA, English), Yale (MA, East Asian Studies) and Northwestern (MM Strategy for Non-Profits), Pinkert returned to Museum of Science and Industry in 1988 on assignment to develop a strategic plan. In 1992 he became vice president for programs. He was invited to create the National Archives Experience on the Mall in Washington, DC, in 2000, developing interactive exhibits and a learning lab illustrating the importance of primary sources. In nearly thirty years of museum management, Pinkert has been passionate about the potential of the museum industry to advance public understanding.*

Lindsay Thompson, PhD, is an associate professor with joint appointments at the Carey Business School and the Bloomberg School of Public Health at the Johns Hopkins University in Baltimore, Maryland. Her research and teaching interests center on values, leadership, and social change in business, society, and organizational culture. Her managerial experience includes technical, leadership and consulting roles in health planning and policy, healthcare, higher education, state government, small business, social enterprise, faith communities, and international nongovernmental organizations. A resident of a transitional neighborhood in Baltimore, Thompson collaborates in city-wide efforts to involve businesses, civic organizations, public officials, and private citizens in transforming distressed and abandoned city neighborhoods into thriving urban communities. Her community leadership work includes involvement in the Maryland Humanities Council, Jewish

Museum of Maryland, Archdiocese of Baltimore, Baltimore City Public Schools, and the Jonestown Planning Council.

Introduction

MARVIN PINKERT took over the leadership of the Jewish Museum of Maryland in the summer of 2012. He succeeded Avi Decter, a successful museum director who left the post with a strong record of substantive and popular state-wide programming, as well as the preparation of a needed expansion plan. The museum is located in downtown Baltimore's Jonestown neighborhood, blocks from the Inner Harbor. It interprets Maryland's Jewish history in its landmark historic sites: the Lloyd Street Synagogue, built in 1845, now the nation's third oldest surviving synagogue structure, and B'nai Israel Synagogue, built to house Chizuk Amuno congregation in 1876 and still home to a vibrant Orthodox community. The museum also includes three exhibition galleries featuring diverse exhibitions that explore, in depth, the Jewish American experience in this region. Despite these existing spaces, when Pinkert joined the organization he learned that many members of the museum's Board of Trustees and staff believed that the museum's physical plant needed to expand, especially to include a classroom and auditorium. This plan would be the foundation for a new capital campaign.

An American Alliance of Museums re-accreditation committee evaluating the museum in 2011, however, raised some questions about the justification for the expansion, and some members of the organized Jewish community expressed their own cautions. Why was the museum contemplating expansion when its attendance was low and stagnant? What unique service would the museum be able to provide with a bigger site that could not be accomplished with more efficient use of the existing facilities? As Pinkert noted, "every element of the expansion plan made sense" from a technical perspective (e.g., collections required additional storage), but he could find "no driving story line" that would guide fundraising and elicit the necessary individual and community support. Hence, before developing an alternative expansion plan launching a major fundraising initiative, Pinkert began working with his Board on a new vision to inspire support and convey the museum's purpose and focus.

The museum's official mission, adopted in 2008 prior to Pinkert's arrival, states that the museum:

> collects, preserves, and studies the history and material culture of Maryland Jewry, including two historic synagogues at our Herbert Bearman campus.

Our exhibitions, programs and activities interpret the American Jewish experience, foster cross-cultural understanding, and promote public discourse about issues in Jewish American life.[1]

Rather than change the mission statement, the Board task force directed its attention to a vision that had tangible consequences for institutional priorities.

The vision of the museum is expressed through the "Four D's"[2]:

- Becoming a **Destination**: "An educational attraction—encouraging more visitors to engage in our historic sites, exhibits, and collections; expanding our public offerings and increasing public awareness of the Museum."
- A site of **Documentation**: Providing access to expert "resources for Jewish study and scholarship—adding to our communal depth of understanding of Jewish identity through the preservation and meaningful examination of the experiences of individuals and communities."
- A site of **Discourse**: "a vibrant center for public dialogue and personal enlightenment—using the platform of the Museum for the discussion of issues of vital interest to the Jewish community and as point of community convening in downtown Baltimore."
- A site of **Discovery**: creating "experiences that reflect a broader context for Maryland Jewish history—drawing connections to individuals and groups, events and trends in American history, to contemporary life, and to our hopes and aspirations for the future."

Taking the Four D's as a blueprint, Pinkert more than doubled the hours that the museum was open to the public; tripled the number of public programs, tying most of them to changing exhibits; and hired the first "visitor services" professional. He also curtailed or terminated activities like publications that were not closely tied to the new vision.

But the most important change was a new attitude about the museum's context. Pinkert made the case to the Board that becoming a "destination" involved not only changes in Jewish Museum of Maryland's internal practices and offerings, but even more critically required change in the perception of the urban environment around the museum campus.

A Neighborhood Focus

Jonestown, originally settled in 1661, is the oldest neighborhood in the city and one of the most historic. By the 1840s, when the Lloyd Street Synagogue was built, it was already a haven for new immigrants, most of them German. In the late nineteenth century Eastern European Jews and Italian Catholics had displaced the Germans. By the time the Jewish Historical Society saved the synagogue from the wrecking ball in 1959, the demographics of Jonestown had begun to change again—now evolving as a predominantly African American community. The violence that erupted after the assassination of Dr. Martin Luther King, Jr., accelerated the demographic shift. In 1984, when a handful of philanthropists converted the Jewish Historical Society into the Jewish Museum of Maryland with its own building for exhibitions, it was perceived as alien to its environment. There would be several proposals to move the museum closer to its Jewish constituency or at least to put more of its energy into outreach and less into its home base.

With Board and staff adoption of the Four D's vision statements, Pinkert began a deeper exploration of the museum's historic Jonestown neighborhood, which had never really recovered from the violence of 1968 and which suffered from longstanding public concerns about safety, an absence of parking, a large number of vacant lots, and economic, business, and residential transition. Pinkert joined the Jonestown Planning Council, a committee of nearby St. Vincent de Paul's Church, and worked with community resident (and Johns Hopkins University faculty member) Lindsay Thompson to revitalize the Historic Jonestown Corporation[3] as a nonprofit legal entity representing the interests of the community.

In addition to the Jewish Museum of Maryland, neighborhood partners in Historic Jonestown, Inc., included the Reginald F. Lewis Museum of Maryland African-American History and Culture, the Star-Spangled Banner Flag House, the Carroll Mansion, the Phoenix Shot Tower, and several other small historic houses. The neighborhood is also home to several social service organizations, such as the Helping Up Mission, the Gallery Church, and The McKim Center. Historic Jonestown, Inc., had existed on paper for some time, having originated an urban heritage walk, but it had not met in three years. Nevertheless, it had a charter and legal recognition, as well as, in the person of Lindsay J. Thompson, neighborhood resident and associate professor at the Carey Business School of Johns Hopkins University, a dynamic new president. Thompson formally assumed this position in 2013.

Recognizing the power of the area's historic, commercial, and cultural fabric, Thompson had created, at the Carey School, a laboratory that leveraged the university's intellectual capital, student energy, and insights in order to address Jonestown's revitalization. She understood that this would be a lengthy process, and that it needed to build on the assets of the neighborhood. In her vision, "Instead of seeing addicts and homeless people as losers to be moved, we looked to harness the social service organizations, the museums, and their volunteers in order to create stronger connections between the people who need help and the people who can help." According to Thompson, "Marvin was the first museum person to understand how the neighborhood—with its cultural and social service organizations—had great potential if its assets could be optimized." Thompson notes that Pinkert quickly understood her efforts at revitalizing the neighborhood by bringing together business, social service organizations, and the cultural institutions. "Marvin Pinkert is a visionary who has been very important to this process."[4]

Accordingly, in addition to working with Historic Jonestown, Pinkert began attending the Jonestown Planning Council meetings. He believed that if the museum built with a focus solely on its own buildings, the space within its walls, and its museum-specific needs, it would miss the opportunity to exploit the potential of the surrounding area. He wanted to explore the possibility of rethinking the museum's location by nesting it deeper into the fabric of the neighborhood. The more he learned, the more he saw the museum's fate dependent on the neighborhood's survival. Bringing more people and organizations into the museum's future planning was essential; a multi-institutional collaboration was the ticket.

Anchoring the Collaborative Planning Process

As soon as the Board completed its vision work (about four months after Pinkert's arrival), Pinkert approached the Board's facilities committee with a suggestion: Let's explore the needs of the community before we proceed with a museum plan, and let's begin with an initial investment of ten thousand dollars to launch a visioning planning process for the neighborhood. After the museum made this initial investment, Pinkert would commit to raising another sixty thousand dollars from outside sources. This was a significant decision, as the museum's finances were tight, and the investment would take priority over a number of other critical expenditures. Several Board members were skeptical that any community study would improve the existing expansion plan. Nonetheless consensus was achieved to move forward, and the Board approved the investment.

Although Pinkert was the key organizer of this neighborhood effort, he had allies in Lindsay Thompson, Joe Cronyn (St. Vincent de Paul), and Bob Gehman (Helping Up Mission), as well as representatives of two enterprises contemplating a move to Jonestown, Sandy Pagnotti (Ronald McDonald House), and Keith Barker (Commercial Development).

The initial ten thousand dollars supported a Request for Proposals to select a firm for the planning process. Eventually, two local foundations contributed a total of seventy thousand dollars for this effort.

As part of the visioning process, the winning planning firm Mahan Rykiel Associates of Baltimore (working with Arnett Muldrow Associates of Greenville, South Carolina) held three work sessions (including focus groups and interviews) involving forty stakeholder groups and more than one hundred participants, including residents and representatives of commercial businesses, social service organizations, and cultural institutions. The process was predicated on building on the neighborhood's "rich cultural history, access to public transportation, and clustering of attractions/institutions . . . in a way that is sensitive and responsive to the human and cultural capital already in place."[5] The four-phase Neighborhood Vision & Master Plan (engage, analyze, envision, and plan) emphasized "cultivating collaboration," gathered data on demographics and existing and potential relationships, and created six goals for the plan. In addition to bringing diverse institutions and community members together to consider the future, the process yielded important new knowledge and insights about the physical fabric of the neighborhood, its tangible and intangible assets, and possibilities for synergies. The six goals emerging from the envisioning process were: (a) embrace authentic identity; (b) celebrate service; (c) provide opportunities for engagement; (d) commit to culture; (e) connect the places; and (f) activate with users.

Outcomes

What has transpired since? In October 2015, Pinkert helped announce the creation of a new neighborhood brand and logo—"an American flag modified with references to the area's history with references to the area's history with the tagline, 'Proudly we hail.'"[6]

"As part of the master plan, institutions and community members have reorganized Historic Jonestown Corp. to act as a nonprofit advocate for the plan's implementation and the neighborhood."[7] There are already some burgeoning new economic development efforts. For example, The Ronald McDonald House Charities of Baltimore, Inc., is building a new multi-million-dollar facility. Among the current neighborhood events, there is an annual museum festival and collaborative participation in the annual Light City event. There are new partnerships among some of the social service organizations, with the Helping Up Mission now partnering with the Baltimore Mission, for example. The UA Center, named for its sponsor, Under Armour, (a Baltimore-based company manufacturing footwear and sports and athletic apparel) is now home to a branch of "The Living Classroom," a nonprofit that serves neighborhood youth and uses the surrounding community to enrich their learning experiences. The National Aquarium will create an education center and holding tanks for animals at the neighborhood's Hindley Creamery development. Things are happening.

According to Thompson, Pinkert, working with other museums, has led the charge to

> open the walls of the museums to the neighborhood. . . . There are four centuries of history in this neighborhood. There are centuries of stories of oppression and resilience. The Jewish Museum and our other local museums are in the cradle of Baltimore's history. They are reminders of our culture not only for Jonestown but for the entire city. These small museums are now our anchors as we move forward. Our historic sites and places are now the defining aspects of the character of this neighborhood, and this is not going to change. Whatever we do, these historic places are the anchors of this place and the way forward.

Finally, concluded Thompson, "museums—in their architecture, documents, and collections—have the important symbolic imagery that helps us unpack this history."

And the Jewish Museum of Maryland?

All that talking with neighbors yielded some unexpected results. The discussion in the vision plan about Jonestown's long history of social justice ended up providing a new theme to tie together the elements of a new expansion plan.

The new plan called for the museum to become the steward of a relocated Holocaust Memorial and a center for education about genocide. In developing its plan the Jewish Museum of Maryland was cognizant of the community's need for additional green space and the potential for educational partnerships with neighborhood charter schools and the Living Classrooms' UA Center.

This new expansion plan not only was approved by the Jewish Museum of Maryland Board, it received the endorsement and support of the Associated Federated Jewish Charities of Greater Baltimore, which incorporated the capital/endowment investment into its own three-year Centennial Campaign.

Better still, the conversations with neighbors had revealed a potential prime site for expansion that had not previously been known to be available.

Though much remains unsettled, it appears that Pinkert's gamble on the Jonestown neighborhood is likely to yield results at least two hundred times the value of the original investment in a community study.

Pinkert's Reflections: Trust and Persistence

As Director Pinkert considered this past three to four years, he noted the importance of trust.

> I went out of my way to ensure that everyone knew that this is a not a study for the benefit of the Jewish Museum of Maryland and that I was putting the needs of the community first. Listening was most important. In addition, we planned many checkpoints along the way, where participants could "check in" regarding their engagement in the process.

Of equal importance, noted Pinkert, was the time spent building an increased level of trust with the Associated. The leadership of this group has been essential to the Jewish Museum's future plans. Pinkert stressed the importance of reciprocity:

> It was important to me to help others, including the Associated, addressing their problems, whenever I could. Sometimes this meant simply correcting misperceptions—on the part of the museum and the Federated Jewish Charities—that had simmered, unattended, for years and were easily addressed.

When tackling a project like this, involving many entities and navigating a variety of changes, including key personnel and shifting partner resources, Pinkert advises,

> Persistence helps. When you hit a roadblock (which I have, repeatedly), back up a few steps and consider whether there is another path in front of you. Too often, when we encounter a barrier, we assume that we won't succeed, and we give up. Know when you need to adjust, know which principles you need to uphold, and keep your eye on your ultimate goals.

Conclusion

Museum Director Pinkert has become a key spokesperson for this broader community revitalization effort. Both Pinkert and Thompson understand that this type of collaboration requires a "long haul" mindset. They are sensitive to the importance of process and for all parties to stay strategic, flexible, and keep learning as they go. Thompson, a classicist by training, cited the poem "Ithaka," as she discussed the significance of the journey itself. "Keep Ithaka always in your mind. Arriving there is what you are destined for. But do not hurry the journey at all. Better if it lasts for years, so you are old by the time you reach the island, wealthy with all you have gained on the way, not expecting Ithaka to make you rich."

An Institutional Commitment to a New Model of Community Collaboration

24

ELISABETH CALLAHAN AND KARLEEN GARDNER

BIOGRAPHIES: ELISABETH CALLAHAN is head of multigenerational learning at the Minneapolis Institute of Art (Mia), where she leads a team of staff who develop innovative, audience-centered programs connecting communities with the museum's collections. She is the co-founder of Museum as Site for Social Action (MASS Action), a national initiative dedicated to equity and social justice in museums. Before her current appointment, she served as the manager of adult programs at the Brooklyn Museum, and manager of public programs and public relations at the Memphis Brooks Museum of Art. She holds a BA in art history from the University of Evansville, an MA in fine and decorative art from Sotheby's Institute London, and a certificate in French language and culture from the Institut Catholique in Paris.

Karleen Gardner, director of learning innovation at the Mia, is committed to developing dynamic, meaningful, and thought-provoking museum experiences for all visitors. Gardner leads initiatives and experiments in interpretation and education, and she works to make the museum accessible and relevant for all audiences. She serves as the lead for the Center for Empathy and the Visual Arts at Mia, and has a special interest in developing strategies for engaging visitors and fostering empathy and global understanding through art. Previously, she served as curator of education at the Memphis Brooks Museum of Art. She received a MSEd as a Kress Leaders Fellow in leadership in museum education at Bank Street College in New York City. Gardner also holds a BA and an MA in art history from the University of Mississippi and a BA in English from the University of Southern Mississippi. In 2008, she was selected as the Tennessee Art Education Association's Outstanding Museum Educator of the Year. Gardner served on the board member of the Museum Education Roundtable from 2012 to 2017 and is currently a peer reviewer for the Journal of Museum Education. *She is a frequent presenter at national and international conferences, and she served as the 2018 Outstanding Educator in Residence for the Singapore Teachers' Academy for the Arts, including presenting the keynote lecture at the Singapore Museum Education Symposium.*

THE MIA, founded as an educational and civic institution, has a long-standing commitment to community at the center of our mission. However, we, like many museums across the country, are pushing ourselves to reexamine what we mean by community and what that commitment looks like.

Mia works with many communities, but in recent years we have come to define *our community* as the surrounding geographic area. The museum is fortunate to be situated in the midst of two neighborhoods, Whittier and Phillips, which are among the most demographically diverse in Minneapolis. A total of 45 percent of the population in Whittier and 80 percent of the population in Phillips identify as Latino, black or African American, American Indian, Asian American, or mixed race. In Whittier, 21 percent of the population identifies as foreign born, and in Phillips, this increases to 35 percent.[1] Whereas people of color and indigenous peoples currently comprise a quarter of the Twin Cities' population, by the middle of this century, this figure will be closer to half of the population.[2]

Despite our location, a survey of Mia's visitorship completed in 2016 indicated that our audience did not reflect the diversity of our neighborhood, with only one-fifth of our audience identifying as people of color. In a year when Mia enjoyed record attendance, the highest in our institution's history, the museum was presented a choice: continue to operate in relative isolation among community members who scarcely know or engage with us, or to work harder to prioritize our community to ensure that we are reflective of and relevant to them.

Kaywin Feldman, Mia's Nivin and Duncan MacMillan director and president, has noted, "because we have free admission, and are presumably accessible to everyone, we might have become complacent in truly engaging our diverse communities." She further asserts that, "while the museum's collection is an asset for the community, we must also recognize that the community is an asset for the museum." Our charge as an institution is to question ourselves openly and honestly on why we may not be welcoming to some community members, particularly visitors of color, and to work intentionally and consistently to address this. "If presence has been privileged over absence, what happens if we start attending to absence?"[3]

The following chapter outlines one way Mia is considering this topic through partnerships with a number of neighborhood-oriented community organizations. It describes, in particular, the museum's collaboration with Hope Community Inc., a nonprofit community development organization located near the museum that is nationally recognized as a model for urban change.

A New Strategic Plan

Under Feldman's leadership, Mia embarked upon a new strategic plan for the term of 2016 to 2021. One of the main focus areas of the *Mia2021* plan is "Engaging Communities," which aims to align the museum to better reflect the changing demographics of the Twin Cities in order to foster future institutional relevance and sustainability. The focus area of the *Mia2021* strategic plan centers around three questions:

1. How can we best serve our community-focused mission when the community is changing at a fast pace?
2. How might we better understand the current needs and interests of our community, defined as the people living in neighborhoods surrounding the museum?
3. How does Mia need to change *internally* to best support these efforts?

In a year when Mia enjoyed record attendance, the highest in our institution's history, the museum is presented a choice: continue to operate in relative isolation among community members who scarcely know or engage with us, or to work harder to prioritize our community to ensure that we are reflective of and relevant to them.

To address these questions, Mia is engaging in active listening with community members to gain a deeper understanding of both barriers to participation and the expectations they have for civic institutions. To respond to what we are hearing from these stakeholders, the museum is committing to a multipronged approach. We will **expand our collection** to be more connected to the communities represented in our neighborhood. We will continue to work collaboratively to **co-create** programming and other initiatives based upon the community's needs and wants. To create authentic relationships, we as museum staff recognize that we must be active, **engaged community members**, onsite and offsite, with residents of the Whittier and Phillips neighborhoods. And finally, to support this work, Mia recognizes it must **create an inclusive culture** and develop internal practices that cultivate cultural responsiveness and support equity.

By the conclusion of the strategic plan's timeframe, and with concerted efforts in this area, Mia hopes to see both internal and external indicators of success. Internally, inclusion will be embedded in our organizational culture and practices, and not seen as an isolated program, but a core institutional value.[4] In our public-facing work, Mia is working toward an institution-wide, cross-departmental commitment to our surrounding communities to become a more engaged and responsive resource. As a public institution, it is our mission and our responsibility—and is to our benefit—to be an accessible and essential resource for the community through our collection and programs. We believe that creating active and sustained relationships with our community members will make both the museum and the community stronger.[5]

Museum as Site for Social Action

Mia is not alone in challenging ourselves to address these issues. There are many museums in the United States and abroad that have made, or are in the process of making, similar strategic shifts. To that end, concurrently with the development of our strategic plan, we initiated the three-year MASS Action project to aggregate and amplify some of the work that museums are doing in this area.

In partnership with over a hundred museum practitioners and thirty institutions, this collaborative project is working to align museums with more equitable and inclusive practices. As the museum field begins to shape its identity in the twenty-first century, MASS Action asks institutions to consider what role and responsibility we have in responding to issues affecting our communities locally and globally; and further, to interrogate how internal practices need to change in order to better inform public practice. As part of this project, a toolkit—part theoretical foundation, part practical exercises—was written by museum professionals who are leading the field in this area, and offers strategies, frameworks, and actions needed to address these important topics and to create greater equity and inclusion in our institutions.

MASS Action practitioners assert that, in order to truly transform the museum space and our relationship with the communities around us, two things must first occur. First, we must acknowledge and address the internal organizational changes that are needed to support this work. "Getting our own house in order is essential if there is to be lasting and effective change in our relations with our communities."[6] Secondly, and just as importantly, museums must confront their institution's legacy, recognizing how and why the museum came to be, and for whom. Addressing this point, authors of the first chapter of MASS Action, "Getting Started: What We Need to Change and Why," write:

> How a museum is sited in a given city—its proximity to pedestrian spaces, its access to mass transit, its long views and visual presence—are all signals of who is and is not welcome in the museum space. Likewise, the accessibility of its entrances, the architectural style of its facade, the scale and navigability of its galleries all contain information about the type of visitor the institution expects to receive and, by extension, the type of visitor who is not explicitly made welcome.[7]

Mia is located in a demographically diverse neighborhood with access to public transportation, so the museum is geographically accessible to many. However, in conversations with community members, we have come to understand that the museum's architecture itself, with its Beaux-Arts façade, is perceived to some as unwelcoming and inaccessible. It is not enough to be a well-located museum with free admission if neighbors do not feel invited in.

In addition to physical structure, historical and social context also informs the conditions under which museums are created and how their roles and purposes are defined. Institutions cannot separate themselves from the collective memories that link their development with structural racism, colonization, historical theft of art and artifacts, abuse of labor, and the destruction or absencing of narratives and alternative interpretations. We must recognize that a "range of emotions necessarily arises for the diverse cultural communities and geographies negatively impacted by this history."[8]

This is particularly relevant to Mia, as the land on which we operate and the collection we display was built on traditional lands of the Dakota people and currently rests a mile away from Little Earth, the largest urban population of Native Americans in the country. How could we propose to build authentic, meaningful relationships within the Native American communities without first acknowledging this legacy? Additionally, a large portion of our local community are of Latin American and East African descent, and yet we have very few objects in the collection that represent the cultures and stories of these populations. How can we expect to build and sustain equitable relationships in these communities without first acknowledging how the lack of representation and cultural exclusion impacts their perceived value within the museum?

A museum must come to accept that its legacy and the subsequent manifestation of its history are real—seen and understood by its communities—and that this no doubt has an impact on patterns of visitorship and engagement, particularly among communities of color.[9] Therefore, it is essential that we acknowledge and accept these realities before we establish relationships within our community; they must inform our actions, intentions, and approach to the foundation of partnerships. *This process of critical self-examination takes time and intention and will occasionally be painful.*[10] This work has indeed been challenging for Mia at times; however, we understand that doing this hard work will help us build and sustain meaningful relationships, leading to long-lasting impacts on both the institution and the community of which we are a part. Therefore, with Feldman's leadership, and under the directives of the *Mia2021* strategic plan, our participation in the MASS Action initiative is creating institutional conversation around our practices and driving the creation of new approaches to both our internal work, as well as our work outside our walls.

Forging a New Kind of Partnership

While encouraging our community to both feel comfortable visiting the museum and empowering them to use the museum as a space to socialize, dialogue, and view and make art are objectives of Mia's ongoing work, we recognize to accomplish these goals means first becoming an active, engaged neighbor and participant in our community to build and earn residents' trust. We must step outside our own walls, supporting work that is, as staff from Hope Community Inc. often describe, "place-based, but not relegated to place."

Though Mia has been bringing art outside its walls for many years through its Art in the Park series, the museum's efforts, historically, have been largely one-off or event-based projects efforts, *transactional* in nature, and not the sustained, ongoing relationships needed for real *transformational* change. To create the environment and structures to support these kinds of relationships would entail a radical departure from our previous structures and models of practice. With the establishment of our relationship with Hope, the museum took a step toward more sustained art-based community work in the neighborhood, and this significant partnership and its vision has now become embedded and woven into the fabric of both of our organizations.

About Hope Community: Celebrating its fortieth year of operation, Hope has established a vital presence in the Whittier–Phillips neighborhoods and has created a critical mass of affordable housing and community-building spaces in the area. The organization is known for its extensive experience and capacity in organizing, building leaders, and supporting community change.

About the Neighborhood: As outlined in Mia's strategic plan, the Whittier and Phillips neighborhoods are vibrant, diverse areas, rich in cultural assets and histories. However, in the mid-twentieth century, the neighborhoods were bisected by a highway and rezoned for business developments, weakening a sense of connection and collective identity in the area. To those from outside the area, they are often seen as "drive through" neighborhoods—places that thousands of people pass through on their way elsewhere, with little understanding of these communities and their cultures. These communities are currently facing major challenges related to future highway reconstruction and concerns of possible gentrification and displacement. Through Hope-led listening sessions, we have learned that people in our neighborhoods want to do all they can to strengthen their connections to one another, to be visible in public processes that impact their communities, and make their neighborhoods places where they are able to continue to live, learn, work, and enjoy.

How Our Partnership Began

Though our two organizations have had some initial conversations over the years, Mia educators began discussions with Hope organizers in earnest in 2015 to learn more about their community-building strategies and to find potential opportunities for partnership. Hope staff were initially cautious, even skeptical, about entering into a partnership with an institution like Mia. While the museum was *talking* about its intention to be more inclusive and community-centered, to many in the community, we still had not yet *shown* real evidence of this commitment. *The museum recognized that we needed community to fulfill our mission and stay relevant, but we had to ask ourselves—after years of perceived and real exclusion, does our community need the museum?* As our director noted, we must do more than offer free admission and expect our community to appear at our door. For Mia, as for other large, predominately white art museums, which have historically been dedicated to aesthetic rather than social concerns, engaging with community members involves showing a long-term commitment to inclusion.

Our relationship developed over time with informal conversations—meeting over coffee once a month to learn more about one another's work, to share upcoming projects and initiatives, and to share successes we were having in our areas and challenges we were facing. Through continued conversations, we began to build trust and establish the foundations of a partnership, finding alignment in our commitment to these neighborhoods, our respect for the histories they represent, and for the people who live here. Recognizing the strengths each organization offers, Hope and Mia staff began to discuss the possibilities and opportunities for a long-term relationship supporting community-centered, art-based initiatives.

In the summer of 2015, we launched our first collaborative community mural, pairing an artist from Hope's longstanding *Power of Vision* mural program with our community partner Centro Tyrone Guzman, a Phillips-based, multiservice community resource for Latinx families. Mia had previously partnered with a group of elders from Centro on an art installation, a crocheted coral reef, which had gone well, and we were looking for other ways to work together. For the mural project, a group of women, all of whom recently migrated to Minnesota from Mexico and Central America, worked together throughout the summer to create a visual representation of pressing issues affecting their lives. They connected with one another through the stories of the losses and violence many had suffered in their home countries, the hardships they faced crossing the border, and the discrimination they experience here in the United States. They also bonded over the individual strength they identified in themselves as women, and the collective strength they found in this group. The resulting mural, on one of Centro's external walls, reflects the group's concerns about human rights and justice for all (im)migrants. To evaluate the program's success, we used a set of indicators to measure our progress toward projected impacts of increased confidence, visual literacy, and skills-building in the participants. In all of these dimensions, we found that this partnership project was deeply successful and would serve as a pilot for Hope and Mia's future work together, providing the vision and foundation for a larger initiative.

Art for Radical Collaboration

In 2016, Hope and Mia staff attended a convening hosted by the Institute of Museum and Library Services and the Local Initiatives Support Corporation to hear a report on their collaborative research project, which explored the role that cultural organizations can play in community revitalization. The premise of the report was that museums and libraries can "magnify their public value by playing a supporting, and sometimes a leading, role in community-wide change efforts."[11] Through this comprehensive study of museum and library initiatives, they identified five key dimensions of effective and rewarding engagement practice, which distinguish these community-based approaches from the more episodic partnerships that are typical of institutions.[12] These characteristics are:

- A full, institutional commitment to the effort;
- An approach co-created between partners;
- A network of partners aimed toward achieving collective impact;
- Significant staff and financial resources dedicated to the efforts; and
- Continual, sustained efforts over time.

With these attributes from the Institute of Museum and Library Services and the Local Initiatives Support Corporation report in mind, and with one major pilot program complete, Hope and Mia began developing the idea for **Art for Radical Collaboration (ARC)**. The goal of this initiative[13] is to engage community members in a creative process that combines arts-based community-building strategies, and community-based models of art practice, to build individual capacity and power and to advance social cohesion and civic engagement.

Why Art?: The emphasis on art as a tool for creating this work is based on our shared belief that art has the power to bring people together, to give voice to community hopes and concerns, and to imagine solutions. It is among Mia's core beliefs that the arts have the power to engage, connect, and transform those who encounter it. "Art sparks curiosity and creativity, breaks down barriers, connects across cultural differences, engages our individual and shared values, and fosters empathy."[14] Therefore, we believe the art museum has the unique opportunity—and carries the responsibility—to use art-making experiences and the art in our collection to leverage this attribute of art. Hope, too, shares in the belief of art as a vehicle for change-making.

> Art is a universal medium, and everyone is an artist in some way. It can move people through emotions, especially those who feel voiceless. Throughout our work we use art and culture to bring people's experience into policy and system challenges, to bring people who feel isolated into the center, to prepare, to communicate and to celebrate.[15]

What Is Radical Collaboration?: Rather than the *illusion* of collaboration—where one person or organization allows for input from another, but retains final authority—we wanted to center a *real* collaborative effort, between Hope and Mia, the organizations and our community, and among community members. Borrowed from the principles of design thinking, radical collaboration is an action-oriented, solutions-focused (rather than problems-focused) approach. It embraces the inclusion of multiple perspectives and speaks to the power that true co-creation has to drive the kind of innovations that can address systemic, far-reaching issues.[16] Our radical collaboration demands that we come to the table as equal partners, acknowledging that everyone has their own expertise. Therefore all collaborators should bring their authentic, intentional selves to the work. This kind of collaboration is important on an individual level, but it also essential on an institutional level to help counterbalance the power dynamic that often shows up in community work.

In addition to arts-based strategies and radical collaboration, we are also employing two additional frameworks to help guide and support this work: collective impact and place-keeping.

Collective Impact: To take this idea of radical collaboration one step further, through ARC we are building a network of cross-sector partnerships with organizations representing wide-ranging areas of experience and expertise (education, health, human services, housing, racial justice) to amplify one another's work along a collective impact model.[17] Because many issues facing communities are complex and systemic, it is believed that a collaborative and coordinated systems approach is needed to support change-making around them.[18]

Place-Keeping: Anticipating that concentrating our efforts in a specified location would realize greater impact, we identified a ten-block (one square mile) area around Mia and Hope to focus on, which we identified by walking the area, using the footpath and bridge that connect the Whittier and Phillips neighborhoods across I-35, and finding the natural boundaries that form around it.

The idea of using arts-based strategies for community engagement within a concentrated area is often associated with "creative place-making." However, this term and process can be interpreted as the need to *make* a place, or to make something of a place that has little value. Gentrification is sometimes the unintended result of this approach, and the nexus of power, money, and art focused on an area when community input and histories are not valued. Mia and Hope will instead approach ARC with the viewpoint of creative place-*keeping*, where the future of a place builds on the history, strengths, and cultures that ground those who make up the community, and where solutions are identified and generated by residents.[19] There is no one more qualified to address community issues than community members themselves. The belief that "people are experts in their own lives" is one of Hope's guiding tenets. As Chaka Mkali, Hope's director of community organizing, has described it, "Those most affected by a problem are best equipped to solve it."[20]

Accordingly, ARC takes a community-generated approach to solutions-finding that emphasizes inclusiveness and active participation amongst residents in the area. This approach builds community capacity and increases people's sense of ownership and involvement in their community, using creative place-keeping strategies to sustain healthy communities as sites of engagement, inclusion, and imagination.

Project Design: Outputs, Outcomes, and Evaluation

Programming

ARC is unique for Mia because, unlike traditional partnerships, which might be managed or coordinated by one staff member, this partnership involves a team from each organization. Mia and Hope staff from all areas and levels of the organization regularly interact. The relationship was fostered in its earliest stages, on Mia's side, by the director of learning innovation, the head of multigenerational learning, and the community arts associate. As the partnership began to take shape, Mia reorganized the Multi-Generational Learning department, refocusing staff priorities in order to create capacity for ARC and other community-generated initiatives, and now has a dedicated staff person to catalyze and support these initiatives in our manager of community arts position. On Hope's side, the director of community organizing and the executive director were the initial stakeholders. In the second year of the partnership, a new staff position, community resilience organizer, was created and serves as a facilitator for many ARC initiatives. In addition, staff from both Hope and Mia are brought in to collaborate on various projects that require their expertise. Mia has a team of staff involved who are experienced in building partnerships, skilled at object-based gallery facilitation and developing art experiences to foster Mia learning goals—creativity, critical thinking, global awareness, and empathy—for people of all ages. Hope staff who are involved have significant experience and capacity in organizing, building and supporting community leadership and community change, and facilitating arts-based experiences. Both organizations also share a roster of talented teaching artists who we work with for many of our programs.

This team-based approach created momentum in a relatively short amount of time. There are currently many activities and efforts connected to ARC, but the basic elements are relationship building, listening/dialogues, co-created programming, and large-scale public art projects.

Relationship Building: Establishing a network of cross-sector partners, artists, and community members to work collaboratively toward collective impact.

Community Listening: Hope is known for their comprehensive approach to organizing and facilitating community listening dialogues. These take a number of forms, but the same framework is applied each time. Starting each project with listening ensures that the direction is coming from the participants.

Community-Generated Programming: A variety of programming, co-created with community artists, organizations, and residents, is regularly offered at Mia and in the neighborhood. Over the past two years, these ranged from conversations on topics such as the intersections of art and social justice, food equity, or racial justice and representation; gallery programming, like Grassroots Gallery Circles, a model developed by a Mia educator that is co-hosted with a community member or organization using art to discuss a relevant topic; events for all ages, like Somali Family Night; or art-making workshops held in public parks and other areas. Some of these take place once; others span the course of months, such as the summer-long series of *Dia de los Muertos* workshops we held with Centro Tyrone Guzman, resulting in a large-scale community *ofrenda* ("offering," a collection of objects placed on a ritual altar during the celebration) displayed at the museum. Many of these programs were already happening in various capacities; we just refocused energies in the neighborhood and aligned them with the goals of ARC.

Power of Vision **Community Mural Program:** Perhaps our largest-scale endeavor in terms of time and investment is the community mural program. Each summer, Hope and Mia undertake two mural projects, pairing an established artist from the neighborhood with a group of community members—artists and others who may not yet think of themselves as artists—to create a large-scale public work of art, which provides a platform for residents to make their voices heard and to make their ideas and identities visible. Over a three-month period, participants connect across cultural differences, share personal stories, take field trips to mural sites across the city to get ideas, visit the museum for inspiration, and learn basic painting techniques. Following this, students create a master sketch and paint the final image at the mural site over several weeks. Over the past few years, we have worked with three groups of elders and teens from Centro, two groups from St. Stephens Human Services (an organization serving adults experiencing homelessness), and most recently, a group of teens from the Somali, Latinx, and Native communities of Phillips and Whittier.

As this work enters its third year, we are thinking about sustainability for ARC, so we are developing two new elements that will serve as platforms or catalysts for future community-generated projects:

Emerging Community Artists Program: To build capacity in human capital, Mia and Hope are currently designing a training program for emerging artists from the area, which will be taught by staff from several partner organizations with expertise in topics ranging from curriculum development to racial equity. Participants will develop new models for an artistic practice that combine methods from the arts, activism, and community organizing, in order to cultivate innovative approaches to engaging with their neighbors and community issues.

Micro-enterprise: To build economic sustainability for these projects, we are also exploring a model of arts-based entrepreneurial opportunities for community members.

Evaluation

In our earliest conversations on the topic, Hope and Mia began framing ARC around the idea of the personal, connective, and collective. The *Personal* addresses the impact this work has on the individual level—the changes in knowledge skills, attitudes, and behaviors. *Connective* references the impact made on the organizational level, the shift in our ability to collaborate with one another and with our community, and the impact on residents' perception of Mia as an engaged neighborhood participant. Finally, *Collective* is the element of impact ARC has on a community level and the social well-being, community cohesion, and civic engagement of the neighborhood.

The project design was somewhat based in a "theory of change" model wherein we define long-term outcomes, break down assumptions, and then design a strategy of approaches to achieve the intended impacts. We

are measuring our progress toward those outcomes using a set of indicators to determine whether the theory underlying the project is correct.[21]
(For example, if a desired outcome is that residents will be more civically
engaged, one possible indicator of this is that we will see an increasing
voter registration rate.) We helped articulate and visualize this process using the format of a logic model to organize our inputs, activities, outputs,
and outcomes.[22] As the best way to measure many of these outcomes is
to talk directly to participants, evaluation tools include surveys, feedback
interviews, and listening sessions (see Table 24.1). It will also include looking at quantitative data about number of participants, as well as external
quantitative data from public records, over time.

Outcomes

Reproduced in the table are the outcomes from the logic model that our
Hope–Mia team developed for individual participants and community impact, which are based on initial feedback from Hope listening sessions, as
well previous research on the social impact of arts participation.[23]

Challenges

Just as the issues that community members are addressing are complex
and systemic, this work, too, is complex—and it pushes the museum to
examine and shift our current systems and modes of operating. This has
caused discomfort for staff at times. As with any project, challenges will
arise, even more so when the project involves creating new ways of evaluating, staffing, and collaborating. In the following, we have outlined some
of the challenges we are facing and the learning that continues to emerge
as a result.

Reporting: As is evident from our projected outcomes, we are working toward big-picture, sustainable systems change. At the moment, traditional museum operations and funding models are not necessarily set up to
support this kind of ongoing work. Here are a few things we have noticed
as we have reported evaluation results to funders, board, and leadership.

First, the impacts of this work will emerge over a relatively long period of time. In the short term, we can evaluate the performance of our
individual programs, but how do we show the progress we are making (or
not) toward our long-term goals in the interim? One of our challenges has
been how to identify and articulate medium-term outcomes—the middle
range between individual program impact now and large-scale community
impact many years in the future.

Table 24.1.

OUTCOME	Individual	Connective	Collective
Artistic/Creative Capacity	Participants experience an increase in creativity and decrease in barriers to artistic expression associated with self, identity, ability, and relationships. Art-making reveals new ideas, ways of thinking, and possibilities and plans for change.	Organization is better prepared to employ art, creative expression, and cultural opportunities as an active contributor to community solution-finding.	Community art projects make community identities visible, voices heard, illuminate issues, and inspire further social or community action toward a shared goal.
Human Capital/Leadership Development	Participants exhibit increased skills (artistic, communication, solution-finding) and confidence, empowerment, and sense of self-efficacy to take action.	Increased ability in communicating, collaborating, and co-organizing.	Shifts in who holds leadership positions. Development of local enterprise.
Civic Engagement Activism, Advocacy	Resident is more engaged in civic life and concerns. Has awareness of issues impacting the community. Feels that they know how to take action, and is making changes that are needed.	Organization is taking intentional action that that serves a civic or social purpose/good. Offers programs, services, or resources that address community needs.	Community is taking intentional and collaborative action to bring about civic or social change. Is more involved in planning and design for policy and public spaces.
Social Cohesion	Decrease in social isolation. Feel more engaged with and connected to neighbors. Increase in inter-cultural and inter-generational understanding. Increased sense of belonging and pride in neighborhood.	Organization is better prepared to sustain comprehensive collaborations with community partners across multiple sectors. Residents feel more engaged connected to museum. Mia is a valued, trusted community partner and resource.	Shared and strengthened sense of community identity. Greater sense of trust and solidarity.

Another challenge is how to measure and quantify the "soft outcomes," such as building relationships between people or organizations, which in some cases are just as important as the formal activities and outcomes.[24] We can state that much of the first year, and a good percentage of time in these following years, has been dedicated to this foundational, though difficult to quantify, work.

One final thing to note is that there is no way to measure direct causality with this work, as there are too many potential variables (a dramatic shift in the economy or major municipal or national events, for example) to absolutely attribute the cause. Depending on the funder or type of museum, this may not satisfy. Despite that, we believe, and research supports, that positive *correlations*—"strong suggestive evidence of the relationship"[25]—can be made between program activities and project outcomes in this kind of work.[26]

Time and Commitment: While institutions traditionally plan projects within discrete windows of time—funding cycles, exhibition dates, etcetera—a community-based practice cannot operate with an end date in mind. This became clear to us in one of our early planning meetings for a three-year grant, when Mia staff began to sketch out a three-year timeline of activities. Mary Keefe, former executive director of Hope stopped us to say, "But what is our 20- to 30-year plan?" She reminded us that, even though we may be talking about a grant with a finite funding period, we must think about this work within a much larger, intentional context.

White-led institutions often reach out to communities of color for grants or exhibitions for finite periods of time, only to drop them months later when the opportunity (program, exhibition, etc.) has ended. This cycle creates exhaustion and distrust, and we must commit ourselves to ending this harmful pattern. This work does not have a beginning, middle, and end; it is ongoing, and thus our commitment to it needs to be as well. This represented a challenging shift in our way of thinking—from transactional to transformational—but eventually came to inform not only our approach to this partnership, but the way we structured our strategic plan, as well.

Additionally, we have come to understand—and this cannot be emphasized enough—that this work takes time. Be prepared and allow adequate time and space for this work. Learning about a community or organization's culture, communication style, and preferences while establishing a relationship takes much more staff time than is typically allotted to traditional programming.

Contribution to Collaboration: Successful partners know that at various times on that journey the partnership will be tested, and that those tests will not only measure the strength and resiliency of the partnership, but will also become the crucible upon which the strength and resiliency of the collaboration will be forged."[27]

While Mia educators and community arts staff were committing to deeper models of collaboration in their work, many museum staff were more accustomed to a model of *contribution*.[28] Contribution is defined as soliciting feedback and input from outside sources, but retaining control over the final product. This was illustrated to us during a funding application: Hope gave us some language to use for the grant narrative, and we rewrote and submitted it with language more aligned with our "institutional voice." This language took a deficit-based approach to describing the neighborhood (focusing on needs), which was in direct conflict with the asset-based approach (focusing on assets/"gifts"/capabilities) that Hope uses. This was the way that the museum had worded grant applications for many years, and we made assumptions about what kind of language the funders wanted. Needless to say, this bred mistrust about the museum's orientation and intent with our partners at Hope. We had a frank conversation, wherein Mia shared our willingness to withdraw the grant application—reinforcing that our long-term partnership was more important than this short-term grant—and through that open discussion, we eventually began to reestablish that trust. In hindsight, our honest discussions, and willingness to recognize where we need new capacities, has strengthened our relationship and helped Mia become more mindful of the new paradigm in which we are operating. A secondary result of this experience is that any Mia or Hope staff who participate in this project now do so with the expectation of fully modeling—and practicing—collaboration and co-creation.

Making It Personal: This project has highlighted staff capacities and new ways of working that are needed to fully embrace and support this work, and the space and time to do so. To truly create radically new models of collaboration, we must also radically shift the way we have been operating for the past one hundred years. Our former silos and structures of work must also change. Perhaps one of our biggest challenges is how to ensure that all museum staff become stakeholders in this work, rather than being housed solely in education or "community outreach" departments or staff positions. How do we ensure that this work is not fringe, but rather seen as core? By making an explicit commitment to this work through its strategic plan, Mia has certainly made an essential first step in this direction. From there, as with any new initiative, sharing information and finding ways to connect and make this work relevant to all departments is key. For certain projects, this is still largely the responsibility of educators, but we are seeing increased interest from curators and other colleagues on how to connect this to their work. Our involvement in the MASS Action project has also provided an opportunity to connect with, share progress, and learn from a coalition of museums who are seeking to make similar shifts in their internal operations.

But ultimately, this work—from the strategic plan directives to the work around the ARC—is far more personal than other kinds of projects. It therefore requires a personal, and professional, commitment. Becoming a more culturally responsive practitioner starts with the internal work and self-reflection that we must do as individuals. Becoming a more active participant in our community is also an individual responsibility. It is meaningless to say that "the museum" needs to be more engaged with our neighborhood if staff are not participating—because the museum *is* its staff as much as its collection and brand. We, as staff, are therefore coming to understand the importance and necessity of "showing up." We must be intentional about our process, modeling what we want to see. Here, again, our strategic plan has created an opening for this to be embedded in each employee's work, just as it has been embedded into performance evaluations and into our goal-setting process as an institution. This may represent a deep shift in practice for many, and may look differently for different departments, so Mia leadership are still navigating as to how to make this consistent and equitable across the institution.

Conclusion

All of the challenges we have faced through this work have brought with them opportunities for learning and for growth. Our partnerships through ARC, under the direction of the *Mia2021* strategic plan and our involvement in MASS Action, has been a deeply rewarding experience for Mia staff. As a result of these and other ongoing efforts, we have begun to see shifts in the museum's and community's perceptions. We have established a strong network of community partners and stakeholders, and the number of museum visitors of color has increased. Mia staff are becoming more culturally responsive, are more aware of community concerns, and our colleagues outside of our education department are increasingly taking our communities into account in their planning and looking for additional op-portunities for collaboration.

If this is a journey, in many ways, Mia has just gotten started. There is a long road ahead of us, and we acknowledge there will likely be many more challenges to face and to learn from as we go. However, we are commit-ted to this work and excited about the direction in which we are heading.

Partnership 3.0   **25**
The Case of the Oregon Museum of Science and Industry

MARSHA L. SEMMEL, FROM INTERVIEWS WITH NANCY STUEBER,
KYRIE KELLETT, LAUREN MORENO, AND MARCIE BENNE

BIOGRAPHIES: NANCY STUEBER is the president of the Oregon Museum of Science and Industry (OMSI) and has served in this capacity since 2000. She has led the development of the organization's twenty-year vision and the accompanying strategic plan focused on mission impact and performance measures. During her tenure, she has led OMSI to financial stability, significantly increased attendance and membership, acquired land for future expansion, and extended statewide reach with a new marine science camp in Newport, Oregon. Stueber has a passion for involving people in science learning, engaging the community, and working to remove barriers to access so that everyone can participate.

Kyrie Kellett, CIP, is a senior learning and community engagement specialist at OMSI and interpretive planning consultant in Portland, Oregon. She specializes in developing new exhibits, programs, and federal grants in collaboration with community partners. She is a National Association for Interpretation Certified Interpretive Planner with over twenty years of experience developing learning experiences for science museums, the National Parks Service, arboreta, environmental organizations, and outdoor youth programs. Her work focuses on the interface of science and culture, building on a bachelor of arts in environmental studies and physics from Whitman College and a master of arts in applied anthropology from Northern Arizona University.

Marcie Benne, PhD, is trained to involve community members in the design of experiences and systems that support their success and well-being. Her motivation is to help people pursue their curiosities and contribute their talents in ways that are meaningful to them. Benne is currently the director of engagement research and advancement at OMSI, where her team involves learners—particularly those that have not been involved with OMSI—in partnership, staff, co-development, and participatory research opportunities related to exhibits and programs. Benne is a founding member of the Informal Learning Leadership Collaborative, a former Visitor Studies Association board member, and a regular facilitator of creative self-expression workshops in her local community.

Lauren Moreno, associate with Catalysis LLC, enjoys guiding collaborative teams to envision, develop, and implement strategic plans and initiatives that better organizations and communities. Prior to joining Catalysis LLC, Moreno served as director of strategic partnerships and programs at OMSI. She has extensive experience leading partnership efforts and designing science communication professional development programs for STEM professionals. She was instrumental in launching Portal to the Public, a nationally renowned framework and network of organizations that connects STEM professionals with public audiences in meaningful conversations. She has served as principal investigator for National Science Foundation funded grants, including Designing Our World, a project designed to empower girls to pursue engineering careers by exploring the collaborative, personal, and altruistic aspects of engineering in partnership with community-based organizations. Moreno's belief in the power of collective action and dedication to facilitating inclusive stakeholder engagement grounds her work.

Introduction: Strategic Plan and Future Visioning

OMSI IS THE LARGEST science center in the state of Oregon, with an annual budget of more than twenty million dollars, serving more than one million people in 2017. In recent years, the museum has evolved its partnership strategies and approaches as it has aligned its assets and goals with a sustained commitment to addressing the needs of diverse communities across the state. OMSI has also honed an understanding of its role in the state's formal and informal science learning ecosystem. Nancy Stueber, at the museum since 1982 and president and chief executive officer since 2000, has worked with board and staff to lead this organizational evolution.

The museum's current twenty-year vision and 2015 to 2020 strategic plan were built on a clear mission and organizational values. OMSI's missions: "Inspire curiosity through engaging science learning experiences, foster experimentation and the exchange of ideas, and stimulate informed action."[1] Its twenty-year vision:

> OMSI, collaborating with partners, will ignite an education transformation at the intersection of science, technology and design, and weave a thriving innovation district into the fabric of Portland, that spreads opportunities across the Northwest.[2]

The planning process brought together OMSI board members and staff as well as results from numerous in-house and community listening sessions. The results reflected a changed orientation to the internal and external museum stakeholders.

Each of the plan's four strategic priorities—state-wide outreach; the development of the museum's Portland campus, known as the OMSI district; "Museum 3.0: Enhancing the Guest and Employee Experience"; and increased contributed income—makes partnership a key strand. The priorities position the museum at various intersections and connecting points, within the city of Portland, the state of Oregon, and the entire Northwest.

A partnership orientation—including local, state-wide, and national collaborations—has deep roots in OMSI's history. One could say that partnerships are part of OMSI's DNA. This chapter highlights a few examples that illustrate the OMSI partnership approach, its evolution, and its integration throughout the museum.

It draws on 2017 interviews with museum President and Chief Executive Officer Nancy Stueber; Marcie Benne, director of engagement research and advancement; Lauren Moreno, former director of strategic partnerships and programs; and Kyrie Kellett, senior learning and community engagement specialist. The examples herein are only a sampling of many and diverse OMSI-related partnerships past and present.

A Culture of Partnerships: Early Examples

Nancy Stueber's first position at OMSI was director of community programs (1982 to 1989); she was vice president for exhibits and played other roles at the museum, including interim president, from 1987 to 1999. The museum had a robust exhibition program, and each of its exhibition projects involved collaboration. For example, Marilyn Eichinger, OMSI president (1985 to 1995), led the Exhibits Research Collaborative (ERC). *Seeking Synergy: Creating a Museum Collaborative That Works*, by Victoria Crawford Coats (OMSI, c. 1994), grew out of the ERC and documented the museum's experience with and guidance for collaborative efforts and examined the benefits and pitfalls of museum collaborations.

The lessons learned from the ERC were applied to a subsequent, OMSI-led, collaborative enterprise. The Small Museum Research Collaborative was established by OMSI in 2004 and lasted for eight years. Funded principally by the National Science Foundation, Small Museum Research Collaborative's purpose was "to create, test, and circulate new small exhibitions and to better understand and serve small museum audiences."[3] The partners, thematically and geographically diverse, included Bootheel Youth Museum, Malden, Missouri; Kidzone Museum, Truckee, California; Las Cruces Museum of Natural History, Las Cruces, New Mexico; the Palouse Discovery Science Center, Pullman, Washington; and ScienceWorks Hands-On Museum, Ashland, Oregon.[4]

During her early years at OMSI, Stueber noted that collaborations, mostly programmatic, were grant-funded, soft-money dependent, and therefore often time-limited and not sustainable. In its most recent OMSI strategic plan, the museum has changed that approach, embedding many of its partnership and community engagement activities deep within its strategic priorities, core operations, and budget. While the museum still seeks (and receives) foundation, corporation, and government grant support, it has adopted a longer-term project horizon for its key partnership initiatives—as well as a different relationship-building process. "It's analogous to building a road," Stueber noted. "With our partnerships and community engagement strategies, we are building a foundation, part of an infrastructure that we hope will carry lots of partnership 'traffic' in the years to come."

Stueber attributed some of the changes in its collaborative approach to the work of the Noyce Leadership Institute (NLI), a multiyear, international, executive leadership program created by the Noyce Foundation in Palo Alto for senior leaders in science-based organizations, especially science centers. The focus of the NLI included building individual self-awareness, adaptive leadership skills, and effective community engagement, with each fellow completing an institution-based strategic community engagement project as part of the institute curriculum. While she had not been a member of any of the seven NLI cohorts, Stueber did serve as sponsor for three OMSI-based Noyce Fellows, a role that included significant involvement in the program. According to Stueber, that experience—as well as the organizational contributions of fellows Ray Vandiver, Marcie Benne, and Jamie Hurd—"shaped my thinking in a deep way, especially about community engagement." Drawing on the tenets of the NLI, the museum has moved from partnerships based on limited duration grant funding to building lasting relationships. This approach, according to Stueber, "forces us to be strategic" in our collaboration decisions. It has also changed the dynamics of the partnership development process.

In addition, the museum has worked with Listen for Good, a nonprofit developing "net promoter scores" for social impact, to develop measurable outcomes for each goal in the strategic plan. Each outcome has a data pipeline and a concurrent visual display, and results are shared regularly with all OMSI staff. "We set up metrics to determine if we are delivering what was expected and if we are making an impact."

A Coastal Presence

Newport, a coastal community, is 133 miles from OMSI's home base in Portland. In 2012, OMSI decided to build a residential camp to consolidate its marine science education programs into a purpose-built, OMSI-owned facility on the Oregon coast, selecting Newport as the location for a Coastal Discovery Center at Camp Gray. OMSI had operated outdoor science education programs in residential camp settings for more than seventy years. They align with the museum's mission by providing immersive, science learning experiences in the natural world that apply what was learned in the classroom. Research has shown that the residential camp setting builds self-confidence, teamwork, and identity as successful learners. Moreover, Oregon had long had Outdoor School as part of the sixth-grade curriculum with OMSI a dominant resource for those programs, as well as school-based three- to five-day programs for all grade levels.[5] In 2016, Oregon voters passed a statewide initiative, Outdoor School for All, which allocated funding from the state budget to school districts. This has increased the demand for residential programs, and OMSI was well positioned to meet it with the increased bed capacity at Camp Gray. OMSI estimated that it would serve one hundred thousand campers at Camp Gray alone over the next twenty years.

This facility would consolidate the museum's coastal camps and complement the existing high desert programming at Camp Hancock located in the John Day Fossil Beds National Monument in central Oregon. The museum recognized its expansion into a small, rural community would be a challenge. They would need to build trust with organizations, especially science- and environmentally related organizations, and other members of the civic, business, and nonprofit community in Newport. As it moved forward with the capital campaign for the center, the museum embarked on a "friend-raising" and listening process within the community. As Stueber noted,

> Two years before we broke ground on our facility, we held a board retreat in Newport. The Executive Director of the Oregon Community Foundation (OCF) helped facilitate a convening with community leaders and members of the OMSI Board of Trustees. The OCF director urged us to go beyond sheer politeness and to candidly express our concerns, as well as our hopes.

Some of the concerns included whether the museum would compete with other area attractions, for funding or customers, especially those focusing on science and the environment.[6] "Before breaking ground, we connected with communities throughout Newport and Lincoln County, listening to the needs of local businesses, schools, tribal members, families, and industry to ensure that our work would be of the highest value to those we serve."[7] As the project was developing, members of the museum staff relocated to Newport to represent OMSI as a member of the Newport Chamber of Commerce, participate in business committee meetings, and meet with various education partners. These included representatives from the Bureau of Land Management, the Confederated Tribes of the Siletz Indians, Oregon State Parks, the Oregon Coast Aquarium, National Oceanic and Atmospheric Administration (NOAA) Fleet Headquarters, and the Hatfield Marine Science Center of Oregon State University, which houses a variety of state agencies, including Oregon Fish and Wildlife, Oregon Marine Fisheries, and NOAA Fisheries. Camp Gray occupies the traditional lands of the Siletz Indian people, and tribal members had been long-time partners with OMSI on culturally based programming, such as Salmon Camp. Tribal elders provided a welcome and blessing for the opening ceremony of Camp Gray. Stueber commented,

> We took a good two years to get to know the people in Newport and to build trust. You might call our approach "deep listening." Still, there were bumps along the way. Some of the STEM partners worried about the impact of the "big museum from the city" on their programs.

There were other insights gleaned from numerous community listening sessions. Parents wanted to have better access for their children to experience the existing, and very popular, OMSI programs and camps in the high desert and other ecosystems throughout the state.

> We modified our programming model to make the camp programs more financially accessible to more people. Although the camp is not entirely free, the fundraising campaign created a scholarship fund designated to provide financial aid for schools and low-income families along the Oregon Coast, with some scholarship funds exclusively for the Siletz tribe. The camp director lives in Newport year-round and is a member of the local Chamber of Commerce. We purchase goods and services locally. We partner with the community on emergency preparedness planning. Creating community benefit and accessibility has been a priority.

By the time the site opened in 2016, community leaders, education partners, and the mayor of Newport welcomed the camp. The Coastal Discovery Center at Camp Gray is now the largest museum-based outdoor science education program in the country, with a stated goal of supporting "a lifetime of stewardship grounded in scientific discovery."[8] In its 2017 annual report, OMSI noted that Camp Gray has continued to bring in new partners, such as the Pacific Northwest College of Art and NW Documentary, to create innovative science-art programming in the area. The museum discovered that many teachers in the local community still had not visited the camp and did not understand the staff's willingness to modify programs to meet their needs. An educator open house helped to expose more teachers and their families to the opportunities at Camp Gray. The Oregon Coast Aquarium has since launched a fundraising campaign, and OMSI is sharing what it learned through its capital campaign.

Deepening Statewide Reach

With OMSI already having state-wide outposts at Newport and Hancock, and given its long history of other state-wide projects, it is not surprising that the current strategic plan maintains a priority to expand "our statewide impact." This goal has also evolved based on OMSI's "with, not for" approach to community engagement and collaborations. In addition to a longstanding traveling program that brings classes, labs, stage shows, and now science festivals to classrooms and communities around the state, the museum has entered into a new series of community listening sessions in three Oregon cities: Newport on the Oregon Coast, Bend in central Oregon, and Eugene in the central Willamette Valley. Several more listening sessions are planned in Pendleton and Umatilla in eastern Oregon. Drawing on collaboration strategies from past experience—and now focused on long-term relationships—OMSI has partnered with a local organization in each of the communities to co-convene the sessions and determine the most effective way that the Portland-based museum, with its unique resources, can add value to the science-related work already underway. In Bend, for example, the main local partner is the High Desert Museum, which focuses on the nature and culture of the state's High Desert region. Accordingly, OMSI staff began discussions with High Desert museum staff, thinking about collaborative possibilities, community needs, and considering who should be invited to the OMSI listening sessions. Through this process, OMSI identified partners in the Bend area for touring its new portable planetarium, funded by NASA, and participated in a local science festival. OMSI and the High Desert Museum have been including each other in grant proposals to fund deeper partnership work.

Another important "essential" in OMSI's current state-wide work is establishing a relationship with the Oregon Community Foundation's field office in the local community. "They can tell us where the needs are, what efforts are making an impact, and who to consult with in the community," Stueber noted. She continued,

> These listening sessions have helped all of us on the OMSI staff to see our connections to the "bigger world" and the needs of our communities—and the role that OMSI can play. We see how OMSI's work contributes to larger community aspirations, especially in rural communities, by breaking down barriers to access so that young people can gain the skills needed to acquire family-wage jobs that will make the communities thrive.

In each case, the museum is working with potential partners to build strong relationships and determine the best form of partnership that addresses the needs of the community and complements existing resources. Instead of beginning with a standalone program, the museum builds on extant networks and organizations to determine what specific, mission-aligned value added it can provide.

Expanding Early Childhood Education
One of the museum's current strategic priorities is expanding early childhood education, especially given recent research that demonstrates that science learning begins at birth and early cognitive development plays a critical role in learning science skills.

As it determined its niche in this work, the museum looked at the early childhood activity throughout the state, including several already established early learning hubs. Through a variety of conversations with key stakeholders, OMSI staff explored the kind of added value it could provide. Ultimately, the museum determined that it could enhance the scientific knowledge and understanding of early brain development among early learning caretakers and teachers. Accordingly, OMSI partnered with Lewis and Clark College's child development program. This partnership was part of OMSI's multiyear participation in the national Learning Labs project headquartered at the Museum of Science Boston. Per the Learning Labs model, Lewis and Clark students conduct research in OMSI's early learning Science Playground. In exchange, they explain their experiments to parents and caregivers and help them understand early cognitive development in their children. OMSI staff provide simple, inexpensive take-home activity ideas for parents and caregivers to reinforce and extend the learning at home. Stueber noted,

> We realized that this parent and caregiver engagement was exactly what was needed, not just for families visiting the museum, but by many of our community-based partner organizations in their work with families. They have identified families and are providing health and nutrition education and parenting techniques. OMSI's focus on brain development and early science learning fills a gap in their offerings. Our staff has drawn on the experience in working with the Lewis and Clark researchers, and is now providing hands-on, culturally specific training with adults and children, not only in the museum, but through partner programs such as Early Head Start, and Impact NW.

The OMSI District

In 2015, the city of Portland began a multiyear process to create a land-use framework for the next twenty years, the 2035 Comprehensive Plan. OMSI's museum is located in a planned re-development area, and the museum owns ten acres of undeveloped land that is a significant asset for its future. To participate in the long range planning process, OMSI developed a twenty-year vision, a first for the museum. While there are many unknowns in such a long planning horizon, it was important to consider the role that OMSI would play in the community in twenty years. Stueber commented,

> OMSI's visioning process began with the staff and board imagining the museum of the future. It was a very helpful process and aligned the staff and board around key principles. Then we convened community listening sessions, beginning with asking community members to share their aspirations for the future. We then shared OMSI's road map and asked people to comment. We asked, "What excites you about this idea? What concerns you?" Thousands of post-it notes were generated. A small staff team worked with our planning consultants to create theme-based categories, and then to generate opportunities based on the ideas. The opportunities we selected became the strategic priorities of our 5-yr. strategic plan and set us on the path toward our 20-year Vision.

As the plan took shape, especially in light of its synergy with the broader Portland city-visioning efforts, a key strategic priority became the "OMSI District," focusing on the museum's existing building and facilities and the surrounding, museum-owned, as-yet-undeveloped area. These master planning efforts for the future OMSI campus expanded beyond the campus proper to include a formal partnership, through a signed Memorandum of Understanding, with Portland Community College, Portland State University, and the Oregon Health Sciences University to explore the concept of an "innovation district" that would include the OMSI campus, these partners, and some other private investments. Part of the project has involved extensive research on innovation districts around the country, which are characterized by research, public education, increased density, transit options, and the ability to live and work nearby. Stueber expressed great hopes for this partnership, although she acknowledged that changing political, social, and economic winds—as well as changes in civic and organizational leadership—could impact the pace of the project. She noted that there have been significant mutual learnings from the process, no matter how the formal Innovation District turns out, and commented on the value of OMSI's Guiding Principles, developed to guide the future campus development.

> The Guiding Principles indicate that the campus development will be successful if, when completed, it is known as: a center of excellence in science teaching and learning; a welcoming and accessible destination for all of the community; a model for sustainability through demonstration projects showcasing sustainable design features; and a revenue generator to support OMSI's mission. These principles align well with the Innovation District partners' goals and proposed outcomes.

Within the Museum

This orientation toward long-term, sustainable relationships has affected the museum's organization chart as well. There is recognition that the quality of audience experiences has an important corollary in employee and volunteer satisfaction. Therefore, OMSI has a strategic priority of "elevating the guest and employee experience," with one of the outcomes "measurable increase in employee satisfaction and retention." A new 2017 position, "head of people and culture," includes responsibilities for working inside and beyond the museum to address equity and diversity, and to increase cultural competency and build solid relationships in both domains. This staff person will help broker ways that OMSI's internal culture can be made even more amenable to a community engagement approach.

Lauren Moreno, OMSI's former director for strategic partnerships and programs, noted the museum's long-term history of partnerships and the general positive attitude about partnerships throughout the museum.[9]

Despite the absence of formal and codified partnership norms, she stated that there is a strong partnership ethos, with little territoriality among different departments. "The norms," she noted, "are implicit." According to Moreno, Chief Executive Officer Nancy Stueber and Chief Operations Officer Erin Graham have long championed the positive value of partnerships, and that value has permeated the museum. Even without detailed criteria, there is a broad, institutional understanding of the strategic role of partnerships.

That said, Moreno discovered as she delved deeper into partnership work that staff members had different perceptions of what partnerships would—or could—be. For example, OMSI has moved to create some formalized partnerships with not-so-usual suspects, including some for-profit vendors like Bon Appetit, the museum's catering and food science initiative partner, formed around mutual goals of food science education and innovative ways to increase earned income to pay for it. Moreno had to overcome a prevailing notion that "money-making partnerships are tainted" in some way. In the case of these types of partnerships, there are financial benefits to both entities as well as learning and community benefits, a boundary-blurring definition of benefits that can require explication.

Moreno noted a spectrum of formalizing documentation that OMSI has used in its partnership work: some are informal, some have contracts and other formal agreements, some have fully codified Memoranda of Understanding. The museum is currently working to develop rubrics that can be used to better document the impacts of its many partnerships.

Kyrie Kellett, a senior learning and community engagement specialist, provided an additional perspective on OMSI's local, community-based partnerships. She discussed a partnership with Verde, a local organization with a mission to serve "communities by building environmental wealth through social enterprise, outreach and advocacy."[10] Kellett, who has been at OMSI since 2006, affirmed that the vast majority of OMSI educational and community programs are collaborative. Like Stueber, she also spoke to the limitations of grant-funded projects in building and sustaining ongoing and trusted community relationships, especially communities of color. Kellett described a "push-pull" attribute of partnerships:

> On the one hand, most federal funders and other grant-makers are promoting (or even requiring) partnerships and collaboration. That is the "push." On the other hand, the "pull" of partnerships has to do with the value-added dimension of working more closely with local entities. As OMSI seeks to increase our community engagement, especially regarding

working with Portland's diverse neighborhoods and their residents, we need to hone a greater understanding of the cultural dimension of this work. It serves OMSI's needs and goals to work with neighborhood-based organizations that have the cultural knowledge, competencies, and perspectives—including foreign language fluency—that OMSI staff may lack.

Moreover, based on their own, often longstanding, community relationships, these organizations have helped broker a more trusted relationship between OMSI and community residents. This trust is important throughout a partnership: Kellett pointed out that some organizations may be suspicious of why the big museum is making contact in the first place. Others, like Verde, may see an immediate win-win possibility in a partnership that holds benefits for each organization.

The Verde Partnership

The relationship with Verde began almost a decade ago, with a National Science Foundation grant that focused on sustainability and climate change. The project's goals were to foster sustainable decision making; promote sustainable practices for developing, designing, and fabricating exhibits; and develop and test an industry standard for sustainable exhibit design and fabrication. The deliverables included a fifteen hundred square foot bilingual (Spanish/English) exhibition at OMSI that engaged the public with everyday personal choices that affect the sustainability of their communities, a bilingual outreach campaign combining an interactive website and cell phone-based "access points" throughout the community, eight bilingual events on various topics related to sustainable living for families, and a website and workshops for exhibit professionals.

Kellett noted that this partnership had a serendipitous beginning: the museum wanted a cultural dimension to the project that involved the Hispanic community, found Verde on the internet, and reached out to them, with an immediate positive response. The five-year grant was funded, with five partners, including OMSI, Verde, Portland Community College, Metro (a regional governmental authority), and the City of Portland.

The project began with a bilingual colloquium, where the partners explored their own understanding of the concept of sustainability. The partners then met once a month for the five-year duration of the project. Verde's main contribution was its deep knowledge and experience with economic equity issues and environmental justice, and its connections to Portland's Latinx community. All in all, the project achieved its promised goals.

Kellett underscored the "down sides" of "soft money," or grant-funded partnerships. In this case, the museum found a way to continue its relationship with Verde beyond the five-year mark by saving some grant money for community mini-grants, a project about neighborhood way-finding linked to public transportation routes, and the co-creation of a bilingual curriculum on transportation for middle school students in five schools. The latter has a career component, bringing transportation engineers, urban planners, and others involved in transportation into the schools.

Despite the paring down of that specific local relationship, Kellet noted that OMSI has moved forward in getting to that "relationship-building mindset" that is so important to successful partnerships. "We've made progress. People here are interested in growth and change." As she reflected on the qualities required for success, Kellet described her ideal partnership scenario: "I'd shift from a project orientation to identifying who we want to partner with and feed that relationship with projects we jointly develop over time."

This is particularly important, added Kellett,

> with communities of color. We want relationships characterized by shared value and reciprocity. These communities have long memories, and many of them have been burned before. We can't use them and then dump them. If we do, it's like a bad boyfriend who calls you only when he needs a date, is lonely, or wants to borrow your truck. Instead, we need to be good friends and true partners, beginning with conversations where we ask them "what are you up to?" and "let's see what we can create together."

Kellett concluded, "We're getting better, and we're learning as we go."

Conclusion
Partnerships at many levels, are central to the current and future work of OMSI. For the museum, core partnership principles include the following:

1. Be clear on how the partnership aligns with OMSI's values and can advance a goal or priority of the strategic plan.
2. Build on OMSI's unique resources, capacity, and strategic plan to add value.
3. Engage in inclusive listening, within the museum, with partners, and within communities.
4. Invest the time to develop trusted relationships with prospective partners.

5. Clarify what "success" means to each prospective partner; articulate the value proposition.
6. Be attentive to the partnership process as it unfolds, and be flexible and responsive to partner needs.
7. Support a partnership "mindset" within the museum and be clear on potential partnership benefits.
8. Create and monitor metrics that track progress toward stated outcomes.

Ultimately, according to Stueber, the challenge is to set the right expectations. "Listen closely but be mindful of what you can and what you can't achieve. Maybe the answer will be a compromise that is achievable and within your purview."

Growing the "Experiment Station" through New Partnerships

26

MARSHA L. SEMMEL, FROM INTERVIEWS WITH DOROTHY KOSINSKI AND SUZANNE WRIGHT

BIOGRAPHIES: DOROTHY KOSINSKI has been the director of The Phillips Collection since 2008. She is the former senior curator of painting and sculpture at the Dallas Museum of Art, and served earlier as an independent curator for the Kunstmuseum Wolfsburg, the Kunstmuseum Basel, and the Royal Academy of Arts in London. In August 2013, Kosinski was appointed by President Barack Obama to the National Council on the Humanities. She currently serves on the Boards of the Sherman Fairchild Foundation and The Morris & Gwendolyn Cafritz Foundation. Kosinski has written and published widely in numerous catalogues and books, as well as many art magazines. She regularly participates in scholarly lectures and has extensive teaching experience at the university level. She received her MA and PhD degrees from the Institute of Fine Arts, New York University, and her BA from Yale University.

Suzanne Wright, director of education and community engagement, has thirty years of experience in art museum education. Under her leadership, The Phillips Collection has developed a nationally recognized portfolio of programs, weaving the visual arts throughout K–12 curriculum and across a lifetime. Most recently, Wright is the project director of Phillips@THEARC, the museum's new creativity campus in Ward 8, an underserved community in Southeast Washington, DC. Other nationally recognized and award-winning highlights include Prism.K12, a national arts integration initiative; the Jacob Lawrence and the Migration Series Teaching Kit; and Art Links to Learning, a museum-in-residence program for Washington, DC schools. Wright received the 2013 Eastern Region Museum Art Educator of the Year Award from the National Art Education Association, and she co-founded the Washington, DC affiliate, Art Education DC, in 2012, serving as its president from 2014 to 2016. Wright has an MA from Tufts University and served as a fellow at the Getty Museum Leadership Institute in 2012.

Introduction

THE PHILLIPS COLLECTION, which bills itself as "America's first museum of modern art," was established in 1921 by Duncan Phillips in Washington, DC, in the aftermath of World War I. Dubbing it "an intimate museum combined with an experiment station" (1926), Phillips served as the museum's director until his death in 1966.

That mantra—intimacy and innovation—governs the museum today, which has been under the leadership of Dorothy Kosinski since 2008. As Kosinski and her leadership team have worked with the board and others in the community, she has leveraged several existing partnerships and taken others to a new level. "I see Washington as our campus," Kosinski noted. "There are so many resources throughout DC—think tanks, embassies, other cultural organizations (both federal and non-federal), universities, each with the capacity to partner." Indeed, the museum's partnership work is so extensive that its Education and Public Engagement office issues an annual *Education/Public Engagement Report* that itemizes and clusters numerous "cultural partners," as well as partners in kindergarten to twelfth-grade education, universities, media, and hospitality. The 2016 report notes that these partnerships are "in line with several of the museum's strategic initiatives—to build relationships with the DC community and foster a global conversation."

This profile focuses on two fairly recent (and still emergent) Phillips Collection collaborations: a six-year partnership, launched in 2015, with the University of Maryland that aims to "dramatically transform scholarship and innovation in the arts," and another, also launched in 2015, with The Town Hall Education Arts and Recreation Campus (THEARC) in the east of the Anacostia area of Washington, DC.

The Phillips Collection and the University of Maryland

The seeds for the University of Maryland collaboration were planted in a number of previous museum/university initiatives. The Center for the Study of Modern Art—established in 2006 under the leadership of then museum director Jay Gates, former Phillips education director Ruth Perlin, and scholar and museum board member Jonathan Fineberg—piloted a partnership with the University of Illinois Champaign–Urbana. "That partnership was brilliantly kick-started by the Phillips' Ruth Perlin and Illinois' Jonathan Fineberg," according to Kosinski. "They experimented with what such a center could be, beyond the rather standard assortment of post docs, interns, and courses." Fineberg, according to Kosinski, is "a force of nature," and Perlin is an "astonishing" voice for her profession. They launched innovative interdisciplinary initiatives, such as "art and the brain," that functioned independently of traditional museum activities like exhibitions and interpretive programs. Perlin's command of the latest developments in museums and museum education, including path-breaking work with digital technology, was critical to the effort.

In addition to the University of Illinois relationship, the Phillips had enjoyed a successful multiyear partnership, codified by a Memorandum of Understanding, with the George Washington University's College of Arts and the Humanities. In addition, there had been previous formal relationships with Georgetown University, the University of Virginia, and New York University.

The University of Maryland enrolled more than forty thousand students at its flagship campus in nearby College Park in 2017. In addition to programs in art history, visual arts, music, theater, dance and performance studies, the university houses the University of Maryland Art Gallery, The Clarice Smith Performing Arts Center, and the DeVos Institute of Arts Management. Wallace Loh assumed the university presidency in 2010.

The university had been seeking a foothold in Washington, DC, for the arts, a partner to enhance its visual arts capacity. Dorothy Kosinski recalls, "Staff in each of our organizations saw our potential compatibility and brought Wallace and me together." Once they met, Kosinski and Loh discovered some "good chemistry" and some common goals. "He's energetic and positive, with a true commitment to enhancing campus offerings. And what's key is that his people share his vision, from the provost, to the deans, to the development department." In an article in *The Washington Post*,[1] Kosinski stated that the relationship was "a transformative marriage." "This is a new series of adventures, beyond the realm of art, with all sorts of multidisciplinary approaches." Loh, who had unsuccessfully brokered a merger with Washington's Corcoran Gallery of Art and its art school, when the Corcoran instead chose an arrangement with the National Gallery of Art and the George Washington University, stated, "I feel like a phoenix rising from the ashes." That unsuccessful endeavor left the university with unfulfilled possibilities, and, perhaps the readiness for a new museum-university partnership, especially with a stable, well-respected museum like the Phillips. "In the sciences, you can't be a great university without great laboratories. It's the same thing with the arts. You have to work with raw materials. This is the art laboratory we don't have." Upon announcement of the partnership, University Provost Mary Ann Rankin noted, "Having an affiliation with an esteemed art museum elevates the university. . . . We've always been strong in STEM, but not so well-known in the fine arts. This is going, in one jump, to put the shine on and take us to another level."

The terms of the Phillips/University of Maryland Memorandum of Understanding are broad in scope and allow for growth and expansion. The museum's website as of September 2017 notes that the relationship is "layered with rich opportunities to collaborate" and "ambitious, entrepreneurial, and risk supportive—essential qualities in today's competitive arts and academic environments." The Phillips' goals were to "expand education programs, reach new and diverse audiences, and pursue key initiatives that align with the museum's strategic mission as an 'experiment station' and institution for learning." The university wanted to "grow its established scholarship and academic programs within the arts, provide unparalleled research and education opportunities for UMD faculty and students, and expand its footprint in the nation's capital."

Partnership Specifics

University of Maryland students, faculty, staff, and alumni association members receive free admission to the Phillips with university identification. University faculty and programming complement the expertise of the museum "and serve as a partner in the exploration of topics related to the museum's collections and programs."

The university is now the primary presenter for all of The Phillips Collections' "Intersections" exhibitions, a series of displays that invite contemporary artists to "explore the intriguing intersections between old and new traditions, modern and contemporary art practices, and museum spaces and artistic interventions."

The Center for the Study of Modern Art is now the University of Maryland Center for Art and Knowledge at The Phillips Collection. According to the museum brochure, it is "the museum's nexus for academic work, scholarly exchange, and innovative interdisciplinary collaborations on issues of production, exhibition, conservation, and theory of modern and contemporary art, as well as culture and politics." Among the many activities under the auspices of the newly rechristened center:

- New arts courses and seminars on art, art history, arts management, museum studies, cultural diplomacy, conservation, and interdisciplinary studies.
- Support for postdoctoral fellows researching modern art, conservation, music, and cultural diplomacy.

- A postdoctoral fellow in virtual culture that exploits the expertise of university faculty in digital investigation in conjunction with the museum's collection and curators.
- Partner for the Phillips International Forum Weekend, established by the museum in 2009.
- Co-publishing the University of Maryland–Phillips Book Prize, a biennial prize for an unpublished manuscript presenting new research in modern or contemporary art.
- Co-presenting a new music series at the museum, in partnership with the University of Maryland School of Music.
- Enhanced programming for Creative Voices DC and other public programs, including programming on the University of Maryland campus, and Conversations with Artists, which brings leading contemporary practitioners to the museum and to the university campus to interact directly with students and faculty.
- Digitizing the museum's archives of books, exhibition catalogues, and correspondence "to preserve the archives in perpetuity and make valuable educational resources easily accessible to scholars, researchers and students around the world."

Finally, the agreement includes plans for developing a new public gallery and hands-on teaching open storage facility in Prince George's County, where the main University of Maryland campus is located. The new facility is planned to be "modest in scale, materials, and design, but bold as an arts/learning space." The gallery will reflect the museum's (and the university's) focus on experimentation and innovation; expand outreach to students and faculty, while broadening public interest in Prince George's County; and foster local economic development. It will enable the museum to put more of its collection of more than four thousand artworks (increased by 25 percent since Kosinski's arrival) on display. Kosinski commented, "I admire Wallace's vision of an innovation district in Maryland, along the purple line [a proposed new subway line], that embodies the creative economy and the urban lifestyle. It is my hope that this Phillips' facility would be a jewel in the University's crown."

Kosinski stressed in an interview that the Phillips Collection has partnership "in its DNA." Nevertheless, she acknowledged that each partnership has to be selected with care and should serve the interests of each party. From the museum's perspective, advantages of the University of Maryland relationship included the university's "brain trust" in a number of areas, including digital innovation, virtual reality, and arts management; the knowledge of university faculty; and the university's "deep enthusiasm and commitment of resources, including financial resources." Moreover, the museum reasoned that this relationship would not entail huge infusions of capital, yet would expand its reach in the physical, intellectual, and virtual realms.

In turn, the university has broad access to the museum. In addition to free admission and the research, presentation, and programming opportunities, the university leadership is represented at every Phillips opening, gala, and other major events. Every Thursday a bus brings forty to fifty University of Maryland students to such museum events as "Phillips after Five." "Our artists go up to campus to do critiques. Our composers go to campus and work with music and performing arts students," commented Kosinski.

The response of each institution's governing bodies? Positive. "Our board sees the transformative potential," noted Kosinski. "We are not anticipating lots of new expenditures. Our goal is to solve problems (like the capacity to exhibit and work with more of the collection) and to unearth and discover creative solutions. I want to not only display and preserve art but to increase access to learning, seeing, studying, curating, teaching, and serving broader communities."

How do the partnership members track their progress? There is a monthly, sixty- to ninety-minute meeting either in Washington, DC, or College Park, involving Kosinski, Deputy Museum Director Klaus Ottmann, and museum development and curatorial staff. They meet with the university provost, a representative from the university's advancement office, and other university staff as needed. "This team gets things done," says Kosinski.

The partnership continues to evolve, with different museum and university staff collaborating in various ways. In 2017 and 2018, for example, a University of Maryland design professor worked with students to reimagine the Phillips' initial gallery experience as a "Welcome Gallery." Museum staff defined the challenge, and students offered various proposals, one of which was adopted by the museum. As Suzanne Wright, Phillips' director of education, noted, "The students learned, and we learned." Another current project involves graduate students in the University of Maryland College of Education, Prince George's County public school teachers, and the Phillips' PRISM program on arts integration.

The Phillips at THEARC

Located in a part of Washington, DC, worlds away from the city's Northwest quadrant that houses The Phillips Collection, THEARC serves a

Washington, DC, population of more than 150,000 residents in the city's Ward 7 and 8, east of the Anacostia River. The area is home to 40 percent of the district's youth, and predominantly African American, with nearly half living at or below the poverty line.[2] Youth in this area have poor records in educational achievement and suffer disproportionately from various health issues.

Founded in 2005 as a campus to provide services and care to Washington's most underserved residents, THEARC celebrated its tenth anniversary in 2015. Its goal:

> THEARC connects individuals and families in need to the resources they require to succeed, offers educational opportunities to at-risk youth, provides programming that appeals to every member of the family, and coordinates an expansive calendar of arts exhibitions, classes and performances.[3]

Managed by the nonprofit Building Bridges Across the River, THEARC's community presence continues to grow, with a planned phase III expansion opened in February 2018.

The community organizations/programs in residence at THEARC's campus include Trinity University, The Washington School for Girls, Boys and Girls Club, Children's National Health System, Children's Health Project of DC, and Covenant House. Resident arts programs include ArtReach, Washington Ballet, and Levine School of Music. There are other programs such as THEARC Farm, a wellness project providing mental health services, and a summer meals program, as well as a workforce center, employment training programs, and reading programs. The facility houses a theater, community meeting room, and recital hall. The ninety-three thousand square foot expansion completed in 2018 includes a black box theater and new partners, including The Bishop Walker School for Boys, the AppleTree Early Learning Public Charter School, and the Phillips Collection.

What inspired the Phillips Collection to embark on this partnership? Director of Education Suzanne Wright discussed this partnership as a natural "next step" in the museum's decades-long commitment to partnerships, especially museums-schools-educators work, with particular attention to underserved communities. The museum's kindergarten to twelfth-grade education programming is rooted in an arts integration approach that embodies the museum's focus on individualized, personalized experiences and experimentation, clear outcomes, and rigorous evaluation. The principal museum-school activities comprise two different programs. The first, PRISM K–12, now a website and national program, uses museum collections to build teacher proficiency in creating "rich, arts–integrated curricula" through a set of six strategies. The strategies—"identify, connect, compare, express, empathize, and synthesize"—can be incorporated into lesson plans and curricula throughout the school. The second program, Art Links to Learning, serves a select number of Washington, DC, elementary and middle schools. This program takes a "whole-school approach to engage teachers, students, and the school community." The participating schools have access to professional development for teachers, in-classroom workshops led by Phillips educators, class visits to the museum, classroom curriculum implemented by teachers, and a culminating community celebration.[4]

For Art Links to Learning, the museum takes on a limited number of schools each year. They are selected through a careful process that has the potential to create an intensive and ongoing relationship. According to Wright, "We start 'dating,' then, if it works, we put a ring on it. This includes a formal memorandum of understanding. At first, we may work with an educator at the school, but then it can develop into a more sustained relationship." Critical elements for the partnership's success: "a stable school and solid principal leadership." The relationship is key. Wright notes that the museum creates deep partnerships with particular schools that last for five years. "At that point, typically, the schools 'graduate,' achieving their mastery in arts integration, and the program becomes self-sustaining. At that point, we back off a bit. The kids at the school will always have free bus trips to the museum. Teachers will always have free professional development if they desire." The museum's more intensive formal engagement ends.

As in other areas of the museum's work, the arrival of Director Kosinski led to a significant ramp up. "We'd done a lot before," noted Wright, "but now we've really upped our game." The enhanced education programming has led to increased emphasis on developing digital resources; more attention to cultural competencies within programming and among museum staff; more partnerships, including the department's annual publication of its partnership report; and the museum's presence at THEARC.

The Phillips' relationship with THEARC began in 2014, spurred by the closure of the Corcoran Gallery of Art (which had sponsored the ArtReach program) and its incorporation into the George Washington University. It was championed by Phillips board member Lynne Horning, who is the chair of the museum's education committee and also on the board of THEARC. With Horning's prompting and Kosinski's endorsement, since this project aligned with the museum's strategic plan and goals,

Wright moved forward in this new relationship, which would include a Phillips satellite in southeast Washington. As she noted, "I'm committed to broadening the educational reach of the museum. I love working with different communities, and, I'm a strategic opportunist. I immediately said, 'Let's do it.'"

By the summer of 2015 there was a museum ad hoc committee that discussed the feasibility of the venture and the $242,000 needed for Phillips construction costs. By the fall, $266,000 had been raised, and the museum board officially approved the project.

The process of crafting the museum's relationship with THEARC took many months. "Lots of relationship-building and trust-building needed to happen. It was very complicated," noted Wright. "There were many bumps in the road. In the end THEARC made space for us." THEARC leadership came to believe that there could be a "both-and" solution to visual arts at the facility, with room for both the George Washington University–Corcoran ArtReach program (which includes various youth, family, and adult afterschool learning opportunities) and the Phillips Collection–University of Maryland presence.

"I have a philosophy about planning meetings," said Wright. "I'm prepared, listening, and collaborative. I show up at every meeting. I try to take the high road in any prospective conflict, always working with the end goal in mind." Those traits paid off in the negotiation process.

Once the relationship with THEARC was formalized, months more of community strategic planning began. With the support of Strategy Arts, a strategic and business planning firm based in Alexandria, Virginia, the museum launched an eight-month community advisory process. The goal was to identify the needs of the community, define specific goals for the Phillips' presence in Anacostia, and pilot the programming.

The Community Advisory Committee comprised fourteen members, including Wright and other members of the Phillips' staff; board member Lynne Horning; the principal of the Washington School for Girls at THEARC; community residents, including a local teacher and the president of the local arts and culture council; the medical director of the Children's Health Project at THEARC; and other THEARC partners and leaders.

In the three meetings that spanned six months, the Community Advisory Committee identified seven areas of need, including changing the city's perception of East of the River communities, providing "third spaces" that were gathering places other than home or school, improving health care and social determinants of health, addressing the neighborhood's socio-economic needs, providing educational opportunities, increasing intergenerational opportunities, and supporting local arts and artists. In addition, Strategy Arts collected and analyzed additional data, including phone interviews with community residents.

The outcome of the process was a June 2017 Planning Report on Phillips@THEARC. It defined five guiding principles that would undergird all museum programs at the facility:

- Based on community needs as identified by the Phillips@THEARC Community Advisory Council;
- Co-created in collaboration with THEARC partners and community organizations, tapping into existing East of the River resources;
- True to the Phillips mission and engagement philosophy;
- A clear investment of Phillips time and resources in East of the River communities; and
- Scale-appropriate to Phillips resources.

These principles helped define four specific goals:

1. Demonstrate an authentic connection and commitment to East of the River communities, developing relationships with THEARC partners and East of the River communities.
2. Create an engaging, inviting, and active atmosphere through the architectural and interior design of the Phillips@THEARC spaces (workshop, gallery/display).
3. Pilot programs in collaboration with THEARC partners that tap into existing community resources.
4. Deepen the Phillips' ongoing school partnerships East of the River, connect these kindergarten to twelfth-grade partnerships to Phillips@THEARC in intentional and innovative ways, and seek out new potential kindergarten to twelfth-grade partners in Wards 7 and 8.

The museum's focus audiences are caregivers (from young parents through grandparents), senior adults, and the kindergarten to twelfth-grade community (teachers, students, families). Accordingly, programs and activities have been developed and piloted for each audience.

Billed as a "new art and wellness program," Phillips@THEARC comprises two main areas. In the Workshop, an environment with floor-to-ceiling magnetic whiteboards and storefront windows, there are a variety of hands-on activities for many community residents. Early programs include

"CreativityTEA," with THEARC partners the Levine School of Music and Double Nickel Theater connecting and celebrating senior community residents and engaging them in activities that spark community storytelling combined with music and art activities. "Create-While-You-Wait" is a

> drop-in and de-stress service designed for caregivers and families visiting THEARC, in conjunction with the Children's Medical Center. There will also be "Creative Care for the Caregiver" programs that combine mindfulness, relaxation and creativity exercises that caregivers can practice at home, and "Tap" into Your Creativity, occasional evening programs for caregivers 'to sip, create, and recreate.

The Living Room Gallery is designed as "an intimate gathering space" displaying works from partnering East of the River programs and organizations. The first exhibition, "The Art of Storytelling," is a collaboration with the Double Nickels Theater, whose mission is to "produce theatrical presentations using reminiscence theatre to reinvigorate the art of conversation and to communicate across generations and cultures," and the Seafarers' Yacht Club, the first African American yacht club in the United States established as the Seafarers' Boat Club in 1945 by First Lady Eleanor Roosevelt and civil rights pioneer Mary McLeod Bethune.

The museum is recruiting people who live or work in Wards 7 and 8 to serve as ambassadors: greeters and activity facilitators for families participating in the "Create-While-You-Wait" drop-in program from Mondays through Saturdays. It remains committed to learning from and with the community and co-creating, with community members, programs and services that address their needs. In spring 2018, the museum hired Monica Jones, a graduate of Howard University with considerable Washington, DC, experience, as the first Phillips@THEARC coordinator. The museum will offer free field trips to the Phillips' main facility for Ward 7 and 8 DC Public Schools and free-of-charge teacher training. The museum has also launched a Friends of the Phillips@THEARC affinity group.

As of this writing, the museum is still developing the ways in which the University of Maryland will be involved. Wright emphasized the need to "go slow" in building trust with the Phillips' new neighbors. "This is about building relationships, one person at a time. Our team needs to comprise those people who are the community. We are acknowledging—and addressing—some previous missteps and learning from the experiences of our other cultural partners at THEARC. We are going slow. We are learning as we go."

Wright concluded the conversation:

> One of my biggest questions is how the Phillips Collection will be changed by this partnership. We started a cultural competency task force last year,

and our staff has been in training to improve our cultural awareness. How will our partnership impact the Ward 7 and 8 communities, and how will our own learnings there change our understanding of ourselves? What will be the impact of Phillips@THEARC be on the museum as a whole?

Indeed, in April 2018, the Phillips announced new steps in moving forward with the diversity focus adopted first in 2013 as part of the museum's strategic plan. Since 2016, a staff-led Inclusion and Diversity Task Force worked to implement changes in the museum's programs and facilities, engaging experts and coaches to explore unconscious bias, and formalizing goals to acquire and display works by underrepresented groups including women, minorities and members of the LGBTQ community. With a major, five-year investment by the Sherman Fairchild Foundation, the museum appointed Makeba Clay as its first chief diversity officer, who will, according to an April 22, 2018, press release, "provide a vision and strategy for robust community engagement which will include enhancing the museum's current partnerships and creating new connections." The grant also makes possible a paid fellowship and series of paid internships. In a May 20, 2018, opinion piece in *The Washington Post*, "Changing the museum leadership model," Kosinski noted her hopes that these positions will

> help eliminate barriers to entry into the field and provide a new cadre of young people with the training and skills to establish credentials. . . . It is increasingly important that museums provide a space where people can connect to one another across perspectives and experiences and relate to their communities' institutions in multiple facets. . . . Our goal is to initiate the transformation of the arts industry in Washington so that it represents the true nature of the city.

Conclusion

The Phillips' ventures with the University of Maryland and THEARC are but two of the museum's partnerships, but they are the two most intensive forged under Kosinski's leadership. As she says,

> My default (to partnership requests) is usually "sure," and our alliances have included arts and schools, arts and aging, arts and embassies, and arts and the academy. These two efforts are a bit different in that they are systemic. They aim to reach beyond the norm, and our hopes are that they are more provocative, ambitious, and transformative in their potential. My thinking is without new money, where is my multiplier? How can I take existing staff and magnify our impact? These partnerships are cost-effective solutions to real organizational problems and community opportunities. All in all, a terrific win-win.

TOOLS, TIPS, AND RESOURCES III

Resources   **27**
Diving Deeper into Partnerships and
Networks

MARSHA L. SEMMEL

WHILE MUCH OF MY LEARNING and experience with strategic partnerships has been of the "seat-of-the-pants" variety, with many lessons learned, occasionally painfully, from wrongheaded expectations, misguided assumptions, insufficient shared communication, and lack of attention to process definition and relationship nurturing, my partnership journey has been immeasurably enriched by actively seeking and consuming a growing body of partnership literature, in the for-profit and nonprofit sectors. The research and practice of partnership and collaboration has grown steadily in recent years due to several factors, among them the realization that many of the community and learning challenges that we face today can only be addressed effectively by a collaborative effort. In addition, the move toward interconnectedness throughout the world, fueled by the inexorable "march" of digital technologies, has amplified traditional interpersonal, social, ideological, geographic, and discipline-based linkages to hyperconnect interest groups; ethnic, cultural, and religious communities; professionals and amateurs; audiences; and learners around the world. Here are some resources and examples containing relevant perspectives, advice, tools, and models—some, but not all, by or for museums. This is by no means a comprehensive list, nor is it in the order of importance, but it does reflect a broad range of thinking and practice on the topic. Each of the preceding chapters includes practical advice and specific pointers, based on actual experience, for the creation, maintenance, and growth of successful partnerships and collaborations.

Partnerships and Collaboration in Nonprofits

In 2002, Jossey-Bass published **The Peter Drucker Foundation's workbook,** *Meeting the Collaborative Challenge: Developing Strategic Alliances Between Nonprofit Organizations and Business.* The workbook, based on the 2000 publication of a book by the same name, notes that it is an increasing necessity for leaders in all sectors to practice "leading beyond the walls" in order to produce "mutual benefits and results" (p. vii). "The challenges our society faces cannot be met—nor our opportunities fully realized—by any one organization or sector alone" (p. vii). The workbook focuses on four dimensions of collaboration: preparation, planning, developing, and renewing nonprofit partnerships with businesses. It is replete with questionnaires and worksheets, drawing substantially on James Austin's "seven C's" of collaboration from his book, *The Collaboration Challenge.* The seven C's are "connection with purpose and people, clarity of purpose, congruency of mission, strategy, and values; creation of value, communication between partners, continual learning, and commitment to the partnership."

Powerhouse Partners: A Blueprint for Building Organizational Culture for Breakaway Results, **by Stephen M. Dent and James H. Krefft,** focuses on how to shape an organizational culture disposed toward successful partnership, from attaining personal mastery to organizational infrastructure, as well as ways to engage in what the authors call "smart partnering." The volume does a deep dive into the characteristics of "traditional" versus "partnering" organizations, with a valuable and detailed focus on organizational culture, from the leader to position descriptions for employees that highlight partnership competencies.

Partnerships: Frameworks for Working Together was produced by the Compassion Capital Fund and administered by the U.S. Department of Health and Human Services. Between 2002 and 2009, Compassion Capital Fund awarded almost thirteen hundred grants to expand the role of nonprofit organizations to provide social services to low income individuals. *Strengthening Nonprofits: A Capacity Builder's Resource Library* was created as part of the resources for training and technical assistance provided to all grantees. This publication provides useful justification for partnerships, outlines types of partnerships as well as the components of successful partnerships (as well as potential barriers to success), and defines key partnership-related terms. It also provides useful checklists for evaluating potential partnerships, beginning the partnership process, establishing and maintaining the partnership, crafting collaborative work plans, and evaluating and monitoring ongoing partnerships.

"**Advancing the Art of Collaboration**," a special section of the *Stanford Social Innovation Review* in April 2017 produced in partnership with BBB's Wise Giving Alliance (Give.org) contained a variety of articles that explored such topics as "Creative vs. Transactional Collaboration," "Building Collaboration into Your Organization," (focusing on culture, people, and leadership), "Hacking Nonprofit Collaboration," (focusing on maximizing social impact), and "The Collaboration Game: Solving the Puzzle," (looking at collaboration through the lenses of economics, game theory, and behavioral sciences).

A December 2014 report entitled "**Making Sense of Nonprofit Collaborations**" published by The Bridgespan Group and authored by Alex Neuhoff, Katie Smith Milway, Reilly Kiernan, and Josh Grehan, presents the results of research about four types of formal collaboration: associations, joint programs, shared support functions, and mergers. Among the research results: more nonprofit collaborations than expected; many successful collaborations; and a desire for more of all types of collaborations, especially shared support functions and mergers" (p. 3). Among the challenges: "lack of funder support for collaboration; difficulty in finding the right partner and negotiating roles; and the downside of well-intentioned funder influence—particularly when it comes to joint programs" (p. 3). Most of the interviewed nonprofits considered "the less integrated forms of collaboration—associations and joint programs—already their way of life, and they believe [sic] the more integrated forms offer the greatest new opportunity for increasing impact through both streamlining costs and freeing up cash for programs, acquiring new capabilities, and expanding the reach of services" (p. 5).

Networks

"**Vertigo and the Intentional Inhabitant: Leadership in a Connected World**," by Bill Traynor and featured in *Nonprofit Quarterly* zeroes in on "network-centric thinking." This seminal article, addressed to network leaders, contends that

> a network environment is dominated by space, and so it is space that should dominate your attention. In a connected environment, the leader has to understand that the power of these environments comes from the space, not the forms that populate the space. Therefore, the critical function of a network's leader is the recognition of—and the creation, preservation, and protection of—space.

Traynor defines space as "time and opportunity," as well as

> accessibility, flexibility, and options. It is the time for unfolding, time for
> adaptation, time and opportunity for intentional and random bumping and
> connecting, time for creation and time for response, time for listening and
> reacting, and time for deconstruction. It is the space in between, around,
> behind, on top of, and underneath all the action, the commitments, the
> transactions. . . . When the space closes, networks die, because in the clut-
> ter of commitments, expectations, structures, programs, partnerships, and
> so forth, there is no more space for adaptation and response.

Traynor emphasizes the importance of space for experimentation. He
suggests three ways to "create and preserve space in a network environment." First, "keep moving the creative, adaptive edge of the network
outward so that the universe of the network expands in three dimensions."
Second, create "an efficient demand environment." He suggests a process
called "resonance testing" that ensures that "only those things that truly
have value get resourced." Finally, "shrink or contract routine and recurring actions to their simplest and most efficient forms." Traynor's group,
Lawrence Community Works in Lawrence, Kansas, adopted a FOLKS
protocol: F (form follows function), O (open architecture is best), L (let it
go), K (keep it simple), and S (solve the problem). Finally, Traynor defines
the leader as not a "mad scientist," but a "mad inhabitant, an intentional
inhabitant, who deploys himself as a key variable to influence the environment from the inside."

In **"Unstill Waters: The Fluid Role of Networks in Social
Movements,"** an article in the Summer 2010 issue of the *Nonprofit
Quarterly*, author Rachel Katcher defined a *social movement* as "a collection
of persons or groups who come together around a common concern."
Typically, their mission is to bring about some type of societal change
relative to their concerns" (p. 54). The article describes the qualities of
these multiorganizational, dynamic, and porous networks, including ways
in which they manage many seemingly contradictory elements, including
the balance between individual autonomy and collective action and accountability.

"Cultivating Leaderful Ecosystems," *Nonprofit Quarterly*, April 21,
2017, by AJA Couchois Duncan, Susan Misra, and Vincent Pan. In this
article, the authors propose five "key nutrients" of "leaderful" ecosystems:

1. Engage the broader system;
2. Intentionally build relationships to embody equity;

3. Be flexible—sometimes more directive, other times more collaborative;
4. Value multiple ways of knowing and the wisdom of multiple voices and perspectives; and
5. Create the space for inner work that is needed for transformation.

In **"You First: Leadership for a New World—The Importance of Open Systems,"** a posting in the *Nonprofit Quarterly* in January 2018, Mark Light warns that even some seemingly expansive ecosystems are still too limited.

> In its quest for preservation and protection of its boundaries, the closed system exhausts all of its resources and collapses. Open systems, on the other hand, get energy from their interactions with the outside world. . . . In open systems, competition keeps everyone on their toes; . . . it keeps the system fresh and excited, and always responsive.

"Leading into Discomfort: Social Sector Leadership in the 21st Century," a May 2012 posting in *Nonprofit Quarterly*, written by the editors in partnership with Robin Katcher, Management Assistance Group, and Jeanne Bell, Compasspoint Nonprofit Services, offers the following advice: Lean into discomfort—being willing to take risks for effective societal change; "Taking Your Place at the Table—and Building the Table If It Isn't There"; and "Taking to the Margins with Purpose."

"Cultivating Systems Leadership in Cross-Sector Partnerships: Lessons from the Linked Learning Regional Hubs of Excellence," a report published in August 2017 by Harder + Company, a community research firm, explored systems leadership in the context of the James Irvine Foundation's Linked Learning Regional Hubs of Excellence (Hubs) initiative. The Hubs project brought together kindergarten to twelfth-grade school districts, postsecondary institutions, workforce intermediaries, employers, and community-based organizations with the goal of increasing "the number of low-income young people who complete high school on time and earn a postsecondary credential by age 25" (p. 5). The report mapped the Hubs learning ecosystem and defined attributes of systems leadership: relationships and trust; co-creation of structures to support the work; open mindset; systems thinking; empowerment; effective communication; incentives and payoffs; a focus on results; and unwavering attention to diversity, equity, and inclusion. It also suggested ways those attributes can be cultivated—individually, through coaching, mentoring, and experiential learning, and collectively, through structured learning activities, learning communities, and communities of practice.

In their winter 2015 piece in the *Stanford Social Innovation Review*, **"The Dawn of System Leadership,"** authors Peter Senge, Hal Hamilton, and John Kania distill three "core capabilities" for honing "commons creating" skills: the ability to see the larger system, fostering reflection and more generative conversations, and shifting collective focus from reactive problem solving to co-creating the future.

Collaboration as Learning Skill

The review of research literature found in the P21 (Partnership for 21st Century Learning) report entitled **"Skills for Today: What We Know About Teaching and Assessing Collaboration"** found "the elements [supporting collaborative skill building] that are common across multiple frameworks include: interpersonal communication; conflict resolution; and task management." The report, also noted that "collaboration skills, like interpersonal communication, conflict resolution, and task management, do not develop on their own but must be explicitly taught." Focusing on these skills can improve students' "commitment to civic participation," workforce success, and advancement.

"Working Better Together: Building Nonprofit Collaborative Capacity," from Grantmakers for Effective Organizations, aimed at funders, states,

> The problems at the heart of the nonprofit sector's work rarely lend themselves to easy answers. In areas ranging from education and environmental protection to social services reform and civil rights, achieving real and lasting impact often means changing complex and dynamic systems. No single organization can succeed in this work on its own.

Accordingly, in order for funders to play their role in fostering collaboration, funders "will need to take a hard look at their core grantmaking practices and assess the degree to which they are encouraging a go-it-alone mindset" (p. 7).

Philanthropy and Collaboration

Based on the realization that there is a "growing need for grantmakers to be more collaborative," Grantmakers for Effective Organizations (GEO) published *Catalyzing Networks for Social Change: A Funder's Guide.*

This guide suggests how networks can be effective frameworks for achieving such positive social benefits as "weaving social ties, accessing new and diverse perspectives, openly building and sharing knowledge, creating infrastructure for widespread engagement, and coordinating resources and action" (p. 5). The resource includes advice about how to work with, and cultivate, a network mindset, the challenges of a networked approach, and assessing network impact.

Another useful GEO-produced resource is **Working Better Together: Building Nonprofit Collaborative Capacity** (2013). The publication describes four "key capacities" for supporting effective nonprofit collaborations: (1) Strong leadership and an open mindset; (2) the ability to share power and responsibility; (3) adaptability and flexibility; and (4) strong connectivity and relationship building. (https://www.geofunders.org/resources/working-better-together-building-nonprofit-collaborative-capacity-694)

"Bolder Together" is a 2011 report on the lessons learned in funder collaboration by the California Civic Participation Funders. Among the group's "takeaways" from their efforts to increase civic engagement among disenfranchised populations:

1. Encourage collaboration over competition;
2. Cover more bases to get to scale;
3. Let local groups lead with their issues, not yours;
4. Create a "container of trust" to hold the work;
5. Invest in long-term movement leadership; and
6. Embrace real-time learning.

The fall 2015 issue of the *Stanford Social Innovation Review* included a special supplement, **"The Power of Philanthropic Partnerships,"** sponsored by the Orfalea Fund. Some thirteen essays explored many dimensions of partnerships, beginning with an essay by Natalie Orfalea, "'Where Two Rivers Meet, the Water Is Never Calm,'" asserting that partnerships are "essential elements of effective philanthropy." In her essay "The Pillars of Partnership" to author Barbara Andersen identifies "six pillars of strategic partnership":

1. Reforms ineffective and/or inefficient systems;
2. Aligns with and advances the missions of all partners;
3. Fosters an entrepreneurial approach to problem-solving;

4. Leverages strengths specific to engaged parties;
5. Focuses on building stakeholder empowerment; and
6. Commits to the attainment of visible, measurable results.

Other Cross-Sector Partnership Variations: Business, Libraries, Archives, Schools

"Building Strong Partnerships with Businesses: Maximizing Your Organization's Workforce Development Potential" is a "pocket guide" for nonprofit leaders created by The Hitachi Foundation.

The Art of Effective Business and Nonprofit Partnerships: Finding the Intersection of Business Need and Social Good by Elyse Rosenblum is another great resource.

"The Ecosystem of Shared Value," by Mark R. Kramer and Marc W. Pfitzer in the *Harvard Business Review*, examines ways in which businesses can partner with other entities, including nongovernmental organizations, governments, and competitors, to achieve financial success, gain the public trust, and achieve social impact.

An in-depth analysis by Jason Alcorn, **"How News Partnerships Work: Commercial and Nonprofit Newsrooms Can Work Together to Benefit and Change Journalism,"** published by the American Press Institute in May 2017 takes a deep dive into a decade-long experience with a model in which nonprofit news organizations partner with commercial news entities in ways that are financially and editorially a "win-win" proposition. These partnerships "fill a need on both sides," "have specific goals," "enable great journalism," and make business sense for both parties. The piece treats issues of intellectual property and includes excerpts of actual sample contracts.

Patricia Montiel-Overall, at the University of Arizona School of Information Resources and Library Science, posits various models of collaboration (as distinct from coordination and cooperation) in her article, **"Toward a Theory of Collaboration for Teachers and Librarians,"** *School Library Media Research*, the research journal of the American Association of School Librarians. She notes many different definitions of collaboration (p. 3) proposes a working definition that applies to teachers and school librarians, and suggests four potential models and related activities.

Science Education for New Civic Engagements and Responsibilities (SENCER) the signature initiative of the National Center for

Science and Civic Engagement, is a national project focused on creating a national network of faculty and other educators who develop and share resources for improving STEM teaching and learning by making connections between STEM and civic issues. The center's vision is to empower citizens as responsible, lifelong learners who can apply the knowledge, values, and methods of science to the complex local and global challenges facing our democracy. Bound together by a shared mission and the SENCER ideals, this network has been dubbed a "community of transformation" by researchers at the University of Southern California.

The University of Miami Scholarly Repository published a white paper on **"Prospects and Strategies for Deep Collaboration in the Galleries, Libraries, Archives, and Museums (GLAMS) Sector,"** which reflects highlights of an Academic Art Museum and Library Summit convened in January 2016. The convening examined three dimensions of sharing within GLAMS: collaborative teaching and learning; collections sharing and exhibitions; and strategic alignments, with participating colleges and universities, providing examples of each. The concluding speaker, Clifford Lynch of the Coalition for Networked Information, urged participants to consider not only the "digital turn" that was affecting these collaborations: "There's also . . . the network turn . . . which takes a turn to the digital as a prerequisite, but goes far beyond that and . . . changes a lot of the rules about everything from inter-institutional collaboration to public engagement and I think in some ways, may have more lasting impacts on our strategies going forward" (p. 13). According to Lynch, this "network turn" could have profound impacts on exhibitions, program, patron-object interaction, discovery and metadata, and professional education (p. 13).

There are a number of useful reports produced by the Institute of Museum and Library Science (IMLS) and its partners that highlight effective collaborations in the service of creating broader learning ecosystems. For example, *Learning Labs in Libraries and Museums: Transformative Spaces for Teens*, published in October 2014 by the Association of Science-Technology Centers and the Urban Libraries Council, with support from IMLS and the MacArthur Foundation, documents research, practice, and impacts on co-created learning environments for teens. (www.imls.gov)

In May 2009, the Harvard Family Research Project published **"From Periphery to Center: A New Vision for Family, School, and Com-**

munity Partnerships" by Heather B. Weiss and Naomi Stephen as a chapter in the *Handbook of School-Family Partnerships* edited by Sandra L. Christenson and Amy L. Reschley, published by Routledge in September 2009. Now reinvented as the Global Family Research Project, the organization continues to focus on broader family/institutional partnerships for effective learning. It connects research, policy, and practice to support inter-organizational collaboration "among child- and family-serving organizations so they can create equitable learning pathways across time and place."

How Cross-Sector Collaborations Are Advancing STEM Learning defined STEM learning ecosystems and their core attributes, identified specific examples, explored strategies for success, and made recommendations for further research and evaluation and future practice.

A growing number of networked-based organizations, including KnowledgeWorks, the STRIVE Network, the Connected Learning Alliance, Education Innovator, Partnership for 21st Century Learning, Ready by 21, and LRNG, routinely publish resources—and offer low-cost or free webinars- on multiorganizational collaborations that support effective community learning ecosystems. These collaborations often include museums.

Museum-Focused Resources

The work of Nina Simon, director of the Museum of Art and History in Santa Cruz, California, is required reading for museum practitioners who are engaging seriously in partnerships that embed a museum in the life, needs, and individuals of a community. From the *Museum 2.0* (museum-two.blogspot.com) to her volumes, *The Participatory Museum* (2010) and *The Art of Relevance* (2016, Museum 2.0, Santa Cruz, CA), Simon has shared her own professional journey toward increasing museum impact on individuals and community. This has shaped her practice as a leader, the culture and organization chart of the museum, the evolving principles that have governed the museum's partnerships, and the many lessons learned (successes and failures) along the way.

"The How of Long Distance Collaboration" offers practical insights about a long-term collaboration of the Levine Museum of the New South, the Birmingham Civil Rights Institute, and the Atlanta History Center devoted to documenting the history of Latinx communities in the region and developing lasting connections to those communities. Its insights consider community listening sessions, staff conversations, project evaluation, and "lessons learned" about creating and sustaining a learning network.

Currently, in my role as adjunct faculty at the Bank Street College Graduate Program in Museum Leadership, I have encountered a most useful "collaboration spectrum" developed by my colleague Janet Rassweiler. The tool, developed by Rassweiler for graduate museum leadership students in a Bank Street course on "Collaboration for Museum Leaders," notes "What kind of relationship will help you best deliver on the work you want to do? It matters less what each relationship is called and more that all participants understand the term to mean the same thing." Rassweiler developed the tool to help emerging museum leaders "think about and describe to others [the] relationships you are in or might build in your work." The Spectrum moves from "competition" to "consultation," "cooperation," "coordination," and "collaboration." It ends with the "collective impact" goal of large-scale social change, requiring shared measurement, a common agenda, and a joint approach.

Among museum-oriented partnership resources is the **"Museums and Community Partnerships: Collaboration Guide,"** published by the Nanoscale Informal Science Education Network in November 2015. This practical how-to guide lays out reasons for collaboration, describes different levels of collaboration, from the less intense "networking" to the more intense "collaboration." For each level, authors note the spectrum of engagement along five dimensions: purpose, commitment, structure, communications, and process. The guide also includes characteristics of successful partnerships, agreements that can be used to formalize partnerships, ways to sustain partnerships, and barriers to success. Finally, it provides examples and additional relevant resources, including a sample Memorandum of Understanding. NISEnet (initially Nanoscale Informal Science Education Network and now National Informal STEM Education Network) is a community of informal educators and scientists dedicated to supporting learning about STEM across the United States.

In 1997, Philadelphia's Franklin Institute co-published, with Girl Scouts of the USA, *Partners in Science: An NSP Guidebook*. The booklet explores the National Science Partnership for Girl Scouts and Science Institutions, funded by the National Science Foundation. Another how-to guide, this booklet focuses on this specific national project and also contains useful hints for any museum/youth-serving organization collaboration. The Franklin continued to forge—and evaluate—museum-community partnerships. In 2013, it published **"Engaging Communities: A Multidisciplinary Review of Core Principles, Frameworks, and Evaluation Strategies for Community Engagement Initiatives"** by Susanna Dilliplane, Annenberg School of Communication, University of Pennsylvania. The paper provides definitions, explores level of community engagement from "outreach" to "collaborate" and "shared leadership," includes key principles of community engagement, three frameworks, and, finally, provides insights into evaluation methods and strategies. A subsequent publication, **"The Franklin Institute's Museum-Community Programs 1993–2014: Lessons Learned,"** by Kirsten Buchner, Insight Evaluation Services, Fairfax, Virginia, evaluated some fourteen museum-community partnership programs.

A Collaboration Workbook: How Six Brooklyn Cultural Institutions Developed a Capacity to Diagnose Community Need and Respond with Collaborative Programs is a valuable guide by Alan Brown, Karen Tingley, and John Shibley. It is based on an Institute of Museum and Library Services–funded project, Heart of Brooklyn, which involved the Brooklyn Botanic Garden, Brooklyn Children's Museum, Brooklyn Public Library, Prospect Park, and Prospect Park Zoo. The report provides a detailed description of the collaborative process, a summary of lessons learned from the collective impact approach, tools developed for the collaboration, and work products.

A 2017 monograph from EmcArts, **"Somewhere Becoming Rain: Adaptive Change Is the Future of the Arts,"** shares learnings from ten years of the National Innovation Labs in the Arts, working principally with museums and performing arts organizations. As it explores new paradigms in the American arts system, from cultural policy, to practice, to audience engagement, to funding, project contributors (including author Richard Evans and contributors Steven Tepper, Jamie Gamble, and Kiley Arroyo), describe the necessary "adaptive capacities" for achieving success in the new paradigm for nonprofit arts organizations. Whereas the old model was characterized by "excellence & access; transactional experiences; institutional creativity; product-driven; and binary distinctions, hierarchies, and permanence," the new paradigm's attributes are "impact and engagement; transformational experiences; distributed and connected creativity; process-driven; and impermanent, contingent, diverse, and horizontal" (p. 15).

According to EmcArts, the seven "essential adaptive capacities" for achieving these new paradigms focus on fostering flexibility, innovation, and re-invention and being highly conscious of the context in which one works ("situation recognition"). Understanding the dynamic ecosystem in which each organization sits requires awareness of—and inclusion of—"a diversity of perspectives," with organizations needing to "become adept at seeking, cultivating, and finding successful external partners," who are often not the "usual suspects." Thus, an essential adaptive capacity is "making collaboration part of the organization's DNA, internally and externally" (p. 47).

> Successful collaborators have learned the delicate balance between trust and reciprocity, with productive conflict as the means to spark new and creative ideas. Power dynamics and misunderstood assumptions can often derail collaborations. Navigating these requires an investment in communications and engagement, and a willingness to be open to thinking differently. (p. 55)

The California Association of Museums has engaged in a focused initiative, **"California Networks for Collaboration."** The goal of the initiative is to bring museums and other partner organizations across California to "reimagine and pilot a dispersed learning model for professional development and statewide collaboration in order to solve pressing issues within the museum field." This multiyear initiative has four phases: discovery, exploration, research, and co-creation, and, at the time of this writing, has just completed phase two. The final reports from the first two phases are posted on the association's website and freely available. The project has been organized based on the principles of collaborative learning environments—interactive, participant-driven, focused on knowledge co-creation, and constructing shared learning. Among the insights from the project so far have been that the most successful interactions have "emphasized intentional networking, collaborative meaning making, and applying shared learning to practice." Each group created its own "knowledge products" that documented their most salient learnings that are being shared across the entire network.

Museum as Process: Translating Local and Global Knowledges (Museum Meanings), by Raymond Silverman, and **"The Interrogative Museum"** by Ivan Karp and Corinne A. Kratz are impressive resources. The Karp/Kratz essay zeroes in on effective museum-community relations in a global context, and provides examples of a variety of projects, from exhibitions, to programs, collections sharing, and documentation. Acknowledging the centrality of collaboration in much of this work—and noting that there is "no cookbook" that can apply to diverse communities—the essay focuses on dimensions of successful collaborative process, especially in international settings.

A Postscript: A Small Selection of Resources Relating to Nonprofit Mergers

"Curating Change: The Merger of Two Historic Women's Organizations" by Sarah Burke and Chloe Singer, June 16, 2017: This case study reviews the merger between the International Museum of Women and the Global Fund for Women in March 2014.

"7 Steps for Making Nonprofit Mergers Work," by Timothy Sandoval. October 20, 2016. *Chronicle of Philanthropy*.

"How to Save a Nonprofit: The Care Steps Required in Mergers and Acquisitions," by Bhakti Mirchandani. This article shares structural details and lessons learned from a formal affiliation between the Hope Community, a nonprofit in East Harlem, and Project Enterprise, a community development financial institution.

"Sharing a CEO: A New Form of Nonprofit Merger Exploration?" by Erin Rubin. April 4, 2018. *Nonprofit Quarterly*. A description of a formal relationship between the YMCA of Michiana (in Indiana) and the YMCA of Southwest Michigan.

Mergers as a Strategy for Success: 2016 Report from the Metropolitan Chicago Nonprofit Merger Research Project by Donald Haider, Katherine Cooper, and Reyhaneh Maktoufi. This important resource analyzes twenty-five nonprofit mergers that took place in Chicago between 2004 and 2014. It includes a tool kit, case studies, and other resources (www.chicagonpmergerstudy.org).

"Chicago Nonprofits Merge to Boost Civic Engagement," by Danielle Holly, describes the planned merger of Chicago Cares and WomenOnCall in order to strengthen their ability to meet the respective missions of both groups.

Success Factors in Nonprofit Mergers examines forty-one nonprofit mergers in Minnesota from 1999 to 2010. The comprehensive study, a joint research project of MAP for nonprofits and Wilder Research, was published in 2012. It includes discussions of the reasons for nonprofit mergers, details of various merger processes, factors involved in merger success, and postmerger outcomes.

Merging Nonprofit Organizations: The Art and Science of the Deal, by John A. Yancy, Barbara Wester Jacobus, and Kelly McNally Koney, published by the Mandel Center for Nonprofit Organizations in Cleveland, Ohio, in 2001, similarly examines the context for nonprofit mergers, partner selection, implementation, and evaluation.

A Final Word: Better Together?

Ten Considerations for Successful Strategic Partnerships

MARSHA L. SEMMEL, ADAPTED FROM A NATIONAL MUSEUM OF AFRICAN AMERICAN HISTORY ND CULTURE CONVENING

Increasingly, museums, nonprofits, corporations, and foundations recognize that achieving meaningful outcomes and addressing significant cultural, societal, and educational challenges requires strategic collaborations and partnerships. In our networked world, no one organization has the resources, or reach, to go it alone. Yet, the root of "collaboration" is "labor": partnerships take work, time, and effort. Here are some final thoughts about forming and sustaining successful partnerships.

1. **Know thyself!** What are you trying to accomplish, and what are you equipped to do on your own? In what ways might partnerships further your organization's (or unit's) goals?
2. **"How can one plus one equal three?"** What are some strategic reasons for joining forces with partner organizations? What might partnerships accomplish that the individual organizations cannot do on their own, while still supporting each partner's mission and goals?
3. **Connect before content**. Who are some likely partners or stakeholders to be approached? Begin to build relationships. Dedicate time to develop trust, brainstorm possibilities, to get to know potential partners; share respective goals. Consider some "unusual suspects." Be open to unforeseen possibilities. Be willing to say "thanks and goodbye" if the prospects are not promising.
4. **Clearly define the partnership and ensure sure that all partners (and required stakeholders) agree to the project and its terms**. Are the goals realistic? Can they be accomplished within the designated timeframe? Are there identified project milestones? How often, and in what way, will the partners meet? What resources (human, fiscal, physical, technological, etc.) will be required (and committed) to launch and manage the partnership? Recognize that partners may contribute different types of support, including people, money, content knowledge, access to (and membership in) the target community, operational infrastructure, and technological expertise.
5. **Identify the "wrangler."** Who will have the responsibility and authority to manage the partnership? Will that person have the necessary time and resources to devote to the project? What does the partnership "organization chart" look like? Is there an advisory body that oversees the day-to-day project management?

6. **Get the right people on the bus.** Are the appropriate people on the partnership team? Do they have the training, skills, knowledge, and resources they need to make the partnership a success? Do they understand their roles? Has the core team mapped the broader project community to ensure that others with influence, needs, or stakes in the project will be kept apprised of the partnership's progress?

7. **"Lean into" the inevitable changes that will occur.** Recognize that successful partnerships are complex, dynamic, and evolving. Understand that new players (individuals and organizations) require attention and orientation. Take small steps. Be willing to modify your course. Be open to new opportunities and outcomes. Consider not only the project, but also the "sticky residue" of the relationships formed by the partnership that could inform future collaborations.

8. **Communicate. Communicate. Communicate.** Consider the many necessary avenues of communication that a successful partnership requires: within the partnership, with the appropriate stakeholders and colleagues within each partner organization, with the target audiences, funders, and other community stakeholders. Agree on talking points and appropriate credits for the partnership announcement and other public communications. Who needs to know what, and when? Who is empowered to be partnership spokespersons?

9. **Periodically, take the project's pulse.** Beyond the project activities themselves, explore partner insights, the nature of evolving relationships, and the impact of changes in the broader environment. Are the partners supporting their own learning capacity by creating feedback loops and sharing information? Are they capturing the effective partnership principles that are emerging? Is there time to reflect on the role of the partnership within the larger organizational or community context?

10. **Document, evaluate, celebrate.** Even if the goals are lofty, is the partnership "right-sized" to be achievable? What will success look like? How are project outcomes defined? Is the evaluation plan flexible enough to accommodate and capture unforeseen outcomes? Is there time to commemorate, and celebrate, project milestones?

Notes

Introduction

1. Stanford Social Innovation Review. 2017. "Advancing the Art of Collaboration." https://ssir.org/advancing_the_art_of_collaboration.

2. Mantel, Hillary. 2009. *Wolf Hall*. London, UK: Henry Holt and Co.

3. Rainie, Lee, and Barry Wellman. 2012. *Networked: The New Social Operating System*. MIT Press, Cambridge, MA. Page ix.

4. Ibid., pages ix–x.

5. For more podcasts, please visit https://www.mckinsey.com/featured-insights/mckinsey-podcast.

6. Hagel III, John, John Seely Brown, and Mariann Jelinek. 2008. "Relational Networks, Strategic Advantage: New Challenges for Collaborative Control." http://www.johnseelybrown.com/RelationalNet.pdf.

7. Ibid., page 3.

8. Ibid., pages 7–8.

9. Winegar, Natasha, Susan Misra, and Ashley Shelton. 2017. "Influencing Complex Systems Change." *Nonprofit Quarterly*. Page 2.

10. Le, Vu. 2017. "Star Trek and the Future of the Nonprofit Sector." *Nonprofit Quarterly*. http://nonprofitaf.com/2017/11/star-trek-and-the-future-of-the-non-profit-sector/.

11. Institute of Museum and Library Services. Date Unknown. "Community Catalyst Initiative." https://www.imls.gov/issues/national-initiatives/communit-catalyst-initiative.

12. Institute of Museum and Library Services. 2009. "Museums, Libraries, and 21st Century Skills." https://www.imls.gov/issues/national-initiatives/museums-libraries-and-21st-century-skills.

13. Connected Learning Alliance. Date Unknown. "What is Connected Learning?" https://clalliance.org/why-connected-learning/.

14. Jung, Yuha, and Ann Rowson Love. 2017. *Systems Thinking in Museums: Theory and Practice*. Lanham, MD: Rowman & Littlefield.

How to Use This Book

1. National Research Council. 2009. *Learning Science in Informal Environments: People, Places, and Pursuits. Committee on Learning Science in Informal Environments.* Philip Bell, Bruce Lewenstein, Andrew W. Shouse, and Michael A. Feder, editors. Board on Science Education, Center for Education. Division of Behavioral and Social Sciences and Education. The National Academies Press, Washington, DC.

Chapter 1

1. Dana, John Cotton. 1999. *The New Museum: Selected Writings by John Cotton Dana*. Lanham, MD: Rowman & Littlefield/American Alliance of Museums.

2. At that time, Conner Prairie was a wholly owned subsidiary of the college.

3. Semmel, Marsha. 2002. "How the West Was One: The Story of a Museum Merger." *Museum News*, pages 38–43.

4. Sheppard, Beverly. 2001. *The 21st Century Learner*. Washington, DC: Institute of Museum and Library Services.

5. Ibid, page 3.

6. Ibid.

7. Ibid, page 9.

8. Ibid, page 10.

9. Kulpinski, D. 2009. *Partnership for a Nation of Learners: Joining Forces, Creating Value*. Washington, DC: Institute of Museum and Library Services.

10. Ibid, page 1.

11. Brown, John Seely, and Thomas, Douglas. 2011. *A New Culture of Learning: Cultivating the Imagination for a World of Constant Change*.

12. Ibid, page 19.

13. Ibid, page 93.

14. Brown, John Seely, and Pendleton-Jullian, Ann. April 20, 2017. "Sense-Making in Our Post AlphaGo World: New Mindsets and Lenses May Be Required." Stanford MediaX Keynote. Page 4.

15. Ibid, page 13.

16. Ibid, page 15.

17. Ibid, page 17.

18. Moore, Mark H. 1995. *Creating Public Value: Strategic Management in Government*. Cambridge, MA: Harvard University Press.

19. While still at IMLS, I contributed an essay, "Museums and Public Value: A US Cultural Agency Example," to *Museums and Public Value: Creating Sustainable Futures*, edited by Carol A. Scott and published in the United Kingdom by Ashgate in 2013.

20. Heifetz, R., Grashow, A., and Linsky, M. 2009. *The Practice of Adaptive Leadership: Tools and Tactics for Changing Your Organization and the World*. Boston, MA: Harvard Business Press.

21. Kotter, John P. 2007. "Leading Change: Why Transformation Efforts Fail," *Harvard Business Review*. https://hbr.org/2007/01/leading-change-why-transformation-efforts-fail. January 2007. Reprint R0701J.

22. Johansen, Bob. 2009. *Leaders Make the Future: Ten Leadership Skills for an Uncertain World*. New York: HarperCollins. Page 140–41.

23. Johansen, Bob, and Ronn, Karl. 2014. *The Reciprocity Advantage: A New Way to Partner for Innovation and Growth*. Oakland, CA: Berrett-Koehler Publishers.

24. Ibid, page 14.

25. Johansen, Bob. 2017. *The New Leadership Literacies: Thriving in a Future of Extreme Disruption and Distributed Everything*. Oakland, CA: Berrett-Koehler Publishers.

26. Ibid, page 77.

27. Ibid, page 78–79.

28. More resources can be found on www.fsg.org.

Chapter 3

1. Oldenburg, Ray. 1989. *The Great Good Place: Cafes, Coffee Shops, Community Centers, Beauty Parlors, General Stores, Bars, Hangouts, and How They Get You through the Day*. New York: Paragon House.

2. Putnam, Robert D. 2000. *Bowling Alone: The Collapse and Revival of American Community*. New York: Simon & Schuster.

3. See note #1.

4. Ignite Talks PBC, 2017. www.ignitetalks.io.

5. National School Reform Faculty and Critical Friends Group, 2017. www.nsrfharmony.org.

6. See note #1.

7. See note #2.

Chapter 5

1. Ackerson, Anne, Hill, Chrystie, Drummond, Christina, et al. 2017. "Nexus Leading across Boundaries (LAB): Layers of Leadership across Libraries, Archives, and Museums." Edited by Nexus LAB Project Team. educopia.org/publications/nexus-layers-of-leadership.

Chapter 6

1. Kelly, J. 1996. *Leisure*, 3rd edition. Boston: Allyn and Bacon.

2. To be accurate, that is only the wealthy majority of humans living within agriculture-based "civilized" societies had the time. Ironically, individuals living

within hunter-gather societies both today and presumably throughout history have typically had considerable leisure time (cf., Diamond, J. 2012. *The World until Yesterday*. New York: Viking).

3. McLean, D. 2015. *Kraus's Recreation and Leisure in Modern Society*, tenth edition. Burlington, MA: Jones and Bartlett Publishers.

4. Falk, J. H., Ballantyne, R., Packer, J., and Benckendorff, P. 2012. "Travel and Learning: A Neglected Tourism Research Area." *Annals of Tourism Research*, 39(2), 908–27. McLean, D., 2015. *Kraus's Recreation and Leisure in Modern Society*, tenth edition. Burlington, MA: Jones and Bartlett Publishers.

5. Kelly, J. R., and Freysinger, V. J. 2000. *21st Century Leisure: Current Issues*. State College, PA: Venture Publishing.

6. Falk, J. H., and Sheppard, B. 2006. *Thriving in the Knowledge Age: New Business Models for Museums and Other Cultural Organizations*. Lanham, MD: AltaMira Press.

7. Quoted in Sandberg, J. 2006. "Farming? Running? It Doesn't Sound Like a Vacation to Me." *Wall Street Journal* online.

8. Sagon, C. 2004. "Formerly known as Sutton Place." F1, *Washington Post*, April 7. Zuboff, S., and Maxmin, D. 2002. *The Support Economy: Why Corporations are Failing Individuals and the Next Episode of Capitalism*. New York: Viking Press.

9. Freysinger, V. J., and Kelly, J. R. 2004. *21st Century Leisure: Current Issues*. State College, PA: Venture Publishing. Obviously, the rich "leisure classes" of former years engaged in this style of leisure long before the twenty-first century, but it is a major shift that it now represents the norm for such a large percentage of the population.

10. Falk, J. H. 2018. *Born to Choose: Evolution, Self, and Well-Being*. New York: Routledge.

11. See review by Falk, J. H. 2016. "Museum Audiences: A Visitor-Centered Perspective." *Loisir et Société/Leisure and Society*, 39(3), 357–70.

12. Falk, J. H., and Sheppard, B. 2006. *Thriving in the Knowledge Age: New Business Models for Museums and Other Cultural Organizations*. Lanham, MD: AltaMira Press.

13. Deloitte. 2015. "Making It Personal: One In Three Consumers Want Personalized Products." https://www2.deloitte.com/uk/en/pages/press-releases/articles/one-in-three-consumers-wants-personalised-products.html. Retrieved February 16, 2017.

14. Prahalad, C. K., and Ramaswamy, V. 2014. "Co-creation Experiences: The Next Practice in Value Creation." *Journal of Interactive Marketing*, 18(3). http://citeseerx.ist.psu.edu/viewdoc/download?doi=10.1.1.474.1975&rep=rep1&type=pdf. Retrieved February 16, 2017.

15. McAdams, D. P. 2008. "Personal Narratives and the Life Story." In O. John, R. Robins, and L. A. Pervin (eds.). *Handbook of Personality: Theory and Research*, third edition. New York: Guilford Press.

16. Prahalad, C. K., and Ramaswamy, V. 2014. "Co-creation Experiences: The Next Practice in Value Creation." *Journal of Interactive Marketing*, 18(3).

http://citeseerx.ist.psu.edu/viewdoc/download?doi=10.1.1.474.1975&rep=rep1 &type=pdf. Retrieved February 16, 2017.

17. Siegel, J. 2005. *The Idea of the Self: Thought and Experience in Western Europe Since the Eighteenth Century*. Cambridge: Cambridge University Press.

18. Bem, D. J. 1972. "Self-Perception Theory." In: L. Berkowitz (ed), *Advances in Experimental Social Psychology*, volume 6, 1–62. New York: Academic Press. Csikszentmihalyi, M. 1990. "Literacy and Intrinsic Motivation." *Daedalus*, 119(2), 115–40. Samdahl, D. M., and Kleiber, D. A. 1989. "Self-Awareness and Leisure Experience." *Leisure Sciences*, 11, 1–10. Steele, C. M. 1988. "The Psychology of Self-Affirmation: Sustaining the Integrity of the Self." In: L. Berkowitz (ed.). *Advances in Experimental Social-Psychology*, volume 21, 261–302. New York: Academic Press. Williams, D. R. 2002. "Leisure Identities, Globalization, and the Politics of Place." *Journal of Leisure Research*, 34(4), 267–78.

19. Kelly, J. R. 1983. *Leisure Identities and Interactions*. London: George Allen and Unwin.

20. Maslow, A. H. 1943. "A Theory of Human Motivation." *Psychological Review*, 50(4), 370–96. *Handbook of Positive Psychology*, 195–206. Oxford: Oxford University Press.

21. Csikszentmihalyi, M. 1990. *Flow: The Psychology of Optimal Experience*. New York: Harper Perennial.

22. Haggard, L. M., and Williams, D. R. 1992. "Identity Affirmation through Leisure Activities: Leisure Symbols of the Self." *Journal of Leisure Research*, 24(1), 1–18.

23. Rounds, J. 2006. "Doing Identity-Work in Museums." *Curator*, 49(2), 133–50.

24. Koke, J. 2010. *AGO Visitor Motivation Study: Cumulative Report*. Technical Report. Toronto: Art Gallery of Ontario.

25. All of these institutions used as a foundation my research on identity-related visit motivations, Falk, J. H. 2009. *Identity and the Museum Visitor Experience*. Walnut Creek, CA: Left Coast Press.

26. Barton, J., and Meszaros, B. 2016. "Extending the Museum Visitor Experience." Society for Experiential Graphic Design. https://segd.org/extending-museum-visitor-experience. Retrieved February 16, 2017.

27. Kostoska, G., Valeri, B., Baez, M., and Fezzi, D. 2013. "Understanding Sharing Habits in Museum Visits: A Pilot Study." In N. Proctor and R. Cherry (eds). *Museums and the Web 2013*. Silver Spring, MD: Museums and the Web. http://mw2013.museumsandtheweb.com/paper/understanding-sharing-habits-in-museum-visits-a-pilot-study/. Retrieved February 16, 2017.

28. Galani, A., Chalmers, M., Brown, B., MacColl, I., Randell, C., and Steed, A. 2003. "Far Away Is Close at Hand: Developing a Mixed Reality Co-Visiting Experience for Local and Remote Museum Companions." Proceedings of ICHIM 2003, Archives and Museum Informatics Europe, electronic edition. http://citeseerx.ist.psu.edu/viewdoc/download?doi=10.1.1.9.6668&rep=rep1&type=pdf. Retrieved February 16, 2017.

29. Winn, A. R. 2012. "The Remembering St. Petersburg Oral History Project: Youth Empowerment and Heritage Preservation through a Community Museum." *Transforming Anthropology*, 20(1), 67–78.

30. Schwartz, D. 2010. "Experiments in Making History Personal: Public Discourse, Complexity, and Community." *Journal of Museum Education*, 35(1), 71–81.

Chapter 8

1. Harwood: The Institute for Public Innovation, American Library Association, Libraries Transforming Communities. Date Unknown. "Libraries Transforming Communities Case Study: Hartford Public Library." Page 7. http://www.ala.org/tools/sites/ala.org.tools/files/content/160310-ppo-ltc-harwood-case-studies-individual-sections-hartford.pdf.

2. Harwood: The Institute for Public Innovation. Date Unknown. "Spokane County: United Way." https://theharwoodinstitute.org/stories/2016/2/3/spokane-county-united-way.

Chapter 9

1. La Piana Consulting. "Chattanooga Museums Administrative Consolidation." https://myforefront.org/sites/default/files/resources/Case%20Study%20Chattanooga%20Museums%20Administrative%20Consolidation.pdf.

2. Honolulu Museum of Art. 2017. "Museum Merger FAQs." https://www.honolulumuseum.org/11588-.

3. Kaleideum Downtown. 2017. "History of Kaleideum Downtown." http://downtown.kaleideum.org/history/.

Chapter 10

1. United States Congress. 2003. H.R. 3491—National Museum of African American History and Culture Act. https://www.congress.gov/bill/108th-congress/house-bill/3491.

2. National Museum of African American History and Culture. "Lift Every Voice Planning Guide." https://nmaahc.si.edu/lift-every-voice-planning-guide.

3. National Museum of African American History and Culture. "Strategic Partnerships." https://nmaahc.si.edu/connect/osp.

4. Ibid.

5. Smithsonian Institution. "Smithsonian 2022: Greater Reach, Greater Relevance, Profound Impact." https://www.si.edu/strategicplan#page-hero-anchor.

Chapter 11

1. Blank, R. 2013. "Science Instructional Time Is Declining in Elementary Schools: What Are the Implications for Student Achievement and Closing the Gap?" *Science Education*, 97(6), 830–47.

2. Tai, R. H., Liu, C. Q., Maltese, A. V., and Fan, X. 2006. "Planning Early for Careers in Science." *Science*, 312, 2243–44.

3. Dabney, K., Tai, R. H., Almarode, J. T., Miller-Friedmann, J. L., Sonnert, G., Sadler, P. M., & Hazari, Z. 2012. "Out-of-School Time Science Activities and Their Association with Career Interest in STEM." *International Journal of Science Education, Part B*, 2:1, 63–79.

4. Ottinger, R. 2006. Noyce Approach to Informal Science Funding. Internal report to the Noyce Foundation Trustees.

5. Falk, J. H., and Dierking, L. D. 2010. "The 95 Percent Solution." *American Scientist* 98, November–December, 486–93. Retrieved from https://www.researchgate.net/publication/299233891_The_95_percent_solution_School_is_not_where_most_Americans_learn_most_of_their_science.

6. Shah, A. M., Wylie, C., Gitomer, D., and Noam, G. 2018. "Improving STEM Program Quality in Out-of-School-Time: Tool Development and Validation." *Science Education* 102(2) 238–59.

7. Assessment Tools in Informal Science (ATIS). Available as a searchable database at http://pearweb.org/atis.

8. Sneider, C. 2011. "Reversing the Swing from Science: Implications from a Century of Research." ITEST Convening on Advancing Research on Youth Motivation in STEM, September 9–11, 2011, Boston College, Boston, Massachusetts. Retrieved from http://www.noycefdn.org/documents/Sneider-The%20Swing%20from%20Science.pdf.

9. Falk, J. H., Dierking, L. D., Staus, N., Wyld, J., Bailey, D., and Penuel, W. "Understanding Youth STEM Interest Pathways within a Single Community: The Synergies Project." *Connected Science Learning*, March 1, page 5.

10. Frameworks Institute. 2016. *STEM Afterschool: It's Time to Activate! A Messaging Toolkit to Make the Case for STEM in Afterschool*. Washington, DC: Afterschool STEM HUB.

11. Allen, P. J., Noam, G. G., and Little, T. D. 2017. "Multi-State Evaluation Finds Evidence That Investment In Afterschool STEM Works." In Ottinger, R. (Editor), *STEM Ready America: Inspiring and Preparing Students for Success with Afterschool and Summer Learning*. Retrieved from STEMReadyAmerica.org.

12. Retrieved from https://www.brainyquote.com/topics/partnerships.

Chapter 12

1. Prince, Katherine, Swanson, Jason, and Saveri, Andrea. 2015. *The Future of Learning: Education in an Era of Partners in Code*. Cincinnati, OH: KnowledgeWorks.

2. Ibid.

3. Bureau of Labor Statistics. 2015. National Longitudinal Surveys. *Bureau of Labor Statistics.* https://www.bls.gov/nls/nlsfaqs.htm.

4. Intuit. 2010. 2020 Report: Twenty Trends that Will Shape the Next Decade. Intuit. http://about.intuit.com/futureofsmallbusiness.

5. Prince, Katherine, Saveri, Andrea, and Swanson, Jason. 2015. *Cultivating Interconnections for Vibrant and Equitable Learning Ecosystems.* Cincinnati, OH: KnowledgeWorks.

6. KnowledgeWorks. 2011. *The Learning Ecosystem of 2025.* Cincinnati, OH: KnowledgeWorks. http://www.knowledgeworks.org/learning-system-2025.

7. Prince, Katherine, Swanson, Jason, and Saveri, Andrea. 2015. *The Future of Learning: Education in an Era of Partners in Code.* Cincinnati, OH: KnowledgeWorks.

8. Prince, Katherine, Swanson, Jason, and King, Katie 2016. *Shaping the Future of Learning: A Strategy Guide.* Cincinnati, OH: KnowledgeWorks. http://www.knowledgeworks.org/shaping-future-learning-strategy-guide.

9. SURGE Columbus. "Who We Are." http://www.surgecolumbus.org/who-we-are.

10. Ancelet, Jeanine, and Coffer, Nancy. 2017. "Columbus Museum of Art *Teen Open Studio Evaluation* Study 2016-2017." Shared privately by the museum.

11. Slootmaker, Estelle. 2017. "Museum School Fulfills Purpose of Original Grand Rapids Public Museum Building," *Rapid Growth.* http://www.rapid growthmedia.com/features/grpublicmuseumschool.aspx.

12. Balboa Park Cultural Partnership. "About the Partnership." https://bpcp.org/about.

13. Balboa Park Cultural Partnership. "About the Learning Institute." https://bpcp.org/learning-institute/about.

Chapter 13

1. See Bevan et al., 2010, and James Irvine Foundation, 2005, for a review on museums partnering with schools; Bodilly, Augustine, and Zakaras, 2008, and Russell, Knutson, and Crowley, 2012, for research on arts organizations partnering with schools; and Barron, Gomez, Pinkard, and Martin, 2014, and Pinkard, Barron, and Martin, 2008, for research on how a digital learning initiative, the Digital Youth Network, coordinated with school activities to further learning.

2. Santo, R. (2017). "Working Open in the Hive: How Informal Education Organizations Learn, Collaborate and Innovate in Networks." Doctoral dissertation. Indiana University, Bloomington, IN.

3. DiMaggio, P., and Powell, W. W. (1983). "The Iron Cage Revisited: Collective Rationality and Institutional Isomorphism in Organizational Fields." *American Sociological Review*, 48(2), 147–60.

4. Small, M. L. (2006). "Neighborhood Institutions as Resource Brokers: Childcare Centers, Interorganizational Ties, and Resource Access among the Poor." *Social Problems*, 53(2), 278.

5. Santo, R., Ching, D., Hoadley, C. M., and Peppler, K. A. (2014). *What Does It Mean to "Work Open" in Hive NYC? A Vision for Collective Organizational Learning.* New York: Hive Research Lab. https://hiveresearchlab.files.wordpress.com/2014/12/what-does-it-mean-to-work-open-in-hive-nyc-hive-research-lab-october-2014.pdf; Santo, R., Ching, D., Hoadley, C. M., and Peppler, K. A. (2016). "Working in the Open: Lessons from Open Source on Building Innovation Networks in Education." *On the Horizon*, 24(3), 280–95; Santo, R. (2018). "Open Source Culture as Inspiration for Design of Educator Learning Networks." In *Networked by Design: Interventions for Teachers to Develop Social Capital*, Yoon & Baker-Doyle, Eds. New York: Routledge.

Chapter 14

1. Mack, Deborah L. 2011. "Libraries and Museums in an Era of Participatory Culture." Edited by Nancy Rogers and Susanna Seidl-Fox. Institute of Museum and Library Services. https://www.imls.gov/publications/libraries-and-museums-era-participatory-culture

2. Noyce Leadership Institute. 2015. Virtual Alumni Program.

3. Cramer, C. H. 1972. *Open Shelves, Open Minds: A History of the Cleveland Public Library*. Cleveland, OH: Press of Case Western Reserve University.

4. Noyce Leadership Institute.

5. Cleveland Public Library. "Cleveland Public Library Strategic Plan 2012-2014: The Future Starts with You." http://www.cpl150.org/wp-content/uploads/2014/12/StrategicPlan_Booklet-2.pdf.

6. Greater Cleveland Food Bank. http://www.greaterclevelandfoodbank.org/.

7. Noyce Leadership Institute.

Chapter 15

1. Americans for the Arts. 2017. "Arts & Economic Prosperity 5: The Economic Impact of Nonprofit Arts & Cultural Organizations & Their Audiences—Balboa Park Cultural District." https://www.sandiego.gov/sites/default/files/ca_balboaparkculturaldistrict_aep5_customizedreport.pdf.

2. Balboa Park Cultural Partnership. 2017. "About the Partnership." https://bpcp.org/about/.

3. Ibid.

Chapter 19

1. Carlin, Bob. 1993. "Final Report: Northside Pittsburgh." November 5, 1993, pages 31–35, www.riversofsteel.com/_uploads/files/northside-final-report.pdf.

2. City Data. 2017. "Pittsburgh: Economy, Major Industries and Commercial Activity," www.city-data.com/us-cities/The-Northeast/Pittsburgh-Economy.html.

3. Pennsylvania Economy League of Greater Pittsburgh. 2017. "The Economic Impact of the Children's Museum of Pittsburgh's Museum Lab Expansion." www.pelgp.org/wp-content/uploads/2016/08/ChildrensMuseumEIReport.pdf.

Chapter 20

1. "The History of Explora." 2016. *New Mexico Kids!* Accessed from Wikipedia: https://en.wikipedia.org/wiki/Explora.

2. Harwood offers a partnership perspective in chapter 8 of this volume.

3. Block, Peter. 2008. *Community: The Structure of Belonging.* San Francisco, CA: Berrett-Koehler Publishers, Inc.

4. The Aspen Institute and Jacobs Center for Neighborhood Innovation. 2012. "Connecting Communities Learning Exchange: A Resident-to-Resident Learning Exchange." https://assets.aspeninstitute.org/content/uploads/files/content/docs/pubs/CCLE-Report_3-14-13_Reduced.pdf.

5. Partnership for Community Action. 2017. "Mission + History." http://forcommunityaction.org/about/mission-history/.

6. Explora. 2017. "Shared Aspirations" Flyer. Printed Media.

Chapter 21

1. Information obtained from personal document sent to Marsha Semmel on January 16, 2017.

2. Institute for Museum and Library Services. 2017. "Museum Grants for African American History and Culture." https://www.imls.gov/grants/available/museum-grants-african-american-history-and-culture.

3. Institute for Museum and Library Services. 2008. "September 2008: Florida African American Museum Exchange Builds Alliance to Preserve History." https://www.imls.gov/news-events/project-profiles/september-2008-florida-african-american-museum-exchange-builds-alliance.

4. Ibid.

5. VIVA FLORIDA. 2018. "About Viva Florida." http://vivaflorida.org/About-Viva-Florida/.

Chapter 22

1. Originally presented as a conference talk at the Association of Academic Museums and Galleries Annual Meeting, Eugene, Oregon, June 2017.

Chapter 23

1. Jewish Museum of Maryland. 2017. "About Us: Mission and Vision." http://jewishmuseummd.org/about-us/mission-vision/.

2. Ibid.

3. Historic Jonestown Corporation. 2017. "Historic Jonestown Corporation." www.historicjonestown.com.

4. Thompson, Lindsay. 2017. Phone interview with Marsha Semmel.

5. Mahan Rykiel Associates and Arnett Muldrow Associates. 2015. "Jonestown Vision Plan: Baltimore, Maryland." http://www.historicjonestown.com/uploads/3/7/7/0/37708449/jonestown_master_plan_final_draft.pdf.

6. Sherman, Natalie. 2015. "With New Logo, Jonestown Wants to Raise Its Profile." The Baltimore Sun. http://www.baltimoresun.com/business/bs-bz-jonestown-branding-20151007-story.html.

7. Ibid.

Chapter 24

1. Minnesota Compass. 2017. "Profiles: Minneapolis-Saint Paul Neighborhoods." www.mncompass.org/profiles/neighborhoods.

2. Lindeke, Bill. 2015. "Chart of the Day: Twin Cities Population (Age and Race) by 2040." https://streets.mn/2015/01/22/chart-of-the-day-tc-population-age-and-race-by-2040.

3. Meszaros, Cheryl, Twyla Gibson, and Jennifer Carter. 2012. "Interpretation and the Art Museum: Between the Familiar and the Unfamiliar," in *Museum Gallery Interpretation and Material Culture*, ed. Juliette Fritsch. New York: Routledge. Page 42.

4. Minneapolis Institute of Arts. 2016. "Engaging Communities." *Mia2021: Strategic Plan*. Page 19.

5. Ibid, page 18.

6. Bryant, Janeen, Kayleigh Bryant-Greenwell, Cinnamon Catlin-Legutko, Gretchen Jennings, and Joanne Jones-Rizzi. 2017. "Moving toward Internal Transformation: Awareness, Acceptance, Action," *MASS Action*. Chapter 2, page 17. www.museumaction.org/resources.

7. Patterson, Adam, Aletheia Wittman, Chieko Phillips, Gamynne Guillotte, Therese Quinn, and Adrianne Russell. 2017. "Getting Started: What We Need to Change and Why." *MASS Action Toolkit*. Chapter 1, page 13. www.museumaction.org/resources.

8. Ibid.

9. Bryant, Janeen, Kayleigh Bryant-Greenwell, Cinnamon Catlin-Legutko, Gretchen Jennings, and Joanne Jones-Rizzi. 2017. "Moving toward Internal Transformation: Awareness, Acceptance, Action," *MASS Action*. Page 22. www.museumaction.org/resources.

10. Ibid, page 27.

11. Walker, Chris, Carlos A. Manjarrez, Lesley Lundgren, and Sarah Fuller. 2015. *Museums, Libraries and Comprehensive Initiatives: A First Look at Emerging Experience*. Washington, DC: Institute of Museum and Library Services. Page 1.

12. Ibid, pages 48–49.

13. We struggle with what exactly ARC is. It is not a "project," as that implies a limited endeavor with a short-term end date. To call it an "initiative" might be better, as community initiatives are community-led and solutions-oriented; however, in the museum context, initiatives are often efforts that are created in response to a needed (or a trend), and not planned with long-term sustainability in mind. "Approach" or "strategy" might be the closest, but do not seem to underscore the weight or breadth of the effort. Most often we just call it our "work." For the purpose of this document, we may use any of these terms interchangeably.

14. Minneapolis Institute of Arts. 2016. "Engaging Communities." *Mia2021: Strategic Plan*. Page 16.

15. HOPE Community. 2017. "Art, Policy, and Power." http://hope-community.org/learn-lead-act/art-policy-power.

16. Hasso Plattner Institute of Design. 2017. "Our Way of Working." Stanford University. https://dschool.stanford.edu/about.

17. "Collective impact" can be defined as "the commitment of a group of important actors from different sectors to a common agenda for solving a specific social problem." From "Collective Impact" by John Kania and Mark Kramer, *Stanford Social Innovative Review*, Winter 2011, page 36.

18. Cleveland, William. 2011. "Arts-Based Community Development: Mapping the Terrain." *A Working Guide to the Landscape of Arts for Change*. Washington, DC: Americans for the Arts. Page 4.

19. U.S. Department of Arts and Culture. 2016. "Human Rights and Property Rights: Placemaking and Placekeeping." www.usdac.gov.

20. 2017. "Art as Community Platform: Transforming Practices of Engagement." Panel discussion held at Mia. September 28, 2017.

21. Kubish, Anne C., Carol H. Weiss, Lisbeth B. Schorr, and James P. Connell. 1995. "Introduction." *New Approaches to Evaluating Community Initiatives*. Washington, DC: Aspen Institute. Pages 1–22.

22. W.K. Kellogg Foundation. 2006. "W.K. Kellogg Foundation Logic Model Development Guide." www.wkkf.org.

23. Williams, Deidre. 1997. *How the Arts Measure Up: Australian Research into Social Impact*. Stroud, England: Comedia; Matarasso, Francois. 1997. *Use or Ornament? The Social Impact of Participation in the Arts*. Stroud, England: Comedia; Ross, Caroline. 2016. *A Creative Placemaking Field Scan: Exploring the Ways Arts and Culture Intersect with Public Safety*. Urban Institute/ArtPlace America, LLC.

24. Compassion Capital Fund. 2010. "Measuring Outcomes." *Strengthening Nonprofits: A Capacity Builder's Resource Library*. www.acf.hhs.gov/sites/default/files/ocs/measuring_outcomes.pdf.

25. Jackson, Maria Rosario, and Joaquin Herranz. 2002. "Culture Counts in Communities: A Framework for Measurement," The Urban Institute.

26. Madan, Renu. 2007. "Demystifying Outcome Measurement in Community Development," Joint Center for Housing Studies of Harvard University and NeighborWorks America.

27. Ibid, page 11.

28. Lashaw, Christine, and Evelyn Orantes. 2017. "Sharing Authority: Creating Content and Experiences," *MASS Action Toolkit*. Minneapolis Institute of Art. Chapter 6, page 106. www.museumaction.org/resources.

Chapter 25

1. Oregon Museum of Science and Industry. 2018. "History and Mission." https://omsi.edu/history-and-mission.

2. Ibid.

3. Oregon Museum of Science and Industry. Date unknown. "Small Museum Research Collaborative." https://omsi.edu/exhibitions/ewpw/smrc.php.

4. Ibid.

5. OMSI has also operated extensive summer camp programs for individual registrants.

6. Oregon Museum of Science and Industry. 2015. "OMSI: Annual Report 2015." https://omsi.edu/sites/default/files/OMSI_Annual_Report_2015.pdf.

7. Ibid, page 10.

8. Oregon Museum of Science and Industry. 2016. "OMSI: Annual Report 2016." Page 8. https://omsi.edu/sites/default/files/OMSI_Annual_Report_2016-web.pdf.

9. Moreno, Lauren. 2017. Personal interview with Marsha Semmel.

10. Verde. 2018. "About Verde." http://www.verdenw.org/about-verde/.

Chapter 26

1. McGlone, Peggy. 2015. "Left at Altar by Corcoran, University of Maryland has New Partner in the Arts." *Washington Post*. www.washingtonpost.com/entertainment/museums/left-at-altar-by-corcoran-university-of-maryland-has-new-partner-in-the-arts/2015/10/04/04feb158-6880-11e5-9223-70cb36460919_story.html?utm_term=.cb1c6c97e2f6.

2. THEARC. 2015. "2015 Annual Report: Celebrating 10 Years of Building Bridges and Families." Page 3. https://issuu.com/thearcdc/docs/2015_annual_report_bbar.

3. Ibid.

4. The Phillips Collection. 2017. "Explore: PRISM.K12." http://www.phillipscollection.org/learn/k-12-education.

Index

About the Author

Marsha L. Semmel is an independent consultant working with foundations, museums, libraries, and other educational and cultural organizations on planning, leadership development, community engagement, and strategic partnerships. She currently serves as senior advisor to the National Center for Science and Civic Engagement in its SENCER (Science Engagement for New Civic Responsibilities) initiative and faculty in the Bank Street College of Education's Graduate Program in Leadership in Museum Education. From 2013 to 2015, Semmel was senior advisor to the Noyce Foundation's Noyce Leadership Institute, a global executive development program for senior staff in informal science learning organizations. Semmel was the director for Strategic Partnerships, deputy for Museum Services, and acting director at the Institute of Museum and Library Services (IMLS) from 2003 to 2013. At the National Endowment for the Humanities (NEH) from 1984 to 1996, Semmel was director, NEH Division of Public Programs, from 1993 to 1996. She has been president and CEO of Conner Prairie, a history museum near Indianapolis, and president and CEO of the Women of the West Museum in Denver. Semmel has served on the boards of the American Alliance of Museums, the Colorado Digitization Program, and ArtTable and currently is a board member of the Institute for Learning Innovation, the Museum of Language Arts, and the Council of American Jewish Museums, as well as chair of the Arlington County Commission for the Arts. She is a member of the Association for Managers of Innovation (AMI), a nonprofit learning community fostering creativity and innovation in organizations and society, and The Museum Group, a consortium of museum consultants founded in 1995 by independent professionals who have held leadership positions in museums.